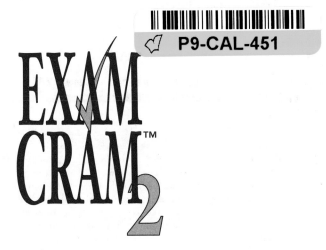

Supporting Users and Troubleshooting a Windows® XP Operating System

Dan Balter

Philip Wiest

CERTIFICATION

Supporting Users and Troubleshooting a Windows® XP Operating System (70-271 Exam Cram)

International Standard Book Number: 0-7897-3149-5

Library of Congress Catalog Card Number: 2003115436

Printed in the United States of America

First Printing: June 2004

07   06   05   04   4   3

Trademarks

All terms mentioned in this book that are known to be trademarks or service marks have been appropriately capitalized. Que Publishing cannot attest to the accuracy of this information. Use of a term in this book should not be regarded as affecting the validity of any trademark or service mark.

Warning and Disclaimer

Every effort has been made to make this book as complete and as accurate as possible, but no warranty or fitness is implied. The information provided is on an "as is" basis. The authors and the publisher shall have neither liability nor responsibility to any person or entity with respect to any loss or damages arising from the information contained in this book or from the use of the CD or programs accompanying it.

Bulk Sales

Que Publishing offers excellent discounts on this book when ordered in quantity for bulk purchases or special sales. For more information, please contact

U.S. Corporate and Government Sales
1-800-382-3419
corpsales@pearsontechgroup.com

For sales outside of the United States, please contact

International Sales
international@pearsoned.com

Publisher
Paul Boger

Executive Editor
Jeff Riley

Acquisitions Editor
Jeff Riley

Development Editor
Steve Rowe

Managing Editor
Charlotte Clapp

Project Editor
Tricia Liebig

Copy Editor
Kris Simmons

Indexer
Chris Barrick

Proofreader
Linda Seifert

Technical Editors
Brian McCann
Mark Soper

Publishing Coordinator
Pamalee Nelson

Multimedia Developer
Dan Scherf

Interior Designer
Anne Jones

Cover Designer
Anne Jones

Page Layout
Michelle Mitchell

CERTIFICATION

Que Certification • 800 East 96th Street • Indianapolis, Indiana 46240

A Note from Series Editor Ed Tittel

You know better than to trust your certification preparation to just any-body. That's why you, and more than 2 million others, have purchased an Exam Cram book. As Series Editor for the new and improved Exam Cram 2 Series, I have worked with the staff at Que Certification to ensure you won't be disappointed. That's why we've taken the world's best-selling certification product—a two-time finalist for "Best Study Guide" in CertCities' reader polls—and made it even better.

As a two-time finalist for the "Favorite Study Guide Author" award as selected by CertCities readers, I know the value of good books. You'll be impressed with Que Certification's stringent review process, which ensures the books are high quality, relevant, and technically accurate. Rest assured that several industry experts have reviewed this material, helping us deliver an excellent solution to your exam preparation needs.

This Exam Cram 2 book also features MeasureUp's powerful, full-featured test engine, which is trusted by certification students throughout the world.

As a 20-year-plus veteran of the computing industry and the original creator and editor of the Exam Cram Series, I've brought my IT experience to bear on these books. During my tenure at Novell from 1989 to 1994, I worked with and around its excellent education and certification department. At Novell, I witnessed the growth and development of the first really big, successful IT certification program—one that was to shape the industry forever afterward. This experience helped push my writing and teaching activities heavily in the cer-tification direction. Since then, I've worked on nearly 100 certification related books, and I write about certification topics for numerous Web sites and for *Certification* magazine.

In 1996, while studying for various MCP exams, I became frustrated with the huge, unwieldy study guides that were the only preparation tools available. As an experienced IT professional and former instructor, I wanted "nothing but the facts" necessary to prepare for the exams. From this impetus, Exam Cram emerged: short, focused books that explain exam topics, detail exam skills and activities, and get IT professionals ready to take and pass their exams.

In 1997 when Exam Cram debuted, it quickly became the best-selling computer book series since "...*For Dummies*," and the best-selling certification book series ever. By maintaining an intense focus on subject matter, tracking errata and updates quickly, and following the certi-fication market closely, Exam Cram established the dominant position in cert prep books.

You will not be disappointed in your decision to purchase this book. If you are, please contact me at etittel@jump.net. All suggestions, ideas, input, or constructive criticism are welcome!

Ed Tittel

I dedicate this book to my loving parents, Maureen and Herb Balter.

—Dan Balter

To Mary Ann.

—Philip Wiest

Contents at a Glance

Table of Contents

. . . .

About the Authors

. . . .

Dan Balter is the Chief Technology Officer for InfoTechnology Partners, Inc., a Microsoft Certified Partner company. He works as an IT consultant and trainer for both corporate and government clients and has worked with several different network operating systems throughout his 20-year career. Dan takes pride in turning complex, technical topics into easy-to-understand concepts. Dan is a Microsoft Certified Desktop Support Technician (MCDST), a Microsoft Certified Systems Administrator (MCSA) on Windows 2000 and Windows Server 2003, and a Microsoft Certified Systems Engineer (MCSE) on Windows NT 4.0, Windows 2000, and Windows Server 2003. He specializes in Microsoft networking technologies, firewalls, virtual private networks (VPNs), and other security solutions in addition to designing and implementing messaging and business solutions for large and small organizations.

Dan is the author of *Exam Cram 2: Managing and Maintaining a Windows Server 2003 Environment* and a co-author for the best-selling books *Exam Cram 2: Windows XP Professional* and *Exam Cram 2: Windows 2000 Professional*, all published by Que Publishing. Dan frequently speaks at conferences across North America, including Advisor DevCon conferences and *Windows & .NET Magazine Connections* conferences. A graduate of USC's School of Business in 1983, Dan has authored more than 300 video-based and CD-ROM–based computer training courses, including instructional titles on installing, configuring, and administering Windows 95, Windows 98, Windows NT, Windows 2000, Windows XP, and Windows Server 2003. He is also a featured video trainer for courses on Microsoft Exchange Server, Microsoft Outlook, and Intuit's QuickBooks small business accounting software. Dan is the video trainer for *ExamBlast–Windows XP Professional* and for the QuickBooks Pro training series on video and CD-ROM from BlastThroughLearning.com.

Dan and his family live in the Santa Rosa Valley area in Southern California, near the city of Camarillo. Dan lives with his lovely wife, Alison; their 8-year-old daughter, Alexis; their 5-year-old son, Brendan; and their golden retriever, Brandy. When he's not writing, researching, or consulting, Dan enjoys traveling with his family, swimming, playing racquetball and basketball, rooting for the Los Angeles Galaxy soccer team and the L.A. Lakers, going for long walks, listening to music, and exploring new age spirituality. Dan can be contacted via email at Dan@TechPartners.info.

Philip Wiest is a nationally known professional technical trainer who has presented more than 1,200 Cisco and Microsoft seminars to more than 37,000 students throughout the United States, Canada, the United Kingdom, and Australia since 1989 for Skillpath Seminars, CompuMaster Seminars, Prime Learning International, and Dun & Bradstreet. He has earned several prominent certifications, including the MCSE; CCNP; CCDA; Network+; Server+; Security+; A+; and, most recently, the new MCDST designation.

He delights audiences by crashing (often with little effort) and then resurrecting (often with much effort) unsuspecting software programs and network applications. His unique, irreverent, solutions-oriented style is at once humorous and insightful.

Philip's clients include The Walt Disney Company, the FBI, American Express, the National Association of Recording Merchandisers, ARCO, Bank of America, KPMG, Sony, EMI Records Group N.A., the National Association of Realtors, Warner Bros., and on and on.

Since graduating from the University of Pennsylvania, he has published more than 200 newspaper and magazine articles, received dozens of national training awards, and completed 15 marathons. He resides in Santa Monica, California, never more than a stone's throw from a keyboard or a microphone.

As one of the first 5,000 professionals worldwide to earn his MCDST, Philip has been named a Microsoft Charter Member for MCDST. Additionally, he has been selected as Certification Magazine's "CertMag 500," the magazine's evaluation and review board of certified experts.

Acknowledgments

Writing is always tough, but it's made much more difficult when you're trying to balance several different projects along with it—all at the same time! Without a doubt, my beautiful wife and my two incredible kids give me the encouragement, support, and the strength that I need to carry on and always see things through to their completion. Alison is much more than just my wife; she's my mentor, my inspiration, and my lifetime partner! My daughter, Alexis, is almost 8 years old now: she never fails to amaze me with her creativity, her love, her warmth, her intelligence, and her willingness to learn. My son, Brendan, is just about 5 years old now, and he is a constant source of happiness, fun, affection, brilliance, and incessant energy! So, first and foremost, I am indebted to my family for their unfailing love and support.

I owe a lot of gratitude to my co-author, Philip Wiest. Without his true persistence and dedication, this book would not have become a reality! Phil, thank you so much for truly partnering with me on this book. I think that you've done a fantastic job, and I trust that those who read this book will agree with me. I also want to offer my heartfelt appreciation to two of my favorite *techno-wizs*: Tim Leonard and Alan Sugano. Tim is a full-time consultant at my company, InfoTechnology Partners, Inc. He has quickly become an invaluable resource, and he is very much responsible for the rapid growth of our company without sacrificing our first-class customer service! Alan Sugano has supplied me with a lot of his technical wisdom, with his wide array of experiences in the IT world, and with an incredible amount of moral support over the years.

Because I enjoy a very active business and personal life, I count my blessings every day for the outstanding individuals who assist my wife and me with an ever-growing list of things that must be attended to. To our nanny, Sonia Aguilar; her husband, Hugo; and their kids, Claudia, Gaby, and Huguito: thank you so much for taking such great care of our kids—we are very fortunate to have you all in our lives! To Edith Swanson, our office manager: thank you for taking such good care of our business matters and, oftentimes, our personal matters! To Dan Holme: thank you for your fantastic insight, your knowledge, your advice, and your support—I truly enjoy our business relationship and our friendship!

To Greggory Peck, thanks for partnering with us on Blast Through Learning (www.BlastThroughLearning.com). I appreciate your patience with me and my wife on project deadlines. Thank you for being an incredible friend! A ton of appreciation has to go to Scott McIntyre, Dave Henson, Derek Melber, Jeremy Moskowitz, Don Jones, and Mark Minasi: I really appreciate all your friendships. You guys all provide me with a lot of inspiration to always keep learning and to be the best author, trainer, and consultant that I can be! To Ron Sharpshair, thank you for all of your guidance, wisdom, and advice, which helps to make me a stronger and better person each and every day! To Carrie Sharpshair, president of Casual Cuisine, thanks for your incredible gourmet meals, which helped me to write this *Exam Cram* guide! Also, to Reverend Mary Lacalle and everyone associated with Unity Center Church of Thousand Oaks: thank you for always being a guiding light, for assisting me in staying on the spiritual path, and for allowing me to have the opportunity to make a difference within our own small community and within the world.

A world of thanks and love go to Herb and Maureen Balter, my mom and dad, for being the terrific parents and grandparents that you are! To my brother and my sister-in-law, Gary and Linda Balter, thanks for all of your love and support! To my in-laws, Charlotte and Bob Roman: your love and caring is never-ending and very much appreciated! To my "medical staff" and great friends, Dr. Steven Perry, D.C. and Dr. Anita Srinivasa, M.D.: your friendship means the world to me and to my family. Thank you for all that you've done and for all that you continue to do for us!

Finally, to Jeff Riley and Steve Rowe at Que Certification: you guys had the patience of heavenly saints while I struggled to complete this book. Thank you so much for hanging in there with me! To everyone else at Pearson Education, thank you for the mutually beneficial ongoing relationship that my wife and I have developed with you over the last several years. So now I'm getting ready for the next big *Exam Cram 2* series book; isn't the Windows "Longhorn" release supposed to come out in the year 2006? Or is it 2007? No matter, I just need to get my hands on the beta version, and I'll be ready.

—*Dan Balter*

Besides my therapist, I can't think of anyone more deserving of my thanks than Mary Ann Llamado, who, along with pursuing her nursing career, has found the time to nurture me as I've never been nurtured and organize me as I've never been organized.

My special thanks also go

—To Bill Cowles, Claudia Mayorga, and Randy Rash of SkillPath Seminars, who, every day that they put a student in front of a teacher, truly make a difference.

—To mentors like Steve Bass and Dan Balter, whose brilliance and irreverence have inspired me to be both amazed and amused by Windows XP.

—To my parents for instilling in me the love of learning and appreciation for the written word.

—And to each and every reader who opens a book and turns a page looking to see what comes next.

—*Philip Wiest*

We Want to Hear from You!

As the reader of this book, *you* are our most important critic and commentator. We value your opinion and want to know what we're doing right, what we could do better, what areas you'd like to see us publish in, and any other words of wisdom you're willing to pass our way.

As an executive editor for Que Publishing, I welcome your comments. You can email or write me directly to let me know what you did or didn't like about this book—as well as what we can do to make our books better.

Please note that I cannot help you with technical problems related to the topic of this book. We do have a User Services group, however, where I will forward specific technical questions related to the book.

When you write, please be sure to include this book's title and author as well as your name, email address, and phone number. I will carefully review your comments and share them with the author and editors who worked on the book.

Email: `feedback@quepublishing.com`

Mail: Jeff Riley
Executive Editor
Que Publishing
800 East 96th Street
Indianapolis, IN 46240 USA

For more information about this book or another Que Publishing title, visit our Web site at `http://www.quepublishing.com`. For information about the *Exam Cram 2* series, visit `http://www.examcram2.com`. Type the ISBN (excluding hyphens) or the title of a book in the Search field to find the page you're looking for.

Introduction

· ·

Welcome to the *70-271 Exam Cram 2*! Whether this book is your first or your twenty-first *Exam Cram 2* series book, you'll find information here that will help ensure your success as you pursue knowledge, experience, and certification. This book aims to help you get ready to take—and pass—the 70-271 exam.

This introduction explains Microsoft's certification programs in general and talks about how the *Exam Cram 2* series can help you prepare for Microsoft's latest MCSE, MCSA, and MCDST certification exams. Chapters 1 through 8 are designed to remind you of everything you need to know to pass the 70-271 certification exam. The two practice tests at the end of the book should give you a reasonably accurate assessment of your knowledge—and, yes, we provided the answers and their explanations for these sample tests. Read the book, understand the material, and you stand a good chance of passing the real test.

Exam Cram 2 books help you understand and appreciate the subjects and materials you need to know to pass Microsoft certification exams. *Exam Cram 2* books are aimed strictly at test preparation and review. They do not teach you everything you need to know about a subject. Instead, the authors streamline and highlight the pertinent information by presenting and dissecting the questions and problems they discovered that you're likely to encounter on a Microsoft test. *Exam Cram 2* authors work hard to bring together as much information as possible about Microsoft certification exams.

Nevertheless, to completely prepare yourself for any Microsoft test, we recommend that you begin by taking the "Self-Assessment" that is included in this book, immediately following this introduction. The self-assessment tool will help you evaluate your knowledge base against the requirements for becoming a Microsoft Certified Desktop Support Technician (MCDST), a Microsoft Certified Systems Administrator (MCSA), and a Microsoft Certified Systems Engineer (MCSE) for the Windows 2000 track and for the Windows Server 2003 track under both ideal and real circumstances.

Based on what you learn from the "Self-Assessment," you might decide to begin your studies with some classroom training or some background reading. On the other hand, you might decide to pick up and read one of the many study guides available from Microsoft or third-party vendors, including the award-winning *Training Guide* series from Que Publishing. We also recommend that you supplement your study program with visits to http://www.examcram2.com to receive additional practice questions, get advice, and follow the most recent developments for the MCDST, MCSA, and MCSE programs.

This book includes a MeasureUp test engine, which simulates the Microsoft testing environment with similar types of questions that you're likely to see on the actual Microsoft exam. We also strongly recommend that you install, configure, and play around with the network operating system software that you'll be tested on: nothing beats hands-on experience and familiarity when it comes to understanding the questions you're likely to encounter on a certification test. Book learning is essential, but without a doubt, hands-on experience is the best teacher of all!

Taking a Certification Exam

After you prepare for your exam, you need to register with a testing center. Each computer-based MCP exam costs $125, and if you don't pass, you can take each again for an additional $125 for each attempt. In the United States and Canada, tests are administered by Pearson VUE and by Prometric. Here's how you can contact them:

➤ *Pearson VUE*—You can sign up for a test by calling 800-837-8734 or via the Web site at http://www.vue.com/ms.

➤ *Prometric*—You can sign up for a test through the company's Web site, http://www.2test.com or http://www.prometric.com. Within the United States and Canada, you can register by phone at 800-755-3926. If you live outside this region, you should check the Prometric Web site for the appropriate phone number.

About This Book

Each topical *Exam Cram 2* chapter follows a regular structure and contains graphical cues about important or useful information. Here's the structure of a typical chapter:

➤ *Opening hotlists*—Each chapter begins with a list of the terms, tools, and techniques that you must learn and understand before you can be fully conversant with that chapter's subject matter. The hotlists are followed with one or two introductory paragraphs to set the stage for the rest of the chapter.

➤ *Topical coverage*—After the opening hotlists and introductory text, each chapter covers a series of topics related to the chapter's subject. Throughout that section, we highlight topics or concepts that are likely to appear on a test, using a special element called an alert:

This is what an alert looks like. Normally, an alert stresses concepts, terms, software, or activities that are likely to relate to one or more certification-test questions. For that reason, we think any information in an alert is worthy of unusual attentiveness on your part.

You should pay close attention to material flagged in Exam Alerts; although all the information in this book pertains to what you need to know to pass the exam, Exam Alerts contain information that is really important. You'll find what appears in the meat of each chapter to be worth knowing, too, when preparing for the test. Because this book's material is condensed, we recommend that you use this book along with other resources to achieve the maximum benefit.

In addition to the alerts, we provide tips that will help you build a better foundation for Windows XP knowledge. Although the tip information might not be on the exam, it is certainly related and it will help you become a better-informed test-taker.

This is how tips are formatted. Keep your eyes open for these, and you'll become a Windows XP guru in no time!

This is how notes are formatted. Notes direct your attention to important pieces of information that relate to Windows XP and Microsoft certification.

➤ *Exam prep questions*—Although we talk about test questions and topics throughout the book, the section at the end of each chapter presents a series of mock test questions and explanations of both correct and incorrect answers.

➤ *Details and resources*—Every chapter ends with a section titled "Need To Know More?" That section provides direct pointers to Microsoft and third-party resources that offer more details on the chapter's subject. In addition, that section tries to rank or at least rate the quality and thoroughness of the topic's coverage by each resource. If you find a resource you like in that collection, you should use it, but you shouldn't feel compelled to use all the resources. On the other hand, we recommend only resources that we use on a regular basis, so none of our recommendations will be a waste of your time or money (but purchasing them all at once probably represents an expense that many network administrators and would-be MCDSTs, MCSAs, and MCSEs might find hard to justify).

The bulk of the book follows this chapter structure, but we'd like to point out a few other elements. Chapters 9 and 11, "Practice Exam 1" and "Practice Exam 2," provide good reviews of the material presented throughout the book to ensure that you're ready for the exam. Chapters 10 and 12, "Answers to Practice Exam 1" and "Answers to Practice Exam 2," offer the correct answers to the questions on the practice tests that appear in Chapters 9 and 11. Appendix A, "What's on the CD?," provides helpful information about the material included on the book's CD-ROM. Appendix B, "Need to Know More?" offers you several books, free email newsletters, and Internet Web sites that contain useful information on Windows XP and related topics. In addition, you'll find a handy glossary and an index.

Finally, the tear-out Cram Sheet attached next to the inside front cover of this *Exam Cram 2* book represents a condensed and compiled collection of facts and tips that we think are essential for you to memorize before taking the test. Because you can dump this information out of your head onto a sheet of paper before taking the exam, you can master this information by brute force; you need to remember it only long enough to write it down when you walk into the testing room. You might even want to look at it in the car or in the lobby of the testing center just before you walk in to take the exam.

How to Use This Book

We've structured the topics in this book to build on one another. Therefore, some topics in later chapters make the most sense after you've read earlier chapters. That's why we suggest that you read this book from front to back for your initial test preparation. If you need to brush up on a topic or if you have to bone up for a second try, you can use the index or table of contents to go straight to the topics and questions that you need to study. Beyond helping you prepare for the test, we think you'll find this book useful as a tightly focused reference to some of the most important aspects of Windows XP.

The book uses the following typographical conventions:

➤ Command-line strings that are meant to be typed into the computer are displayed in monospace text, such as

```
net use lpt1: \\print_server_name\printer_share_name
```

➤*New terms* are introduced in italic.

Given all the book's elements and its specialized focus, we tried to create a tool that will help you prepare for—and pass—Microsoft Exam 70-271. Please share with us your feedback on the book, especially if you have ideas about how we can improve it for future test-takers. Send your questions or comments about this book via email to feedback@quepublishing.com. We'll consider everything you say carefully, and we'll respond to all suggestions. For more information on this book and other Que Certification titles, visit our Web site at http://www.quepublishing.com. You should also check out the new *Exam Cram 2* Web site at http://www.examcram2.com, where you'll find information updates, commentary, and certification information.

Thanks for making this *Exam Cram 2* book a pivotal part of your certification study plan: best of luck on becoming certified!

Self-Assessment

. . . .

Welcome to the self-assessment for this *Exam Cram 2* book. This is designed to help you evaluate your readiness to tackle the Microsoft Certified Desktop Support Technician (MCDST) certification. It should also help you to understand what you need to know to master the main topic of this book—namely, Exam 70-271, "Supporting Users and Troubleshooting a Microsoft Windows XP Operating System." You might also want to check out the Microsoft Skills Assessment home page—http://www.msmeasureup.com/test/home.asp on the Microsoft Training and Certification Web site. Because the MCDST credential can serve as a stepping-stone to the higher-level certifications, such as the Microsoft Certified Systems Administrator (MCSA) and the Microsoft Certified Systems Engineer (MCSE) credentials, this chapter also examines your current level of knowledge and experience for the road leading to these higher-level titles.

In addition to looking at the Microsoft Skills Assessment page, it's a good idea to browse through the home page for the 70-271 exam itself—http://www.microsoft.com/learning/exams/70-271.asp—as well as the home page for the MCDST certification at http://www.microsoft.com/learning/mcp/mcdst/default.asp (see Figure SA.1). But before you tackle this book's self-assessment, let's talk about concerns you might face when pursuing an MCDST, MCSA, or MCSE credential and what an ideal MCDST, MCSA, or MCSE candidate might look like.

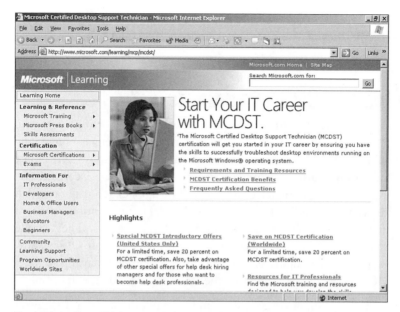

Figure SA.1 The MCDST certification home page.

MCDSTs in the Real World

In the next section, we describe the ideal MCDST, MCSA, and MCSE candidates, knowing full well that only a few real candidates actually meet that ideal. In fact, our description of those ideal candidates might seem downright scary, especially with the changes that have been made to the Microsoft Certified Professional program to support Windows Server 2003, Windows XP, and Windows 2000. But take heart: Although the requirements to obtain the MCDST, MCSA, and MCSE certifications might seem formidable, they are by no means impossible to meet. However, you need to be keenly aware that getting through the process takes time, involves some expense, and requires real effort.

Increasing numbers of people are attaining Microsoft certifications. You can get all the real-world motivation you need from knowing that many others have gone before, so you will be able to follow in their footsteps. If you're willing to tackle the process seriously and do what it takes to obtain the necessary experience and knowledge, you can take—and pass—all the certification tests involved in obtaining the MCDST, MCSA, or MCSE credentials. In fact, at Que Publishing, we've designed the *Exam Cram 2* series and the *MCSE Training Guide* series to make it as easy for you as possible to prepare for these exams. We've also greatly expanded our Web site, http://www.examcram2.com, to provide a host of resources to help you prepare for the complexities of Windows XP, Windows 2000, and Windows Server 2003.

The Ideal MCDST Candidate

Ideally, MCDST candidates should have experience supporting users who operate Microsoft Windows XP Professional in a business environment, and they should also have some familiarity with Microsoft Windows XP Home Edition in a nonbusiness environment. People seeking MCDST certification are expected to have experience using many of the application programs that ship with Windows XP Professional and the Home Edition, such as Microsoft Internet Explorer and Microsoft Outlook Express. They should also be well versed in the popular programs of the Microsoft Office suite, which are widely relied upon by the majority of PC users today. Candidates for the MCDST credential must pass the following two Microsoft exams:

➤ *Exam 70-271*—Supporting Users and Troubleshooting a Microsoft Windows XP Operating System

➤ *Exam 70-272*—Supporting Users and Troubleshooting Desktop Applications on a Microsoft Windows XP Operating System

The 70-271 and 70-272 exams serve to validate that a candidate can successfully answer, or know when to escalate, all technical support calls from workstation users. Candidates should be able to resolve operating-system issues by offering technical support over the telephone, by connecting to a user's computer remotely, and by working directly at a user's workstation. They should have a good working knowledge of how to function and troubleshoot issues in a workgroup setting as well as within an Active Directory domain environment. MCDST candidates should understand how users are affected by the different features that are available in each of these network environments.

Putting Yourself to the Test

The following series of questions and observations is designed to help you figure out how much work you must do to pursue Microsoft certification and what kinds of resources you can consult on your quest. Be absolutely honest in your answers, or you'll end up wasting money on exams that you're not yet ready to take. There are no right or wrong answers—only steps along the path to certification. Only you can decide where you really belong in the broad spectrum of aspiring candidates. Two things should be clear from the outset, however:

➤ Even a modest background in computer science will be helpful.

➤ Hands-on experience with Microsoft products and technologies is an essential ingredient in certification success.

Educational Background

The following questions concern your level of technical computer experience and training. Depending upon your answers to these questions, you might need to review some additional resources to get your knowledge up to speed for the types of questions that you will encounter on Microsoft certification exams:

1. Have you ever taken any computer-related classes? [Yes or No]

If Yes, proceed to Question 2; if No, proceed to Question 3.

2. Have you taken any classes on computer operating systems? [Yes or No]

If Yes, you will probably be able to handle Microsoft's architecture and system component discussions. If you're rusty, you should brush up on basic operating-system concepts, especially virtual memory, multitasking regimes, user-mode versus kernel-mode operation, and general computer security topics.

If No, you should consider doing some basic reading in this area. We strongly recommend a good general operating-systems book, such as *Operating System Concepts* by Abraham Silberschatz and Peter Baer Galvin (John Wiley & Sons). If this book doesn't appeal to you, check out reviews for other, similar, books at your favorite online bookstore.

3. Have you taken any networking concepts or technologies classes? [Yes or No]

If Yes, you will probably be able to handle Microsoft's networking terminology, concepts, and technologies. (Brace yourself for frequent departures from normal usage.) If you're rusty, you should brush up on basic networking concepts and terminology, especially networking media, transmission types, the Open Systems Interconnect (OSI) reference model, and networking technologies such as Ethernet, Token Ring, Fiber Distributed Data Interface (FDDI), and Wide Area Network (WAN) links.

If No, you might want to read one or two books in this topic area. The two best books that we know are *Computer Networks* by Andrew S. Tanenbaum (Prentice-Hall) and *Computer Networks and Internets* by Douglas E. Comer and Ralph E. Droms (Prentice-Hall).

Hands-On Experience

The most important key to success on all the Microsoft tests is hands-on experience, especially when it comes to Windows Server 2003, Windows XP, Windows 2000, and the many add-on services and components around which so many of the Microsoft certification exams revolve. If we leave you with only one realization after you take this self-assessment, it should be that there's no substitute for time spent installing, configuring, and using the various Microsoft products on which you'll be tested. The more in-depth understanding you have of how these software products work, the better your chance in selecting the right answers on the exam:

1. Have you installed, configured, and worked with the following:

   ➤ Windows 2000 Professional? [Yes or No]

   If Yes, make sure you understand the concepts covered in Exam 70-210.

   If No, you should obtain a copy of Windows 2000 Professional and learn how to install, configure, and maintain it. Pick up a well-written book to guide your activities and studies (such as *MCSE Windows 2000 Professional Exam Cram 2*), or you can work straight from Microsoft's exam objectives if you prefer.

   ➤ Windows XP Professional? [Yes or No]

   If Yes, make sure you understand the concepts covered in Exam 70-270, Exam 70-271, and Exam 70-272.

   If No, you should obtain a copy of Windows XP Professional and learn how to install, configure, and maintain it. Pick up a well-written book to guide your activities and studies (such as *MCSE Windows XP Professional Exam Cram 2*), or you can work straight from Microsoft's exam objectives, if you prefer.

   ➤ Windows 2000 Server? [Yes or No]

   If Yes, make sure you understand the concepts covered in Exam 70-215.

   If No, you should consider acquiring a copy of Windows 2000 Server and learn how to install, configure, and administer it. Purchase a well-written book to guide your activities and studies (such as *MCSE Windows 2000 Server Exam Cram 2*), or you can work straight from Microsoft's exam objectives.

➤ Windows Server 2003? [Yes or No]

If Yes, make sure you understand basic concepts as covered in Exam 70-291. You should also study the TCP/IP interfaces, utilities, and services for Exam 70-293, and you should implement security features for Exam 70-298.

If No, you must obtain one or two machines and a copy of Windows Server 2003. (A trial version is available on the Microsoft Web site.) Then, you should learn about the operating system and any other software components on which you'll also be tested. In fact, we recommend that you obtain two computers, each with a network interface, and set up a two-node network on which to practice. With decent Windows Server 2003–capable computers selling for about $500 to $600 apiece these days, this setup shouldn't be too much of a financial hardship. You might have to scrounge to come up with the necessary software, but if you scour the Microsoft Web site, you can usually find low-cost options to obtain evaluation copies of most of the software that you need.

You can download objectives, practice exams, and other data about Microsoft exams from the Training and Certification page at **http://www.microsoft.com/traincert**. You can use the "Exams" link to obtain specific exam information.

Use One Computer to Simulate Multiple Machines

If you own a powerful enough computer—one that has plenty of available disk space, a lot of RAM (at least 512MB), and a Pentium 4–compatible processor or better—you should check out the VMware and Virtual PC virtual-machine software products that are on the market. These software programs create an emulated computer environment within separate windows that are hosted by your computer's main operating system—Windows Server 2003, Windows XP, Windows 2000, and so on. On a single computer, you can have several different operating systems running simultaneously in different windows! You can run everything from DOS to Linux, from Windows 95 to Windows Server 2003. Within a virtual-machine environment, you can "play" with the latest operating systems, including beta versions, without worrying about "blowing up" your main production computer and without having to buy an additional PC. VMware is published by VMware, Inc (an EMC company). You can get more information from its Web site at **http://www.vmware.com** (see Figure SA.2). Virtual PC was purchased from Connectix Corporation in 2003 and is now published by Microsoft. You can find out more information on this product at **http://www.microsoft.com/windowsxp/virtualpc** (see Figure SA.3).

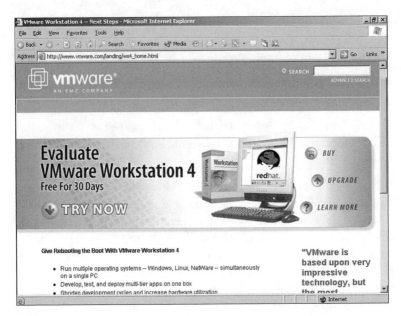

Figure SA.2   The home page for VMware Workstation 4.

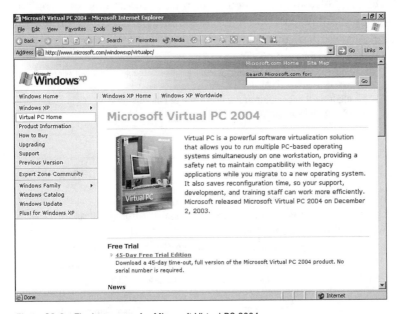

Figure SA.3   The home page for Microsoft Virtual PC 2004.

For any and all of these Microsoft operating systems exams, the Resource Kits for the topics involved always make good study resources (see Figure SA.4). You can purchase the Resource Kits from Microsoft Press (you can search for them at **http://www.microsoft.com/learning/Books/default.asp**), but they also appear on the TechNet CDs, DVDs, and Web site (**http://www.microsoft.com/technet**). Along with the *Exam Cram 2* books, we believe that the Resource Kits are among the best tools you can use to prepare for Microsoft exams. Take a look at the Windows Deployment and Resource Kits Web page for more information: **http://www.microsoft.com/windows/reskits/default.asp**.

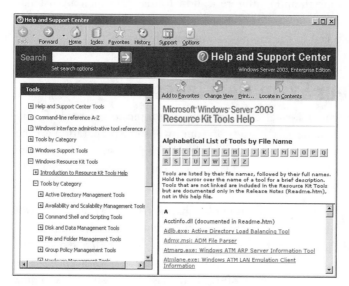

Figure SA.4   Viewing the alphabetical list of tools for the Windows Server 2003 Resource Kit.

2. For any specific Microsoft product that is not itself an operating system (for example, SQL Server), have you installed, configured, used, and upgraded this software? [Yes or No]

If Yes, skip to the next section, "Testing Your Exam Readiness." If No, you must get some experience. Read on for suggestions about how to do this.

Experience is a must with any Microsoft product exam, be it something as simple as FrontPage 2002 or as challenging as SQL Server 2000. For trial copies of other software, you can search Microsoft's Web site, using the name of the product as your search term. Also, you can search for bundles such as BackOffice, Enterprise Servers, Windows Server System, or Small Business Server.

If you have the funds, or if your employer will pay your way, you should consider taking a class at a Microsoft Certified Training and Education Center (CTEC). In addition to classroom exposure to the topic of your choice, you get a copy of the software that is the focus of your course, along with a trial version of whatever operating system it needs, as part of the training materials for that class.

Before you even think about taking any Microsoft exam, you should make sure you've spent enough time with the related software to understand how to install and configure it, how to maintain such an installation, and how to troubleshoot the software when things go wrong. This time will help you in the exam—and in real life!

Testing Your Exam Readiness

Whether you attend a formal class on a specific topic to get ready for an exam or use written materials to study on your own, some preparation for the Microsoft certification exams is essential. At $125 a pop—whether you pass or fail—you'll want to do everything you can to pass on your first try. That's where studying comes in.

We include two practice tests in this book (Chapters 9 and 11), so even if you don't score too well on these tests the first time, you can study the practice exams more and then tackle the tests again. We also have practice questions that you can sign up for online through http://www.examcram2.com. The MeasureUp CD-ROM in the back of this book has sample questions to quiz you; you can purchase additional practice questions from http://www.measureup.com. If you still don't hit a score of at least 70% after practicing with these tests, you should investigate the other practice-test resources that are mentioned in this section.

For any given subject, you should consider taking a class if you've worked with the self-study materials, taken the test, and still been unsuccessful. The opportunity to interact with an instructor and fellow students can make all the difference in the world, if you can afford that luxury. For information about Microsoft classes, visit the Training and Certification page at http://www.microsoft.com/traincert/training/find/findcourse.asp for locating training courses offered at Microsoft CTECs.

If you can't afford to take a class, you can visit the Training and Certification pages anyway because they include links to free practice exams and to Microsoft-approved study guides and other self-study tools. Even if you can't afford to spend much money at all, you should still invest in some low-cost practice exams from third-party vendors. The Microsoft Training and

Certification "Assess Your Readiness" page at http://www.microsoft.com/traincert/assessment offers several skills-assessment evaluations that you can take online to show you how far along you are in your certification preparation.

The next question deals with your personal testing experience. Microsoft certification exams have their own style and idiosyncrasies. The more acclimated that you become to the Microsoft testing environment, the better your chances will be to score well on the exams:

1. Have you taken a practice exam on your chosen test subject? [Yes or No]

   If Yes, and if you scored 70% or better, you're probably ready to tackle the real thing. If your score isn't above that threshold, you should keep at it until you break that barrier.

   If No, you should obtain all the free and low-budget practice tests you can find and get to work. You should keep at it until you can break the passing threshold comfortably.

 When it comes to assessing your test readiness, there is no better way than to take a good-quality practice exam and pass with a score of 70% or better. When we're preparing ourselves, we shoot for 80% or higher, just to leave room for the "weirdness factor" that sometimes shows up on Microsoft exams.

Assessing Readiness for Exam 70-271

In addition to the general exam-readiness information in the previous section, there are several things you can do to prepare for the Exam 70-271. As you're getting ready for the exam, you should visit the *Exam Cram 2* Web site at http://www.examcram2.com. We also suggest that you join an active MCSE/MCSA email list and email newsletter. Some of the best list servers and email newsletters are managed by Sunbelt Software and *Windows & .NET Magazine*. You can sign up for Sunbelt's newsletters at http://www.sunbelt-software.com. You can register for the *Windows & .NET Magazine* "Update" newsletters at http://www.winnetmag.com/.

Proven Microsoft exam veterans also recommend that you check the Microsoft Knowledge Base (available on its own CD as part of the TechNet collection, and on the Microsoft Web site, at http://support.microsoft.com) for "meaningful technical support issues" that relate to your exam's topics.

Although we're not sure exactly what the quoted phrase means, we have also noticed some overlap between technical-support questions on particular products and troubleshooting questions on the exams for those products.

Take on the Challenge!

After you assess your readiness, undertake the right background studies, obtain the hands-on experience that will help you understand the products and technologies at work, and review the many sources of information to help you prepare for a test, you'll be ready to take a round of practice tests. When your scores come back positive enough to get you through the exam, you're ready to go after the real thing. If you follow our assessment regime, you'll not only know what you need to study, but you'll know when you're ready to set a test date at Pearson VUE (http://www.vue.com) or Prometric (http://www.prometric.com). Go get 'em: good luck!

Installing the Windows XP Desktop Operating System

Terms you'll need to understand:

✓ Unattended installations
✓ Windows Update
✓ Dynamic updates
✓ FAT, FAT32, and NT File System (NTFS)
✓ Microsoft Product Activation (MPA)
✓ Retail, Original Equipment Manufacturer (OEM), Open, Select, and Enterprise licensing types
✓ Setup Manager
✓ Answer files
✓ Uniqueness database files (UDBs)
✓ Remote Installation Services (RIS)
✓ Preboot Execution Environment (PXE) network cards
✓ User State Migration Tool (USMT)
✓ Files and Settings Transfer (FAST) Wizard
✓ Service Packs (SPs) and slipstreaming

Techniques you'll need to master:

✓ Performing attended and unattended installations
✓ Performing upgrade installations
✓ Using Setup Manager to create and modify answer files
✓ Installing Windows XP from an RIS server
✓ Troubleshooting application compatibility issues
✓ Establishing dual-boot or multiple-boot configurations
✓ Migrating user settings and data with the USMT and the FAST Wizard
✓ Troubleshooting installation failures
✓ Installing Service Packs and slipstreaming installation files

Microsoft designed Windows XP Home Edition and Windows XP Professional to be powerful in their capabilities yet relatively simple to install and get up and running. However, the apparent simplicity in installing Windows XP can be deceiving. Buried "under the hood" of Microsoft's latest desktop operating system lie many advanced features, such as the ability to perform an unattended installation using a preconfigured answer file. Windows XP Professional, the business edition, also offers you the option to install from a preconfigured image on an RIS server and the power to boot a computer that has no operating system on it using a PXE-compliant network card so that you can just sit back and watch as Windows XP gets *automagically* installed.

After you successfully install Windows XP onto a desktop computer, certain licensing provisions require that you use MPA, whereas other licensing types completely bypass MPA. This chapter explores the many subtleties about installing Windows XP as well as describes the various releases and minimum operating requirements for each edition of Windows XP.

Flavors of the Windows XP Operating System

Microsoft Windows XP comes in two distinct *flavors*, or editions. Each edition is designed for specific environments and types of usage. All editions of Windows XP are built on the reliability and the security of the Windows 2000 engine, but Windows XP has been greatly enhanced with several new features compared to Windows 2000. These new features include the Internet Connection Firewall (ICF), Dynamic Updates during installation, System Restore, Remote Assistance, Remote Desktop Connections, and native CD-burning capabilities, among several others. Each edition of Windows XP and its intended use is detailed in the following list:

➤ *Windows XP Home Edition*—This edition is designed for the home user and contains a subset of the features in Windows XP Professional. *It cannot be a member of a Windows NT or an Active Directory domain, and it cannot act as a Remote Desktop server*. It works well for composing and editing general-purpose documents; for browsing the Internet; for using email applications; and for editing multimedia content such as photos, music, audio, and video files.

➤ *Windows XP Professional*—This edition is designed for the business user, replacing Windows 2000 Professional. It offers several features that are not available under the Home Edition, such as acting as a Remote

Desktop server, joining a Windows NT or Active Directory domain, native file encryption, support for up to two processors, System Restore, Device Driver Rollback, and Automated System Recovery.

Hardware Requirements and Installation Issues

Even though Windows XP Home Edition and Windows XP Professional target different types of users, these two operating systems have the same minimum hardware requirements. Unfortunately, the minimum hardware specifications as stated by Microsoft do not truly reflect the "horsepower" needed for Windows XP to perform well in the "real world," especially when it comes to using such demanding applications as computer-aided design programs and multitasking several different programs simultaneously. Most people find that Windows XP performs fairly well with 256MB of memory, but that it performs even better with 512MB of RAM or more. The minimum hardware specifications are as follows:

➤ A personal computer with a Pentium-based or Pentium-compatible processor running at a clock speed of at least 233Mhz

➤ 64MB RAM (but Microsoft recommends at least 128MB RAM)

➤ One 1.5GB hard disk drive with at least 650MB of available disk space

➤ Super VGA (or better) video display adapter and monitor capable of 800×600 resolution or higher

➤ CD-ROM or DVD drive

➤ Keyboard input device

➤ Mouse or compatible pointing device

Before installing Windows XP, you should check the BIOS version and supported features that are part of your computer (see Figure 1.1). Motherboard manufacturers burn the BIOS instruction code (programming) into the Complementary Metal Oxide Semiconductor (CMOS) chip that is built into each PC's motherboard. In most cases, you can update the version of the BIOS stored on the computer by contacting the motherboard or computer manufacturer. It is best to install the latest BIOS from your hardware vendor before tackling the XP Professional installation. Features such as Plug and Play and Advanced Configuration and Power Interface (ACPI) are important for the full functionality of Windows XP.

ACPI allows the operating system to control power management and is responsible for the core Plug-and-Play functions in Windows XP. If you first install Windows XP on a system that does not support ACPI and later upgrade the system to support ACPI, you will most likely encounter a Windows Blue Screen Stop Error message, also commonly known as the Blue Screen of Death (BSOD). The Hardware Abstraction Layer (HAL) for ACPI is not the same as that of Advanced Power Management (APM), which is used if ACPI is not supported.

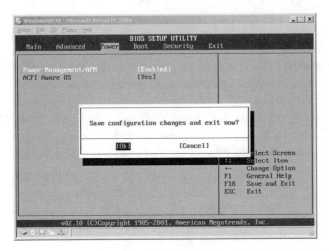

Figure 1.1 An example of the BIOS Setup Utility for American Megatrends, Inc.

After you verify that the computer meets, or exceeds, the minimum hardware requirements, you should check whether the various components that make up your system, such as the video display adapter and the network interface card (NIC), are compatible with Windows XP. To verify compatibility, you should check the Hardware Compatibility List (HCL) on the Windows XP installation CD. However, the HCL stored on the CD gets outdated quickly. You should visit http://www.microsoft.com/whdc/hcl to obtain the most current information possible.

Licensing Issues and MPA

Technically, Microsoft "licenses" each of its software products to individuals, companies, and organizations; it does not "sell" its software. When money is exchanged for Microsoft's (and many other software publishers') software products, ownership is not granted to the buyer. As the End User License Agreement (EULA) states, the purchaser is buying a license to use the software in accordance with the terms of the EULA contract and copyright law. For Microsoft server products, the person or entity "buying" the software must purchase a license for each server product.

Additionally, the licensed entity must purchase a separate Client Access License (CAL) for each user or device that will be connecting to the server software. For example, if your organization is using Windows Terminal Services, each Terminal Server (Remote Desktop Connection) user or device must also have a Terminal Server Client Access License (TSCAL), or each user or device must qualify to use a built-in TSCAL, to connect to Windows Terminal Servers. Microsoft offers a total of seven types of software licensing:

➤ *Full Packaged Product*—You can purchase full retail products in the box at stores such as Staples or Office Depot or from any one of a number of online resellers via the Internet. This low-volume purchase option is designed for consumers and small businesses that need fewer than five licenses. Media (CD-ROM, DVD-ROM) ships in each package.

➤ *OEM Licensing*—The term OEM applies to companies such as IBM, Dell, and Hewlett-Packard (HP). These companies manufacture and sell personal computers with Microsoft operating systems pre-installed, such as Windows XP. Microsoft sells OEM versions of its operating systems software to these manufacturers, specifically for pre-installing the software on new computer systems.

 OEM software and licensing is prohibited from being sold as a standalone software product. Retail (Full Packaged Product) product key codes do not work on OEM versions of Microsoft software; OEM product key codes do not work on retail versions.

➤ *Open Licensing*—This is the entry-level volume-licensing program for corporate, academic, charity, and government customers that need at least five licenses per product or more. The Open, Select, and Enterprise licensing programs are more economical than purchasing retail packages. This program is designed for small- to medium-sized companies.

➤ *Select Licensing*—This volume licensing program is designed for corporate, academic, and government customers who have decentralized purchasing and need at least 250 licenses per product or more.

➤ *Enterprise Agreement Licensing*—This volume licensing program is designed for corporate customers who have centralized purchasing and need at least 250 licenses per product or more.

➤ *Enterprise Subscription Agreement Licensing*—This volume licensing program is also designed for corporate customers that need at least 250 licenses per product or more, and these software products are licensed on a subscription basis.

➤ *Academic, Charity, and Government Licensing*—Microsoft also offers programs designed specifically for educational institutions, charitable organizations, and government agencies. These licensing programs offer reduced rates to qualified organizations.

You must purchase media separately for a nominal fee for Open, Select, Enterprise, Academic, Charity, and Government Licensing.

Understanding Microsoft Licensing

Microsoft licensing generally offers three licensing modes—*Per Server, Per Device* or *Per User*, and *Per Processor*. When buy a new computer that comes with an operating system, or when you install an operating system such as Windows XP Professional on a computer, Microsoft grants you a user license to use that software on that specific machine. Computers running desktop operating systems are often referred to as *clients*. Per-server licensing requires a CAL for each user or device that accesses a particular server. In this mode, CALs are associated with specific servers. If you choose the per-server option, you must purchase at least as many CALs for a given server as the maximum number of clients that might connect to that server at any point in time.

Just because you have Windows 9x/NT/2000/XP running on a computer does *not* automatically grant you any type of built-in license for accessing server computers running Microsoft operating systems on a local area network. CALs are required for connecting to and making use of server resources, such as file sharing and printing. CALs are required *in addition* to purchasing the operating system for workstations.

If you choose the per-device or per-user option, each CAL is associated with a specific user, computer, or device. Clients, therefore, are entitled to connect to *any* server on the network as long as each client (user or device) possesses a CAL for each type of server being accessed (for example, one CAL for Windows Server 2003, one CAL for SQL Server, one CAL for Exchange Server, and so on). Not all but selected server products offer per-processor licensing, such as SQL Server 2000. *With per-processor licensing, CALs are not required*. The server itself is licensed based on the number of processors installed in the server.

Microsoft permits organizations to make a one-time–only switch from per-server licensing to per-device or per-user licensing. Microsoft does not permit switching from per-device or per-user licensing to per-server licensing.

To keep track of software licensing for the different types of licensing options, Windows 2000 Server and Windows Server 2003 install the Licensing tool by default. You need to work directly with the proper licensing server if you want to manage software licenses for an entire site.

Using the Licensing Tools

Windows Server 2003 actually installs two licensing utilities by default. The Licensing icon in the Control Panel lets you configure licensing for the local server (see Figure 1.2). Under Active Directory for Windows Server 2003, if you click Start, All Programs, Administrative Tools, Licensing on a domain controller (DC) computer, you can launch the Enterprise Licensing tool for sites and domains (see Figure 1.3). To use either licensing tool, *you must have the License Logging service running* on the server that you are working on. By default, the License Logging service is *not* started automatically. You must be a member of the Administrators group for the local server or for the domain on which you want to manage licensing.

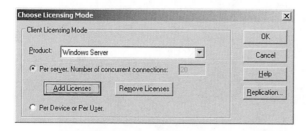

Figure 1.2   The Choose Licensing Mode utility for managing software licenses on the local server.

Figure 1.3   The Enterprise Licensing tool for managing software licenses for Active Directory sites and domains.

Using Volume License Key Codes and MPA

Microsoft operating systems such as Windows XP and Windows Server 2003 require that you enter a specific 25-character Volume License Key (VLK) code during the installation of each copy of the software that you install. For retail (Full Packaged Product) versions and OEM versions, you must also *activate* each copy of the software that you have installed. This procedure is referred to as MPA or as Windows Product Activation (WPA), as shown in Figure 1.4. Because the activation procedure has also been implemented in other Microsoft products, such as Office XP and Office 2003, the broader term, MPA, is more applicable. Microsoft implemented product activation in an effort to reduce software piracy.

Microsoft gives you *30 days* after the first time you use the product in which to activate *Windows XP* and *Office 2003*; Microsoft allows you *60 days* after installation in which to activate *Windows Server 2003*. If users do not activate the software within the appropriate time frame, Windows XP stops functioning; Office 2003 goes into *reduced functionality* mode (read-only mode); Windows Server 2003 can only be accessed using the Administrator account under Safe Mode. For Volume Licensing customers, these products do not require Microsoft Product Activation: they are shipped as already activated.

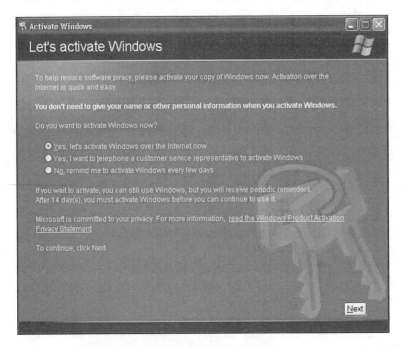

Figure 1.4   The Activate Windows dialog box for Windows XP.

For retail and OEM versions of Windows XP, if you add, remove, or change several hardware components on your computer at the same time, you might be prompted to reactivate Windows XP. For example, if you were to power off your PC and add new memory, swap out the old network card for new one, and swap out the old video card for a different one, Windows XP might require you to reactivate it the next time you start the computer. This step can occur to ensure that you are not trying to install (clone) Windows XP onto another computer without being properly licensed. Placing a phone call to MPA and explaining the situation should allow you reactivate fairly easily.

Performing an Attended Installation of Windows XP

You can install Windows XP Professional in one of two ways—*attended* and *unattended*. An attended installation is simply a straightforward *interactive* setup where the user must respond to prompts from the setup program to complete the installation process. An unattended installation is a great way to automate the installation procedure, especially if you need to install several computers at the same time using standardized settings. One popular method for performing unattended installations requires an answer file, which is a text file that contains the necessary and optional configuration parameters for the setup program to follow as it installs Windows XP Professional on the computer.

Understanding the Installation Steps

You can install Windows XP directly from the setup files stored on its CD-ROM media, from its setup files copied onto the computer's hard drive, or from its setup files stored on a network drive. Microsoft does not publish Windows XP setup files on floppy disk. The Windows XP installation process is divided into the following six major stages:

1. *Text-Mode Phase*—This first stage runs in a text-mode environment, similar to the legacy MS-DOS operating system interface. Setup copies files from the CD-ROM (or from another location where the setup files are stored) onto a temporary folder on the computer's hard drive. After the copy process finishes, the system restarts.

2. *GUI Phase*—This second stage launches into GUI mode, which has the typical Windows look and feel. During the initial portion of the GUI phase, Setup starts the *Collecting Information* stage to survey the overall configuration of the computer system and to detect hardware devices installed on the system.

3. *Dynamic Update*—At this stage, Windows XP Setup attempts to locate and use a live connection to the Internet so that it can search for and download any updated installation files from Microsoft.

4. *Preparing Installation*—During this stage, the user is prompted for important answers about how the system should be configured. This stage is the interactive portion of the Setup program. The installation cannot continue until the user addresses each dialog box presented. The Windows XP Start menu items are also installed during this stage.

5. *Installing Windows*—This stage deals with implementing the configuration settings that the user has requested by addressing the questions in each of the dialog boxes that appear during the Preparing Installation stage. After this stage finishes, the system restarts.

6. *Finalizing Installation*—This stage begins as the computer restarts following the Installing Windows stage. The Setup program detects the display settings and attempts to set the best screen resolution for the monitor and video display adapter installed. For Retail and OEM versions, the Windows *Out Of Box Experience* (OOBE) launches to assist users with setting up an Internet connection (optional), registering their copies of Windows XP (optional), activating their copies of Windows XP (mandatory within 30 days), and entering at least one username into the system.

Installing the Windows XP Operating System

To perform a clean install (as opposed to an upgrade), you can boot the computer directly from the Windows XP Professional CD, if your computer supports booting from the CD or DVD drive. If the computer does not support booting from the CD drive, you can boot using an MS-DOS boot floppy that contains device drivers for the CD drive, or you can boot from a Windows 98 Startup disk, which already contains drivers for most CD drives. From a command prompt, you need to navigate to the I386 folder so that you can run the winnt.exe command: it is a 16-bit setup program that can be launched from an MS-DOS or Windows 98 Startup environment. You cannot run the setup.exe program that resides on the root of the CD-ROM under the MS-DOS or Windows 98 Startup environment. After you start the Windows XP Setup program, follow these steps for a successful installation:

1. Press the Enter key to begin the installation process in the first stage (Text-Mode Phase).

2. Press the F8 key to agree to the EULA.

3. Use the arrow keys to select an existing disk partition on which to install Windows XP, or create a new disk partition within unpartitioned space on a disk, as shown in Figure 1.5.

4. Press the Enter key to continue with the installation.

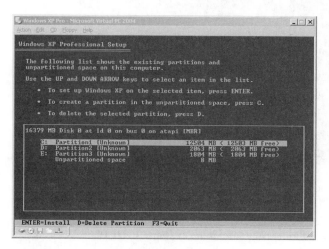

Figure 1.5   Choosing an installation partition.

5. If you choose to install on a new partition, Setup prompts you to format it before the installation can continue. If you selected an existing partition, Setup asks you whether or not you want to format it. *Formatting deletes all data stored on the partition!* Your options (shown in Figure 1.6) are FAT file system (Quick or normal format) or NTFS (Quick or normal format). Select the appropriate options and press the Enter key to continue.

The FAT and FAT32 file systems are inherited from the days of MS-DOS and Windows 9x. The preferred file system for Windows XP, Windows 2000, and Windows Server 2003 is NTFS. NTFS offers file-level security, file encryption, file compression, storage space optimization, and much greater reliability than FAT or FAT32, among many other features. The only tangible benefit that FAT or FAT32 offers compared to NTFS is backward compatibility with previous operating systems such as Windows 95, Windows 98, and Windows Me. This compatibility is especially important in dual-boot and multiboot configurations, where two or more operating systems must co-exist on the same computer. Other than that, remember that NTFS is the ticket!

6. Windows XP Setup then proceeds to format the installation partition (if necessary). Next, Setup analyzes the hard disks installed on the computer and creates a list of files that need to be copied to a temporary folder on the hard disk. After the Setup files are copied, Setup restarts the computer so that the second stage of the installation (GUI Phase) can commence.

Figure 1.6 Selecting a file system and a formatting option for the installation partition.

7. Upon restart, the Collecting Information stage (GUI Phase) begins. The Dynamic Update stage quickly follows and then the Preparing Installation stage launches. During this portion of the installation, all three of these stages appear to run simultaneously.

8. The first question asked of the user involves Windows XP's Regional and Language Settings. If you're located within the United States, you shouldn't have to change the Standards and Formats setting or the Text Input Language settings. Click the Next button to continue.

9. A second dialog box immediately follows and prompts the user to enter his or her name and the organization name (if any) for licensing purposes. Click Next to continue.

10. The third dialog box requires the user to enter the 25-character VLK product code for licensing enforcement. Type in the product key and click Next to proceed.

11. The fourth dialog box prompts you to enter a name for this computer, and as an option, you can enter a password for the default administrator user account. (FYI: Windows XP Home Edition does give you the option to enter a password for the administrator.) Type in a computer name and an administrator password and click Next to continue.

12. The fifth dialog box asks you to verify or set the correct date, time, and time zone information for the computer. Click Next to move onto the next step.

13. At this point, the Setup program installs networking software components, if the computer has at least one network adapter or modem installed. The default components are The Client for Microsoft Networks, File and Print Sharing, the Quality of Service (QoS) Packet Scheduler, and the TCP/IP network protocol. Under Windows XP, TCP/IP cannot be uninstalled.

14. The sixth dialog box prompts you to choose from two types of Networking Settings: Typical or Custom. Click one of these options and click Next.

15. If you select Custom settings, you can manually configure the system's networking components and you can also install or uninstall the default components (except for TCP/IP). In addition, you can enable or disable each component by marking or clearing its check box (see Figure 1.7). Click Next to continue.

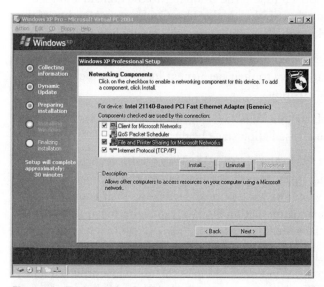

Figure 1.7   The Networking Components dialog box.

16. Accept the default option setting to make the computer a member of a workgroup, or select the option to make the computer a member of a domain (see Figure 1.8). Type the name of a workgroup or accept the default. Click Next to continue.

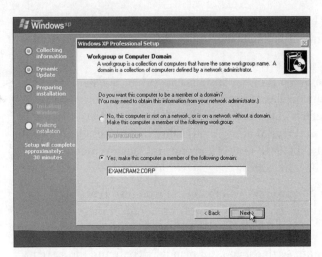

Figure 1.8 The Workgroup or Computer Domain dialog box.

17. If you selected Yes, Make This Computer a Member of the Following Domain in Step 15, you must now type the name and password of a user who is authorized to join the computer to the domain and then click OK. If you selected No...Make This Computer a Member of the Following Workgroup, the installation process simply continues.

18. At this point, Setup copies the installation files from the temporary folder on the hard drive to their permanent location on the chosen installation disk partition.

19. After the main Installing Windows stage completes, the system restarts and the Finalizing Installation stage begins.

20. For Retail and OEM versions, the Windows OOBE launches to assist users with setting up an Internet connection (optional), registering their copies of Windows XP (optional), activating their copies of Windows XP (mandatory within 30 days), and entering at least one username into the system.

21. For standalone PCs and workgroup computers, Windows XP automatically logs on to the Windows desktop as the username provided during the OOBE. For these computers, the Windows Welcome screen appears whenever you log off or if you log on with a password. For computers that are members of a Windows domain, the Log On to Windows dialog box appears; you need to type in your username and password, and you can select to log on to the local computer or to the domain from the Log On to drop-down list box.

Performing Unattended Installations of Windows XP

If you need to roll out several Windows XP computers all at once, or if you find that you need to re-install machines over and over again using the same configuration settings, then you really need to know how to install Windows XP without requiring any user intervention. You can take on the job of performing unattended installs in any one of the following ways:

➤ Create an answer file and install from the Windows XP CD-ROM.

➤ Create an answer file and install from a network server share.

➤ Install from an RIS server under Windows 2000 Server or Windows Server 2003.

➤ Install from a system image file created by a third-party software product and applied in conjunction with the sysprep.exe tool from Microsoft.

Automating CD-ROM and Network Installations

By storing all the required answers to the questions posed by the Windows XP Setup program, you can easily automate the installation process to provide for an unattended installation. After all, the only user intervention required is to answer each prompt that appears during the initial part of the Text-Mode Phase and during the Preparing Installation stage of Setup. You can create a Windows XP Setup answer file manually, if you want, but it is much easier to use the setupmgr.exe tool. Many software tools and utilities ship on the Windows XP Professional CD-ROM. The deployment tools are stored within a compressed cabinet file (.cab) located in the \support\tools folder. If you double-click the deploy.cab file, you can view the deployment tools. The deploy.cab file contains just nine files, including the setupmgr.exe file, which is the executable file for the Windows XP Setup Manager. To use these tools, simply drag and drop all nine of them into a folder on your computer's hard drive.

Creating Answer Files with Setup Manager

Unattended answer files are text files that provide all the necessary answers to the questions posed by the Windows XP Setup program to allow for automated installations. After you copy the Windows XP deployment tools onto your computer's hard drive, you can double-click the setupmgr.exe file to launch the application. Microsoft has updated the Windows XP deployment tools more than once since Windows XP was initially released. At the time that this book was published, there were three versions of Setup Manager for Windows XP and later operating systems—Windows XP, Windows XP SP1, and Windows Server 2003.

The steps that follow use the original version that shipped on the Windows XP CD-ROM. Therefore, depending on the version of Setup Manager that you use, some of the options displayed might be slightly different. The terms "Windows 2002 Server" and "Windows .NET Server" both refer to the Windows Server 2003 product family. To create a new answer file using Setup Manager, follow these steps:

1. Click Next for the Welcome to the Windows Setup Manager Wizard window.

2. Leave the default option Create a New Answer File (Create New) selected and then click Next.

3. Make sure that the Windows Unattended Installation (Unattended Setup) option is selected and then click Next to continue.

4. Select the Windows product that you want to install and click Next:

   ➤ Windows XP Home Edition

   ➤ Windows XP Professional

   ➤ Windows 2002 Server, Advanced Server, or Data Center

5. Select the level of user interaction that you want to offer during the installation process (see Figure 1.9):

   ➤ Provide Defaults (User Controlled)

   ➤ Fully Automated

   ➤ Hide Pages (Hidden Pages)

   ➤ Read Only

   ➤ GUI Attended

You can download updated deployment tools for Windows XP from Microsoft's Web site. The updated Windows XP SP1 Deployment Tools page allows you to download the **xpsp1DeployTools_en.cab** file at the following URL: **http://www. microsoft.com/downloads/details.aspx?FamilyID=7a83123d-507b-4095-9d9d- 0a195f7b5f69&DisplayLang=en**. You should always check for recent updates before you start to implement your Windows XP deployment plan.

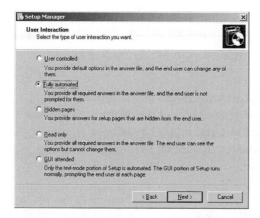

Figure 1.9 The User Interaction dialog box for Setup Manager SP1.

6. Click Next.

7. Select whether you want to create a distribution folder (share) where the Windows XP Setup files are located, if you want to modify an existing distribution share, or if you want to run Setup unattended from the Windows XP CD, and then click Next.

8. Specify the location of the Windows XP Setup files so that they can be copied to the distribution folder on the network and then click Next.

9. Type in a location or click Browse to specify the location of the distribution folder.

10. Type in the share name for the distribution folder (see Figure 1.10) and click Next.

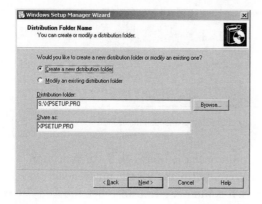

Figure 1.10 Specifying a distribution folder and assigning its share name for the network.

11. You must accept the terms of the EULA for Microsoft Windows, if you choose the Fully Automated unattended installation option. Click to select the I Accept the Terms of the License Agreement check box and then click Next.

12. At this point, the Setup Manager settings dialog box appears, where you can customize several different aspects of the unattended installation. Type in the default username and organization name and click Next. (You can also jump around from setting to setting by clicking each option in the left column.)

> Setup Manager has three sections of customization settings: General Settings, Network Settings, and Advanced Settings.

13. Specify display settings or accept the defaults and click Next.

14. Specify a time zone or accept the default and click Next.

15. For a fully automated installation, you must specify a Windows product key (see Figure 1.11). Type in the key and click Next.

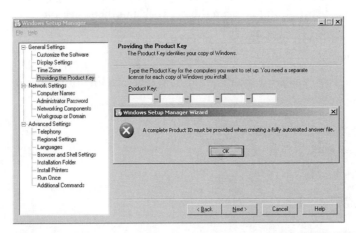

Figure 1.11 Typing in a product key for a fully automated unattended installation.

16. At the Computer Names option, under the Network Settings section, you must provide at least one computer name for the unattended installation. You can type in each computer name and click the Add button and you can click the Import button to import computer names from a text file. These computer names are stored in another text file whose name has the .udb extension. Alternatively, you can select the

Automatically Generate Computer Names Based on the Organization Name check box. Click Next to continue.

 For unattended installations, you can assign computer names and specify other settings using a *Uniqueness Database file* (**.udb**). You must specify name and location of the UDB file on the command line when you launch the Windows XP installation. A UDB file is a text file whose values *override the values stored in the unattended answer file* during an installation. On the command line, you specify the name of the UDB file with the **/UDF** switch, *not* **/UDB**. You can learn more about using UDB files in the section "Using UDB Files" later in this chapter.

17. Under the Network Settings section, you can customize local administrator password settings, you can configure settings for networking components, and you can specify that the newly installed computer joins a particular workgroup or domain. Click Next or select a different option in the left column to continue.

18. Under the Advanced Settings section, you can customize telephony settings, regional settings, languages options, and several other items. Click Next or select a different option in the left column to continue.

19. Click the Additional Commands option from the left column and click Finish to save your custom settings to an answer file. Type in the path (or click Browse) and type in the filename for the answer file. The default location is the distribution folder that you specified. The default answer filename is unattend.txt.

20. Click OK after you enter the answer filename and location (or accepted the defaults), and Setup Manager saves the files to disk and then copies the Windows XP setup files to the distribution folder that you specified.

21. After the file copy procedure finishes, Setup Manager notifies you whether all the necessary components for an unattended installation have been put in place, and you can exit the program.

Using UDB Files

As we mentioned previously, UDB files are used to override the values stored in an answer file (see Figure 1.12). When you specify multiple computer names when creating or modifying an answer file in Setup Manager, the appropriate UDB file is created for you by Setup Manager. If you specify the /UDF parameter on the command line for setup.exe, without any UDB filename, the Setup program prompts the user to insert a floppy disk that contains a UDB file with the default name of $Unique$.udb during the installation.

To specify the UDB file to be used, you must use the syntax `/udf:name_of_UDB_file.udb` as one of the command-line parameters for `setup.exe`.

Launching Unattended Installations

After you create or modify an answer file in Setup Manager, the program generates the files necessary for performing unattended installations based on the criteria you specified. In the previous step-by-step example for using Setup Manager, the program creates three files (using default filenames) in the `S:\XPSETUP.PRO` folder for unattended installations:

➤ `unattend.txt`—This is the unattended answer file.

➤ `unattend.udb`—This is the UDB file.

➤ `unattend.bat`—This is an MS-DOS–style batch file command that simplifies the unattended installation command-line syntax by preconfiguring the command line for you.

 The Windows XP Setup Manager allows you to manually modify the answer file (**unattend.txt**) using any text editor, such as **Notepad.exe**, and your changes remain intact even if you choose to make more modifications to the file later using Setup Manager. Setup Manager maintains any changes that you make to the answer file manually—so you can make changes to answer files using both a text editor and Setup Manager.

If you want to perform an unattended installation using the Windows XP CD-ROM, you must name or rename the answer file `winnt.sif` and copy it onto a floppy disk. The floppy disk must be inserted into the computer's floppy disk drive prior to launching the Setup program for an unattended installation to work. An unattended answer file looks something like the following abbreviated example:

```
;SetupMgrTag
[Data]
    AutoPartition=1
    MsDosInitiated="0"
    UnattendedInstall="Yes"
[Unattended]
    UnattendMode=FullUnattended
    OemSkipEula=Yes
    OemPreinstall=Yes
[GuiUnattended]
    AdminPassword=*
    EncryptedAdminPassword=NO
    TimeZone=4
    OemSkipWelcome=1
[UserData]
    ProductID=XXXXX-XXXXX-XXXXX-XXXXX-XXXXX
```

```
FullName="Authorized User"
OrgName="Exam Cram 2 Corporation"
ComputerName=*
```

A UDB file looks something similar to the screenshot in Figure 1.12 and the batch file that gets created by Setup Manager looks something like this:

```
@rem SetupMgrTag
@echo off
rem
rem This is a SAMPLE batch script generated by the
➥Setup Manager Wizard.
rem If this script is moved from the location where it was generated,
➥ it may have to be modified.
rem
set AnswerFile=.\unattend.txt
set UdfFile=.\unattend.udb
set ComputerName=%1
set SetupFiles=\\DC1\XPSETUP.PRO\I386
if "%ComputerName%" == "" goto USAGE
\\DC1\XPSETUP.PRO\I386\winnt32 /s:%SetupFiles% _ /unattend:
➥%AnswerFile% /udf:%ComputerName%,%UdfFile% _ /makelocalsource
goto DONE
:USAGE
echo.
echo Usage: unattend ^<computername^>
echo.
:DONE
```

Using this example, to start the unattended installation for a workstation to be named Station01, you first need to connect to the distribution share on the network where the Windows XP installation files and answer files are located. As an alternative, you could burn a CD with all these files on it. After that, you can use the unattend.bat file to begin the installation. At a command prompt, if you navigate to the distribution share, you can type unattend station01 and the unattended installation begins.

Understanding Setup Programs and Command-Line Switches

On the root of the Windows XP CD-ROM, you can see the setup.exe executable program file that you can use to launch attended installations from 32-bit environments, such as Windows 98, Windows Me, Windows NT 4.0, and Windows 2000. Also on the CD-ROM in the I386 folder, you can find the winnt.exe and the winnt32.exe executable programs. You can only run the winnt.exe setup program under 16-bit operating systems, such as MS-DOS and Windows 95 or Windows 98 startup environments. You can only run the winnt32.exe setup program under 32-bit operating systems, such as those previously mentioned.

Figure 1.12 A UDB file generated by Setup Manager.

The major advantages of winnt.exe and winnt32.exe is that they both accept various customizable parameters (also known as switches or options) on the command line when you execute them; the setup.exe program does not accept command-line parameters. If you run the winnt.exe /? or the winnt32.exe /? command at a command prompt, you can view all the various command-line options that are available. Some of the biggest differences between winnt and winnt32 appear in Table 1.1.

Table 1.1 Major Differences in Command-Line Options Between the winnt and the winnt32 Setup Programs	
winnt 16-Bit	**winnt32 32-Bit**
Supports 16-bit operating systems only.	Supports 32-bit operating systems only.
/u:answer_filename	**/unattend:**answer_filename
Dynamic Update not supported.	**/dushare**—Specifies location of downloaded Dynamic Update files.
Dynamic Update not supported.	**/duprepare**—Prepares the downloaded Dynamic Update files to be shared.
Dynamic Update not supported.	**/dudisable**—Turns off the Dynamic Update feature during Setup.
/e—Specifies a program to be run after the GUI phase of the Setup program.	**/cmd**—Specifies a program to be run before the final GUI phase of the Setup program.
Check Upgrade Only not supported.	**/checkupgradeonly**—Checks for upgrade compatibility with Windows XP.

Table 1.1 Continued	
winnt 16-Bit	**winnt32 32-Bit**
Syspart not supported.	**/syspart:*drive_letter*—**Allows you to copy the Setup files to a hard disk partition and mark it as active, and then you can install the disk onto another computer and run Setup.
Recovery Console installation not supported.	**/cmdcons—**Installs the Recovery Console on a functioning Windows XP computer. You can only run it after Windows XP is already installed.

You can manually launch an unattended installation from the command line without utilizing a batch file created by Setup Manager. The following two examples demonstrate how you can fire off an unattended installation for a new workstation named Station01 using a mapped network drive under a 16-bit environment and under a 32-bit environment:

➤ *MS-DOS and Windows 9x startup environments:*

```
WINNT.EXE /s:Z:\i386 /u:unattend.txt /udf:station01,unattend.udb
```

➤ *Windows 9x, Windows NT 4.0, and Windows 2000 environments:*

```
WINNT32.EXE /s:Z:\i386 /unattend:unattend.txt
/udf:station01,unattend.udb
➥ /dushare:Z:\i386\updates
```

Automating Installations with RIS

You can use RIS to deploy Windows XP Professional and Windows 2000 Professional over a network from a remote installation server. You can use RIS to install Windows XP Professional to a computer with a blank hard drive or to reinstall Windows XP Professional to repair a corrupted installation.

The main goal of RIS is to reduce total cost of ownership (TCO) by having one central location for either the end users or administrators to install current Windows desktop operating systems. To install Windows XP Professional using RIS, a user presses the F12 key during the boot process to boot from the network and download the small installation files needed to launch the installation process from an RIS server. If a workstation's network card does not support the PXE standard for booting from the network, you may create a boot floppy disk instead. The following three steps are involved in making RIS work and they are discussed in detail in the next sections:

➤ Configuring the workstations

➤ Setting up or verifying that the proper network services are in place, including at least one RIS server

➤ Creating the Windows XP or Windows 2000 Professional images

Configuring Workstations

You can have a workstation computer connect to an RIS server in two ways. The first method is to install a peripheral connection interface (PCI) network adapter that contains an onboard PXE ROM chip. You then have to configure the computer's BIOS to boot from the PXE network adapter. When the computer boots from the PXE network adapter, it attempts to get an IP address from a Dynamic Host Configuration Protocol (DHCP) server. After the network adapter obtains an IP address, the user is prompted to press the F12 key to locate an RIS server.

The second method for connecting a workstation computer to an RIS server is with a network adapter that is not PXE-compliant. You can use an RIS boot disk for network adapters manufactured by such companies as 3Com and Intel. You can use the `rbfg.exe` utility to create an RIS boot disk. After you install RIS on a server, you can find the utility at `<RIS_server_drive_letter>:\RemoteInstall\Admin\i386\rbfg.exe`.

Configuring and Verifying Network Services

Before you can install and configure RIS, several prerequisites must be in place on the network. The following is a list of the requirements the network must meet before you can use RIS:

➤ *DHCP server*—The client needs to obtain an IP address from a DHCP server during the boot process. You cannot configure RIS until a DHCP server is available. A Windows Server 2003 or a Windows 2000 Server DHCP server cannot give out IP addresses to clients unless it is *authorized* to do so under Active Directory.

➤ *Active Directory and Domain Name System (DNS)*—When the network adapter has an IP address, it needs to find an RIS server. The client finds an RIS server by querying a DNS server to find where an Active Directory DC is located. Active Directory then tells the client (workstation computer) where an RIS server can be found. Although Active Directory and DNS are required for RIS, a Windows Internet Naming Service (WINS) server is *not* required.

➤ *At least one RIS server*—Obviously, the network must supply at least one RIS server with at least one downloadable system image before you can perform an RIS installation.

➤ *A separate drive letter for RIS images*—RIS demands its own drive partition or volume on the RIS server. You cannot install RIS on a system or a boot partition (or volume, for dynamic disks), which usually means that you cannot use the C: drive. RIS stores its system images using *single instance storage* (SIS). SIS technology stores only one copy of each file. Any duplicate copies are not stored on disk; they are referenced using pointers to the single copy already stored on the hard drive to save disk space. This is why RIS needs its own drive letter. It is recommended that you reserve at least 2GB for an RIS disk partition or volume.

After you meet these four conditions for an RIS installation, you are ready to start deploying workstations over the network using RIS. You can create and use an unattended answer file (remboot.sif) to fully automate your RIS installations.

Creating Windows XP Professional RIS Images

The Remote Installation Services Setup Wizard creates the first image of Windows XP Professional for you. However, that image provides only an *attended* installation of the operating system, not an *unattended* installation. You can create additional images that contain the operating system as well as any necessary applications and configuration settings. RIS installs a utility called riprep.exe that you can use to create images of the operating system and any installed applications. The functionality of riprep.exe is similar to that of a third-party disk imaging application, such as Norton Ghost by Symantec.

Unfortunately, riprep.exe has some definite limitations. It can only create an image of the C: drive of a computer. If a computer contains a C: drive and a D: drive, only the C: drive is stored as part of the image. Also, when you apply the image to a computer via RIS, any *existing disk partitions or volumes* are *deleted!* The entire hard drive is repartitioned as a single drive letter and the new disk partition or volume is then formatted with the NTFS. If you can work within these parameters, you can easily configure and deploy riprep.exe images.

The first step is to install and completely configure Windows XP Professional to your exact liking and specifications on a workstation computer. Be sure to test the installation thoroughly because it becomes your model image for deployment. The key to successful riprep.exe deployments is that the operating system, the settings, and the application programs are all installed, configured, and working properly *before* you create and deploy the image. You need to perform the following steps to create a Windows XP Professional image using `riprep.exe`:

1. Log on to the Windows XP Professional computer whose image you want to upload to the RIS server. This machine is known as the master or model computer.

2. Install Windows XP Professional and any applications that users might need.

3. For the user account that you've logged on as to set up the model Windows XP computer, copy its user profile to the Default User profile and grant modify permissions to it for authenticated users.

4. Connect to the REMINST sharepoint on the RIS server. Run `riprep.exe` from the network path `\\<RIS_Server_Name>\REMINST\Admin\I386\`.

5. The Remote Installation Preparation Wizard launches. You need to provide the RIS server name on which the image should be placed and the name of the folder to which the image should be copied.

6. Provide a user-friendly name for the image (such as Sales or Accounting).

After you complete these steps, `riprep.exe` removes the unique attributes, such as the security IDs (SIDs) and the computer name from the master/model computer and, thereby, from the system image. After removing the unique attributes from the Windows desktop operating system, `riprep.exe` copies the image to the designated RIS server. At this point, when the master/model computer restarts, it boots into the Windows Mini-Setup Wizard and you have to perform a partial re-installation of Windows. During an RIS workstation installation, the client computer boots remotely and then downloads the image onto its hard drive. The computer must reboot after downloading the RIS image so that the Mini-Setup Wizard can launch and ask you the unique identifying information for the new workstation, which was removed from the `riprep.exe` image.

NOTE You can use Setup Manager to create answer files for RIS images to take advantage of unattended installations. The default filename is **remboot.sif**, simply a renamed version of the **unattend.txt** default answer filename for automating unattended installations.

Downloading an RIS Image to a Workstation

After you configure an RIS server with one or more images, users can boot their computers from an installed, PXE-compliant network adapter and press F12 to locate an RIS server. If the computer does not have a PXE-compliant network adapter installed, you can create a special RIS boot floppy disk from the RIS server. The server then displays a welcome screen. The user simply presses the Enter key to go to the next screen. Next, the user must log on to the Active Directory domain. After the user logs on, the user sees a list of RIS images to choose from. The user selects an image from the list, and RIS first reformats the entire C: drive and then downloads the image to the target computer. After about 30 to 40 minutes, the user has a clean installation of the operating system with all the appropriate configuration settings and all the required applications already installed and set up.

 You can find out more about RIS installations and image cloning deployments at **http://www.microsoft.com/windows2000/en/datacenter/help/default.asp?url=/w indows2000/en/datacenter/help/sag_RIS_Default_topnode.htm**. You can learn more about third-party disk imaging products, such as Ghost and Ghost Enterprise edition from Symantec Corporation, at **http://enterprisesecurity.symantec. com/products/products.cfm?productid=3&EID=0**.

Automating Installations with Third-Party Disk Imaging Tools

In addition to deploying workstation system images under RIS, you can also take advantage of third-party disk imaging utilities, such as Ghost by Symantec Corporation or DriveImage, among many other brands. DriveImage was previously published by PowerQuest Corporation, which was recently acquired by Symantec. Because Microsoft operating systems such as Windows 2000 and Windows XP are based on Windows NT technology, the installed system on each computer requires a unique machine SID to distinguish it from all other systems. You also cannot have two or more Windows NT, Windows 2000, or Windows XP-based computers with the same NetBIOS name, the identical hostname, the exact same IP address, or any other unique identifying features on the same network. For these reasons, third-party disk image copies of Windows XP/2000/2003–based computers must be modified to retain their own unique identities.

The System Preparation tool (sysprep.exe) from Microsoft prepares a master image of a computer that runs Windows 2000 Professional or Windows XP

Professional along with any installed software applications. You must use the sysprep.exe tool in conjunction with third-party disk imaging software if you want to roll out multiple workstations using disk images. *Disk imaging software* makes an exact mirror copy of whatever is on the computer's hard drive, including all the unique settings of Windows 2000 or Windows XP, to a file (or spanning multiple files) on disk. The System Preparation tool removes all the unique settings from a Windows desktop computer before the computer is imaged. sysprep.exe is easy to use, but you must follow several specific steps to use it. The first step is to create a folder called sysprep in the %systemdrive% folder (for example, c:\sysprep).

To use the System Preparation tool, you must extract it from the deploy.cab file and place it in the sysprep folder. You need to extract both the sysprep.exe file and its helper file named setupcl.exe. The next step is to install and configure all the application programs that you want to be included as part of the disk image. After you accomplish that step, you can run sysprep.exe from the sysprep folder. Sysprep.exe removes all the settings from the operating system and then either restarts or powers down the computer (see Figure 1.13). You then need to reboot the computer with some type of boot disk (often an MS-DOS or a Windows 9x startup floppy disk or CD-ROM) so that you can run the disk imaging software to create an image of the computer's entire hard drive or an image of just the bootable drive.

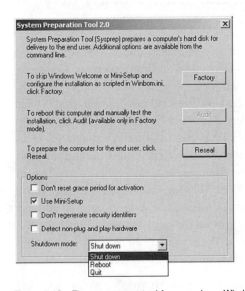

Figure 1.13   The **sysprep.exe** tool for preparing a Windows XP disk image.

Most drive imaging utilities give you different options for where to store computer system images—an external hard drive, an internal hard drive, writable CD or DVD media, or a network drive. To load an image onto another computer, you simply need to point the disk imaging software to where the *source* system image file is located, and the program transfers (copies) the image onto the hard drive of the target computer. After the image transfer finishes, you need to restart the target computer. Upon restart, thanks to the sysprep.exe tool that prepares the image before it gets copied, the Windows Mini-Setup Wizard launches. This version is a scaled down and quicker version of the normal Windows installation routine. The wizard prompts you to put back the unique configuration settings that sysprep.exe removes from the system image. The SID is generated automatically during the Mini-Setup installation. However, you have to manually enter the several missing pieces of information when prompted, such as the new computer name, the username, network settings, and so forth.

The Mini-Setup Wizard requires you to enter a fair amount of information for every computer to which you apply the image. You can use Setup Manager, as discussed earlier in this chapter, to create an answer file that must be named sysprep.inf (a renamed version of the unattend.txt answer file used for automating unattended installations). This file provides the necessary responses for the Mini-Setup Wizard to answer all the installation prompts. The sysprep.exe utility accepts several useful optional parameters when you run it from the command line, as shown in Figure 1.14. These options include -quiet to not display confirmation dialog boxes, -pnp to force Plug and Play to re-enumerate devices on the next reboot, and -clean to clean out critical devices.

 For **sysprep.exe**, the **–reseal** option is the one to remember: this selection prepares the operating system to be imaged before the disk imaging software is used. When you use disk imaging together with a **sysprep.inf** answer file from Setup Manager, the end result is the unattended install of the third-party disk image. The **sysprep.inf** file answers all the questions required during the Mini-Setup installation.

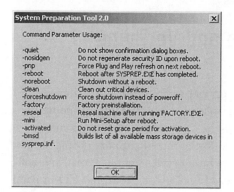

Figure 1.14   Available command-line–only options for **sysprep.exe**.

You must place **sysprep.inf** in the **sysprep** folder or on a floppy disk, which are the default locations where the Mini-Setup Wizard looks for the answer file (it checks the **sysprep** folder first) after you apply the image.

Performing Upgrade Installations

Windows XP supports several different upgrade paths. The easiest and most seamless upgrades occur when you migrate from Windows 2000 Professional to Windows XP Professional and when you migrate from Windows XP Home Edition to Windows XP Professional. You can perform an unattended upgrade by specifying the /unattend option on the winnt32.exe command line. With this method, all the custom user configuration settings from the previous operating system are carried over to Windows XP and no user interaction is needed during the setup process. You can upgrade directly to Windows XP Home Edition or Windows XP Professional from the following Microsoft operating systems:

➤ Windows 98 and Windows 98 Second Edition (SE)

➤ Windows Me

➤ Windows NT 4.0 Workstation with SP5 or higher

➤ Windows 2000 Professional

➤ Windows XP Home Edition (supports an upgrade to Windows XP Professional only)

 Microsoft does *not* support any upgrades to Windows XP Home Edition or Professional from Window 3.x, Windows 95, or Windows NT 3.5 or 3.51 Workstation. Additionally, you cannot upgrade (downgrade) any Microsoft server operating system (Windows NT 4.0 Server, Windows 2000 Server, Windows Server 2003) to any edition of Windows XP.

Planning the Upgrade and Verifying Compatibility

Because a computer's operating is critical to its proper functioning, you should always treat an upgrade as a serious potential threat to the computer's well-being. Upgrades from MS-DOS–based systems, such as Windows 98 and Windows Me, are especially vulnerable to incompatibility problems. You should review a computer's current operating system, applications, and configuration settings before forging ahead blindly with the install CD in hand

and clicking setup.exe. Check on the following items before performing an upgrade to Windows XP:

➤ *Hardware and software issues*—The Microsoft Windows Upgrade Advisor (also known as the Windows XP Readiness Analyzer) can point out areas of potential conflict and incompatibility with the current operating system. You can run this tool directly from the Windows XP CD-ROM. At a command prompt, type <CD *drive letter*>:\i386\winnt32.exe /checkupgradeonly and press Enter to run the program.

➤ *Special disk controller drivers*—For third-party small computer system interface (SCSI) or Redundant Array of Independent Disks (RAID) controllers, you might need to press the F6 key during the initial text mode of the setup process. If you miss this selection and Setup continues, you will most likely end up with an error specifying that the boot device is inaccessible, requiring you to start the installation all over again.

➤ *File system options*—Windows XP has three options to choose from for its file system: FAT, FAT32, and NTFS. NTFS is the best option because it supports compression, disk quotas, encryption, mount points, and remote storage.

➤ *Software utilities*—Windows XP employs a newer version of NTFS that can cause conflicts with pre-XP versions of antivirus tools and disk defragmenting software. You should remove such applications before you perform the upgrade.

➤ *Windows 9x data compression*—You must uncompress any drives that have been compressed with either Windows 95 or Windows 98 compression features such as DriveSpace or DoubleSpace. Windows XP is not compatible with these compression schemes. The same holds true for any third-party data compression tools: be sure to uncompress the data and then remove these types of utilities to insure a smoother upgrade experience.

➤ *Computer system firmware (BIOS)*—As a rule of thumb, newer BIOSs support newer operating systems better. Consider installing the most recent BIOS update for your computer's motherboard.

➤ *Virus scanners/antivirus software*—At a minimum, be sure to disable any antivirus utility during the upgrade installation. Often, it's recommended to uninstall the existing antivirus software, perform the upgrade, and then install a more recent, compatible version of antivirus software. Many third-party utilities and older software programs can be impediments to a successful upgrade.

➤ *Legacy or incompatible software*—It's often advisable to uninstall any third-party network protocol stacks, network client software, disk utilities, or other products that are not explicitly designed for or certified to work with Windows XP.

➤ *Back up data and previous operating system files*—You cannot fully recover from a failed operating system upgrade without valid, recent backups. Of course, data backups are paramount, but operating-system backups can be almost as important. An operating-system image copy stored on some type of external media can prove to be a lifesaver (or at least a jobsaver) if Murphy's Law comes into play. (In case this expression is foreign to you, Murphy's Law supposedly states that "whatever can go wrong will go wrong!")

Maintaining Compatibility with Legacy Applications

After you successfully upgrade a system to Windows XP, some older programs might not work properly or might not function at all. Fortunately, Windows XP provides built-in application compatibility support for legacy software programs. If you right-click an executable file and select Properties, you can click the Compatibility tab, where you can configure the application to run in a specific compatibility mode (see Figure 1.15). The available compatibility modes are as follows (note that Windows NT 3.5 and 3.51 compatibility modes are not available):

➤ Windows 95

➤ Windows 98/Windows Me

➤ Windows NT 4.0 (SP5)

➤ Windows 2000

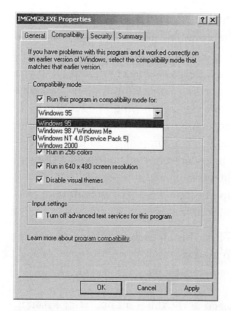

Figure 1.15   The available application compatibility mode settings under Windows XP.

Installing the Windows XP Upgrade

Running the Windows XP installation routine is fairly straightforward, but the Setup program does still prompt you for responses to certain questions as it performs the upgrade. To run an unattended upgrade installation, go to the I386 folder on the Windows XP CD-ROM and type `winnt32 /unattend` either in the Start, Run box or at a command prompt. When you invoke this option, the Setup program copies over all the user settings from the operating system that is being upgraded: no user input is needed and Setup runs completely unattended.

After upgrading to Windows XP from Windows 98, Windows 98 SE, or Windows Me, you actually have the option of *uninstalling Windows XP* and reverting to the previous operating system! To remove Windows XP from a computer that was upgraded from one of these operating systems, double-click the Add/Remove Programs icon in Control Panel. Find the Windows XP item in the list of installed software. Select the Windows XP option from the list and click the appropriate Remove/Uninstall button to uninstall Windows XP from the computer and return to the version of Windows 98 or Windows Me that was installed previously.

Unfortunately, if you convert the file system on the boot or system partition to NTFS, *you cannot use the uninstall option.* This uninstall option does not exist for upgrades from Windows NT 4.0 Workstation or Windows 2000 Professional.

Installing Windows XP with One or More Operating Systems

Windows XP is designed to co-exist with one or more Microsoft operating systems installed on the same computer. If you install Windows XP in addition to one other operating system, you have a *dual-boot* configuration. If you install Windows XP in addition to two or more operating systems, you have a *multiboot* configuration. The Windows XP Setup program automatically installs a dual-boot or a multiboot configuration when one or more Microsoft operating systems already exist on a computer. You should investigate third-party products if you want to dual-boot or multiboot Windows XP with non-Microsoft operating systems such as Linux or OS/2 to ensure compatibility. When setting up a computer for a dual-boot or multiboot configuration, keep the following guidelines in mind:

➤ Install the oldest operating system first. Install each additional operating system in the sequence of oldest to newest.

➤ Install each operating system into its own drive letter on the hard drive.

➤ Maintain file system compatibility across the different operating systems by using the file system accessible to all the installed OSs on the computer. This often means using FAT or FAT32, not NTFS. Windows 9x and Windows Me do not support NTFS. Windows NT 4.0 does not support FAT32, but it does support FAT and NTFS.

Migrating User Settings to Windows XP

You might choose to *migrate* a user to a new Windows XP computer rather than upgrade the existing computer because the hardware might simply be too old to support the hefty requirements of Windows XP. In this scenario, a user gets a brand new machine with (presumably) new versions of applications, but what about the user's previous settings for the Windows desktop, the various preferences for his or her programs, and the user's favorites and files stored in the My Documents and My Pictures folders? Well, the Windows XP *FAST Wizard* copies these important items from a user's old computer to the new computer using a GUI interface. For command-line aficionados, you can use the *USMT*.

The FAST Wizard is available from the Windows XP Start menu, under Start, Programs, Accessories, System Tools. The wizard collects and then stores the necessary user information from the user's previous computer, and then you need to run the wizard again on the new Windows XP computer so that it can copy the user's information onto the new PC (see Figure 1.16). The FAST Wizard requires that you transfer the user's information using a serial cable connection, a network connection, or removable media to temporarily store the migration data. You can migrate user settings and files using the FAST Wizard from the following operating systems:

➤ Windows 95

➤ Windows 98 and Windows 98 SE

➤ Windows Me

➤ Windows NT 4.0

➤ Windows 2000

➤ Windows XP

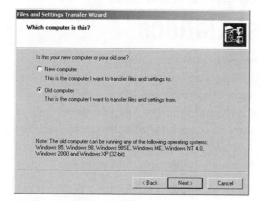

Figure 1.16   The FAST Wizard.

Migrating User Settings with the USMT

The USMT is a more robust utility than the FAST Wizard, but it is also more complex to use. The advantage of the USMT is that it offers customizable options that the FAST Wizard does not support. The USMT uses several .dll files; however, it employs only two executable files— scanstate.exe and loadstate.exe. The USMT tools are located on the Windows XP CD-ROM in the Valueadd\MSFT\USMT folder. Ideally, you should copy the entire USMT folder to a central server computer that will store each user's migration settings and files.

By mapping a network drive to the folder on a server where you placed the USMT programs, you must first run the scanstate command at a command prompt on the old (*source*) computer to transfer the user's data to the server. Next, on the user's new Windows XP (*target*) computer, you also need to map a network drive letter to the share on the server where the USMT programs and the user migration data are stored. By running the `loadstate` command at a command prompt, you can transfer the user's settings and files to the new machine. To view the various options that are available with both the `scanstate.exe` and the `loadstate.exe` USMT tools, type either `scanstate /?` or `loadstate /?` at a command prompt. You can remember the USMT sequence of events this way:

➤ `scanstate` = *source* (old) computer

➤ `loadstate` = *target* (new) Windows XP computer

Updating and Troubleshooting Windows XP Installations

Updating computer operating systems has become a necessary chore for network administrators; this task is no longer an optional activity. Microsoft and other vendors release software patches (hotfixes) and SPs for their products on a regular basis. How to effectively and efficiently deploy these updates depends on several factors, including an organization's software update testing policies, the number of computers in the organization, and the degree of control required over the software update implementation process.

Troubleshooting failed installations of Windows XP is another area that can cause a network administrator's hair to turn gray or fall out prematurely. If you are aware of many of the common causes of failed installations, you can more quickly assess the situation and try to fix the problem. The following sections address the issues about how to update Windows XP with patches and SPs and how to recognize the symptoms of common Windows XP installation problems.

Keeping Windows Systems Up-to-Date

In today's fast moving world of technology, security for our computer systems has become paramount. New security vulnerabilities are being discovered constantly, so it is vital that Windows operating systems get updated with the latest security patches on an ongoing basis. For individual computers or for a small group of computers, you might choose to use the Windows Update Web site—http://windowsupdate.microsoft.com.

However, to maintain updates on numerous computers, such as hundreds or thousands of workstations, you should go with a more centralized and robust solution, such as Microsoft's Software Update Services (SUS), Microsoft's follow-up to SUS—Windows Update Services (WUS), Microsoft's Systems Management Server (SMS) product, or a third-party solution such as UpdateExpert by St. Bernard Software.

In addition to the Windows Update Web site, you can usually download update hotfixes individually from Microsoft's Web site or FTP site. Almost always, a Microsoft Knowledge Base (KB) article and a related Microsoft Security Bulletin accompany and explain the reasons and the importance of each individual update (see Figure 1.17).

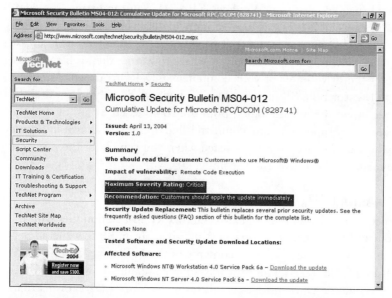

Figure 1.17   A Microsoft Security Bulletin with its associated KB Article number (828741) in parentheses.

Installing SPs

Microsoft tends to publish software patches (SPs) or hotfixes rather frequently—especially whenever new security vulnerabilities are discovered. SPs are published much less frequently, and Microsoft plans a release schedule for each SP. SPs are operating-system–specific. You cannot install an SP designed for Windows 2000 on Windows XP: the SP setup program (update.exe) does not permit you to install an SP on an incompatible operating system. However, an SP designed for Windows XP is meant to be installed on both the Home and Professional editions. The SPs designed for Windows 2000 are meant to be installed on both the Professional and Server editions.

> SPs designed for 32-bit systems cannot be installed on 64-bit systems. Microsoft publishes separate SPs for 64-bit editions of its operating systems.

For individual systems, you can usually install an "express" version of an SP via the Windows Update Web site. For multiple computers, you should download the network install version of an SP so that you can deploy it to multiple machines simultaneously over the network. Network versions of SPs are downloaded as compressed executable files which are usually named something such as xpsp1.exe (Windows XP SP1). You can extract the compressed SP executable files to a local or network drive by using the /x option on the command line. For example, if you click Start, Run; type x:\xpsp1.exe /x; and click OK, you are prompted for where to extract the SP files (where x: denotes the drive letter of your computer's CD-ROM drive). After you successfully extract the SP files to a local or network drive, you can find the update.exe file in the update folder. Both the compressed SP utility and the update.exe utility support several command-line options, as shown in Figure 1.18. Note that the /x option is *not* listed when you run either the xpsp1.exe /? command or the update.exe /? command.

Slipstreaming SPs

The process of updating the original Windows XP installation files with the files from an SP is called *slipstreaming*. You can apply an SP to a shared network folder by copying the entire contents of the Windows XP CD-ROM into a shared folder on a server or workstation computer. This shared folder with the Windows XP Setup files is called the *distribution share* (or distribution folder). From the Update folder within the distribution share, you need to run the command update.exe -s:[path], where the path must be replaced with the location of the Windows XP Setup files that you want updated (the distribution share).

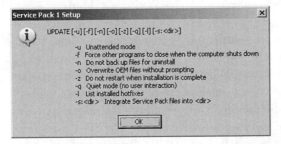

Figure 1.18 The SP1 Setup message box detailing the available command-line options for installing SPs.

Do not include the **I386** folder name as part of the path because the SP looks for the **I386** folder by default. In fact, if you do *not* place the Windows XP installation files within a folder named **I386** at the end of the uniform naming convention (UNC) or drive letter path, the slipstream process fails. For example, if the **I386** folder is located within a share named **xpsetup** on a server named **server01**, you need to type the following command to slipstream the SP into the original Windows XP Setup files:

Update.exe –s:\\server01\xpsetup

If you add the **I386** folder name to the path, the SP looks for the **I386** in the **\\server01\xpsetup\i386\i386 path** and it fails to locate the files.

If you install Windows XP by using the slipstreamed distribution method, the original installation files are merged with the updated SP files. Using this method can save you a lot of time and helps you avoid having to re-apply an SP after each installation. If you don't have the opportunity or ability to create a slipstreamed distribution share, you can apply an SP after completing a successful install by running **update.exe** (or the compressed SP executable file) on the local computer. If you install any new services or components after applying the SP, Windows XP can obtain the files it needs for those items from a slipstreamed installation folder. In this way, you can add new services and components to a system without having to re-apply the SP.

Troubleshooting Installation Problems

Windows XP should install on most new computers without too much difficulty. However, there are some common reasons that it might not install properly. The following is a list of typical installation problems:

➤ *Media errors*—These are problems you encounter with the distribution CD-ROM. You should make sure the problem exists with the media itself, not with access to the media. If you place the Windows XP Professional CD-ROM in a shared drive for installation, too many people could be using the drive at one time. This situation could generate some errors. However, if only one person is connected to the shared drive and errors persist, you should get a replacement for the Setup CD-ROM. In addition, you should always restart failed installations that are due to media errors.

➤ *Incompatible CD-ROM or DVD drive*—There are many specifications for CD-ROM and DVD drives. You can install Windows XP from most drives, but there are some exceptions. If the CD-ROM or DVD drive is not compatible, you need to replace it or copy the distribution files onto the local hard drive or on another computer connected to the LAN. Also, as mentioned earlier in this chapter, the Windows XP CD-ROM is bootable and can be installed from compatible drives. If the CD-ROM can't boot, you need to ensure that the drive is compliant and that the boot order in the BIOS has been set to the CD-ROM or DVD drive.

Also, the controller card for the CD-ROM or DVD drive could be failing, or the drive itself could be failing.

➤ *Installation halts or errors*—If a Stop error occurs during the installation, it is typically the result of incorrect or incompatible drivers. You need to obtain the correct and current drivers and restart the installation process. Also, the installation might stop just after the copy or text phase due to a warning that the master boot record has a virus. This warning typically results when the BIOS has enabled the virus warning option. You should turn off this option and restart the installation. As a final measure, you need to ensure that all devices are on the HCL.

➤ *Lack of disk space*—Windows XP needs more available free disk space than its predecessors. You should ensure that at least 650MB of free space is available.

➤ *Dependency failures*—For the installation to complete successfully, all services must be able to start when needed. Several Windows XP services depend on other services to start first. For example, if the drivers for the network adapter cannot load, that affects all services that depend on the network adapter's successful installation. As a result, the computer cannot join a domain.

➤ *Problems joining a Windows Server domain*—If the network adapter has initialized, but the computer still can't join a domain, you should verify that one or more DNS servers for the domain are online and that you are pointing the workstation to the correct IP address for the organization's DNS servers. You also need to verify that you typed the domain name correctly. If problems persist, you can temporarily install the computer to a workgroup to complete the installation.

Exam Prep Questions

1. What can you use in conjunction with an answer file to override settings in the answer file during a fully automated installation of Windows XP Professional?

   ❏ A. A **sysprep.inf** file
   ❏ B. An **unattend.txt** file
   ❏ C. An **unattend.udb** file
   ❏ D. An **unattend.bat** file

   Answer C is correct. A UDB file is used to override values stored within an answer file. Answer A is incorrect because a sysprep.inf is used as an answer file for automating the Mini-Setup Wizard after a system image (created with a third-party tool) has been copied onto a computer's hard drive. Answer B is incorrect because an unattend.txt is used as an answer file for unattended installations. Answer D is incorrect because an unattend.bat is created by Setup Manager to automatically launch an unattended installation, preconfiguring the required command-line options for the setup.exe program.

2. Which of the following types of Windows XP licensing and media require MPA after a successful installation? (Select all correct answers.)

   ❏ A. Open licensing and media
   ❏ B. Select licensing and media
   ❏ C. OEM licensing and media
   ❏ D. Enterprise licensing and media
   ❏ E. Retail licensing and media

   Answers C and E are correct. OEM and Retail Licensing and CD-ROM media require MPA within 30 days of installation. Answer A is incorrect because Open licensing does not require MPA. Answer B is incorrect because Select licensing does not require MPA. Answer D is incorrect because Enterprise licensing does not require MPA.

3. Which of the following methods allow you to create and edit an answer file for an unattended installation? (Select all correct answers.)

- ❑ A. **Sysprep.exe**
- ❑ B. **Setupmgr.exe**
- ❑ C. **Notepad.exe**
- ❑ D. **Setup.exe**
- ❑ E. **Winnt.exe**
- ❑ F. **Winnt32.exe**

Answers B and C are correct. The Windows XP Setup Manager (setup-mgr.exe) is available on the Windows XP CD-ROM, and it creates and edits answer files. You can also create and edit answer files with any text editor program, such as notepad.exe. Answer A is incorrect because sysprep.exe prepares a system to be imaged by third-party disk imaging software. Answer D is incorrect because setup.exe launches the Windows XP installation program. Answer E is incorrect because winnt.exe is the Windows XP installation program for 16-bit environments, such as MS-DOS. Answer F is incorrect because winnt32.exe is the Windows XP installation program for 32-bit environments, such as Windows 98 or Windows NT 4.0 Workstation.

4. Which of the following command lines correctly launches an unattended Windows XP installation using an answer file named **unattend1.txt**, specifies a uniqueness database file, and turns off the Dynamic Update feature?

- ❑ A. **Winnt32.exe /s:Z:\i386 /u:unattend1.txt /udb:station01,unattend1.udb /dudisable**
- ❑ B. **Winnt.exe /s:Z:\i386 /u:unattend1.txt /udb:station01,unattend1.udb / dudisable**
- ❑ C. **Winnt32.exe /s:Z:\i386 /unattend:unattend1.txt /udb:station01,unattend1.udb /dudisable**
- ❑ D. **Winnt32.exe /s:Z:\i386 /unattend:unattend1.txt /udf:station01,unattend1.udb /dudisable**
- ❑ E. **Winnt.exe /s:Z:\i386 /unattend:unattend1.txt /udf:station01,unattend1.udb /dudisable**

Answer D is correct. The winnt32.exe (32-bit) installation program uses the /unattend: option and the /udf: option (not /udb), and the /dudisable option disables Dynamic Updates. Answer A is incorrect because winnt32.exe uses the /unattend: option (not /u:), and it uses the /udf: option (not /udb). Answer B is incorrect because the winnt.exe (16-bit) program uses the /udf: option (not /udb), and the /dudisable option is not available. Answer C is incorrect because winnt32.exe uses the /udf: option (not /udb). Answer E is incorrect because winnt.exe (16 bit) uses the /u: option instead of /unattend:, and it does not offer the /dudisable option.

5. Select two methods that you can use to copy over files and user configuration settings from a computer running Windows 95 to a new computer running Windows XP Home Edition. (Select all correct answers.)

   ❑ A. Norton Ghost by Symantec Corporation

   ❑ B. RIS

   ❑ C. USMT

   ❑ D. **Riprep /transfer**

   ❑ E. FAST Wizard

   Answers C and E are correct. Both the USMT and the FAST Wizard copy files and user settings from a previous computer to a Windows XP computer (Home Edition or Professional). The FAST Wizard is a graphical tool; the USMT is a command-line utility. Answer A is incorrect because Ghost is a third-party utility that copies system disk images and clones them onto other computers. Answer B is incorrect because RIS remotely installs an operating system onto a computer by first formatting the C: drive; it does not transfer settings from one computer to another. Answer D is incorrect because the Riprep.exe command creates an operating system image to be uploaded to an RIS server.

6. Under the USMT, which of the following commands do you need to run and on which computer do you need to run them to transfer user files and settings from a Windows Me computer to a Windows XP computer?

   ❑ A. First run **loadstate.exe** on the Windows Me computer and then run **scanstate.exe** on the Windows XP computer.

   ❑ B. First run **scanstate.exe** on the Windows XP computer and then run **loadstate.exe** on the Windows Me computer.

   ❑ C. First run **scanstate.exe** on the Windows Me computer and then run **loadstate.exe** on the Windows XP computer.

   ❑ D. First run **loadstate.exe** on the Windows XP computer and then run **scanstate.exe** on the Windows Me computer.

   Answer C is correct. When you use the USMT programs, you must first run the scanstate.exe command on the original (source) computer, which in this case is Windows Me. For the second step, you need to run the loadstate.exe program on the Windows XP (target) computer to transfer the user's files and settings to the new PC. Answers A, B, and D are incorrect because you have to *first* run the scanstate.exe command on the source PC (Windows Me) *before* you can run the loadstate.exe command on the target PC (Windows XP).

7. How can you perform an unattended installation of Windows XP Home Edition from the local CD-ROM drive without running the Setup program from a network location and without running Setup from the local hard drive?

- ❑ A. Create an answer file using Setup Manager, name it **unattend.txt**, and copy it to a floppy disk. Insert the floppy disk into the A: drive before you launch Windows XP Setup.
- ❑ B. Create an answer file using Setup Manager, name it **winnt.sif**, and copy it to a floppy disk. Insert the floppy disk into the A: drive before you launch Windows XP Setup.
- ❑ C. Create an answer file using Setup Manager, name it **sysprep.inf**, and copy it to a folder that you create on the C: drive named **sysprep**. Launch the Windows XP Setup program.
- ❑ D. Create an answer file using Setup Manager, name it **remboot.sif**, and copy it to a floppy disk. Insert the floppy disk into the A: drive before you launch Windows XP Setup.

Answer B is correct. You must rename the unattended answer file to winnt.sif and copy it to a floppy disk if you want to perform an unattended installation using the only Windows XP CD-ROM. Answer A is incorrect because the unattended answer file stored on the floppy disk must be named winnt.sif. Answer C is incorrect because sysprep.inf is stored in the c:\sysprep folder only when you want to automate the Mini-Setup Wizard after using third-party imaging software to clone a disk image onto a computer. Answer D is incorrect because the unattended answer file stored on the floppy disk must be named winnt.sif, not remboot.sif, which is optionally used for RIS installations.

8. Which of the following features must be supported in a LAN environment if you want to boot new workstations from the network and then install Windows XP on them using an RIS server? (Select all correct answers.)

- ❑ A. NWLink
- ❑ B. DHCP
- ❑ C. Internal DNS servers
- ❑ D. Active Directory
- ❑ E. PXE-compliant network adapters on the workstations
- ❑ F. PXE-compliant network adapters on the RIS server
- ❑ G. A separate drive letter on the RIS server for RIS images
- ❑ H. **Sysprep.exe**
- ❑ I. Setup Manager

Answers B, C, D, E, and G are all correct. To use RIS to install system images, you need DHCP running on the network, at least one internal DNS server, Active Directory up and running, a PXE-compatible network adapter on each workstation, and a separate drive letter for the RIS images on the RIS server. Answer A is incorrect because the NWLink protocol is an optional protocol under Windows 2000/2003/XP, and it is not required for RIS installations. Answer F is incorrect because PXE-compliant network adapters are not required on RIS servers. Answer H is incorrect because the sysprep.exe utility is not used for RIS installations. Answer I is incorrect because the Setup Manager is not a required component for RIS installations; it can be used as an option to specify disk partitioning and formatting settings.

9. Which of the following operating systems cannot be upgraded to Windows XP Home Edition or Windows XP Professional? (Select all correct answers.)

❑ A. Windows 95 OSR2
❑ B. Windows NT 4.0 Workstation SP4
❑ C. Windows 2000 Professional SP1
❑ D. Windows 2000 Server SP4
❑ E. Windows Me
❑ F. Windows 98 SE

Answers A, B, and D are correct. You cannot upgrade any edition of Windows 95, Windows NT 4.0 Workstation must have at least SP5 installed, and you cannot upgrade (downgrade) any Microsoft server operating system to Windows XP. Answer C is incorrect because you can upgrade Windows 2000 Professional with SP1 installed to Windows XP. Answer E is incorrect because you can upgrade Windows Me to Windows XP. Answer F is incorrect because you can upgrade Windows 98 and Windows 98 SE to Windows XP.

10. Which of the following commands successfully slipstreams Windows XP SP1 into the original Windows XP Setup files? For each possible answer, **r:** represents the computer's CD-ROM drive where the Windows XP SP1 CD is located and the **xpsetup.pro** folder represents where the **I386** folder is located that contains original Windows XP Professional Setup files.

❑ A. r:\xpsp1.exe –s:\\server01\xpsetup.pro.
❑ B. r:\xpsp1.exe –s:\\server01\xpsetup.pro\i386.
❑ C. r:\update\update.exe –s:\\server01\xpsetup.pro.
❑ D. r:\update\update.exe –s:\\server01\xpsetup.pro\i386.

Answer A is correct. The SP1 executable file for Windows XP is named xpsp1.exe, the correct option is -s:<folder path>, and the correct folder that contains the I386 subfolder is xpsetup.pro (the I386 subfolder is assumed). Answer B is incorrect because the SP installation program will not be able find the Windows XP Setup files in the \\server01\xpsetup.pro\i386\i386 folder and the slipstream process will fail. Answers C and D are incorrect because before you can run the update.exe program, you must first extract all the SP files onto a local or network drive by specifying the /x option on the xpsp1.exe command line. For example, if you run the command r:\xpsp1.exe /x, you'll be prompted for where to copy the uncompressed SP files. The update.exe program is *not* stored in an uncompressed, usable format on the SP CD-ROM.

Configuring and Troubleshooting Resources

Terms you'll need to understand:

- ✓ Simple File Sharing
- ✓ Share permissions
- ✓ NT File System (NTFS)
- ✓ Effective Permissions
- ✓ Encrypting File System (EFS)
- ✓ Local printers and print jobs
- ✓ Printer permissions
- ✓ Network printers and print jobs
- ✓ Offline files/client-side caching

Techniques you'll need to master:

- ✓ Configuring shared folder permissions
- ✓ Configuring NTFS file and folder permissions
- ✓ Working with NTFS encrypted files
- ✓ Troubleshooting printing
- ✓ Connecting to network printers
- ✓ Working with offline files settings

Knowledge workers need to access data and printers—a lot. As a desktop support technician, your responsibility, like the Fire Department, is to be there when needed, ready to rescue lost data and lost print jobs. Supporting shared resources and troubleshooting access to those shared resources are two of the most important jobs that a desktop support technician faces. Fortunately, Windows XP comes well-equipped with plenty of tools to maintain a reliable network infrastructure.

Managing and Troubleshooting Shared Folders

Windows XP introduces alternative ways to grant folder permissions to network users. You can choose either standard file sharing or the new Simple File Sharing option.

Managing and Troubleshooting Simple File Sharing

Simple File Sharing eliminates the complexity of setting individual file and folder permissions. In short, when you access a shared folder under Simple File Sharing, you do so as the guest account.

Simple File Sharing is enabled by default when the computer running Windows XP Professional is standalone or a member of a workgroup. This Simple File Sharing check box is ignored when the computer is a member of a Windows domain.

Simple File Sharing creates a Shared Documents folder, inside of which it creates two subfolders, Shared Pictures and Shared Music. Remote users who access a shared folder over the network always authenticate as the guest user account when Simple File Sharing is enabled.

The properties sheet for a shared folder under Simple File Sharing configures both share permissions and NTFS permissions (if the shared folder is stored on an NTFS volume) simultaneously: you cannot configure the two permissions separately.

Under Simple File Sharing, a shared folder is not private unless the folder resides on an NTFS volume. Anyone logged on locally can access the files if he is on a FAT16- or FAT32-formatted volume.

To disable Simple File Sharing on a standalone system or on a computer that is a member of a workgroup, perform the following steps:

1. Open a window in either My Computer or Windows Explorer.

2. Click Tools, Folder Options from the menu.

3. Click the View tab.

4. Clear the Use Simple File Sharing (Recommended) check box under the Advanced Settings section.

5. Click OK.

The Shared Documents, Shared Pictures, and Shared Music folders are not available if the Windows XP Professional computer is a member of a Windows domain.

Because under Simple File Sharing (see Figure 2.1), you are connected as the guest account, the network connections used by remote-management utilities and remote Registry tools also use the guest account. Of course, the guest account must be enabled on computers configured with Simple File Sharing.

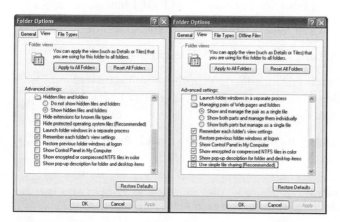

Figure 2.1   Windows XP Home Edition Folder Options (left) and Windows XP Professional Edition Folder Options (right).

Simple File Sharing, if enabled, improves your computer's security. Why? Because anyone who connects, including an Internet hacker, connects *automatically* as the guest account, not as the ever-dangerous local administrator—an account that oftentimes is left wide open with a blank password.

Considering a blank password? Having a blank password prevents any remote logon activity. You cannot use accounts with blank passwords to log on to the computer over the network, nor to utilize the **RunAs** command. Only users at the physical computer console can use Windows XP Professional with blank passwords.

Be careful, however. If your computer is not in a physically secure location, you should assign passwords to all local user accounts. Failure to do so allows anyone with physical access to the computer to easily log on by using an account that does not have a password. This is especially important for portable computers, which should always have strong passwords on all local user accounts.

Creating and Removing Shared Folders

When Simple File Sharing is disabled, sharing folders under Windows XP is similar to setting up shared folders in the past. Shared folders are often referred to simply as *shares*. From the graphical user interface (GUI), you can use the Windows Explorer (or My Computer) to right-click any available folder you want to make available to users over the network. To create a shared folder on a Windows XP computer, follow these steps:

1. Open My Computer or Windows Explorer.

2. Right-click the folder that you want to share and select Sharing and Security.

3. From the Sharing tab, click the Share This Folder button.

4. Type the new shared folder's name in the Share Name box.

5. Optionally, type in a description in the Description box.

6. In the User Limit section, either accept the default setting of Maximum Allowed or click Allow This Number of Users and type in the number in the spinner box.

7. Click OK to create the shared folder with default share permissions (see Figure 2.2).

Under Windows XP, the default share permissions are Everyone: Allow Read, *not* Everyone: Allow Full Control as in earlier versions of Windows.

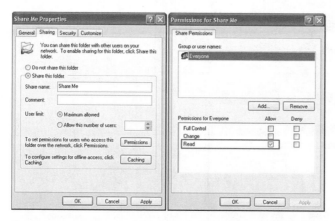

Figure 2.2   Creating a new shared folder using default share permissions.

You can share a single folder and use more than one name. To do so, click the New Share button that appears at the bottom of the Sharing tab on an existing shared folder. Use this technique if you need to create multiple network links to the same folder. (Idea: One link might be public, and one might be private using the $ symbol as the last character in the share name to hide it from the browser.)

To remove a share when you have multiple shares for the same physical folder, select the share from the Share Name drop-down list box and click the Remove Share button at the bottom of the dialog box. To stop sharing the folder entirely, click the Do Not Share This Folder option button at the top of the dialog box; this action removes all shares from the network browse list, and the folder is no longer accessible by remote users as a network shared folder.

The command line is often an efficient alternative to the GUI.

Using the net share command at the command prompt, you can easily create new shared folders. To create a shared folder, type **net share name_of_share=driveletter:\path** and press Enter. For example, to create a shared folder named companypayroll for the folder c:\Payroll, at a command prompt type **net share companypayroll=c:\payroll**. To remove the share, type **net share companypayroll /delete**.

Microsoft also provides a tool for supporting and troubleshooting shared folders. The Shared Folders Microsoft Management Console (MMC) snap-in, shown in Figure 2.3, provides a central location for managing shared folders. It is a node within the Computer Management console, or you can enable it individually by typing **fsmgmt.msc** in the Start, Run dialog box.

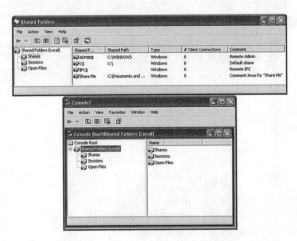

Figure 2.3 Viewing shared folders from the Shared Folders Microsoft Console **fsmgmt.msc** (above) and with the shared folders snap-in inserted into a custom MMC (below).

In Windows XP, Microsoft added a wizard to create shares in the Shared Folders snap-in. The Create Shared Folder Wizard (see Figure 2.4) gives you the ability to customize both share permissions and NTFS folder permissions (if the folder resides on an NTFS drive).

Share permissions are separate and different from (NTFS) file-system security permissions. Share permissions only affect remote users when they access shared folders over the network. NTFS permissions, on the other hand, are more granular than share permissions and apply to both folders and files.

Share permissions apply only to shared folders; you cannot apply them to individual files.

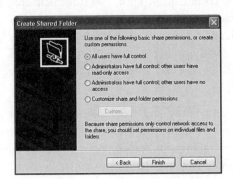

Figure 2.4 Specifying folder permissions for a share with the Create Shared Folder Wizard's dialog boxes.

If you are a member of a Windows 2000 or 2003 domain, you can publish shares in Active Directory from the Shared Folders snap-in, but not from

Windows Explorer or My Computer (see Figure 2.5). Publishing shares in Active Directory enables users to locate shared resources by querying Active Directory rather than by browsing My Network Places. Users can locate published shares using different search criteria, such as keywords. As you can see in Figure 2.5, the publish tab of a shared folders properties dialog box allows you to add a description, the name of an owner, and specific keywords for searches to each share. Imagine putting a project number or customer account number in the keyword field.

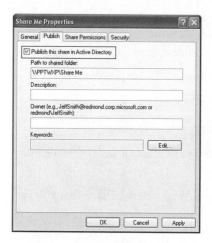

Figure 2.5 Publishing a share to the Active Directory.

Connecting to Shared Resources on a Microsoft Windows–Based Network

Users and desktop support technicians have several options with which to connect to shared network resources. These options include the following:

➤ Type a Universal Naming Convention (UNC) path in the Start, Run dialog box in the format *servername**sharename*.

➤ Navigate to the share through the My Network Places window.

➤ Employ the net use command from a command prompt window.

If you want to connect to a shared folder named demos that resides on a Windows computer named MRKTG44, click Start, Run; type \\MRKTG44\demos; and click OK. At this point, you are connected to that shared resource, provided that you possess the proper user ID, password, and security permissions to access the shared folder.

You can connect to a network share from My Network Places. To use the My Network Places window, perform the following steps:

1. Click Start, My Network Places.

2. In the right-hand Network Tasks section, click the Add a Network Place link, which reveals the Add Network Place Wizard.

3. Click Next, click Choose Another Network Location, and then click Next again.

4. Enter the Internet or network address, or click Browse to locate the network share by viewing the available network resources. You can connect to one of the following types of resources:

   ➤ A shared folder using the sample syntax \\server\share

   ➤ A Web folder using the sample syntax http://webserver/share

   ➤ An FTP site using the sample syntax ftp://ftp.domain.name

5. Click Next to enter a name for the network place or accept the default name.

6. Click Next again to view a summary of the Network Place that you are adding.

7. Click Finish to establish the connection to the shared folder, provided that you have the proper permissions. A list of network resources to which you have already connected appears within the My Network Places window.

For Command-Line Enthusiasts: The **net use** Command

Accessing a Share with an Alternate Security Context

As a desktop support technician, you might sometimes need to access a share with an alternate security context. You can connect to a network resource by appending one of the following password/username extensions to the end of the **net use** command:

➤ [password |*] /USER:[domainname\]username

➤ [password |*] /USER:[dotted domain name\]username

➤ [password |*] /USER:[username@dotted domain name

The /USER: option enables the user to complete the command with a different user account. For example, if I'm logged on to computer01 as **DomainABC\PhilW**, I can use the **net use** command to log on to server15 as the administrator and be prompted for a password with the command **net use \\server15\share1\ * /user:domainABC\administrator**.

As mentioned earlier in the discussion of multiple share names for the same folder, administrators can create their own hidden shares simply by adding a dollar symbol to the share name of any shared folder. Administrators can view all the hidden shares that exist on a Windows XP computer from the Shared Folders MMC snap-in. When you create your own hidden shares, any users can connect to them provided that they know the exact UNC path and that they possess the necessary permissions for accessing that shared folder.

Windows XP, along with Windows Server 2003, Windows 2000, and Windows NT, automatically creates specific shared folders by default every time you start Windows. These default shares are often referred to as *hidden* or *administrative* shares because a dollar symbol ($) is appended to each share name, which prevents the shared folder from appearing on the network browse list. Users might not realize that these "unadvertised" shares exist.

Microsoft Windows networking conceals hidden shares when users navigate through My Network Places. The NETLOGON, SYSVOL, and User Authentication Module for Macintosh (UAM) volume shares on Windows Server operating systems are not hidden; these administrative shares are visible to all users. The default hidden administrative shares on desktop operating systems include the following:

➤ *C$, D$, E$, F$, etc.*—These shares are created automatically (by default) for the root of each available drive letter on the local computer.

➤ *ADMIN$*—This share exposes the %systemroot% folder to the network (for example, C:\Windows).

➤ *IPC$*—This share is used for interprocess communications (IPCs). IPCs support communications between objects on different computers over a network by manipulating the low-level details of network transport protocols. IPCs enable the use of distributed application programs that combine multiple processes working together to accomplish a single task. The IPC$ share is on every Windows-based server; it enables you to authenticate using a different set of user credentials to a remote server.

➤ *PRINT$*—This share holds the printer drivers for the printers installed on the local machine. When a remote computer connects to a printer over the network, it downloads the appropriate printer driver.

Although you can temporarily disable the default hidden shares or administrative shares, you cannot delete them without modifying the Registry (which is not recommended) because they are re-created each time the computer restarts. You can connect to an administrative hidden share, but only if you provide a user account with administrative privileges along with the appropriate password for that account.

Controlling Access to Shared Folders by Using Share Permissions

When you create a new share under Windows XP Professional or Windows Server 2003, the default share permissions are Everyone: Allow Read.

Share permissions determine the level of access to files and folders stored within the share for remote users accessing the share over the network; local users accessing local files are not affected by share permissions.

For the highest level of security, use NTFS (file-system) permissions in addition to share permissions to ensure that local users accessing the files are also subject to any restrictions you've configured. To enable network access, you must create a share, but you should use NTFS settings because they apply to both local and network users and because NTFS security provides a wider variety of permission levels.

Share permissions offer only three levels of security access: Read, Change, or Full Control. Each permission level can be allowed (Allow check box marked), implicitly denied (Allow check box cleared), or explicitly denied (Deny check box marked). The share permissions and their levels of access are as follows:

➤ *Read*—This default permission lets users view folder names and filenames, view data within files, and execute application program files.

➤ *Change*—This permission allows all Read permissions and also lets users add folders and files, change data within files, and delete folders and files.

➤ *Full Control*—This permission grants the same privileges as the Change permission for share permission purposes. It also permits users to change NTFS file-level and folder-level permissions for files and folders stored on NTFS drives.

Customizing share permissions is optional when creating a shared folder; the Everyone: Allow Read permission is automatically assigned to all new shares. You can change the default share permissions for a new share or for an existing share. To modify share permissions, follow these steps:

1. Right-click the shared folder in Windows Explorer or My Computer and select Sharing and Security.

2. Click the Permissions button.

3. Select a user or group name that is listed.

4. Mark the appropriate Allow or Deny check box for the permission that you want to configure: Read, Change, or Full Control.

5. Click the Add button to add a user or group to the list.

6. Select the user or group that you added and mark the appropriate Allow or Deny check box for the permission that you want to configure: Read, Change, or Full Control.

7. To remove a user or group that is listed, select it and click the Remove button.

8. Click OK for the Share Permissions dialog box and then click OK for the folder's properties sheet to save the settings.

Monitoring, Managing, and Troubleshooting Access to Files and Folders Under NTFS

NTFS offers numerous features, like auditing and encryption, that help administrators maintain and safeguard applications and data. Although you can control access to shared network folders by managing share permissions, Windows XP NTFS provides a more robust access control solution. In addition to offering administrators more granularity of security access control over files and folders than network share permissions, NTFS permissions reside at the file-system level, which allows administrators to manage one set of access control settings for both local users and network users.

You can apply NTFS security permissions to files, folders, and printers for specific users; specific groups of users; and, under Active Directory, to specific computer accounts. Windows XP Professional provides four local users by default: administrator, HelpAssistant, SUPPORT_*xxxxxxxx* (xxxxxxxx represents a unique number for your Windows XP system), and guest. The guest user account, HelpAssistant, and the SUPPORT_*xxxxxxxx* account are disabled by default.

The administrator user account is all powerful on the local machine; you can rename it, but you cannot delete it. The HelpAssistant account is supposed to be disabled by default (this is true with Windows XP Service Pack 1 [SP1]). It has a randomly generated strong password and is used during a Remote Assistance session to allow the "expert" to log on to the "novice" computer.

Nine local groups are created automatically: Administrators, Backup Operators, Guests, HelpServicesGroup, Network Configuration Operators, Power Users, Remote Desktop Users, Replicator, and Users.

Windows XP also has system groups whose memberships change dynamically.

At a given point in time, a user using a Windows XP computer in a particular manner is a member of one or many special built-in system groups.

For example, when a user logs on to a computer remotely over the network, that user's account becomes a member of the Network system group for the duration of that session. Table 2.1 outlines various built-in system groups.

Table 2.1 Built-In System Groups Under Windows XP Professional	
Built-In System Groups	**Description**
Everyone	This group includes all nonanonymous users who access the computer. The best practice is to avoid using this group. If you enable the guest account, any user can become authorized to access the system, and the user inherits the rights and permissions assigned to the Everyone group.
Authenticated Users	These users have valid user accounts on the local system, or they possess a valid user account within the domain of which the system is a member. It is preferable that you use this group over the Everyone group for preventing anonymous access to resources. The guest account is never considered an authenticated user.
Creator Owner	This is a user who creates or takes ownership of a resource. Whenever any member of the Administrators group creates an object, the Administrators group is listed as the owner of that resource in lieu of the actual name of the individual who created it.
Network	This group contains any user accounts from a remote computer that access the local computer via a current network connection.
Anonymous Logon	This group contains any user who accesses the computer without a name, password, or domain. Users cannot log on to the system both as an Interactive user and an Anonymous Logon user at the same time. In Windows XP, this group is *not* a member of the Everyone group.
Dialup	This group contains any user accounts that are currently connected via dial-up networking.

Table 2.1 Continued	
Built-In System Groups	**Description**
Interactive	This group contains any user who logs on to the computer locally or using a Remote Desktop client connection.
Terminal Server Users	This group contains any user who accesses a Terminal Services Server running in Terminal Service 4.0 compatibility mode.

Controlling Access to Files and Folders by Using NTFS Permissions

Basic NTFS permissions, as shown in Figure 2.6, represent predefined advanced NTFS permissions, and you apply them per user and per group. Individual file permissions differ slightly from the permissions that apply to folders. Table 2.2 highlights the basic permissions available for both folders and files.

In many instances, basic permissions are sufficient for granting or denying fundamental privileges to both users and groups. Best practice dictates that it is more efficient assigning permissions to groups of users rather than to individual users. Above all, standards save time and help simplify networks.

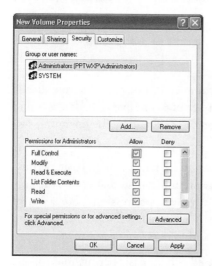

Figure 2.6   Viewing default basic NTFS permissions.

Table 2.2 Basic NTFS Security Permissions for Folders and Files	
Permission Name	**Levels of Access**
Read	View and list folders and files; view attributes, extended attributes, and permissions of folders.
Read & Execute	Run program files; view and list folders and files; view attributes, extended attributes, and permissions of folders and files.
List Folder Contents (folders only)	View and list folders and files; run program files.
Write	Add files to a folder.
Modify	View and list folders and files; view the contents of files; write data to files; add folders and files; delete folders, files, and file contents; view and set attributes and extended attributes.
Full Control	View and list folders and files; view the contents of files; write data to files; add folders and files; delete folders, files, and file contents; view and set attributes and extended attributes; change permissions for folders and files; take ownership of folders and files.

NOTE

The List Folder Contents permission is inherited by folders, but not by files. It appears only when you view folder permissions and drive volume permissions. Read & Execute is inherited by both files and folders and is always present when you view file or folder permissions.

By default, NTFS security permissions are inherited from an object's parent. An administrator, however, can manually override the default inheritance and explicitly configure permission settings.

When you create a new NTFS drive volume, Windows XP automatically assigns default basic NTFS permission settings for five default users and groups. Advanced NTFS permissions are also assigned by the operating system.

As a desktop support technician, you need to be familiar with basic permissions, understand their effect on objects, and understand that each basic permission is a combination of individual advanced permissions. For a list of special permissions, go to the Windows XP Help and Support Center and search for "Special permissions for files and folders."

The five default groups and their associated default basic permissions follow:

➤ *Administrators*—Allow Full Control.

➤ *Creator Owner*—No basic permissions set for the root of the drive volume; all check boxes are cleared.

➤ *Everyone*—No basic permissions set for the root of the drive volume; all check boxes are cleared.

➤ *System*—Allow Full Control.

➤ *Users*—Allow Read, Allow Read & Execute, and Allow List Folder Contents.

An object's NTFS security permissions are automatically inherited from its parent container.

For example, a file's NTFS permissions are inherited from its folder; a sub-folder's NTFS permissions are inherited from its parent folder. Folders stored in the root of a drive volume inherit their NTFS permissions from the drive volume's permissions, which are set by default.

Inheritance is the default behavior for NTFS permissions; if you remove inherited permissions, explicit permissions take their place. When a file or folder has inherited the permissions from the parent folder, the Allow and Deny check boxes for NTFS basic permissions are shaded and not changeable.

By clicking the Advanced button at the bottom of the Security tab, you can work with the Advanced Security settings dialog box, as shown in Figure 2.7.

To disable inheritance, uncheck the Inherit from Parent the Permission Entries that Apply to Child Objects... check box. By clearing this check box, you can choose to copy the existing inherited permissions and turn them into explicit permissions, or you can remove them entirely and manually establish new explicit permissions. As soon you clear the check box, the Security message box appears, and you must choose one of the following options:

➤ Copy the existing inherited permissions.

➤ Remove the existing inherited permissions.

➤ Cancel the action and leave the inherited permissions intact.

NTFS security permissions are cumulative. A user's effective NTFS permissions are the accumulation of permissions assigned to them directly and permissions they acquire indirectly by also being a member of a group. Further, Deny entries always override Allow entries for the same permission type (Read, Write, Modify, and so on).

Figure 2.7 Using Advanced Security Settings to disable inheritance of NTFS permissions (notice the enclosed area).

NTFS security permissions apply to all users whether they are local or remote; share permissions apply only to remote users accessing files and folders over the network. When a user accesses a file across a network connection, the effective permissions on the file or folder are the product of both NTFS permissions and Share permissions.

If you apply both share permissions and NTFS permissions to a shared folder, the permissions they have in common will apply. For this reason, it is considered a best practice to set either restrictive share permissions or restrictive NTFS permissions, but not both.

The easiest way to manage permissions on NTFS-formatted drives is to share folders with the setting Allow: Full Control. Then, use NTFS permissions to control access. This technique simplifies the process of determining the actual network permissions because the NTFS permissions alone determine a user's effective permissions on an object.

To change NTFS security permissions, you must be the owner of the file or folder whose permissions you want to modify, or the owner must grant you permission to make modifications to the object's security settings.

Groups or users who are granted Allow: Full Control on a folder can delete files and subfolders within that folder regardless of the permissions protecting those files and subfolders.

To view or assign basic NTFS permissions on a file or a folder for users and groups, follow these steps:

1. Open Windows Explorer or My Computer, right-click a file or folder stored on an NTFS drive volume, and select Properties.

2. Click the Security tab.

3. To add a user or group to the list of Group or User Names, click the Add button.

4. Type the user or group name in the Enter the Object Names to Select box or click the Advanced button to pick from a list of user and group names.

5. Click OK to close the Select User, Computer, or Group dialog box.

6. To remove a user or group, select the name and click Remove.

7. To assign permissions to a user or group, select the name and mark the Allow or Deny check box for each permission that you want to assign.

8. Click OK to save your settings and close the properties window.

NTFS advanced permissions are called *special* permissions. These special permissions are the building blocks of basic permissions. In Windows XP, special permissions give administrators granular control over exactly what types of security access users can have over files and folders. Special permissions are somewhat hidden from view. They allow administrators to fine-tune access control entry (ACE) security settings. From the Security tab of a file or folder's properties sheet, click the Advanced button to view, add, modify, or remove special NTFS permissions.

When you click the Advanced button, you see the Advanced Security Settings dialog box, which shows each ACE assigned to every user and group that has permissions on that resource. To remove a permission entry, select the entry and click the Remove button.

To view or edit existing individual special permission entries, as shown in Figure 2.8, select one of the users or groups listed and then click the Edit button. When you click the Edit button, the Permission Entry dialog box appears. This dialog gives administrators a fine level of control over the access allowed to individual users and groups on specific resources.

From the Permission Entry dialog box, you can perform the following tasks for the specified user or group:

➤ Click the Change button to change the user or group listed in the Name box so that this permission entry applies to some other user or group.

➤ Click the Apply Onto drop-down list box to specify exactly where these special permissions should apply.

➤ Change the permission entries themselves by marking or clearing the Allow or Deny check box for each permission that you want to assign.

Figure 2.8 Viewing special NTFS permissions.

There's good news for desktop support technicians who are overwhelmed by estimating true permissions when multiple NTFS settings, both basic and advanced, intersect.

Windows XP provides a way for desktop support technicians to view current effective permissions from the Advanced Security Settings dialog for a file or folder. Local administrators logged into non–domain-member computers cannot view NTFS effective permissions for domain users.

The Effective Permissions tab, as shown in Figure 2.9, calculates effective permissions based on user permissions, group permissions, and inherited permissions.

The effective permissions feature does not consider share permissions when calculating effective permissions.

To view effective permissions on a file or a folder for a user or group, follow these steps:

1. Open Windows Explorer or My Computer, right-click a file or folder stored on an NTFS drive volume, and select Properties.

2. Click the Security tab.

3. Click the Advanced button to display the Advanced Security Settings dialog box.

4. Click the Effective Permissions tab.

5. Click the Select button, type a user or group name for which you want to view effective permissions, and click OK. (Click the Advanced button and then click Find Now to select from a list of user and group names.)

6. View the effective permissions for the user or group that you selected, as shown in Figure 2.9.

7. Click OK to close the Advanced Security Settings dialog box and then click OK to close the properties sheet.

Figure 2.9   Viewing NTFS effective permissions for a user or a group.

Understanding and Troubleshooting "Access Denied" Messages

Okay, there's nothing as frustrating as "access denied."

As a desktop support technician, when different factors control access to files and folders, users might not be able to access files that they need. In these instances, you must diagnose and fix the problem. The major contributing factors for access control issues are

➤ Shared folder permissions

➤ NTFS permissions

➤ EFS-encrypted files

If you review these three major factors in the sequence listed, you should be able to solve most access-control issues. Share permissions do not apply to local users trying to access local folders and files. NTFS permissions and EFS encryption apply to both local and network users.

For remote users attempting access files over the network, always check the share permissions first. Also, the default share permissions are Everyone: Allow Read for Windows XP Professional and Windows Server 2003.

Share permissions have no effect on local file access by local users; local access includes users interactively logged on to a computer and users logged on to a computer via Terminal Services (Remote Desktop Connections).

After you verify the share permissions for a folder, check the NTFS permissions. NTFS permissions apply to all users—whether they are local users or network users. Be sure to review all special NTFS permissions, not just the basic NTFS permissions. Right-click the folder or file in question, select Properties, and click the Security tab. Click the Advanced button to view and adjust the special NTFS permissions, if necessary.

Also, from the Advanced Security Settings dialog box, click the Effective Permissions tab and check the effective permissions for each user and group that you are investigating. These measures should reveal why users can't access the folders or files that they need.

After you verify and make any necessary changes to the share permissions and NTFS permissions to allow users to access the files and folders that they need, be sure to check for EFS encryption if the access problem still persists.

To check a file or folder for EFS encryption, right-click the object and select Properties. From the General tab, click the Advanced button to display the Advanced Attributes dialog box, as shown in Figure 2.10.

If the Encrypt Contents to Secure Data check box is marked, the object is encrypted: encryption limits access to the user who originally encrypted the file, any users who have been granted shared access to the encrypted file, and the designated Data Recovery Agent (DRA).

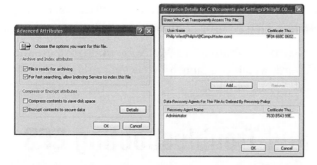

Figure 2.10   Encryption settings (left) and adding additional users who can transparently access this file (right).

If the file is encrypted and users who need to access the file do not have shared access, you need to add those users to the Users Who Can Transparently Access This File list box in the Encryption Details dialog box. The Encryption Details dialog box appears when you click the Details button from the Advanced Attributes dialog box.

You can use the **cipher.exe** tool at a command prompt to encrypt files, unencrypt files, list files and folders that are encrypted, and perform many other EFS-related activities. Type **cipher.exe /?** and press Enter to display the syntax and options for this command.

Optimizing Access to Files and Folders

To optimize access to files and folders, users and desktop support technicians can create shortcuts to local files and folders, map drive letters to remote shared folders, or add network places to My Network Places.

To create a shortcut, select the file or folder using the right mouse button and choose Create Shortcut.

You can also drag the object and drop it on the Start menu to create a shortcut to the file on your Start menu.

You can also create a shortcut and place it in the All Users profile folder to make it available to all users who use the computer.

To map a drive letter to a remote share, use the command net use x: \\servername\sharename, where x is an unused local drive letter and \\servername\sharename is the name of the remote share. You can substitute an asterisk for the drive letter to automatically assign the next available drive letter on your system.

You can also map a network drive using the My Network Places menu bar, clicking Tools, and selecting Map Network Drive.

To add network place (a network shortcut) to My Network Places, use the Add Network Place Wizard, which you launch by clicking Add a Network Place in the My Network Places window.

Managing and Troubleshooting EFS

NTFS supports data encryption. Just as with NTFS data compression, you set data encryption as an advanced attribute for a file or folder. EFS encryption and decryption is transparent to users. You can either compress or encrypt files and folders, but you can't use both compression and encryption on the same file or folder.

Folders that are encrypted using EFS set the encryption attribute on files that are moved or copied into them; those files automatically become encrypted once they reside in that folder. Files that are encrypted using EFS remain encrypted even if you move or rename them. Encrypted files that you back up or copy also retain their encryption attributes as long as they reside on NTFS-formatted drive volumes or the backup program is designed for Windows XP.

You can encrypt and decrypt files and folders from the GUI by using Windows Explorer and My Computer, as well as from the command line by using the cipher.exe tool. Encrypted folders and files appear in green in My Computer and the Windows Explorer. You can turn off this default color distinction by clicking Tools, Folder Options, View in My Computer or the Windows Explorer. To encrypt a file or folder from the GUI, follow these steps:

1. Open Windows Explorer or My Computer.

2. Right-click the file or folder that you want to encrypt or unencrypt and select Properties.

3. On the General tab, click the Advanced button.

4. From the Advanced Attributes dialog box, mark (or clear) the Encrypt Contents to Secure Data check box to encrypt (or unencrypt) the file or folder that you selected. Click OK to close the Advance Attributes

dialog box and then click OK for the properties sheet to apply this setting. (When you encrypt a folder, you are prompted to select between applying this setting to the folder only, or, to the folder, subfolders, and files.)

5. To share access to an encrypted file, click the Details button from the Advanced Attributes dialog box. You cannot share access to encrypted folders.

6. From the Encryption Details dialog box, click the Add button to add more users' EFS certificates to the encrypted file to share access with those users, as shown in Figure 2.10.

7. From the Select User dialog box, click the user whose EFS certificate you want to add for shared access to the encrypted file and click OK. You see only certificates for users who have encrypted a folder or file previously.

8. Click OK for the Encryption Details dialog box.

9. Finally, click OK for the Advanced Attributes dialog box and then click OK for the properties window.

After a file has the encryption attribute, only the user who originally encrypted the file, a user who has been granted shared access to the encrypted file, or the DRA who was the DRA at the time the file was encrypted may access it. DRAs are users who are designated as recovery agents for encrypted files. Only these users have the ability to decrypt any encrypted file regardless of who has encrypted it. DRAs do not need to be granted shared access to encrypted files; they have access by default. Any other users who attempt to access an encrypted file receive an Access Is Denied message.

NOTE A user with the necessary NTFS access permissions can still move encrypted files within the same drive volume or delete them entirely; therefore, the enforcement of proper NTFS permissions remains extremely important for encrypted files.

The default DRAs are as follows:

➤ The local administrator user account on Windows 2000 non-domain member (standalone) computers. Standalone Windows XP and standalone Windows Server 2003 computers have no DRAs by default.

➤ The domain administrator user account on Windows Server 2003 or Windows 2000 Server domain controllers and for Windows Server 2003, Windows XP, and Windows 2000 domain member computers.

Working with Local and Network Printers

Who hasn't received a phone call from a frustrated user unable to print a file? Yes, the wires are connected. Yes, there is paper in the printer. Yes, the printer is turned on. Now what?

Managing Local Printers and Print Jobs

You manage print devices in Windows XP Professional from the Printers and Faxes folder, which is accessible from the Control Panel or by clicking Start, Printers and Faxes.

Within the Printer and Faxes folder are printers that enable you to view and manage the print jobs they are forwarding to the actual physical printers.

Double-click any of the printers listed to view the print queue they are controlling.

It is important to know whether a printer is offline. If the printer is offline, as shown in Figure 2.11, no amount of "wishful thinking" will make queued documents print until the printer status is returned to online.

When Use Printer Online appears, this means the printer is currently offline.

Figure 2.11 When a printer is offline, the File menu displays Use Printer Online.

Controlling Access to Printers

Printing in Windows XP comes with many options. To Microsoft, printers are software that link to the physical printers on your network. As software, the printers can be configured in multiple fashions to suit your business needs.

You can configure who has permission to use or manage the printers, as shown in Figure 2.12. You can configure when printers are available. You can configure multiple printers to point to the same physical printer and give each printer a unique priority number.

All these choices are properties of the printer.

Right-click one of the available printer icons in the Printers and Faxes folder and choose Properties, to configure that printer's settings and options. The printer Properties dialog box contains six tabs (seven tabs for a color printer): General, Sharing, Ports, Advanced, Security, Device Settings, and Color Management (for a color printer).

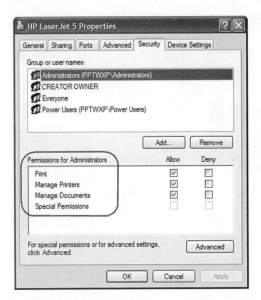

Figure 2.12   Controlling access to a printer using permissions.

Connecting to a Local Printer

If you are working with a USB printer, it is, by definition, Plug and Play compatible and *should* be recognized and installed automatically. In the real world, this might not always be the case.

To manually add a local printer to your system, follow these steps:

1. Log on as an administrator or a member of the Administrators group.

2. Click Start, Printers and Faxes to open the Printers and Faxes window.

3. Click the Add a Printer link from the Printer Tasks pane. The Add Printer Wizard appears. Click Next to continue.

4. Click the Local Printer button. If the printer that you are adding is not Plug and Play compatible, you can clear the Automatically Detect and Install My Plug and Play Printer check box. If the printer is Plug and Play compliant, Windows XP Professional automatically installs and properly configures it for you.

5. If the printer is not Plug and Play, the Select a Printer Port dialog box appears. Click the port you want to use from the Use the Following Port drop-down list, or click the Create a New Port button and choose the type of port to create from the drop-down list.

6. Click Next.

7. Select the printer Manufacturer and Model. Click the Have Disk button if you have a DVD-ROM, CD-ROM, or disk with the proper printer drivers from the manufacturer. Click the Windows Update button to download the latest drivers available from Microsoft's Web site. You should strive to only use drivers that have been digitally signed by Microsoft, for compatibility.

8. Click Next.

9. Enter a name for the printer. The name should not exceed 31 characters, and best practice dictates that the printer name should not contain any spaces or special characters. Specify whether this printer will be designated as the system's default printer.

10. Click Next.

11. In the Printer Sharing dialog box, click the Share Name button if you want to share this printer with the network. Enter a share name for the printer; it's a good idea to limit the share name to 14 or fewer characters and to omit spaces within the share name.

12. Click Next.

13. Enter an optional location name and comment.

14. Click Next.

15. Click Yes and then click Next when prompted to print a test page; it's always a good idea to make sure that the printer has been set up and is working properly.

16. Click Finish to exit the Add Printer Wizard.

Managing Network Printers and Print Jobs

When you physically connect a printer and then share that printer with the network, a Windows XP Professional workstation becomes a print server.

You can configure many of the properties of your Windows XP Professional print server by selecting File, Server Properties from the Printers and Faxes window. The next sections outline lists of the values you can adjust.

The General Tab

From the General tab, you can work with the following settings:

➤ Add or modify printer location and comment information.

➤ Set printing preferences such as portrait or landscape orientation.

➤ Select paper source and quality.

➤ Print a test page.

When garbled text appears in printed files, printing a test page might determine the source of the problem.

If a test page fails to print, always suspect a physical problem first. Try an alternate cable. If a new cable fails to solve the problem, you might want to try alternate printer driver software.

Printing and keeping a test page, just after you install a printer or change its ink, is a great way to create a baseline to which you can compare future documents.

The Sharing Tab

The Sharing tab displays the following options:

➤ Share the printer, change the network share name, or stop sharing the printer.

➤ Install additional printer drivers for client computers that use different operating systems or different Windows NT CPU platforms, as shown in Figure 2.13.

If you elect to install additional drivers, you are asked to provide a path to the additional driver files.

Because these drivers will be inherited by client computers, it is a good practice to test the drivers first before deploying them through a shared printer.

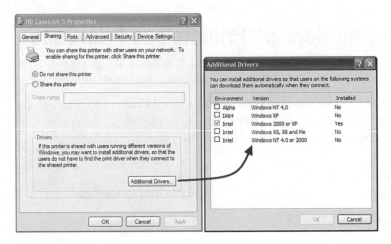

Figure 2.13   You can configure Windows XP with multiple printer drivers.

The Ports Tab

On the Ports tab, you have these configuration options:

➤ Select a port to print to.

➤ Add, configure, and delete ports.

➤ Enable bidirectional printing support.

➤ Enable printer pooling, which enables you to select two or more identical print devices that are configured as one logical printer; print jobs are directed to the first available print device.

Faulty port configuration and port drivers can also cause printing problems.

You can test a parallel port by sending some text to it. For example, type `dir` `> lpt1` at a command prompt from a directory with a lot of files, such as `c:\Windows`. As long as the printer is not a PostScript printer, this test determines whether the printer port driver and the printer are working. If you can print from the command line, the hardware is probably okay; suspect a software problem.

If the printer is connected to a serial interface and documents are not printing properly, check the configuration of the serial port. Are the baud rate and parity configured properly?

For USB printers, check whether the USB printer port is properly installed and selected. You might need to go to Device Manager and delete an improperly installed and configured USB device.

Finally, if you can print from DOS but you cannot print a file with Notepad or WordPad, suspect the Windows printer driver, which is configured on the Advanced tab.

The Advanced Tab

Besides the printer driver, the Advanced tab provides a lot of interesting settings for a desktop support technician. Imagine being able to control the availability of the printer or the priority of print jobs sent to the printer, as shown in Figure 2.14.

The Advanced page enables you to

➤ Set time availability limits.

➤ Set print job priority.

➤ Change the printer driver or add a new driver.

➤ Spool print jobs and start printing immediately, or start printing after the last page has spooled.

➤ Print directly to the printer; do not spool print jobs.

➤ Hold mismatched documents.

➤ Print spooled documents first.

➤ Retain documents after they are printed.

➤ Enable advanced printing features (such as metafile spooling) and enable advanced options (such as Page Order, Booklet Printing, and Pages Per Sheet); advanced options vary depending upon printer capabilities.

➤ Set printing defaults.

➤ Select a different print processor: ready-to-print (RAW), Enhanced Metafile (EMF), or Text.

➤ Specify a separator page.

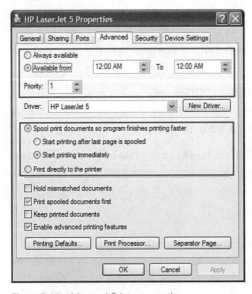

Figure 2.14 Advanced Printer properties.

Troubleshooting printing problems often starts with configurations in the Advanced page.

When printing is not centered, the paper size and type might not be configured properly under Printing Defaults at the bottom of the Advanced tab.

When a document fails to print, is it due to insufficient printer memory to support complex pages? When printing with a laser printer, consider reducing the dots per inch (dpi) to reduce the amount of memory required for the page to print. When a print job freezes, it might be due to insufficient hard drive space for spooling. If you suspect spooler-related problems, you can configure them in the Advanced tab and you can log spooling events by configuring Print Server properties.

To access Print Server properties, in the Printers and Faxes window menu bar, click File and click Server Properties to open the Print Server property box displayed in Figure 2.15.

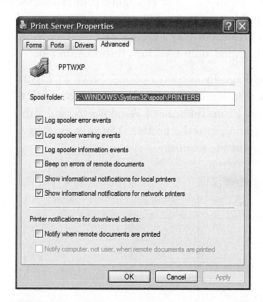

Figure 2.15   Print Server properties, advanced troubleshooting options.

 Be familiar with the Advanced tab of Printer properties and the Advanced tab of Print Server properties in Windows XP. They are useful sources of printer troubleshooting options and information.

The Security Tab

To control user access to printers and printer settings, you can configure the following security settings with the Security tab:

➤ Set permissions for users and groups (similar to NTFS file and folder permissions): Allow or Deny the Print, Manage Printers, and Manage Documents.

➤ Set up printer auditing (similar to NTFS file and folder access auditing) via the Auditing tab by clicking the Advanced button.

➤ Take ownership of the printer (similar to taking ownership of NTFS files and folders) via the Owner tab by clicking the Advanced button.

➤ View the effective permissions for the printer (similar to viewing the effective permissions for NTFS files and folders) via the Effective Permissions tab by clicking the Advanced button.

The Device Settings Tab

The Device Settings tab enables you to view or configure printer-specific settings. The available settings on this tab depend on the manufacturer and the model of the printer. Not all printers display a Device Settings tab. Some printers, such as the Epson C80, display only a Version Information tab.

In the Device Settings tab, the Page Protection option, shown in Figure 2.16, is designed to improve the printing of complex documents from printers with insufficient memory. Page Protection causes Windows to render the entire page in memory before sending it to the printer. A printer must have 1MB of installed memory to support the feature.

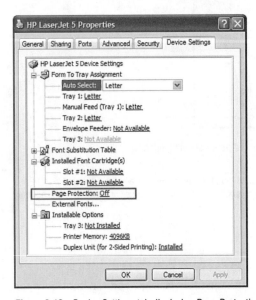

Figure 2.16   Device Settings tab displaying Page Protection.

Additionally, users can install supplemental memory in a printer to improve performance. For Windows to recognize the supplemental memory, you might need to increase the value for Printer Memory that appears in the Device Settings tab.

Color Management Tab

The Color Management tab, which appears only on printers that support color management, enables you to select a color profile with which to translate colors to your printer. These profiles provide information to Windows about the color capabilities of the printer.

Using the IPP

Internet Printing Protocol (IPP), also known as Web printing, enables users to connect to and manage shared printers through a browser, as shown in Figure 2.17.

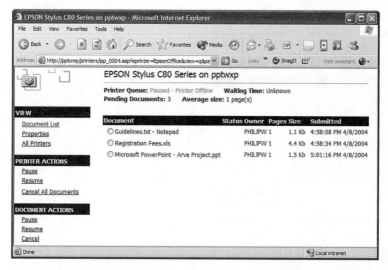

Figure 2.17 Viewing print jobs on a shared Epson Stylus C80 printer using a Web browser.

A computer running Windows XP can be an IPP server if you install the World Wide Web Service and Printers Virtual Directory from the Windows Components Wizard in Add Remove Programs, shown in Figure 2.18.

After installing the World Wide Web Service and Printers Virtual Directory, you must restart the Print Spooler service. You do not have to restart the computer.

Users connecting to your shared folders can use one of two available URLs to connect to the print server or to a specific print share:

➤ http://*print_server_name*/printers—Connects to the Web page for the Printers and Faxes folder on the Windows XP print server computer.

Shared fax devices are not shown in the browser window, as seen in Figure 2.19.

➤ `http://print_server_name/printer_share_name`—Connects to the Web page for the print queue folder for the printer that you specify, shown in Figure 2.17.

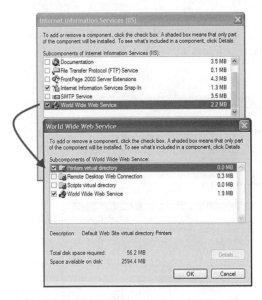

Figure 2.18   Installing Internet printing in Windows XP.

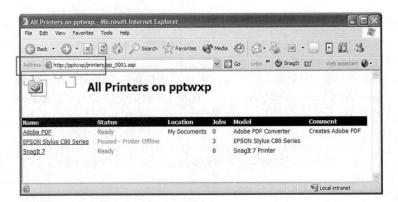

Figure 2.19   Shared printers viewed through a Web browser.

Configuring and Troubleshooting Printer Permissions

With printer permissions, as shown in Figure 2.20, you can control who can use a printer. For security reasons, you might need to limit user access to certain printers. You can also use printer permissions to delegate responsibilities for specific printers to users who are not administrators.

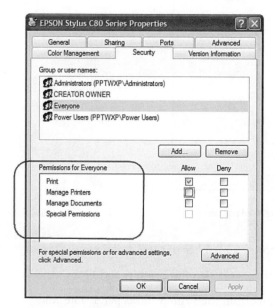

Figure 2.20   Controlling printer security using permissions.

Windows XP Professional provides three levels of printer permissions: Print, Manage Documents, and Manage Printers.

➤ Print permissions allow a user to send documents to the printer.

➤ Manage Documents allows a user to pause, cancel, restart, and rearrange *all* the documents in the print queue. These permissions apply only to documents sent to the printer after the user is given Manage Documents permission.

➤ Manage Printers allows a user to share printers, change printer spool settings, configure user permissions, change printer properties, and pause and restart the printer.

You can resolve the complex results of overlapping or intersecting printer permissions using the printer's Effective Permissions page. Access the Effective Permissions page, shown in Figure 2.21, by clicking Advanced on the Security page of the Printer Properties dialog box.

Connecting to a Network Printer

You can use the Add Printer Wizard from the Printers folder. To connect to a network printer, follow these steps:

Figure 2.21 Effective Permissions on shared printers.

1. Log on as an administrator or a member of the Administrators group.

2. Click Start, Printers and Faxes to open the Printers and Faxes window.

3. Click the Add a Printer link from the Printer Tasks pane. The Add Printer Wizard appears. Click Next to continue.

4. Click the option button labeled A Network Printer, or a Printer Attached to Another Computer.

5. Click Next.

6. Follow one of these options:

   ➤ Select Browse for a Printer, and then click Next.

   ➤ Select Connect to This Printer, type in the UNC path for the printer, as shown in Figure 2.22, and then click Next.

   ➤ Select Connect to a Printer on the Internet or on a Home or Office Network, type in the URL address for the printer, and then click Next.

7. If you choose to browse for a printer, locate the printer from the Browse for Printer dialog box and then click Next.

8. Click Yes or No when prompted to make the printer the system's default, and click Next.

9. Click Finish to exit the Add Printer Wizard.

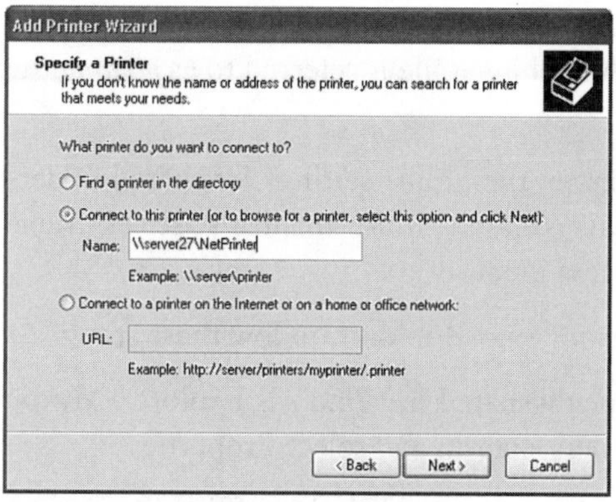

Figure 2.22   Connecting to a network printer.

You can also connect to a network printer via the command line by using the `net use` command. The syntax is as follows:

```
net use lptx: \\print_server_name\printer_share_name
```

Printer ports lpt1, lpt2, and lpt3 are represented by `lptx`. The `net use` command is the only way to connect client computers that are running MS-DOS to network printers.

Keep in mind that the `net use` command utilizes a NetBIOS name. For devices to connect across the network that use a NetBIOS name, name resolution is required. In other words, incorrect or absent Domain Name System (DNS), Windows Internet Naming Service (WINS), LMHOSTS, or HOSTS files can prevent printer recognition. To troubleshoot name-resolution problems, test the command by substituting the IP address of the remote device.

Managing and Troubleshooting Offline Files

Offline files provide an excellent way to have access to network files, even when you're not connected to the network.

From the perspective of the client, users can make almost any shared file available offline by right-clicking it and making it available offline. When you make a file available offline, there might be an apparent increase in the speed of network performance because the offline file is "preferred" by

Windows when you open a network file. If the two files are identical, the locally cached file opens. Manually caching a file is referred to as *pinning* the file.

From the perspective of the file server, the offline settings for shared folders default to manual caching. That is, users must manually select Make Available Offline from a file's context menu.

To configure other offline settings for shared folders, follow these steps:

1. Right-click a folder that is already shared in Windows Explorer, My Computer, or the Shared Folders snap-in and select Properties.

2. If you're using the Shared Folders snap-in, click the Offline Settings button from the General tab. If you're using Windows Explorer or My Computer, click the Offline Settings button from the Sharing tab.

3. Select one of the available options for offline files, as shown in Figure 2.23:

   ➤ *Automatic Caching of documents*—When a user opens a network file, it is cached automatically on the local hard drive.

   ➤ *Automatic Caching of Programs and Documents*—When a user opens a network file or runs a network application, the documents or the .exe is cached automatically on the local hard drive. Windows always checks whether the locally cached document has been updated on the server before it chooses which one to open. Windows always opens the locally cached executable without checking the server first.

   ➤ *Manual Caching of Documents*—Users must choose which files to store offline. This is the default setting.

4. Click OK for the Offline Settings dialog box and then click OK for the share's properties sheet to save the settings.

Offline files are synchronized, by default, when a user attempts to open the network file. If the network file is newer, the network file opens. If the files have the same time, date, and size, the local file opens.

Users can schedule periodic synchronization of offline files to ensure that they have the latest versions of all files. This task is especially important for users with mobile computers who are disconnected from the network while traveling.

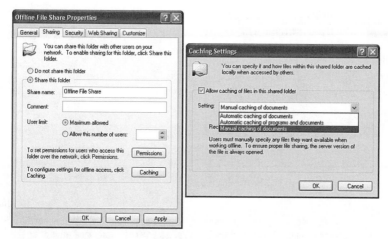

Figure 2.23 Configuring a share's offline settings.

Synchronization settings appear in the Explorer Menu under Tools, Synchronize and include options based on logons and logoffs as shown in Figure 2.24, or a chronological schedule, as shown in Figure 2.25.

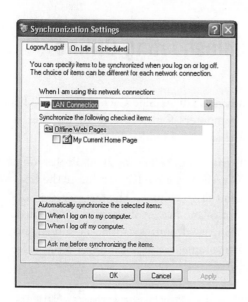

Figure 2.24 Configuring synchronization settings.

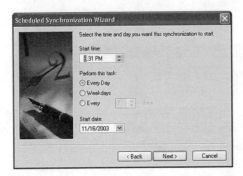

Figure 2.25 Using the Scheduled Synchronization Wizard.

 You can also configure offline settings from the command line using the **net share** command. Type **net share /?** and press Enter at a command prompt to view the proper syntax and available options for this command. The **/cache: setting_name** is an optional parameter for this utility. You can type **net share name_of_shared_folder /cache:manual** for manual caching, **net share name_of_shared_folder /cache:programs** for automatic caching of network programs and data files, **net share name_of_shared_folder /cache:documents** for automatic caching of data files only, or **net share name_of_shared_folder /cache:none** to turn off offline files for the share.

Configuring and Troubleshooting Offline Files

The Offline Files feature is also known as Client-Side Caching (CSC). The default location on Windows XP computers for storage of offline files is %systemroot%\CSC (for example, C:\Windows\CSC), a hidden system folder.

You can use the Cachemov.exe tool from the Windows 2000 Professional Resource Kit or the Windows 2000 Server Resource Kit to relocate the CSC folder in Windows XP onto a different drive volume. The Cachemov.exe utility moves the CSC folder to the root of the drive volume that is specified. After you move the CSC folder from its default location, all subsequent moves place it in the root of the drive volume; Cachemov.exe never returns the folder to its original default location.

 The default cache size is configured as 10% of the client computer's available disk space. You can change this setting by selecting Tools, Folder Options from the menu bar of any My Computer or Windows Explorer window. The Offline Files tab of the Folder Options dialog box displays the system's offline files settings, as shown in Figure 2.26.

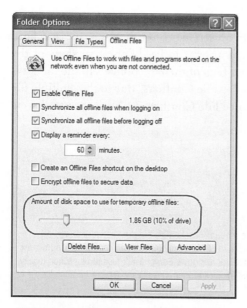

Figure 2.26   Configuring a share's offline settings.

Automatic caching of folders can slow down performance if the number of files or the sizes of files in shared folders is prohibitive. In addition, the amount of disk space for temporary offline files is attributed to automatically cached files. It does not limit the number of manually cached (pinned) files you configure.

You can use group policies in an Active Directory domain to configure local offline file settings. When managing many computers running Windows XP, it might be easier to configure one offline file group policy and link it to the domain, a site, or an organizational unit.

Troubleshooting Synchronization Issues

To troubleshoot synchronization issues or to make sure, before you leave the office, that you have all the necessary files cached locally, you can use the Offline Files dialog box.

The Offline Files dialog box, shown in Figure 2.26, is available in the Windows Explorer menu bar under Tools, Folder Options, Offline Files, View Files. It displays a list of all locally cached files and enables you to cache files immediately to make sure they are up-to-date.

When synchronization fails, it might be due to lack of network connectivity. It might be due to a discrepancy between the client and the server system time. Check system clocks and check connectivity.

Offline files work best with shared folders to which a limited number of users have access. For example, when two users work on the same file and both configure offline caching, ultimately there can be different versions of the same file on three computers. When each of them reconnects to the file server, they might be required to "Resolve File Conflicts" due to the multiple file versions. As you might guess, Resolve File Conflicts enables a user to do one of the following:

➤ Keep her version.

➤ Keep the network version.

➤ Keep both versions.

You can use offline files to manually cache files over the network stored on any Windows computer that uses the SMB protocol. You can configure Windows 9x, Windows 2000, Windows XP, or Windows Server 2002 files to be cached locally. You cannot use offline files for files stored on NetWare servers because they do not use SMB.

Exam Prep Questions

1. You're a desktop support technician.

   The network is set up as a workgroup and all users log on to their computers by using their own local administrator accounts. A user named John is using a computer running Windows XP that had been used previously by another user in another department. John stores confidential files on the computer and wants to ensure that only he has access to those files. Company policy prohibits encrypting files. How might you make sure that former users do not have access to John's files?

   ❑   A. John needs to lock down all his files with NTFS permissions.

   ❑   B. John needs to disable the former user's account.

   ❑   C. John needs to delete all former users' accounts.

   ❑   D. John needs to change the password of his administrative account.

   Answer C is correct. The only way to prohibit other users from accessing files or changing permissions on his computer is to delete all former administrative accounts because he can never know whether a former user of the computer might have created multiple administrative accounts to which she knows the password. Answer A is incorrect because although locking down files with NTFS is effective, you cannot lock out an account that has the right to take ownership of the files. Answer B is incorrect because an account that can be disabled can also be enabled again. Answer D is incorrect because changing the administrator account's password does not stop another account with administrative privileges from accessing files locally.

2. You're a desktop support technician for a company. A user named Roger uses a Windows XP Professional computer that contains a folder named **CSFs**, which is shared as **CSFDocuments**. The folder is shared to all users with read and modify permissions. Roger then creates a second sharepoint to the **CSFs** folder and names it **CSFDocs**. Users report they are unable to modify files when using the new **CSFDocs** share but are able to modify files when they use the original **CSFDocuments** share.

   What is the most likely reason for this?

   ❑   A. Roger configured the files in the **CSFDocs** folder with different NTFS permissions.

   ❑   B. Roger created the shared folder named **CSFDocs** and did not edit its permissions.

   ❑   C. The files in the **CSFDocs** folder are already in use when users access the folder.

   ❑   D. In Windows XP, when you create two shares to the same folder, only one of them can have read and write attributes.

Answer B is correct. The default attributes of a shared folder in Windows XP is Read Only. This question tests your ability to show that you know the new default share permissions. Answer A is incorrect. NTFS attributes are attached to the files themselves, not the shared folder. Therefore, Roger cannot be using different NTFS permissions for the files. Answer C is incorrect because files that are in use would have been opened as read-only whether accessed from either share. Answer D is incorrect because different shares created for the same folder are independent from one another.

3. You're a desktop support technician for a company.

   Your user needs to reconnect a computer running Windows XP to a network printer named Printer1. The printer is connected to a computer running Windows Server 2003 named **\\W2KS.** Using Remote Assistance, you connect to the user's computer and then run the Add Printer Wizard. Using the least administrative effort, how would you connect the workstation to the printer?

   ❏ A. Map a printer port to the remote printer with the command **net use LPT1 \\Printer1\W2KS**.

   ❏ B. Map a printer port to the remote printer with the command **net use LPT1 \Printer1\\W2KS**.

   ❏ C. Map a printer port to the remote printer with the command **net use LPT1 \\W2KS\Printer1**.

   ❏ D. Map a printer port to the remote printer with the command **\\Net Use Lpt1: W2KS\Printer1**.

   Answer C is correct. This question probes your knowledge of standard command-line syntax for accessing a shared printer. Answer C shows the correct syntax for mapping to a network printer. Answers A, B, and D are incorrect because the format for mapped printer is
   `\\servername\printername`.

4. You are a desktop support technician for your company.

   A user reports that his printer is "not working!" The printer is connected directly to the computer. The cabling appears connected properly. The correct printer driver appears to be installed properly. The print queue displays none of the previous print jobs sent by the user. How would you troubleshoot the problem?

   ❏ A. Instruct the user to press F5.

   ❏ B. Instruct the user to click the Use Printer Online command.

   ❏ C. Remotely stop the print spooler.

   ❏ D. Remotely start the workstation.

The correct answer is B. Clicking the Use Printer Offline command puts the printer "online" again. Answer A is incorrect: Pressing F5 (refresh) only updates the print list; it does not test printing capabilities. Answer C is incorrect; the spooler service needs to be stopped and then *restarted*. If you stop the spooler service, no jobs ever print. Answer D is incorrect; restarting the workstation service is not a support technician's first choice in troubleshooting printing problems.

5. You are a desktop support technician for your company.

   A sales rep arrives in your office and needs to print several documents created while on a recent business trip. She attaches her laptop to a printer using a USB cable. The four documents she created while out of the office are visible in the print queue, but they are not printing. You need to ensure that the printer is working properly and prints the four waiting print jobs.

   What should you do?

   - ❑ A. Reboot the computer.
   - ❑ B. Restart the print spooler.
   - ❑ C. Click the Use Print Online option.
   - ❑ D. Delete the files from the print queue.

   The correct answer is C. You must ensure the printer knows that it is online again. Answer A is incorrect; rebooting the computer eliminates the print jobs. Answer B is incorrect; restarting the print spooler is not the first choice for a desktop support technician under these circumstances. Answer D is incorrect; deleting the print jobs from the print queue also sacrifices those documents.

6. You are a desktop support technician for your company. All client computers run Windows XP Professional.

   A computer running Windows Server 2003, named **Server2k3**, where users store their personal files, supports automatic caching for all shared folders. Other network file servers also have caching available for shared folders.

   A user named John needs to be able to access his personal files when traveling with a portable computer. How would you ensure that he is able to access his files on **Server2K3** at all times but not files on other servers?

   - ❑ A. Configure a local group policy on John's laptop with an offline exception.
   - ❑ B. Configure the folders on **Server2K3** for automatic caching.
   - ❑ C. Use NTFS permission to control which files John is able to cache locally.
   - ❑ D. Remove John from the local Administrators group on his laptop.

The correct answer is B. Automatic caching stores files locally that are opened by a user. NTFS security prevents users from opening others' files. Answer A is incorrect; there is no offline policy that needs to be constructed to achieve the objective. Answer C is incorrect because NTFS does not include references to offline caching. Caching is a folder configuration, not a file configuration. Answer D is incorrect because John's membership in the local Administrators group has no bearing on offline file caching.

7. You are a desktop support technician for your company.

   Your network is configured as a workgroup and the company recently replaced John's Windows 2000 Professional client computer with a new Windows XP Professional computer. Afterward, John reports that he can't specify individual user permissions on a folder he is attempting to share. What should you do?

   ❑   A. Instruct John to enable Simple File Sharing.
   ❑   B. Instruct John to disable Simple File Sharing.
   ❑   C. Instruct John to use NTFS security instead of Share permissions.
   ❑   D. Instruct John to use **RunAs** with an administrator account.

   The correct answer is B. This is a question on Simple File Sharing. Simple File Sharing prevents the ability to share folders to individuals or groups. Answer A is incorrect; enabling Simple File Sharing prevents granular security. The folder is shared, in Simple File Sharing, to the guest account. Answer C is incorrect; NTFS security is not an option when Simple File Sharing is enabled on a workgroup member. Answer D is incorrect; administrator credentials provide no extra benefit when Simple File Sharing is enabled.

8. You are a desktop support technician. A user in your company, Fred, receives an "access denied" message when he tries to configure a printer from within an application.

   What is a possible cause of this error message?
   ❑   A. Fred is not an administrator.
   ❑   B. Applications do not allow users to configure printers.
   ❑   C. Fred does not have the appropriate permission to change printer configurations.
   ❑   D. Printer configurations cannot be adjusted.

   Answer C is correct. Fred does not have an appropriate permission to change printer configurations. As a desktop support technician, to resolve this problem, you might modify the printer's access control list (ACL). Answer A is incorrect; you do not need to be an administrator to make printer configuration changes. Answer B is incorrect; permissions, not applications, allow or disallow printer configuration changes. You can access printer properties within applications such as Excel 2003. Answer D is incorrect; printer configurations can be modified.

9. You are a desktop support technician for your company. A user named John reports that documents do not print completely or come out garbled from his printer, which connects to a computer running Windows XP. What do you recommend that John do?

❑ A. The printer driver is incorrect. Install the correct printer driver.

❑ B. Purchase a new printer.

❑ C. Inspect the HCL.

❑ D. Try printing a test page.

❑ E. Check the cables connecting the printer to the computer or the network.

Answer E is correct. Always suspect the simplest solution first and have the user check the physical connection to the printer. Answer A is incorrect. By installing the correct driver for the printer, you can eliminate garbled printing; however, this step is not something for the user to perform. Answer B is incorrect; purchasing a new printer would not be your first recommendation. Answer C is incorrect; the Hardware Compatibility List might not include your printer, even though it is compatible with Windows XP. Answer D is the next logical option after you have the user check the physical connection.

10. You are a desktop support technician for your company. A user named John reports that when he attempts to print a document, he hears the hard disk thrashing, and the document doesn't print. What is the most likely reason?

❑ A. The hard drive has crashed.

❑ B. You are using the wrong driver for the hard drive.

❑ C. You have chosen to print to a file.

❑ D. There is insufficient hard disk space for spooling. You should create more free space on the hard disk.

Answer D is correct. From the evidence provided in the question, it sounds as if there is insufficient hard-disk space for spooling. You should either create more free space on the hard disk by using Disk Cleanup or Defrag or consider disabling spooling and printing directly to the printer. Answer A is incorrect; a crashed hard drive would most likely result in a greater number of symptoms. Answer B is incorrect because the wrong driver for the hard drive would prevent all drive activity. Answer C is incorrect because printing to a file should not cause the hard disk to thrash.

Need to Know More?

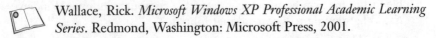

Wallace, Rick. *Microsoft Windows XP Professional Academic Learning Series*. Redmond, Washington: Microsoft Press, 2001.

Balter, Dan and Derek Melber. *MCSE/MCSA Exam Cram 2: Windows XP Professional*. Indianapolis, Indiana: Que Certification, 2002.

Stanek, William R. *Microsoft Windows XP Professional Administrator's Pocket Consultant*. Redmond, Washington: Microsoft Press, 2003.

Barker, Gord and Robert L. Bogue. *MCSE Training Guide (70-270): Windows XP Professional*. Indianapolis, Indiana: Que Publishing, 2002.

Microsoft Windows Team. *Microsoft Windows XP Professional Resource Kit Second Edition*. Redmond, Washington: Microsoft Press, 2003.

Search the Microsoft Product Support Services Knowledge Base on the Internet: http://support.microsoft.com. You can also search Microsoft TechNet on the Internet: http://www.microsoft.com/technet. Find technical information using keywords from this chapter, such as share permissions, NTFS permissions, offline files, shadow copies, Remote Desktop Connections, Terminal Services, file systems, printing and faxing, and EFS.

Managing and Troubleshooting Desktop Storage

Terms you'll need to understand:

✓ Basic versus Dynamic disks
✓ Partitions, volumes, and logical drives
✓ Simple, spanned, and striped volumes
✓ The **diskpart.exe** utility
✓ NT File System (NTFS) volumes
✓ The **convert.exe** utility
✓ Troubleshooting disk drives
✓ Troubleshooting removable storage
✓ Disk defragmentation

Techniques you'll need to master:

✓ Using the Disk Management console
✓ Monitoring and troubleshooting disks using the Performance console
✓ Using the Disk Defragmenter and Disk Cleanup Wizard
✓ Selecting a file system for Windows XP Professional
✓ Using **convert.exe** to convert a File Allocation Table (FAT) volume to NTFS
✓ Using **diskpart.exe** to manage disk drives and volumes from the command line
✓ Creating simple, spanned, and striped volumes
✓ Converting from Basic to Dynamic disks and back again
✓ Troubleshooting disk drives, CD-ROM, and Universal Serial Bus (USB)–based storage.

For a desktop support technician, the number of distress calls from wayward users who have lost their files can be daunting. However, the storage options supported in Windows XP combine a lot of the old and a bit of the new in terms of things Windows XP can do.

Disk storage is more than about finding lost files. In this chapter, we cover how to support and troubleshoot hard disks and explore available options under Windows XP for creating partitions, formatting drive volumes, and managing disk administration.

Disk Storage Administration

If you are familiar with managing and troubleshooting hard disks and volumes under Windows 2000, you'll be comfortable working with disk-storage administration in Windows XP. For desktop support technicians who are familiar with Windows NT 4, Windows XP Professional introduces some new concepts, such as *Basic* and *Dynamic disk storage*.

Basic Disks

A Windows XP Basic disk, similar to the disk configuration under earlier versions of Windows, is a physical disk with primary and extended partitions. As long as you use the FAT file system, Windows XP Professional and Home editions, Windows 2000, Windows NT, Windows 9x, and MS-DOS operating systems all can access Basic disks.

On a Basic disk, you can create up to three primary partitions and one extended partition, four primary partitions, or one extended partition with logical drives.

Windows XP supports FAT primary partitions up to 4GB in size. Windows 9x/Me and MS-DOS support only 2GB primary partitions.

If you discover you've created a partition that's too small, you cannot *extend* it using the Disk Management Microsoft Management Console. However, if you use the DiskPart.exe command-line utility shown in Figure 3.1, you can extend a Basic disk partition to contiguous unallocated space. The partition must use the NTFS format and cannot be the system or boot partition.

Figure 3.1   The DiskPart utility, which enables you to extend partitions and convert Basic disks to Dynamic disks.

Basic disks store their configuration information in the master boot record (MBR), which is stored on the first sector of the hard drive. The configuration information consists of the disk's partition information.

Basic disks support spanned volumes (volume sets), striped volumes (stripe sets), mirrored volumes (mirror sets), and Redundant Array of Independent Disks (RAID) Level 5 volumes (stripe sets with parity) that were created (and named) under Windows NT 4.

Mirrored and RAID-5 volumes are fault-tolerant volumes designed to withstand single disk failures. They are only available under the Windows 2000 Server or Windows Server 2003 family of server operating systems. Windows XP does not support these types of volumes on either Basic or Dynamic disks.

Dynamic Disks

A Windows XP Dynamic disk is a physical disk that does not use conventional *partitions* or *logical* drives. A Dynamic disk is a single partition that can be divided into separate *volumes*. You can even resize a volume "on the fly" (without a reboot).

Dynamic disks are combined into collective "disk groups," which helps to organize them. All Dynamic disks in a computer are members of the same disk group. Each disk in a disk group stores replicas of the group's configuration data in a region known as the Logical Disk Manager (LDM) metadata partition.

This configuration data is stored in a 1MB region at the end of each Dynamic disk and is the reason you must have at least 1MB of empty disk space for the LDM to convert a disk from Basic to Dynamic.

Dynamic disks can contain an unlimited number of volumes; you are not restricted to four volumes per disk, as you are with Basic disks, and those volumes can be extended if they are formatted with NTFS. To convert a volume from FAT to NTFS, use the `convert.exe` *volume*: `/FS:NTFS` command, where *volume* is the logical letter of the drive.

Locally, regardless of the type of file system, only computers running Windows XP Professional, Windows 2000, or Windows Server 2003 recognize Dynamic disks. Windows XP Home Edition does not offer Dynamic disks. Dynamic disks are not supported on portable computers.

Managing Basic and Dynamic Disks

Basic and Dynamic disks are Windows XP's way of managing hard disk configuration. If you're migrating to Windows XP from Windows NT 4, the Dynamic disk concept might seem unfamiliar in the beginning, but once you understand the differences, working with Dynamic disks is not complicated. You can format partitions with FAT16, FAT32, or NTFS on a Basic or a Dynamic disk. FAT and NTFS are discussed later in this chapter.

From the Disk Management console, you can only format a dynamic volume as NTFS. You must use Windows XP Explorer to format a dynamic volume as FAT or FAT32. Table 3.1 compares the terms used with Basic and Dynamic disks.

Table 3.1 A Cross-Reference of Terms Used with Basic and Dynamic Disks	
Basic Disks	**Dynamic Disks**
Active partition	Active volume
Extended partition	Volume and unallocated space
Logical drive	Simple volume
Mirror set	Mirrored volume (server only)
Primary partition	Simple volume
Stripe set	Striped volume

Table 3.1 Continued	
Basic Disks	**Dynamic Disks**
Stripe set with parity	RAID-5 volume (server only)
System and boot partitions	System and boot volumes
Volume set	Spanned volumes

You can convert a Basic disk to a Dynamic disk using the DiskPart command-line utility mentioned earlier or the Disk Management MMC shown in Figure 3.2.

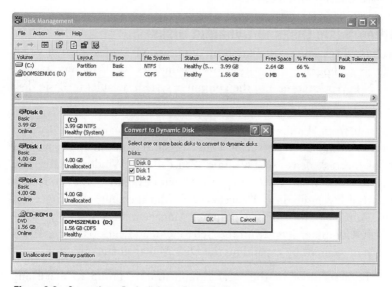

Figure 3.2 Converting a Basic disk to a Dynamic disk.

If you are upgrading from Windows 98 or Windows Me to Windows XP Professional, do not make changes to your disk configuration, such as converting to Dynamic disks and volumes, if you ever want to uninstall XP and revert back to the previous operating system.

Dynamic disks have some additional limitations. You can install Windows XP on a dynamic volume that you converted from a Basic disk, but you can't extend either the system or the boot partition. Additionally, any disk troubleshooting tools you've used might not be able to read the dynamic Disk Management database!

Dynamic disks are only supported on desktop or server systems that use Small Computer System Interface (SCSI), Fibre Channel, Serial Storage Architecture (SSA), Integrated Drive Electronics (IDE), Enhanced IDE

(EIDE), Ultra Direct Memory Access (DMA), or Advanced Technology Attachment (ATA) interfaces.

Dynamic disks are not supported on portable computers, removable disks (such as Jaz or Zip drives), and disks connected via USB or FireWire (IEEE 1394) interfaces. If you need to configure an IEEE 1394 disk drive to dynamic, see Knowledge Base Article 299598. They are also not supported on Windows XP Home Edition.

They are also not supported on hard drives with a sector size larger than 512 bytes. Cluster disks—groups of several disks that serve to function as a single disk—are not supported either.

Converting Basic Disks to Dynamic Disks

When you perform a new installation of Windows XP Professional or when you perform an upgrade installation from Windows 98, Windows Me, or Windows NT Workstation 4.0, the computer system defaults to Basic disk storage.

If you upgrade from Windows 2000 Professional (or if you import a "foreign disk" from Windows 2000 Server or a later version), you can configure one or more of the disk drives as Dynamic. You can use Windows XP's Disk Management console (an MMC snap-in), shown in Figure 3.2, to convert a Basic disk to a Dynamic disk. To access Disk Management, click Start, All Programs, Administrator Tools, Computer Management. Or simply right-click the My Computer icon from the Start menu and click Manage. You'll find Disk Management by expanding the Disk Management category.

You must be a member of the local Administrators group to make any changes to the computer's disk management configuration. Before you upgrade disks, close any programs that are running on those disks.

As mentioned earlier, for the conversion to succeed, any disks to be converted must contain at least 1MB of unallocated space. Disk Management automatically reserves this space when creating partitions or volumes on a disk, but disks with partitions or volumes created by other operating systems might not have this space available. (This space can exist even if it is not visible in Disk Management.)

Windows XP requires this minimal amount of disk space to store an LDM database, which is maintained by the operating system that created it.

Because the LDM is maintained by Windows XP Professional, you cannot multi-boot Windows XP Professional with any other operating system if you have only one disk.

To convert a Basic disk to a Dynamic disk using the Disk Management console, perform the following steps:

1. Open the Disk Management tool.

2. Right-click the Basic disk you want to change to a Dynamic disk and then click Convert to Dynamic Disk.

Because the conversion from Basic to Dynamic is per physical disk, all volumes on a physical disk must be either Basic or Dynamic. When converting from a Basic to a Dynamic disk, you do not need to restart your computer unless you are converting the system or boot partitions or if the partition contained the page file.

To change or convert a Basic disk to a Dynamic disk from the Windows XP command line, perform these steps:

1. Open a command prompt window, type `diskpart`, and press Enter.

2. Type `commands` or `help` to view a list of available commands.

3. Type `select disk 0` to select the first hard disk (`select disk 1` to select the second hard disk, and so on) and press Enter.

4. Type `convert dynamic` and press Enter.

5. Type `exit` to quit the `diskpart.exe` tool and then restart the computer to have the new configuration take effect (see Figure 3.1).

You can use the DiskPart utility to create mount points for hard drives through empty folders on NTFS drives. In other words, rather than define a volume with a drive letter, you can link it back to an empty folder on an NTFS formatted drive.

You also can use DiskPart to import foreign disks into computers running XP. This technique is explained in the section "Moving Disks to a Different Computer."

In addition to using `diskpart.exe`, you can manage FAT, FAT32, and NTFS file systems with the `fsutil.exe` command-line utility.

`Fsutil.exe` manages disk quotas, reparses (mount) points, and performs several other advanced disk-related tasks. Type `fsutil` at a command prompt to view a list of supported commands (see Figure 3.3).

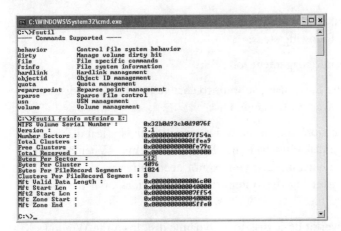

Figure 3.3 The Windows XP **fsutil.exe** command provides file system information, including sector size.

When you convert a Basic disk to a Dynamic disk, any existing partitions on the Basic disk become simple volumes on the Dynamic disk. Any existing striped volumes or spanned volumes become dynamic striped volumes or dynamic spanned volumes.

Reverting Dynamic Disks to Basic Disks

To revert from a Dynamic disk back to a Basic disk, you must remove all volumes from the Dynamic disk first. After you change a Dynamic disk back to a Basic disk, you can create only partitions and logical drives on that disk.

Converting to a Dynamic disk is effectively a one-way trip. To convert from a Dynamic disk back to a Basic disk, you must delete all dynamic volumes. This is a considerable downside! If you find yourself needing to do it, however, first back up your data, convert the disk to Basic, and then restore your data.

To convert a Dynamic disk to a Basic disk, perform the following steps:

1. Open Disk Management.

2. Right-click the Dynamic disk you want to change back to a Basic disk and then click Convert to Basic Disk.

Moving Disks to a Different Computer

When you relocate a Dynamic disk from one computer to another, you are moving the disk from one disk group to another. Initially, the disk is perceived as "foreign" when it is connected.

When you connect a foreign Dynamic disk, you need to rescan all drives and then *import* the *foreign* disk. This procedure updates the disk's metadatabase. Importing a disk merges the disk's information with the LDM database on the host computer.

Along with disk configuration information, the LDM database stores drive letter assignments. Imported drives keep their original drive letters unless the letters are used by the new host system. If a driver letter is already in use, the system assigns the next available drive letter. To eliminate conflicts, you can remove the drive letters from the volumes before moving the disk.

Because volumes can span multiple disks, when you move multidisk volumes, always move all the disks that compose the volume.

Don't move a disk that contains system or boot volumes to another computer unless you need to recover data. You might also encounter problems if you attempt to move the Dynamic disk back to its original computer. However, you can successfully move Basic disks that have system or boot volumes in this manner because they don't contain a dynamic LDM database.

You can use the `diskpart.exe` command-line tool or Disk Management to import disks.

To relocate disks to another computer, perform the following steps:

1. First, before you disconnect the disks, look in Disk Management and make sure the status of the volumes on the disks is "healthy." If the status is not healthy, repair the volumes before you move the disks.

2. Turn the source computer off, remove the physical disks, and then install the physical disks on the target computer. Restart the target computer.

3. Open Disk Management.

4. Click Action and then click Rescan Disks.

5. The disk that you move is designated Dynamic/Foreign instead of Dynamic. Right-click the disk and click Import Foreign Disks.

6. The Foreign Disk Volumes dialog box appears, indicating the size, condition, and type of the volume on the imported drive.

7. Click OK to add the disks.

Be sure to move all disks that are part of a volume set or a stripe set. If you move only some of the disks that are members of a volume set or stripe set, you render the set unusable. You might even damage the set and lose the data stored on the set if you do not move all the set's disks.

Reactivating Missing or Offline Disks

With LDM, every disk knows about every other disk in your system. When a disk can't be located, it does not disappear from Disk Management. It is simply designated "missing," as shown in Figure 3.4.

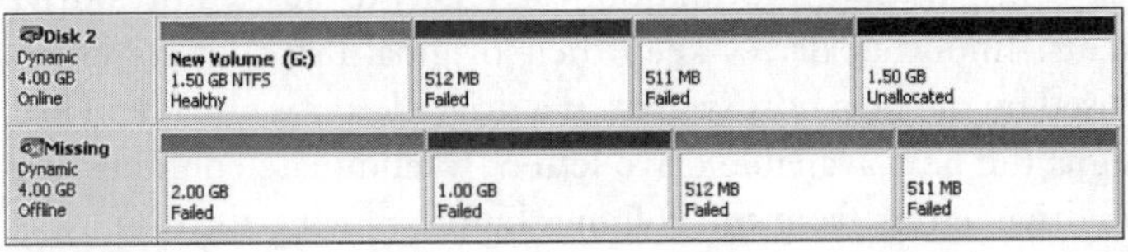

🖵Disk 2 Dynamic 4.00 GB Online	New Volume (G:) 1.50 GB NTFS Healthy	512 MB Failed	511 MB Failed	1.50 GB Unallocated
🖵Missing Dynamic 4.00 GB Offline	2.00 GB Failed	1.00 GB Failed	512 MB Failed	511 MB Failed

Figure 3.4 A drive designated as missing.

A Dynamic disk might be labeled missing when it is corrupted, powered down, or disconnected. Only Dynamic disks can be reactivated—not Basic disks.

Disks are labeled missing because other disks in the disk group share LDM information that *expects* the disk to be connected and functioning.

To reactivate a missing or offline disk, perform the following steps:

1. Open Disk Management.

2. Right-click the Offline disk whose status is missing and then click Reactivate Disk.

3. The disk should be titled Online after the disk is reactivated.

Working with Basic Partitions

Windows XP Basic disks support partitions and logical drives and recognize volumes created using Windows NT 4 or earlier operating systems.

Before Windows 2000, Basic disks supported all volume types: basic volumes, volume sets, stripe sets, mirror sets, and stripe sets with parity (also known as RAID-5 sets).

Under Windows XP, you can create Basic partitions only on Basic disks. Because Windows XP Professional is considered a desktop (client-side) network operating system, it does not support any type of fault-tolerant volumes—even on Dynamic disks. Only Microsoft server operating systems support fault-tolerant features such as mirrored volumes and RAID-5 volumes (stripe sets with parity), and those configurations can only reside on Dynamic disks.

Keep in mind that these Windows fault-tolerant configurations are operating system features. Independent, non-OS RAID arrays, such as Serial ATA RAID host adapters, provide similar benefits with much less system overhead.

Using Partitions and Logical Drives on Basic Disks

To *extend* a Basic partition, the partition must be formatted as NTFS, it must be adjacent to contiguous unallocated space on the same physical disk, and it can be extended only onto unallocated space that resides on the *same physical disk*. You can only extend a Basic partition with the diskpart.exe utility, as shown in Figure 3.5, and not through the Management Console.

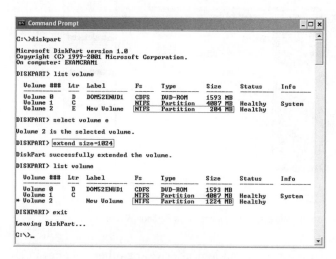

Figure 3.5 Using the **diskpart.exe** utility to extend partition E.

Creating or Deleting a Partition or Logical Drive

To create or delete a partition or logical drive, you can use the diskpart.exe command-line tool, shown in Figure 3.1, or use the Disk Management console, shown in Figure 3.6.

To create or delete a partition of logical drive, follow these   steps:

   1. Open the Disk Management console.

   2. To create a new partition, right-click an unallocated region of a Basic disk and then click New Partition.

To create a new logical drive, right-click an area of free space in an extended partition and then click New Logical Drive to start the Create Partition Wizard.

3. Select Primary Partition, Extended Partition, or Logical Drive as appropriate and follow the instructions presented by the wizard to define the size and format of the new storage space.

4. To remove a partition, select Delete Partition from the partition's context menu.

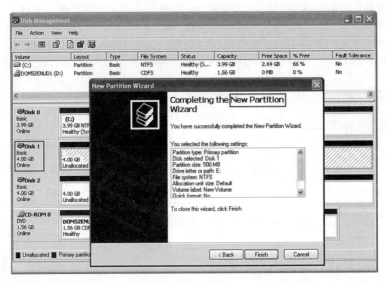

Figure 3.6 Dividing Basic disks into partitions using the New Partition Wizard.

In Windows XP, you must delete all logical drives or other volumes in an extended partition before you can delete the extended partition.

Be careful. If you choose to delete a partition or logical drive, all the data on the deleted partition or logical drive is lost. You cannot recover data stored on deleted partitions or logical drives. You cannot delete the system partition, boot partition, or any partition that contains an active paging file.

Dynamic Volumes

What were once called *sets* (such as mirror sets and stripe sets) under earlier operating systems are called *volumes* (such as mirrored volumes and striped volumes) in Windows XP.

Dynamic volumes are the only type of volume you can create on Dynamic disks.

Dynamic disks eliminate the four partitions per disk limitation of Basic disks. You can install Windows XP Professional onto a dynamic volume; however, the volume must already contain a partition table. (It must have been converted from Basic to Dynamic under Windows XP or Windows 2000.)

 You cannot install Windows XP onto *dynamic volumes* that were created under Windows 2000, Windows XP, or Windows Server 2003 *from unallocated space*.

Only computers running Windows XP Professional, Windows 2000, or Windows Server 2003 can access dynamic volumes. The five types of dynamic volumes are simple, spanned, mirrored, striped, and RAID-5. Windows XP Professional supports only simple, spanned, and striped dynamic volumes, shown in Figure 3.7.

Volume	Layout	Type	File System	Status	Capacity	Free Space	% Free	Fault Tolerance	Overhead
(C:)	Partition	Basic	NTFS	Healthy (System)	3.99 GB	2.81 GB	70 %	No	0%
New Volume (E:)	Simple	Dynamic	NTFS	Healthy	2.50 GB	2.49 GB	99 %	No	0%
New Volume (F:)	Spanned	Dynamic	NTFS	Healthy	1.50 GB	1.49 GB	99 %	No	0%
New Volume (G:)	Simple	Dynamic	NTFS	Healthy	1.50 GB	1.49 GB	99 %	No	0%
New Volume (H:)	Striped	Dynamic	NTFS	Healthy	1021 MB	1013 MB	99 %	No	0%

Disk 0	
Basic 3.99 GB Online	(C:) 3.99 GB NTFS Healthy (System)

Disk 1				
Dynamic 4.00 GB Online	New Volume (E:) 2.00 GB NTFS Healthy	New Volume (F:) 1.00 GB NTFS Healthy	New Volume (E:) 512 MB NTFS Healthy	New Volume (H:) 511 MB NTFS Healthy

Disk 2				
Dynamic 4.00 GB Online	New Volume (G:) 1.50 GB NTFS Healthy	New Volume (F:) 512 MB NTFS Healthy	New Volume (H:) 511 MB NTFS Healthy	1.50 GB Unallocated

CD-ROM 0	
DVD (D:) No Media	

■ Unallocated ■ Primary partition ■ Simple volume ■ Spanned volume ■ Striped volume

Figure 3.7 Simple (E, G); spanned (F); and striped (H) dynamic volumes displayed in Disk Management.

By default, Disk Management uses solid colors to represent the five different types of dynamic volumes. Table 3.2 lists the colors Disk Management uses by default.

Table 3.2 Colors Used by Disk Management to Represent Drives	
Object	Color
Unallocated	Black
Extended partition	Green
Logical drive	Blue
Mirrored volume	Brick (server only)
Primary partition	Dark blue
Striped volume	Cadet blue
RAID-5 volume	Cyan (server only)
Free space	Light green
Simple volume	Olive
Spanned volume	Purple

You must be an administrator or a member of the Administrators group to create, modify, or delete dynamic volumes.

Simple Volumes

A *simple volume* consists of disk space on a single physical disk. It can consist of a single area on a disk or multiple areas on the same disk that are linked together.

To create a simple volume, perform the following steps:

1. Open Disk Management.

2. Right-click the unallocated space on the Dynamic disk where you want to create the simple volume and then click New Volume.

3. Using the New Volume Wizard, shown in Figure 3.8, click Next, click Simple, and then provide the volume's size and formatting details.

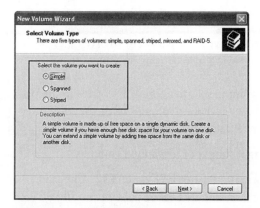

Figure 3.8 Using the New Volume Wizard for Dynamic disks to create different types of dynamic volumes.

Spanned Volumes

A spanned volume consists of disk space from more than one physical disk. You can add more space to a spanned volume by extending it at any time.

To create a spanned volume, perform the following steps:

1. Open Disk Management.

2. Right-click the unallocated space on one of the Dynamic disks where you want to create the spanned volume and then click New Volume.

3. Using the New Volume Wizard, click Next, click Spanned, and then follow the instructions on your screen.

Here are guidelines for spanned volumes:

➤ You can create spanned volumes on Dynamic disks only.

➤ You need at least two Dynamic disks to create a spanned volume.

➤ You can extend a spanned volume onto a maximum of 32 Dynamic disks.

➤ Spanned volumes cannot be striped.

➤ Spanned volumes are not fault-tolerant.

Extending Simple or Spanned Volumes

To extend a simple or spanned volume, perform the following steps:

1. Open Disk Management.

2. Right-click the simple or spanned volume you want to extend, click Extend Volume, and then follow the instructions on your screen.

In general, you cannot extend a volume that maintains its entries in the partition table. This includes the system and boot volumes of the operating system used to convert the disk from Basic to Dynamic.

Here are guidelines for extending a simple or a spanned volume:

➤ You cannot extend *volumes* formatted using FAT or FAT32. You can extend a volume if it is formatted using NTFS or contains no file system.

➤ You cannot extend a volume that was converted from Basic to Dynamic by the Windows 2000 Disk Management tool.

➤ If you extend a simple volume across multiple disks, it becomes a spanned volume.

➤ After you extend a Windows XP dynamic volume onto multiple disks, you cannot stripe it.

➤ You cannot extend a system volume or boot volume.

➤ After a spanned volume is extended, deleting any portion of it deletes the entire spanned volume.

➤ You can extend both simple and spanned volumes onto a maximum of 32 Dynamic disks.

➤ Spanned volumes write data to subsequent disks as each disk volume fills up. Therefore, a spanned volume writes data to physical disk 0 until it fills up, then writes to physical disk 1 and so on. If a single disk in the spanned volume fails, only the data contained on that failed disk is lost.

Striped Volumes

Striped volumes store data in stripes across two or more physical disks. Data in a striped volume is allocated evenly and across (in stripes) the disks of the striped volume. Storing files in this manner increases the write/read speed to and from your disks.

To create a striped volume, perform the following steps:

1. Open Disk Management.

2. Right-click unallocated space on one of the Dynamic disks where you want to create the striped volume and then click New Volume.

3. Using the New Volume Wizard, click Next, click Striped, and then follow the instructions on your screen.

Here are the guidelines for striped volumes:

➤ You need at least two physical, Dynamic disks to create a striped volume.

➤ You can create a striped volume onto a maximum of 32 disks.

➤ Striped volumes are not fault-tolerant and cannot be extended or mirrored.

Troubleshooting Issues on Basic and Dynamic Disks

As a desktop support technician, you configure Dynamic disks and dynamic volumes in specific circumstances; you need to be aware when each is appropriate and be prepared to recover data should the disks or volumes fail.

If you upgrade a computer running Windows 2000 Professional that has hard drives configured as volume sets or stripe sets, you must back up all the data stored on each volume set or stripe set first because Windows XP Professional does not support volume sets or stripe sets on a Basic disk.

➤ Under Windows 2000 Professional, volume sets and stripe sets are supported on Basic disks for backward compatibility to NT 4.0 workstations. However, you cannot create such sets on Basic disks in Windows 2000.

➤ Under Windows XP Professional, volume sets and stripe sets are strictly not supported during installations. Windows XP Professional Setup does not allow an installation to complete if stripe sets or volume sets are present on Basic disks.

To migrate data on volume sets or stripe sets stored on Basic disks from Windows 2000 Professional to Windows XP Professional, perform the following steps:

1. Under Windows 2000, back up the data.

2. Under Windows 2000, use the Disk Management console to convert the Basic disks to Dynamic disks.

3. Upgrade the operating system to Windows XP Professional.

Installing Windows XP on a Dynamic Disk

If you create a dynamic volume from unallocated space on a Dynamic disk, you cannot install Windows XP on that volume because Windows XP Setup recognizes only dynamic volumes that are in the volume's partition table.

(Partition tables exist on basic volumes and in dynamic volumes that are the result of an upgraded Basic disk. They do not appear on new dynamic volumes.)

Wait, there's more!

Let's say you are able to upgrade a basic volume to dynamic (by converting the Basic disk to a Dynamic disk). You can install Windows XP on that volume, but you cannot extend the volume because the volume information lives in the partition table.

You can install Windows XP onto a dynamic volume if

➤ The volume was upgraded from Basic to Dynamic by Windows 2000.

➤ The volume is one on which you've run `diskpart retain` to add an entry to the partition table.

➤ The volume is a simple volume that is the boot or system volume.

Extending a Volume on a Dynamic Disk

After you convert a Basic disk to Dynamic, you can extend dynamic volumes that you create. In fact, you can extend volumes and make changes to disk configuration in most cases without rebooting your computer.

If you want to take advantage of these features in Windows XP, you must change or upgrade a disk from Basic to Dynamic status, as covered earlier in this chapter.

Therefore, if you want to create more than four volumes per disk or want to extend, stripe, or span volumes onto one or more Dynamic disks, and your computer runs only Windows XP, use Dynamic disks.

Upgrading from Windows NT 4 with Basic Disks

Windows XP Professional does not support volume sets or stripe sets on a Basic disk.

If you need to upgrade a computer running Windows NT 4 that has hard drives already configured as volume sets or stripe sets, you must first back up all the data stored on each volume set or stripe set.

To migrate data on volume sets or stripe sets from Windows NT 4 to Windows XP Professional, perform the following steps:

1. Under Windows NT 4, back up the data.

2. Delete the volumes.

3. Upgrade the operating system to Windows XP Professional.

4. Convert the appropriate hard disks from Basic to Dynamic disks.

5. Create the appropriate volumes.

6. Restore the backed-up data.

Diagnosing Hard-Disk Problems

As a desktop support technician, when a disk or volume fails, you want to know how to detect the failure and how to recover the data quickly.

The Disk Management snap-in makes it easy to locate problems. In the Status column of the list view, you can view the status of a disk or volume. The status also appears in the graphical view of each disk or volume, as shown in Figure 3.9.

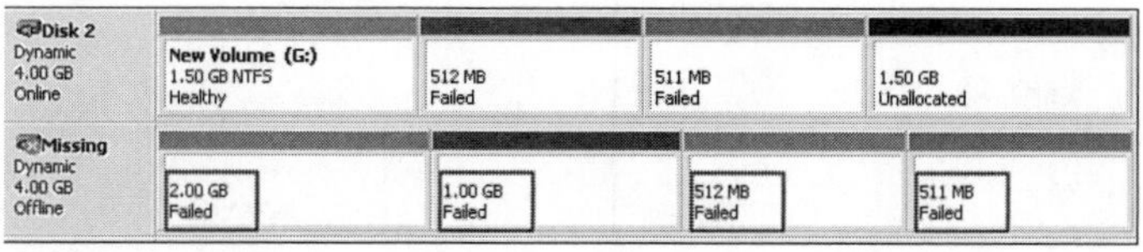

Figure 3.9   A failed drive affecting spanned and striped volumes but not a simple volume on a healthy drive. (Disk 3 is missing.)

To diagnose disk and/or volume problems, perform the following steps:

1. Open Add Hardware in the Control Panel. Click Next. Windows XP tries to detect new Plug and Play devices.

2. Click "Yes, I Have Already Connected the Hardware", and then click Next.

3. Choose the device you want to diagnose and fix, and then click Next.

4. The Add Hardware Wizard informs you of the device's current status. Click Finish to invoke the Hardware Troubleshooter as part of the Help and Support Center, or click Cancel to exit the Add Hardware Wizard.

You can also troubleshoot hardware problems using the Device Manager.

To access the Device Manager, right-click the My Computer icon from the Start menu and select Properties. Click the Hardware tab and then click the Device Manager button. Expand the hardware category that you need to troubleshoot and right-click the device that you want to inquire about.

Select Properties from the context menu to display the properties window for that device, as shown in Figure 3.10. All the pertinent information about the device is available from this window, including its device status as determined by the operating system.

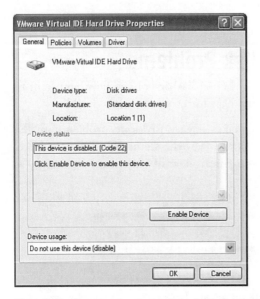

Figure 3.10 The properties sheet for a hard disk that shows its device usage as "disabled" in Device Manager.

Deteriorating performance is sometimes a precusor to hardware failure. You can monitor disk performance with the Performance console.

The Windows XP performance-monitoring tool, shown in Figure 3.11, consists of two parts: *System Monitor* and *Performance Logs and Alerts*. The MMC snap-in is simply named Performance. With System Monitor, you can collect and view real-time data about disk performance and activity in graph, histogram, or report form. Performance Logs and Alerts enables you to configure logs to record performance data and to set system alerts to notify you when a specified counter's value is above or below a defined threshold.

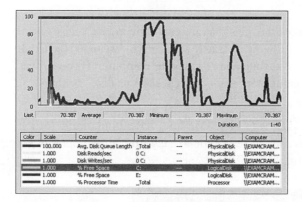

Figure 3.11   The Windows XP System Monitor.

To open Performance, perform the following steps:

1. Click Start, Control Panel.

2. In the Control Panel, double-click Administrative Tools, and then double-click Performance. You use System Monitor within Performance to monitor disk activity.

For measuring disk performance, Windows XP maps physical drives to logical drives by applying the same instance name. For example, if a computer contains a dynamic volume that consists of two physical hard disks, the logical drives might appear as Disk 0 C: and Disk 1 C:, which denotes that drive C spans physical disks 0 and 1.

For a PC that has three logical volumes on one physical disk, the instance appears as 0 C: D: E:.

Detecting and Repairing Disk Errors

In the Windows 2000 operating systems, the ScanDisk utility detected and fixed disk errors. In Windows XP, desktop support technicians can use the Error-checking tool (chkdsk.exe) to check for file-system errors and bad sectors on your hard disk. To run the Error-checking tool, perform the following steps:

1. Open My Computer and right-click the local disk you want to check.

2. Select Properties.

3. Click the Tools tab.

4. Under Error-checking, click Check Now.

5. Under Check Disk Options, select Automatically Fix System Errors, Scan for and Attempt Recovery of Bad Sectors, and click Start.

If the volume to be checked has files that are currently in use, such as some of the operating system files, you are asked whether you want to reschedule the disk checking for the next time you restart your computer. If you say yes, when you restart your computer, Windows checks the disk, as shown in Figure 3.12.

If the volume being checked is NTFS, Windows XP automatically logs all file transactions, replaces bad clusters automatically, and stores copies of key information for all files on the NTFS volume.

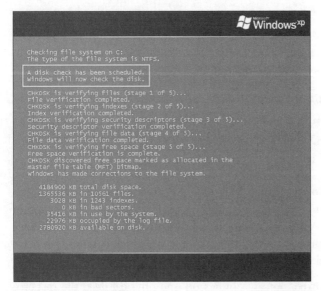

Figure 3.12 Error-checking process running on drive C: upon a system restart. (This is a composite screen shot.)

Supporting CD and DVD Playback and Recording Devices

With Windows XP Professional, users can save information such as photos and software to a compact disc (CD) without installing third-party software. Because CD-recordable (CD-R) and CD-rewritable (CD-RW) drives have become standard parts of the desktop architecture, desktop support technicians need to understand their capabilities and limitations.

Writing Files and Folders to CD-R and CD-RW Media

To copy files or folders to a CD, follow these steps:

Insert a blank, writable CD into the CD recorder. (You need a blank, writable CD and a CD drive [CD burner] that has the capability of writing CDs.)

Open My Computer and then select the files and folders you want to write to the CD.

In the My Computer task pane under File and Folder Tasks, click Copy This File, Copy This Folder, or Copy the Selected Items.

In the Copy Items dialog box, click the CD recording drive and then click Copy.

In My Computer, double-click the CD recording drive. Under CD Writing Tasks, click Write These Files to the CD.

 NOTE   Standard CDs hold 650MB of information. High-density CDs hold at least 700MB of information. You must have enough space on your hard drive to temporarily hold the files you want to copy to the CD or the operation will fail. The local hard drive serves as Windows XP's temporary staging area for data being written to recordable or rewritable CD media.

When you are writing files, to optimize your computer for optimal writing speed, Microsoft recommends that you redirect the temporary files created by the write process to another local drive or partition, as shown in Figure 3.13.

When the process of copying is complete, the last page of the CD Writing Wizard, shown in Figure 3.14, enables you to create another CD like the one you just created.

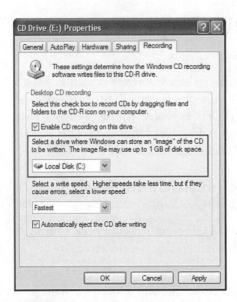

Figure 3.13 How to modify the location for temporary CD files.

Figure 3.14 The CD Writing Wizard copying files to a CD.

To create multiple CDs with the same files, click Yes, Write These Files to Another CD, and insert another blank, writable CD into the CD recording drive.

To erase files from a CD, follow these steps:

1. Double-click the CD recording drive to display the content.

2. Under CD Writing Tasks, click Erase This CD-RW.

3. The CD Writing Wizard enables you to delete the content of the CD-RW.

Erasing a CD-RW deletes all the files on the CD. You cannot specify individual files. Not all CDs are erasable; a CD-R disc is not erasable.

Many software programs like Roxio's Direct CD and Copy-to-Disk use the Universal Disk Format (UDF), which is a standard published by the Optical Storage Technology Association (OSTA). Windows XP reads UDF versions up to 2.01 using the udfs.sys driver.

Windows XP writes data to CDs using the Joliet and International Organization for Standardization (ISO) 9660 CD File System (CDFS) formats. When Windows XP writes audio to CD, it uses the Red Book format. UDF is a successor to the ISO 9660 CDFS.

Therefore, if you are using a CD-RW disk, you can erase files and append files to a disk that already has files if the disk was originally formatted using Windows XP. However, to modify existing CD-RW disks formatted with UDFS, you need extra software.

Configuring CD-R/CD-RW Device Settings

You can limit a user's ability to burn CDs using Windows Explorer.

By configuring the group policy value User Configuration /Administrative Templates/Windows Components/Windows Explorer/Remove CD Burning Features, you can prevent users from using the Windows Explorer CD burning features.

This setting does not prevent third-party CD burners.

If you are trying to troubleshoot reading and writing problems, you can stop the drive from automatically ejecting the CD and you can change the speed with which data is written to the drive. Each of these are hardware properties, shown in Figure 3.13.

Following is a list of other troubleshooting solutions:

1. Don't interrupt the flow of data to the CD recorder.

2. When creating a CD, the CD recorder must receive a *constant* flow of data from the hard disk. If the flow of data is interrupted, the CD continues to spin but the writing laser does not have any information to copy onto the disc. When this happens, the writing process stops and users end up with a useless CD. To maintain a constant flow of data, heed these guidelines:

➤ Record at a lower write speed.

➤ Close any other programs that are running.

➤ Disable any screen savers that might begin suddenly during writing.

3. Don't run out of available disk space for the CD recording process:

➤ When creating a CD, Windows uses available free space on the hard disk to store temporary files.

➤ To free up disk space, run the Disk Defragmenter tool, run the Disk Cleanup Wizard, delete unneeded data files, and empty the Recycle Bin.

➤ If you have more than one partition or disk drive, select one for the temporary file storage area that has sufficient disk space.

4. Ensure that the CD and the CD recorder are clean and dust free.

5. If the CDs from one manufacturer keep failing, try a different brand.

Configuring and Troubleshooting Removable Storage

Pen drives, thumbnail drives, flash drives, and memory cards are all data storage destinations.

Windows XP provides numerable drivers for such devices; however, because they are relatively new, they might come with interesting "challenges."

For example, you can extend the Disk Quotas feature of Windows XP to apply to removeable media using a group policy. This might frustrate users attempting to store files, such as MP3 files, on removable media. The value is stored in Group Policies under `Computer Policy/Administrative Templates/System/Disk Quotas/Apply Policy to Removable Media`. Use `gpedit.msc` to edit the local policy.

Saving files to removable media can create other challenges, as shown in Figure 3.15. For example, to avoid errors when writing to media, don't disconnect FAT16-formatted removable storage devices prematurely. If a user ejects a FAT16-formatted removable-storage device, problems could be caused by the 8-second write-flush delays—a delay originally created on those file systems for performance reasons.

FAT16 partitions range from 16MB to 2GB. This size was once common for hard disks and has become popular again as removable-storage sizes increase. (FAT12 volumes do not have this problem because they are primarily used for floppy disks and are not designed to use a write-behind delay.)

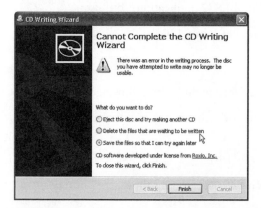

Figure 3.15   The CD Writing Wizard—unable to write to a disc.

If a removable-storage device is formatted with the FAT16 file system and users eject the device approximately 5–8 seconds after data was written to the device, they will have abandoned the write-flush delay on FAT16 file systems. This can lead to unexpected consequences:

➤ A user's storage device might remain in a "nonflushed" state.

➤ Users might lose data that is stored on their removable-storage device.

➤ Users might experience problems or receive error messages when they insert the removable-storage device into other host devices.

In short, don't eject removable media prematurely.

In addition, not everyone is permitted to format and eject removable media. The local policy `Computer Configuration/Windows Settings/Security Settings/Local Policies/Security Options/Devices:Allowed to Format and Eject Removable Objects` controls those privileges. By default, only administrators are allowed to format and eject removable objects.

When users work with disks, disk-reading problems can occur when they try to open a file, execute a program from disk, or switch disks while using programs that require multiple disks. They might receive error messages referring to problems reading the disk or copying specific files. Following are examples of Microsoft error messages:

➤ A device attached to the system is not functioning.

➤ Unable to read drive letter.

➤ A required file, `kernel32.dll`, was not found.

➤ Application name is not a valid WIN32 application.

➤ An error reading from file [Installer Error 1305].

➤ Insufficient memory.

Other problems users might experience include the following:

➤ When they insert the disc in the drive or read a disc, the computer freezes or hangs (see "dies").

➤ The disc does not eject from the drive.

➤ Reading from the disc takes an *unbelievably* long time.

As a desktop support technician, what can you do? The following troubleshooting guidelines might provide some ideas:

➤ Don't forget the obvious. If you experience problems with a DVD disc, make sure that you insert the DVD into a DVD drive, not a CD-ROM drive.

➤ Examine the disc for obvious physical damage such as warping or large scratches. If the disc is damaged, contact the manufacturer for a replacement CD.

➤ Clean the CD-ROM or DVD-ROM disc using a disc cleaning kit or gently wipe the silver side of the disc with a soft, lint-free cotton cloth. Do not use paper cloth because it can scratch the disc. Resist the temptation to use a circular motion because it also can scratch the disc. Wipe the disc from the center outward.

➤ Clean the disc by using a water-dampened cloth or a commercial CD cleaning solution or DVD cleaning solution. Dry the disc thoroughly before you put it into the drive.

➤ If your computer has multiple CD-ROM drives, CD-R drives, CD/RW drives, or DVD drives, test the disc in another drive. For DVDs, make sure that the drive has a DVD logo. If the disc works in another drive, the original drive might be faulty.

➤ If the disc appears clean yet does not work in another drive, it is probably damaged and must be replaced.

➤ You can clean the disc drive by using a CD-ROM drive cleaning disc or DVD drive cleaning disc.

If users are experiencing problems with a CD-ROM drive in Windows XP, you can also consider the following actions:

Verify that the hardware is compatible with Windows XP by making sure that the CD-ROM drive is listed on the Windows hardware compatibility list (HCL).

➤ For a SCSI CD-ROM drive, make sure that the SCSI controller is listed on the Windows HCL.

➤ If the CD-ROM drive or SCSI controller is not listed on the Windows HCL, contact the device manufacturer, obtain a Windows-compatible device driver, or consider replacing the device.

You should also verify that the CD-ROM drive is installed according to the manufacturer's specifications. Don't forget to open the case and check master/slave/cable-select jumpering on the drive and for the proper cabling.

If it is a SCSI CD-ROM drive, check the following:

➤ Is the SCSI bus is terminated correctly? On a SCSI bus, the last SCSI device needs a special terminator.

➤ Verify the CD-ROM SCSI ID. The SCSI ID of the CD-ROM drive is normally set to SCSI ID 2 or higher. Ensure that the CD-ROM drive is not configured to use a SCSI ID already assigned to another device.

➤ Verify that the SCSI ID of the SCSI controller is set to SCSI ID 7.

➤ Verify that no other adapters are configured with settings that conflict with the SCSI controller's settings.

➤ Search the Windows XP Event Viewer for error messages related to the CD-ROM drive or SCSI controller.

➤ Open Device Manager to see whether it detects the SCSI controller and the CD-ROM drive. Does Device Manager indicate that the devices are working properly?

If users have installed an IDE CD-ROM drive, make sure they are using a device driver that is designed for the IDE controller to which the CD-ROM drive is attached.

If the manufacturer does not provide a specific driver for the IDE controller, install the IDE controller driver that comes with Windows XP. This driver is compatible only with IDE CD-ROM drives that are Advanced Technology Atachment Packet Interface (ATAPI) 1.2–compliant. By contacting the CD-ROM's manufacturer, you should be able to verify the ATAPI compliance level of the CD-ROM drive.

If you are trying to install a CD-ROM drive that uses a proprietary, non-SCSI interface, check the following:

➤ Make sure that the correct device driver is installed by running Windows XP Setup and selecting Add/Remove SCSI Adapters on the Options menu.

➤ Review the Windows XP "read me" file (readme.wri) and the Windows XP catalog, available online at http://www.microsoft.com/windows/catalog/.

Users might report that Windows does not recognize their CD-ROM drives. Start Windows Explorer and look for a drive letter assigned to the CD-ROM drive.

If the CD-ROM drive does have a drive letter, try to view a folder by using the CD-ROM drive. Make sure that you insert a data CD into the CD-ROM drive.

If AutoPlay is enabled on a drive, there might a short delay of up to 10 seconds before the CD or DVD is recognized and displayed in My Computer. Try disabling AutoPlay on the drive.

If you can read a data CD but cannot play a music CD, use one of the following strategies:

➤ In Control Panel, start Sounds and Audio Devices, click the Hardware tab, and then make sure that the CD/DVD drive is listed along with Audio Codecs.

➤ If these items are not listed, use the Add/Remove Hardware program in Control Panel to reinstall necessary drivers.

➤ If the system is configured to dual-boot to another operating system, check whether the CD-ROM drive functions in the other operating system. If the CD-ROM drive does not function properly in MS-DOS or in another operating system, contact the drive manufacturer.

The desktop support technician needs a few tricks up his or her sleeve to test the CD further. Here are a few sleights of hand:

➤ Turn off all other programs. Software might be interfering with reading the disc. This problem can occur with anticrash software, antivirus software, or firewall software running in the background. Starting the computer without unnecessary software might enable you to read from the disk.

To eliminate interfering programs, do a clean boot of XP and quit any remaining programs:

1. Close all programs that are running.

2. Press Ctrl+Alt+Del. In the Windows Security dialog box, click Task Manager.

3. In Windows Task Manager, click Applications.

4. No programs should appear under the Task list. If any programs appear, click the program name, and then click End Task.

Again, attempt to read from or write to the media.

If a user installed the Windows XP upgrade over Windows 95, 98, or Me, and the DVD-ROM stopped working after the upgrade, it might be that the drive is being treated as DMA (direct memory access). Switch the CD-ROM drive or DVD drive to DMA mode from Programmed Input/Output (PIO), as shown in Figure 3.16.

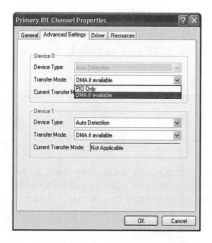

Figure 3.16 Drive configuration changes, mode options: DMA and PIO.

PIO is a method of moving data between devices that sends data through the processor. DMA is a newer alternative to PIO in which data from an attached device goes directly to memory, bypassing the processor. To switch between PIO to DMA mode, follow these steps:

1. In Control Panel, double-click Administrative Tools, and then click Computer Management.

2. Click System Tools, and then click Device Manager.

3. Click to expand IDE ATA/ATAPI controllers.

4. Click the specific controller for which you want to configure DMA/PIO settings.

5. Click the Advanced Settings tab.

6. In the Transfer Mode box, click either PIO Only or DMA if available.

The Disk Defragmenter Tool

Disk Defragmenter rearranges files, programs, and unused space on your computer's hard disks, allowing programs to run faster and files to open more quickly. Putting the pieces of files and programs in a more contiguous arrangement on disk reduces the time the operating system needs to access them.

To run Disk Defragmenter, perform the following steps:

1. Click Start, (All) Programs, Accessories, System Tools, and then click Disk Defragmenter. Alternatively, you can right-click a drive letter in My Computer, select Properties, click the Tools tab, and click Defragment Now.

2. Select which disks you want to defragment and any additional options you want to set.

3. Click the Defragment button to start the defragmentation process.

 Windows XP Professional ships with a command-line version of the disk defragmenter—**defrag.exe**. You can run this program within a batch file or inside of a Windows script, which in turn can be scheduled to run automatically using the Scheduled Tasks folder.

On NTFS volumes, Windows XP reserves a portion of the free space for a system file called the master file table (MFT). The MFT is where Windows stores all the information it needs to retrieve files from the volume. Windows stores part of the MFT at the beginning of the volume. Windows reserves the MFT for exclusive use, so Disk Defragmenter cannot and does not move files to the beginning of volumes.

Disk Cleanup helps free up space on your hard drive by searching your drives and then showing you a list of temporary files, Internet cache files, and potentially unnecessary program files that you can safely delete. You can instruct Disk Cleanup to delete none, some, or all of those files. To use the Disk Cleanup Wizard, perform the following steps:

1. Click Start, (All) Programs, Accessories, System Tools.

2. Click the Disk Cleanup icon and follow the onscreen instructions.

Exam Prep Questions

1. You are a desktop support technician, and you support computers running Windows XP in a Windows Server 2003 domain. Domain policy explicitly prohibits using Windows Explorer burn CDs. However, Mary Ann is able to burn a CD. What is the most likely reason?

   ❑ A. Mary Ann is using a third-party application to create or modify CDs using a CD writer.

   ❑ B. Mary Ann is using Internet Explorer to create a CD.

   ❑ C. Mary Ann is a member of the Power Users group.

   ❑ D. The policy only applies to Windows Server operating systems.

   Answer A is correct. The group policy value User Configuration, /Administrative Templates/Windows Components/Windows Explorer/Remove CD Burning Features prevents users from being able to use the Windows Explorer CD burning features. It does not prevent users from using third-party applications to create or modify CDs using a CD writer. Answer B is incorrect because Internet Explorer, with the policy enabled, explicitly prevents copying information to a CD. Answer C is incorrect because being a member of the Power Users group does not eliminate the effect of the policy. Answer D is incorrect because the policy applies to Windows Server and Windows XP operating systems.

2. You are a desktop support technician for a large company and you support computers running Windows XP. A user, Joshua, wants to convert one of the hard drives connected to his Windows XP Professional desktop computer from a Basic disk to a Dynamic disk. In the Disk Management console, he right-clicks the physical disk designated as Disk 1, but the option to Convert to Dynamic Disk is unavailable. Why would the option to convert the drive to a Dynamic disk be disabled?

   ❑ A. There are already drive volumes with data stored on that physical disk.

   ❑ B. The drive is an external drive connected via USB or IEEE 1394 (FireWire) bus connections.

   ❑ C. The drive is an external Fibre Channel device.

   ❑ D. The drive has a sector size of 512 bytes.

   Answer B is correct. Hard disks connected via USB or FireWire (IEEE 1394) buses are not supported for Dynamic disks by default. Answer A is incorrect because you are allowed to convert disks with existing drive volumes and data to Dynamic disks; you cannot convert back to a Basic disk without deleting all existing volumes (and therefore the data on those volumes). Answer C is incorrect because Dynamic disks do support Fibre Channel drives. Answer D is incorrect because Dynamic disks require drives with 512 or fewer bytes per sector.

3. You are a desktop support technician. A user, Toby, wants to convert physical hard disk 2 on his Windows XP Professional desktop computer from a Basic disk to a Dynamic disk using only the command line. Is a command-line tool available to accomplish this task? If so, what is the name of this utility and does it differ from the Disk Management console?

   ❑   A.   The command-line tool is called **diskperf.exe**. Only administrative users may use it.

   ❑   B.   No command-line tool equivalent to the Disk Management MMC exists.

   ❑   C.   The command-line tool is called **diskpart.exe**. You must restart the computer for the conversion process to take effect.

   ❑   D.   The command-line tool is called **convert.exe**. You do not need to restart the computer for the conversion to take place unless you are converting the boot disk.

   Answer C is correct. Diskpart.exe is the command-line equivalent to Disk Management. You must restart the computer for the conversion to take effect. Answer A is incorrect because diskperf.exe enables and disables hard disk performance counters on earlier versions of Windows; it does nothing for converting Basic disks to Dynamic disks. Answer B is incorrect because a command-line utility with functionally equivalent to Disk Management does exist—diskpart.exe. Answer D is incorrect because you use the convert.exe command-line tool to convert a FAT or FAT32 volume to NTFS.

4. You are a desktop support technician. A user complains that he is running low on available disk space for critical database records he is importing into his sales database. The data resides in a partition on a Basic disk on a computer running Windows XP. If you suggest converting to a Dynamic disk, what types of storage solutions would the conversion provide? (Select all correct answers.)

   ❑   A.   Spanned volumes

   ❑   B.   Extended volumes

   ❑   C.   RAID-5 volumes

   ❑   D.   Simple volumes

   ❑   E.   Volume sets

   ❑   F.   Striped volumes

   ❑   G.   Mirrored volumes

Answers A, D, and F are correct. Spanned volumes enable you to store data sequentially over two or more physical disks, but Windows XP displays the disks as one logical drive volume. Simple volumes are the most fundamental dynamic volumes, with each simple volume residing on only one physical disk. Striped volumes are also supported under Windows XP, enabling you to store data in stripes across two or more physical disks, but Windows XP displays the disks as one logical drive volume. Answer B is incorrect because there is no such volume as an extended volume on a Dynamic disk. Answer C is incorrect because Windows XP Professional does not support the fault-tolerant RAID-5 volume configuration. Answer E is incorrect because volume sets were supported for Basic disks under Windows NT; they are known as spanned volumes under Windows XP. Answer G is incorrect because Windows XP Professional does not support the fault-tolerant mirrored volume configuration.

5. You are a desktop support technician. A user, Hazel, has a Windows XP Professional computer that has two physical hard drives installed. Both disks have been converted to Dynamic disks. The first disk (disk 0) has a capacity of 20GB with a drive C (system and boot) volume of 2GB, a drive D volume of 7GB, and 11GB of unallocated free space. The second disk (disk 1) has a capacity of 30GB with 20GB of unallocated free space. Hazel needs to extend drive D (a simple volume) on her computer so that the volume has an increased amount of total disk space—from 7GB to 14GB. How can you accomplish this without deleting any existing data? (Select all correct answers.)

   ❑   A. Repartition and reformat drive C.
   ❑   B. Extend drive D to an area of free space on disk 1.
   ❑   C. Extend drive D to an area of free space on disk 0.
   ❑   D. Convert disk 1 to Basic and extend the volume.

Answers B and C are correct. You can extend a simple volume on a Dynamic disk onto unallocated free space of additional Dynamic disks up to a maximum of 32 Dynamic disks; this process automatically turns the volume into a spanned volume. You can also extend a simple volume on a Dynamic disk onto an area of unallocated free space on the same Dynamic disk. Answer A is incorrect because repartitioning and reformatting a disk deletes any data stored on the disk. Answer D is incorrect because converting a disk from Dynamic to Basic deletes any data stored on the disk.

6. You are a desktop support technician. To make accessing several different hard drive volumes and removable drives easier on a local Windows XP computer, you want your users to be able to access each drive volume through different folder names located on the same drive letter. How can you accomplish this?

❑   A. Use the **subst.exe** command-line utility to specify each folder as a unique drive letter.

❑   B. Use the Disk Management console to create mount points for each hard drive volume letter through empty folders on the same FAT or FAT32 volume.

❑   C. Use **diskpart.exe** to create mount points for each hard drive volume letter through empty folders on the same NTFS volume.

❑   D. Use **diskperf.exe** to create mount points for each hard drive volume letter through empty folders on the same NTFS volume.

Answer C is correct. You can use either diskpart.exe or the Disk Management MMC snap-in to create mount points for a drive letter through empty NTFS folders. Answer A is incorrect because the subst.exe command associates a specific drive letter path with a different drive letter root folder. Answer B is incorrect because you can only create mount points on empty NTFS folders. Answer D is incorrect because diskperf.exe enables and disables hard-disk performance counters on earlier versions of Windows.

7. You are a desktop support technician. What is the easiest way to convert an NTFS drive volume configured as drive D to the FAT32 file system without losing any existing data? Assume that the volume is not the system or boot volume.

❑   A. Use the command **convert d: /fs:fat32**.

❑   B. Use the command **convert d: /fs:-ntfs**.

❑   C. Use the Disk Management console to revert the volume back to FAT or FAT32.

❑   D. Back up all the data stored on the NTFS drive volume, use **diskpart.exe** or the Disk Management console to delete the volume, create a new volume, format the volume as FAT32, and then restore the backed-up data.

Answer D is correct. Windows XP does not offer a conversion tool for converting an existing NTFS volume to FAT, to FAT32, or to any other file system. You must back up all the data on the volume, create a new volume, format it, and restore the data. Answer A is incorrect because the `convert.exe` command does not support the conversion to the FAT or FAT32 file systems. Answer B is incorrect because the `convert.exe` command-line tool only supports a conversion to NTFS; prepending a minus sign (-) to the NTFS parameter is not supported. Answer C is incorrect because the Disk Management console only supports reformatting an existing NTFS drive volume to convert it to the FAT or FAT32 file system.

8. You are a desktop support technician. A user complains that she cannot copy a 100MB folder onto a USB 2.0 pen drive that she has been issued for transferring files. What is the most likely reason she is unable to store the files on the pen drive?

   ❑ A. You have a strict disk quota policy that uses default settings.
   ❑ B. Because you cannot limit the enforcement of a disk quota on removable media, the drive must be faulty.
   ❑ C. You have enabled the Apply Policy to removable media policy.
   ❑ D. She is logged on with local administrator privileges.

   Answer C is correct. In the group policy feature, you can enable the computer policy `Administrative Templates/System/Disk Quotas/Apply Policy to Removable Media`. This policy extends disk quotas to include removable media. Answer A is incorrect. By default, disk quota policies do not apply to removable media. Answer B is incorrect. You *can* apply disk quotas to removable media. There is no evidence that the pen drive is faulty. Answer D is incorrect; logging on with local administrator privileges does not necessarily prohibit a user from being able to store files to removable media.

9. You are a desktop support technician. Layla is attempting to format a USB 2.0 pen drive in her computer. However, the format option is not available. How can you make the format option available to her?

   ❑ A. Using group policies, enable the program **format.exe** for Layla's account.
   ❑ B. Using group policies, remove Layla's name from Restricted Groups.
   ❑ C. Add Layla's name to the local Administrators group on her computer.
   ❑ D. Modify the local policy on the machine, Allowed to Format and Eject Removable Objects.

Answer D is correct. By modifying the local policy `Computer Configuration/Windows Settings/Security Settings/Local Policies/Security Options/Devices:Allowed to Format and Eject Removable Objects` (administrators). By default, only administrators are allowed to format and eject removable media. Answer A is incorrect; there is no program named `format.exe`. Answer B is incorrect. Restricted Groups is designed to control membership in local groups on computers running Windows XP. Removing Layla's name from the Administrators group does not elevate his privileges; more than likely, it reduces them. Answer C is incorrect; adding Layla's name to the local Administrators group will possibly enable him to use the format option, provided that the policy in the local machine is configured to allow administrators to format removable media. However, it is not advisable to add users to the local administrators group to provide them with specific privileges; it is more secure to elevate their permissions in a more specific way.

10. You are a desktop support technician. When Bob attempts to install a software program from CD and is unable to do so, a message appears that says "the feature cannot be found".

    The CD is visible in Explorer. He can copy files from the CD to the hard drive.

    Bob tries to install the program on another computer, and when he double-clicks the program **setup.exe**, the program proceeds successfully.

    Bob's original computer has sufficient disk space on which to install the software. What is a possible reason for Bob's inability to install the software on his computer running Windows XP?

    ❑ A. A policy that prevents installation from removable media is in place on Bob's computer.

    ❑ B. This function is not supported by Windows XP.

    ❑ C. The CD is corrupt and unreadable.

    ❑ D. It's a faulty driver. Use driver rollback to replace the CD-ROM driver.

    Answer A is correct. If the policy `User Configuration/Administrative Templates/Windows Components/Windows Installer/Prevent Removable Media Source for Any Install` is enabled, when a user tries to install a program from removable media, the process fails. If you disable the setting, or do not configure it, users can install from removable media. Answer B is incorrect; Windows XP supports CD-based software installation, by default. Answer C is incorrect; the CD is readable in other computers and can be used to copy files. Answer D is incorrect. There is no evidence of a driver problem.

Need to Know More?

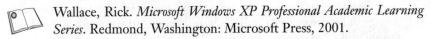

Wallace, Rick. *Microsoft Windows XP Professional Academic Learning Series*. Redmond, Washington: Microsoft Press, 2001.

Balter, Dan. *MCSE Exam Cram 2 Windows XP Professional*. Indianapolis, Indiana: Que Certification, 2002.

Bott, Ed and Carl Siechert. *Microsoft Windows XP Inside Out, Deluxe Edition*. Redmond, Washington: Microsoft Learning, 2002.

Simmons, Curt and James Causey. *Microsoft Windows XP Networking Inside Out*. Redmond, Washington: Microsoft Learning, 2002.

Stanek, William R. Microsoft Windows XP Professional Administrator's Pocket Consultant. Redmond, Washington: Microsoft Press, 2003.

Search the Microsoft Product Support Services Knowledge Base on the Internet: http://support.microsoft.com. You can also search Microsoft TechNet on the Internet: http://www.microsoft.com/technet. Find technical information using keywords from this chapter, such as FAT, FAT32, NTFS, Basic disk, Dynamic disk, drive partition, drive volume, simple volume, spanned volume, striped volume, managing digital media, and disk management.

Setting Up and Troubleshooting Hardware Components and Device Drivers

. . . .

Terms you'll need to understand:

✓ Device Manager
✓ Driver signing
✓ Driver roll back
✓ Add Hardware Wizard
✓ **sigverif.exe**
✓ Plug and Play versus managed hardware
✓ Windows Update
✓ Network adapter or network interface card (NIC)
✓ Universal Serial Bus (USB) devices
✓ Hibernation versus standby mode

Techniques you'll need to master:

✓ Installing, configuring, and troubleshooting hardware devices and drivers
✓ Updating drivers and system files
✓ Rolling back drivers to a previous version
✓ Managing and troubleshooting driver signing

The expression *computer hardware* includes any physical device that is connected to a computer which is controlled by the computer's processors. It includes equipment connected to the computer at the time that it is manufactured as well as equipment that you add later.

Modems, disk drives, CD-ROM drives, printers, network cards, keyboards, display adapter cards, and USB cameras are all examples of devices. Each device attached to a system must also have a corresponding software driver, which allows the device to interface (communicate) with the computer's operating system.

Supporting and troubleshooting hardware devices and their associated drivers is vital to maintaining a productive network. Administering, diagnosing, and resolving desktop hardware-related issues is where productivity and this chapter begin.

Managing and Troubleshooting Hardware Devices and Drivers

Windows XP offers full support for Plug and Play (PnP) devices and offers limited support for non–Plug and Play devices. Be sure to always consult the latest Windows XP hardware compatibility list (HCL) before installing a new device to verify that the device is supported. You can access the online version of the HCL at http://www.microsoft.com/whdc/hcl/search.mspx.

Although devices are tested with varieties of hardware and software combinations, it is a still a good idea to test devices yourself to be certain that they will work with Windows XP and the specific hardware and software upon which you and your users depend.

For a device to work properly with Windows XP, you must install software (a device driver) on the computer. Each hardware device has its own unique device driver, which the device manufacturer typically provides. However, Windows XP includes many device drivers that might work better with Windows XP than the manufacturers' own drivers. Look for Microsoft to recommend using its own drivers for a given device rather than those of the manufacturer because Microsoft understands the inner workings of the operating system better than anyone else.

Because Windows XP manages your computer's resources and configuration based on PnP standards, you can install many PnP hardware devices without restarting your computer. Windows XP automatically identifies (enumerates) the new hardware and installs the necessary drivers. Windows XP fully supports computers with BIOS versions that are compliant with the Advanced Configuration and Power Interface (ACPI) specification. Windows XP also supports computers with certain BIOS versions that are compliant with the older Advanced Power Management (APM) specification.

Installing, Configuring, and Managing Hardware

You might need to configure devices on Windows XP machines using the Add Hardware Wizard in the Control Panel or by clicking the Add Hardware Wizard button from the Hardware tab on the System Properties window. Keep in mind that in most cases, you need to be logged on to the local computer as a member of the Administrators group to add, configure, and remove devices. Many devices completely configure themselves without any administrator intervention at all; other devices require some administrative effort.

Installing PnP Devices and Non-PnP Devices

Connect the device to the appropriate port or slot on your computer according to the device manufacturer's instructions. If the new device is not immediately discovered by the operating system, you might need to start or restart your computer. Plan for necessary downtime on production computers. PnP is an enormous convenience, but it is not a replacement for preparedness. If you are prompted to restart your computer, do so when it is appropriate. For PnP devices, Windows XP should detect the device and then immediately start the Found New Hardware Wizard. If a new device does not immediately install, you might need to use a special setup driver disk, CD-ROM, or DVD from the manufacturer that ships with the device. If you are still unable to install the device, or if you are installing a non-PnP device, perform the following manual installation steps:

1. Click the Add Hardware icon in the Control Panel.

2. Click Next and then click Yes, I Have Already Connected the Hardware. Click Next again.

3. Scroll down the Installed Hardware list to the bottom, select Add a New Hardware Device, and click Next.

4. Select one of the following options:

> *Search for and Install the Hardware Automatically (Recommended)*—Do this step if you want Windows XP to try to detect the new device that you want to install.

> *Install the Hardware That I Manually Select from a List (Advanced)*— Do this step if you know the type and model of the device you are installing and you want to select it from a list of devices.

5. Click Next, and then follow the instructions on your screen.

6. You might be prompted to restart your computer, depending on the type of device.

Troubleshooting Installed Devices with the Add Hardware Wizard

Sometimes, an installed hardware device is not automatically recognized by the Windows XP PnP enumeration. If an installed device fails to be discovered or fails to function, a desktop support technician should troubleshoot the device by performing the following steps:

1. Click the Add Hardware icon in the Control Panel.

2. Click Next and then click Yes, I Have Already Connected the Hardware. Click Next again.

3. Select the installed hardware device that you are having trouble with and click Next.

4. Follow the subsequent instructions on your screen. Click Finish to launch the Hardware Update Wizard or to go through a hardware troubleshooter from the Windows XP Help and Support Center shown in Figure 4.1, depending on the device in question, to try to resolve the problem. Otherwise, click Cancel to exit the Add Hardware Wizard.

Troubleshooting Hardware with Device Manager

The Windows XP Device Manager is quite similar to the Device Manager in Windows 2000. The Device Manager window displays hardware devices connected to the computer. Device Manager gives administrators the power to update device drivers, enable or disable devices, uninstall devices, scan for hardware changes, roll back drivers, and even work with resource settings for devices, all in one centralized interface.

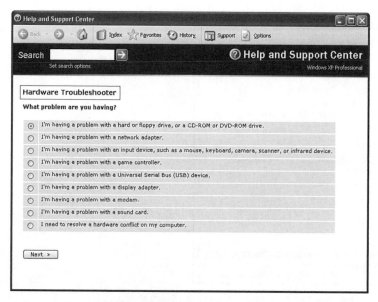

Figure 4.1 The Hardware Troubleshooting Wizard.

To run Device Manager, follow these steps:

1. Right-click My Computer from the Windows desktop or from the Start menu and select Properties. Alternatively, you can double-click the System icon from the Control Panel.

2. From the System properties window, click the Hardware tab and then click the Device Manager button.

By default, Device Manager categorizes and displays devices into logical groups such as computer, disk drives, display adapter, and so on. To work with an individual device, click the plus symbol to expand the appropriate category and then right-click the device itself and select Properties to display its properties sheet. Devices that are not set up or functioning properly have their categories automatically expanded, and each problem device appears with a yellow question mark or an exclamation point to denote a problem with the device.

To enable or disable a device, use its properties sheet and click the Device Usage drop-down list box to select either Use This Device (Enable) or Do Not Use This Device (Disable), as shown in Figure 4.2.

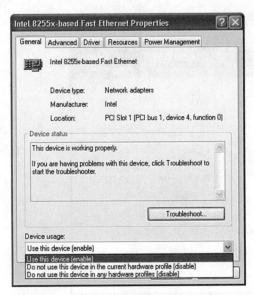

Figure 4.2   The properties sheet for a network adapter from Device Manager.

To install or reinstall a driver for a device, access its properties dialog box and click the Update Driver button (as shown in Figure 4.3) from the Driver tab and follow the onscreen instructions. You might need the CD-ROM or disk containing the device drivers from the manufacturer.

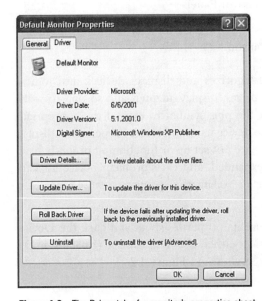

Figure 4.3   The Driver tab of a monitor's properties sheet.

Managing Device Drivers and System Updates

Keeping drivers and system files updated ensures that your operating system performs at its peak. Microsoft recommends using Microsoft digitally signed drivers whenever possible. Microsoft has thoroughly tested Microsoft digitally signed drivers for compatibility with Windows XP, so these drivers are more stable than unsigned drivers. The driver.cab cabinet file is stored in the \i386 folder on the Windows XP CD-ROM, and this file contains all the drivers that Windows XP works with at the time that the operating system is released to manufacturing. This cabinet file is copied to the %systemroot%\Driver Cache\i386 folder when Windows XP is installed.

Whenever a driver is updated, Windows XP looks in the driver.cab file first. The location of driver.cab is a Registry key, shown in Figure 4.4, and you can change the value with the Registry Editor (regedit.exe) and by navigating to HKLM\Software\Microsoft\Windows\CurrentVersion\Setup\DriverCachePath.

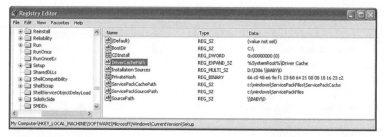

Figure 4.4 The **DriverCachePath** value name in the Windows XP Registry specifying where the **driver.cab** file is located.

Automatic Updating of Device Drivers and System Files

Windows XP supports automatic updates for critical operating system files. In Windows XP, you must be logged on as a member of the Administrators group to install updated components or to change Automatic Updates settings. If the computer is a member of an Active Directory domain, group policy settings might further restrict your ability to modify these settings and install updated components. To turn on, turn off, or modify Windows XP Automatic Updates notification settings, follow these steps:

1. Log on to the computer as the administrator or as a member of the Administrators group.

2. Right-click My Computer from the Start menu or the Windows desktop and select Properties.

3. Click the Automatic Updates tab.

4. To enable automatic updates, be sure that the Keep My Computer Up to Date check box is marked; it is the default setting. To disable automatic updates, clear this check box.

5. When automatic updates are enabled, select from one of three available notification settings:

   ➤ Notify Me Before Downloading Any Updates and Notify Me Again Before Installing Them on My Computer.

   ➤ Download the Updates Automatically and Notify Me When They Are Ready To Be Installed. (This option is the default selection.)

   ➤ Automatically Download the Updates, and Install Them on the Schedule That I Specify. (You must then choose the day and time when you want the updates downloaded and installed.)

6. Click OK to accept the new settings.

 After the successful installation of certain updated components, Windows XP might prompt you to restart the computer. As a best practice, you should always restart the machine immediately as instructed. Failure to follow these instructions can result in an unstable or nonfunctioning workstation. Because you must restart the computer after an update, you should install updates only during nonproduction hours.

You should also consider turning off the Automatic Updates feature so that you can manually install all updates on nonproduction workstations in a test environment first. As a general rule, you should always test updates first before installing them on production workstations and servers.

Windows XP reminds you about downloading or installing automatic updates by placing an auto-update icon in the notification area of the system tray (located in the right corner of the taskbar). If you choose not to install one or more updates that you downloaded to your PC, Windows XP deletes those update files from your computer. If you later decide that you want to install any of the updates that you previously declined, click the Declined Updates button on the Automatic Updates tab of System Properties. If any of the previously declined updates still apply to your system, Windows XP displays them the next time that the system notifies you of newly available updates.

Manually Updating Device Drivers

Automatic updates might be convenient but they won't update all device drivers. To update drivers on individual components, such as network cards or small computer system interface (SCSI) disk controllers, perform the following steps:

1. Open Device Manager and expand the device category where the device that you want to update is located.

2. Perform one of these two steps:

   ➤ Right-click the device that you want to update, select Update Driver from the right-click menu, and follow the onscreen instructions.

   ➤ Right-click the device that you want to update and select Properties from the right-click menu. Click the Driver tab, click the Update Driver button, and follow the onscreen instructions.

Updating Drivers and System Files with Windows Update

Windows Update is a Microsoft database of important operating system files such as drivers, patches, help files, and other components stored on public Microsoft Web servers that you can manually download to keep your Windows XP installation up to date. However, once again, before you get too carried away with ease of updating a mission-critical workstation from a Web page on the Internet, remember that you should always test patches and fixes before applying them.

Only operating system files are included in Windows Update. Other applications, such as Microsoft Office, must be manually updated with security hotfixes and service releases to keep those programs current.

A link to Windows Update, by default, is listed under Start, All Programs in Windows XP. When the program runs, click Scan for Updates and follow the onscreen instructions to review and install all or some of the applicable updates.

You must be logged on as a member of the Administrators group to complete the installation of various Windows Update components or procedures. If the computer is a member of an Active Directory domain, group policy settings might prevent you from updating any system files or drivers.

Using the Driver Roll Back Feature

Driver roll back is a new feature in Windows XP. If you encounter problems with a hardware device after you install an updated driver for it, you can revert to the previously installed software driver for that device by using the Roll Back Driver option (see Figure 4.3) within Device Manager.

Managing and Troubleshooting Device Conflicts

You can configure, diagnose, and modify settings for hardware devices using the Device Manager.

For example, each resource assigned to a device—a memory address range, interrupt request (IRQ), I/O port, Direct Memory Access (DMA) channel, and so on—must be unique or the device will not function properly. For PnP devices, Windows XP attempts automatically to ensure that these resources are configured uniquely. When a device has a resource conflict or is not working properly, Windows displays a yellow circle with an exclamation point next to the device's name. If a device has been improperly installed or if it's been disabled, Windows displays a red X next to the device name in Device Manager.

If you are having trouble with a particular device, sometimes it's helpful to simply uninstall the device's driver, reboot the computer, and then attempt to reinstall the driver. Because PnP devices automatically invoke an installation procedure, if you do not want the operating system to try to install a particular device whenever the computer restarts, disable the device rather than uninstall its driver.

Occasionally, two devices require and can share the same resources; this does not always result in a device conflict—especially if the devices are PnP-compliant. Sometimes, two or more devices can share resources, such as interrupts on Peripheral Connection Interface (PCI) devices. It all depends on the drivers and the computer. For example, Windows XP might share IRQ 9 or IRQ 10 among multiple PCI devices, such as USB host controllers, SCSI adapters, and audio controllers. In many instances, you cannot change resource settings for PnP devices because no other settings are available.

When you install a non-PnP device, the resource settings for the device are not configured automatically. In some cases, you might have to manually configure these settings. Such a configuration is called *forced hardware*, and the System Information Utility (msinfo32.exe) lists them under System Summary, Hardware Resources, Forced Hardware.

The appropriate range of resource settings should appear in the device's user manual. If you need to change resource settings for a device, follow these steps:

1. Open Device Manager and expand the device category where the device is located.

2. Right-click the device for which you want to adjust its resource settings and select Properties.

3. Click the Resources tab and clear the Use Automatic Settings check box (if available). If the Use Automatic Settings check box is dim (unavailable), you cannot change the resource settings for this device.

4. Choose one of the following courses of action:

   ➤ Click the Settings Based on drop-down list box to select from the predefined list of settings.

   ➤ Click a Resource Type item shown in the Resource Settings list box and then click the Change Setting button (see Figure 4.5) to individually modify the resource's setting. Change the setting and click OK. Repeat this action for each resource setting that you want to change.

5. Click OK for the device's properties sheet to return to the Device Manager window.

Generally, you should not change resource settings manually because when you do so, the settings become static and Windows XP has less flexibility when allocating resources dynamically to other devices. If too many resource settings are static, Windows XP might not be able to install new PnP devices. In addition, if you manually change resource settings to incompatible values, the device might lose functionality.

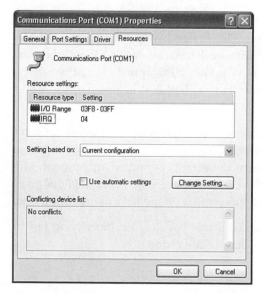

Figure 4.5 Adjusting resource settings for a device, such as COM1.

Uninstalling and Reinstalling Device Drivers

If you need to uninstall a driver for a particular device, open Device Manager and locate the device that you want to uninstall. Right-click the device name and select Uninstall. Click OK in the Confirm Device Removal dialog box. The driver for an installed device is not deleted from the system when the device is uninstalled. When the computer restarts, Windows XP attempts to reinstall the PnP device unless you explicitly designate the device as "disabled" from its properties sheet in Device Manager. If you need to reinstall a driver for a non-PnP device, perform the following steps:

1. Right-click My Computer and select Properties.

2. Click the Hardware tab and click the Add Hardware Wizard button to launch the wizard and then click Next.

3. Click Yes, I Have Already Connected the Hardware and then click Next.

4. Select the device that you want to reinstall from the Installed Hardware list box and click Next.

5. Follow the instructions that the wizard displays to finish the reinstallation process.

Managing and Troubleshooting Driver Signing

Microsoft touts its digital signatures for device drivers as a method for determining the overall reliability of software drivers. Windows XP uses the same type of driver-signing process as Windows 2000 to make sure that drivers have been certified to work correctly with the Windows Driver Model (WDM).

Depending on the driver signing policy configured on a Windows XP computer, you might be allowed to install non-digitally signed drivers without any warning, you might be warned but still permitted to proceed with installing non-digitally signed drivers (see Figure 4.6), or you might be completely prevented from installing drivers that do not have digital signatures.

For more information about signed driver policies, see "Specifying Driver Signing Options from the GUI" later in this chapter.

Figure 4.6   The Driver Signing Options dialog box for specifying unsigned device driver installation behavior.

If your computer is experiencing a device-driver problem, it might be because it is using a driver that was not correctly (or specifically) written for Windows XP. To search your system and locate unsigned drivers, use the Signature Verification tool, `sigverif.exe`. To use this digital-signature verification tool, perform the following steps:

1. Click Start, Run; type `sigverif.exe`; and click OK to launch the program.

2. Click the Advanced button.

3. Select the option Look for Other Files That Are Not Digitally Signed.

4. Mark the Include Subfolders check box.

5. Click the Logging tab to make any changes for the log file and then click OK. Note the log file name: `sigverif.txt`.

6. Click Start to run the signature-verification process.

7. After the process finishes, the Signature Verification Results window appears. Review the list of unsigned drivers and click Close to exit. You can review the results again later by double-clicking the `sigverif.txt` log file located by default in the `%systemroot%` folder (for example, `C:\Windows`).

Specifying Driver Signing Options from the GUI

Windows XP offers administrators some control over whether users can install digitally signed drivers. Signed drivers are software device drivers that have been tested by Microsoft for compatibility with Windows XP (or other versions of Windows). Microsoft issues a catalog (*.cat) file that contains a digital signature for each device driver which successfully passes its compatibility test. Manufacturers then distribute the associated catalog file as part of each device driver's set of installation files. Unsigned drivers are drivers that either have not been tested or drivers that are actually not compatible with specific versions of Windows: these drivers do not have catalog files included as part of their sets of installation files.

To change the system's driver-signing options, shown in Figure 4.6, right-click My Computer, select Properties, click the Hardware tab, and click the Driver Signing button. Select one of the following actions, for the operating system to take when you attempt to install an unsigned device driver:

➤ *Ignore*—This option bypasses driver-signing checks, allowing the user to proceed with the driver installation even if a driver is not signed.

➤ *Warn*—This option issues a dialog box warning if an unsigned driver is encountered during a device driver installation. It gives the user the option of continuing with the installation or terminating the device driver's setup. This setting is the default.

➤ *Block*—This option is the most restrictive of the three settings. To prevent the installation of any unsigned device drivers, you should select this option.

When you are logged on to the computer as the administrator or a member of the Administrators group, the Administrator Option for driver signing is also available. If you mark the Make This Action the System Default check box, the driver-signing setting that you have chosen will become the default setting for all other users who log onto this server.

NOTE Nonadministrator users can make the driver signing policy for a given system more restrictive than the current default setting; however, they cannot make the driver signing policy more relaxed.

Specifying Driver Signing Options Using Policy Settings

Instead of modifying the driver-signing options from the GUI, you can manipulate Windows XP driver-signing options using either a local policy setting or a group policy object (GPO) setting. Both the local policy setting and the group policy setting appear in the Local Policies, Security Options container named Devices: Unsigned Driver Installation Behavior. The three options for the unsigned driver behavior policy are the same as the options in the System Properties window shown earlier in Figure 4.6; they are just worded differently, as shown in the bulleted list in Step 3. To configure driver-signing options using local policy for a computer running Windows XP, follow these steps:

1. Click Start, Run; type `gpedit.msc`; and click OK.

2. Expand the `Computer Configuration¦Windows Settings¦Security Settings¦Local Policies` node and select the Security Options subnode.

3. Double-click the Devices: Unsigned Driver Installation Behavior policy, select one of the following options, and click OK:

> *Silently Succeed*—Selecting this setting ignores whether a driver is signed or not, allowing the user to proceed with the driver installation.

> *Warn But Allow Installation*—Selecting this setting issues a dialog box warning if an unsigned driver is encountered during a device installation. It gives the user the option of continuing with the installation or terminating the device's setup.

> *Do Not Allow Installation*—This option is the most restrictive of the three settings. To prevent the installation of any unsigned device drivers, you should select this option.

4. Exit from the Local Security Settings console.

Of course, because GPOs are applied via the local, domain, site, organizational unit (LDSO) methodology, local policy settings can be overridden by group policy settings within an Active Directory environment. Configuring the group policy for Devices: Unsigned Driver Installation Behavior is quite similar to working with the local policy setting; however, you must use the Group Policy Object Editor Microsoft Management Console (MMC) snap-in instead of the Local Security Settings MMC snap-in.

Working with USB Controllers and Hubs

Windows XP offers built-in support for many USB devices. Because all USB devices fully support PnP, USB peripherals can be easily connected to (and disconnected from) Windows XP computers that have USB ports by using standard USB cables and connectors. Windows XP Home and Windows XP Professional with Service Pack 1 (SP1) provide support for the USB 2.0 specification and are fully backward compatible with the USB 1.1 standard. In theory, USB devices can be safely connected and disconnected while the computer is running. Windows XP detects USB devices when they are plugged in to the computer and attempts to install the proper device driver for each detected USB device. If Windows XP cannot locate an appropriate device driver, it prompts you to insert a driver disk or CD-ROM from the manufacturer of the device.

To support USB, a computer needs either a USB host controller built in to the motherboard or a USB controller adapter card installed. The USB host controller directs all USB traffic and also serves as a hub to which USB devices connect. You can connect additional (external) USB hubs to connect multiple USB devices to the host controller, which is also known as the *root hub*. Hubs are either self-powered or bus-powered. Some devices, such as mice and keyboards, can function when plugged into bus-powered USB hubs. Other devices, such as external hard drives, printers, and scanners, might require more power than bus-powered hubs can provide. You should connect these kinds of USB devices to self-powered hubs. USB supports up to a maximum of 127 devices connected to one USB host controller (root hub) with no more than 7 tiers (7 layers of USB hubs daisy-chained together). You can use no more than five external hubs in one physical chain of hubs. Each device can be no more than 5 meters away from the port of the hub it is connected to.

 USB devices that install and function properly under Windows 98, Windows Me, or Windows 2000 are not guaranteed to work under Windows XP. Be sure to check for upgraded drivers before you upgrade a computer to Windows XP. Verify that USB peripherals are on the Windows XP HCL, or check with the USB device vendor regarding compatibility with Windows XP.

Viewing Power Allocations for USB Hubs

USB devices must share electrical power. The USB root hub is allocated a certain amount of power that any USB hubs and USB devices connected to it must share. As you add USB devices, less power is available to each connected device. To view power allocations for USB hubs, perform the following steps:

1. Open Device Manager.

2. Expand the entry for Universal Serial Bus Controllers.

3. Right-click USB Root Hub and then click Properties.

4. Click the Power tab to view the power consumed by each device in the Attached Devices list.

As mentioned, hubs for USB devices are either self-powered or bus-powered. Self-powered hubs (hubs plugged into an electrical outlet) provide maximum power to the device, whereas bus-powered hubs (hubs plugged only into another USB port) provide minimum power (see Figure 4.7). You should plug devices that require a lot of power, such as cameras and hard drives, into self-powered hubs.

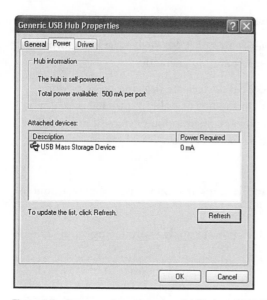

Figure 4.7   Power requirements and availability for a USB hub.

 In Device Manager, the Universal Serial Bus Controllers node appears only if you have a USB port installed on the computer. The Power tab appears only for USB hubs.

Troubleshooting USB Devices

Sometimes, when you install a USB device on a computer, the computer might start functioning poorly or the system might even freeze entirely. In such a scenario, power off the computer, wait about 60 seconds, and then power it back on. You might even need to completely disconnect the power for some newer devices that are power-management–aware. If that doesn't help, try one or more of the following steps:

➤ Follow the manufacturer's installation instructions, which might require that you run a setup program before connecting the USB device to the computer.

➤ Connect the device to a different computer to verify that it is not defective.

➤ Plug the device directly into a USB root hub on the back of the computer instead of plugging it into a USB hub that is daisy-chained off the root hub.

➤ Look at the Windows XP event log for USB-related error messages.

➤ Check Device Manager to verify that all USB devices on the Universal Serial Bus Controllers tree are operating correctly.

➤ Check whether one or more USB devices are drawing more power (more than 500 milliamps) than the bus or hub can provide. Use a separate power adapter for high power consumption devices (if available) or use a self-powered USB hub for such devices.

➤ Replace the USB cables.

➤ Make sure that no more than five hubs are connected in one continuous chain.

➤ Make sure that your computer's power supply is producing ample power. If necessary, replace it.

Working with NICs

Most, if not all, NICs on the market today are PnP PCI devices that Windows XP recognizes and installs automatically. If necessary, you can attempt to install non-PnP network adapters, or PnP NICs that are not detected automatically by using the Add New Hardware applet in the Control Panel. You can access the Network Connections applet from the Control Panel or by clicking Start, Settings, Network Connections if you use the classic Start menu. The following options are available from the Advanced menu of the Network Connections window:

➤ *Operator-Assisted Dialing*—You can enable or disable this feature for dial-up connections.

➤ *Dial-up Preferences*—You configure location information for dial-up connections with this option for settings such as country/region, area code/city code, carrier code, outside line access code, and tone or pulse dialing. You also can configure Autodial, Callback, and Diagnostics settings from this option.

➤ *Network Identification*—This option displays the Computer Name tab from the System Properties window, where you can change the computer's NetBIOS name and join the computer to a domain or a workgroup.

➤ *Bridge Connections*—You can join multiple network connections to form a network bridge by first selecting the connections in the Network Connections window and then clicking this option.

➤ *Advance Settings*—You can make changes to the binding order of protocols, bind and unbind protocols to network adapters, and modify the network provider order by selecting this option.

➤ *Optional Networking Components*—You can install or remove Windows XP additional networking components such as Management and Monitoring Tools (such as Simple Network Management Protocol [SNMP] and Windows Management Instrumentation [WMI]-SNMP Provider), Networking Services (such as Internet Gateway Device Discovery and Control Client, IPv6 Connection Firewall, Peer-to-Peer, Routing Information Protocol [RIP] Listener, Simple TCP/IP Services, and Universal Plug and Play), and Other Network File and Print Services (such as print services for Unix computers) by selecting this option.

Configuring Networking Connections and Protocols

Each network adapter has its own separate icon in the Network Connections folder. Right-click a network adapter icon (network connection) to access its properties.

In the properties dialog box, you can install protocols, change addresses, or perform any other configuration changes for the connection. The properties window for each network connection has three tabs: General, Authentication, and Advanced. The General tab displays the network adapter (NIC) for the connection along with the networking components for the connection. (Client for Microsoft Networks, File and Printer Sharing for Microsoft Networks, and Internet Protocol are the defaults.) You can also install, configure, and uninstall networking components from the General tab.

On the Authentication tab you can enable or disable IEEE 802.1x authentication. It is enabled by default. You can select the Extensible Authentication Protocol (EAP) to be used on the system from the EAP Type drop-down list box: Message Digest 5 (MD5)-Challenge, Protected EAP (PEAP), or Smart Card or Other Certificate (default). On the Advanced tab, you can turn on or off the Internet Connection Firewall (ICF) feature and the Internet Connection Sharing (ICS) feature. When you mark the check box for ICF, click the Settings button to configure advanced settings for ICF, as shown in Figure 4.8. The Services tab for ICF allows you to select which services (or ports) should be open for passing data through an Internet connection.

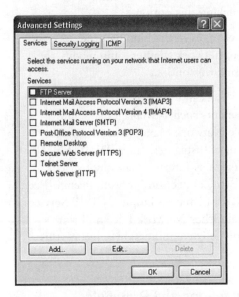

Figure 4.8   The Advanced Settings dialog box for configuring open ports under ICF.

Transmission Control Protocol/Internet Protocol (TCP/IP) is the default protocol installed by Windows XP, and it cannot be uninstalled. The properties window for Internet Protocol (TCP/IP) provides a new tab not present under Windows 2000 Server—Alternate Configuration (see Figure 4.9.) By using the Alternate Configuration tab, you can set up alternate IP settings that will be used if no Dynamic Host Configuration Protocol (DHCP) server is available. By clicking the Advanced button from the Internet Protocol (TCP/IP) Properties window, you can add default gateway IP addresses and metrics, configure Domain Name System (DNS) settings, configure Windows Internet Naming Service (WINS) settings, and set up TCP/IP filtering.

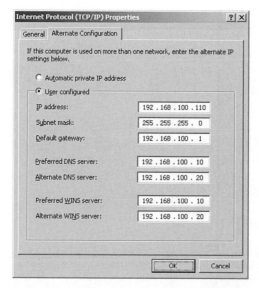

Figure 4.9   The Alternate Configuration tab on the TCP/IP Properties dialog box.

Setting Up Wireless Networking Support

Windows XP Home Edition and Windows XP Professional both include support for the IEEE standard 802.11 for wireless networks. The Wireless Configuration service is installed and enabled at startup by default. This service is responsible for handling the automatic configuration of wireless network adapters.

Wireless network support under Windows XP includes a new roaming feature that enables the operating system to detect a move to a new wireless access point and forces re-authentication to verify appropriate network access at a new location. By default, wireless network support under Windows XP uses the zero client configuration feature to automatically configure and use IEEE 802.1x authentication on the wireless network. (It includes the different "flavors" of wireless networking—802.11a, 802.11b, 802.11g, and so on.)

You can configure wireless networking settings by opening the Network Connections applet from the Control Panel, right-clicking the wireless connection you want to modify, and selecting Properties. Using the wireless connection's Properties dialog box, you can enable or disable the automatic wireless configuration, set up or disable IEEE 802.1x authentication, and specify a connection to a wireless network with or without a Wired Equivalent Privacy (WEP) Network Key, as shown in Figure 4.10.

Figure 4.10 Configuring Wireless Network connection properties.

Configuring and Troubleshooting Video Display Devices

When Windows XP is installed, your system's BIOS selects the primary video display adapter based on PCI slot order. You can install and configure additional video adapters by using the Display applet or the Add Hardware applet in the Control Panel.

Video problems often occur for one of three reasons:

➤ An incorrect video device driver is installed.

➤ The display settings for the video adapter are configured incorrectly.

➤ The graphics hardware acceleration setting is set too high.

If you select an incorrect video driver or if you configure a video driver's settings incorrectly, your Windows XP system can become unusable or even display the "blue screen of death." Fortunately, Windows XP offers several ways to restore the previous (functional) video display settings. When you restart the computer, press the F8 key as Windows XP is restarting, which enables you to select one of the following startup options (see Figure 4.11) from the Windows Advanced Options menu:

➤ *Safe Mode*—Enables you to manually update, remove, or even roll back the problem video driver.

➤ *Enable VGA Mode*—Boots the system using the current driver in standard VGA 640×480 resolution. You can then correct any incorrect video settings. Unlike Safe Mode, all other device drivers are loaded.

➤ *Last Known Good Configuration (Your Most Recent Settings That Worked)*—Enables you to revert the system's Registry and device-driver configurations to the last time that a user started the computer and logged on successfully.

```
Windows Advanced Options Menu
Please select an option:

    Safe Mode
    Safe Mode with Networking
    Safe Mode with Command Prompt

    Enable Boot Logging
    Enable VGA Mode
    Last Known Good Configuration (your most recent settings that worked)
    Directory Services Restore Mode (Windows domain controllers only)
    Debugging Mode

    Start Windows Normally
    Reboot

Use the up and down arrow keys to move the highlight to your choice.
```

Figure 4.11 The Windows Advanced Options startup menu.

Configuring Multiple-Monitor Support

Windows XP continues to support multiple-monitor functionality that effectively increases the size of your desktop. Multiple displays still must use PCI or Accelerated Graphics Port (AGP) port devices to work properly with Windows XP. PCI or AGP video adapters that are built into the motherboard are also supported under the multiple-monitor feature.

 You can combine up to 10 individual monitors to create a desktop large enough to display numerous programs, management consoles, and other windows.

Arranging Multiple Monitors

With multiple monitors, one monitor always serves as the primary display. It's the monitor on which you see the Logon dialog box when you start your computer. Most application programs, system windows, and dialog boxes display themselves on the primary monitor when you initially open them.

However, you can rearrange program windows, the Windows Explorer window, dialog boxes, and the like, and you can place them on the monitor of your choice. You can even set different resolutions and different color depths for each monitor. You can also connect multiple monitors to individual graphics adapters or to a single adapter that supports multiple outputs; computers with these types of video display adapters can take full advantage of the DualView feature of multiple-monitor support.

To arrange multiple monitors, perform the following steps:

1. Open the Display applet in the Control Panel.

2. Click the Settings tab.

3. Click and drag each monitor icon to the position that represents the physical arrangement of the monitors on your desk. Click either OK or Apply to view the changes. You can also click the Identify button to briefly flash each monitor's identifying number on each monitor's screen as assigned by Windows XP.

The positions of the monitor icons determine how you move windows and other objects from one monitor to another. For example, if you are using two monitors and you want to move objects from one monitor to another monitor by dragging them left or right, place the monitor icons side by side, as shown in Figure 4.12. If you want to move objects between monitors by dragging them up and down, place the monitor icons one above the other.

Figure 4.12 Arranging monitor icons in the Display Properties dialog box for the multiple monitor feature.

Troubleshooting the Multiple Monitor Feature

The default refresh frequency setting is typically 60Hz, although your monitors might support a higher setting. A higher refresh frequency might reduce flicker on your screens, but choosing a setting that is too high for your monitor could make your display unusable and might even damage your hardware. If the refresh frequency is set to anything higher than 60Hz and one or more of the monitor displays goes black when you start Windows XP, restart the system in Safe Mode. Change the refresh frequency for all monitors to 60Hz. If you are using unattended installation for computers, you might need to double-check this setting in your unattended installation script file, commonly named `unattend.txt`, to ensure that it is configured for 60Hz.

Managing Tape Backup Devices

Windows XP provides a high degree of flexibility and control for tape backup devices. You can back up or restore from tape devices, enable or disable specific tapes in your library, insert and eject media, and mount and dismount media. Tape devices are not the only media that the Backup Utility program supports. You can back up to network shares; to local hard drives; or to removable media such as Zip disks, Jaz disks, USB hard drives, and IEEE 1394 (FireWire) hard drives. Backing up to tape is still popular, however, despite some of its drawbacks.

The Windows XP Backup Utility does not support backing up directly to CD-R, CD-RW, DVD-R, DVD-RW, DVD+R, or DVD+RW media. You can copy files directly to a CD-R or a CD-RW disc, or you could copy a backup file that had been created by the Backup Utility to a CD-R or CD-RW disc. During a restore, the Windows XP Backup Utility can read directly from CD-R or CD-RW media to perform the restore procedure. Unfortunately, if the backed-up data to be restored exceeds the capacity of a single CD, both the backup and restore procedures become very labor-intensive and not very automated.

If the tape device is PnP-compliant, Windows XP ought to detect the device and install the appropriate drivers as well as allocate system resources for the device. If you are using a tape device that is not PnP-compliant, use the Add Hardware applet in the Control Panel to install the drivers and assign resources for the device. Use Device Manager to enable, disable, or adjust the settings for any tape device.

Upgrading a System from Uniprocessor to Multiprocessor

Unlike Windows 95, 98, and Me, Windows XP Professional supports up to two processors (CPUs). Windows XP Home does not include multiprocessor support. When more than one processor is present in the computer at the time that the operating system is installed, Windows XP Professional installs either the ACPI Multiprocessor Hardware Abstraction Layer (HAL) or the Multiprocessor Specification (MPS) Multiprocessor HAL. These HALs allow the operating system to support symmetric multiprocessing (SMP), which distributes processing tasks among the installed CPUs. If Windows XP is installed with just one CPU (a uniprocessor system) and you later want to add one or more processors (to create a multiprocessor system), you must use the Hardware Update Wizard to install a new HAL, to enable support for multiple processors.

To install support for multiple CPUs, perform the following steps:

1. Right-click My Computer and then select Properties.

2. Click the Hardware tab and then click the Device Manager button.

3. Expand the Computer node and note the type of support you currently have.

4. Right-click the icon for the current type of PC that is installed and select Update Driver to launch the Hardware Update Wizard.

5. Select the option Install from a List or Specific Location (Advanced) and click Next.

6. Click the option Don't Search. I Will Choose the Driver to Install and click Next.

7. Select the appropriate type of computer from the Model list box, or click the Have Disk button if you have a disk or CD from the manufacturer, and then click Next.

8. Click Finish to exit from the wizard. You must restart the computer for the change to take effect.

Changing a computer's HAL is never trivial. You should take great care whenever attempting to install a HAL. To upgrade the BIOS from supporting APM to ACPI, you'll need to reinstall Windows XP so that the operating system will properly support that type of upgrade.

Supported Multiprocessor HAL Updates

Windows XP supports only a few specific HAL updates because the installation of an incorrect HAL can render the operating system unusable. For a computer with the MPS Multiprocessor HAL installed, you can update the system to either of the following two HAL options:

➤ Standard PC HAL

➤ MPS Multiprocessor HAL (this is a re-installation option)

For a computer with the ACPI Multiprocessor HAL installed, you can update the system to any one of the following three HAL options:

➤ MPS Multiprocessor HAL

➤ ACPI PC HAL

➤ ACPI Multiprocessor HAL (this is a re-installation option)

 You cannot switch to the MPS Uniprocessor HAL or the ACPI Uniprocessor HAL if the computer already has a Multiprocessor HAL installed. *To install a Uniprocessor HAL for Multiprocessor HAL systems, you must reinstall Windows XP.*

Managing and Troubleshooting Hardware Profiles

A *hardware profile* stores configuration settings for a collection of devices and services. Windows XP can store multiple hardware profiles so that you can easily enable or disable devices to meet different needs depending on the circumstances.

Imagine a computer that has one or more external hard drives or tape backup drives connected. If those devices interfere with the computer when it's in production, you can boot the computer and use a hardware profile that disables those devices.

You create and manage hardware profiles using the System applet in the Control Panel or by right-clicking My Computer and choosing Properties. Inside the System applet, click the Hardware tab and click the Hardware Profiles button to open the Hardware Profiles dialog box

At installation, Windows XP creates a single hardware profile called Profile 1 (Current), which you can rename. To configure a new hardware profile, copy the default profile and rename it appropriately.

To configure hardware devices for the new profile, restart the computer and select the profile you want to configure. You enable or disable devices in a hardware profile using the device's properties dialog boxes in Device Manager. You enable or disable services in a hardware profile by using the Services MMC snap-in. The computer does not need to be restarted with a specific hardware profile when you configure services.

When more than one hardware profile exists, Windows XP displays the Hardware Profile/Configuration Recovery Menu each time the computer restarts, as shown in Figure 4.13.

 Do not confuse hardware profiles with user profiles: the two are not related! Hardware profiles deal with devices and services settings for the entire computer; user profiles deal with user configuration settings for individual users.

```
      Hardware Profile/Configuration Recovery Menu

This menu allows you to select a hardware profile
to be used when Windows is started.

If your system is not starting correctly, then you may switch to a
previous system configuration, which may overcome startup problems.
IMPORTANT: System configuration changes made since the last successful
startup will be discarded.

      Office
      Santa Monica
      Palo Alto
      Kansas City
      Vacation


Use the up and down arrow keys to move the highlight
to the selection you want. Then press ENTER.
To switch to the Last Known Good configuration, press 'L'.
To Exit this menu and restart your computer, press F3.
```

Figure 4.13   The Hardware Profile/Configuration Recovery Menu.

Managing Power Configurations and Settings

Using Power Options in Control Panel, you can create power configurations designed to extend battery life on laptops, create automatic power alarms, and monitor battery power levels.

Power schemes allow you to specify when to automatically turn off the monitor, turn off the hard disk, go into standby mode, or go into hibernation mode when your computer is either plugged in or using battery power. You can specify one setting for battery power and a different setting for AC power.

When Windows XP goes into standby, it turns off the monitor and hard disks while maintaining power to memory. When you bring the computer out of standby, your desktop appears exactly as you left it. You might want to save your work before putting your computer on standby because, while your computer is on standby, information maintained in memory is not saved to your hard disk. If there is an interruption in power, information in memory is lost.

To save even more power, Windows uses hibernation mode. The hibernate feature turns off your monitor, saves everything in memory on disk, and turns off the computer completely. When you restart the computer, your desktop is restored exactly as you left it.

Hibernation takes longer, of course, due to the transfer of all memory-stored data to the hard drive. Standby, however, is faster because it does not transfer the current data stored in memory to the hard drive.

You can be sure to expect a number of questions on the exam to come out of hibernation and standby. Your understanding of these options is likely to be tested.

Configuring and Troubleshooting ACPI Issues

The power options, like standby and hibernate, vary depending on the computer's hardware configuration. To use power options, the computer must be ACPI-compliant, meaning that all components are capable of power management. If one or more components are not capable of power management, you might either not have ACPI functionality or you might experience erratic behavior.

To take full advantage of PnP, you must use an ACPI computer, running in ACPI mode, and the hardware devices must be PnP. In an ACPI computer, the operating system, not the hardware, configures and monitors the computer.

ACPI lets the operating system direct power to devices as they need it, preventing unnecessary power demands on your system.

Configuring and Troubleshooting System Power Options

A number of concepts and considerations are crucial to supporting power management in Windows XP machines.

Users should put their computers in hibernation when away from the computer for an extended time or overnight. When they restart the computers, their desktops are restored exactly as they left them.

Typically, a user turns off his monitor or hard disk for a short period to conserve power. If he plans to be away from his computer for a while, the user should put his computer on standby, which puts the entire system in a low-power state.

To automatically put your computer into hibernation, you must be logged on as an administrator or a member of the Administrators group or Power Users group to complete this procedure, and you must have a computer that is set up by the manufacturer to support this option; you must have a computer whose components and BIOS support this option. If the Hibernate tab is unavailable, your computer does not support this feature.

If your computer is connected to a network, network policy settings might also prevent you from completing this procedure. Hibernation mode must be enabled before you can put a computer into hibernation. To enable hibernation mode, access Power Options in the Control Panel, and perform the following steps:

1. Open Power Options: click Start, (click Settings for the Classic Start menu), click Control Panel, click Performance and Maintenance, and then click Power Options.

2. Click the Hibernate tab, select the Enable Hibernation check box, and then click Apply. (If the Hibernate tab is unavailable, your computer does not support this feature.)

3. Click OK to close the Power Options dialog box.

4. Click Start, and then click Shut Down. In the What Do You Want the Computer to Do drop-down list, click Hibernate.

Laptops in standby mode might be security risks. For security purposes, you can configure Windows to always prompt you for a password when you resume. Follow these steps to complete this:

1. Open Power Options in Control Panel.

2. Click the Advanced tab, and then click Prompt for Password When Computer Resumes from Sleep. The password for which you will be prompted when the computer resumes is the password for the currently logged-on user account.

Do you want to configure Windows to notify users of impending loss of power? In the Alarms menu of the Power Options dialog box, you can set a low battery alarm, a critical battery alarm, or both. By default, the low battery alarm sounds when 10% of the battery power remains. A critical battery alarm sounds when your battery is down to 3% power. You can also combine these alarms with text messages and automatic hibernation to prevent loss of data.

When battery drainage occurs quickly, consider the amount of power your computer is consuming and the age of the battery. Both can reduce battery performance.

Exam Prep Questions

1. You are a desktop support technician. A user has a Windows XP laptop computer that he would like to configure to hibernate after 10 minutes. However, no hibernate option exists in the Power Options dialog box. You discover that the BIOS on the laptop computer is not ACPI-compliant.

   You download the latest BIOS update from the manufacturer's Web site and successfully install it. However, when you attempt to start the system after the update, the boot process fails and the system stops responding.

   Which of the following actions should you perform?

   ❑   A.   Reinstall Windows XP.

   ❑   B.   Restore from backup.

   ❑   C.   Enable ACPI support in the BIOS.

   ❑   D.   Go to Safe Mode and modify the hibernation options there.

   The correct answer is A. During installation of XP, if the system BIOS is ACPI compliant, XP installs the appropriate HAL to support ACPI. However, the installation on the laptop was made on a non-ACPI compliant foundation and therefore commanded a different version of HAL, one that will not boot the system once the BIOS is upgraded. Of the four answers, only one will update HAL to comply with the new BIOS. Answer B is incorrect. It will not change HAL. Answer C is incorrect; the problem is that ACPI is enabled, either automatically or by a command. If you could disable ACPI support, this might enable you to boot the laptop, but many ACPI BIOS settings are automatic. Answer D is incorrect because the system will not boot.

2. You are a desktop support technician for an insurance company that issues digital cameras to claims adjusters in the field. An agent who has a computer running Windows XP attaches his camera to a PC Card. The agent complains that while he is on flights to and from customer sites, his laptop battery drains very quickly while he works on reports. He does not use the camera while traveling between customers. He would like to extend the life of his battery as long as possible.

   Which of the following actions would you perform?

   ❑   A.   Configure a low-battery alarm notifying the agent when his battery drains to 15%.

   ❑   B.   Create an additional hardware profile in which the PC Card is disabled.

   ❑   C.   Enable Hibernation mode when the laptop is idle.

   ❑   D.   Enable Standby mode when the laptop is idle.

Answer B is correct. You use a second hardware profile designed to enable the PC Card only when the digital camera is needed and to disable the PC Card when the camera is not needed. This solution helps conserve battery power on flights. Answer A is incorrect; a low-battery alarm does not help to elongate battery life. Answer C and D elongate battery life, but the agent is using the laptop while on flights, and therefore automatic activation of either standby or hibernation is unlikely.

3. You are a desktop support technician. A user cannot install a network printer on her computer running Windows XP. She needs to print documents soon, and the only printer with sufficient capacity is this printer that will not install.

How can you help the user install the network printer?

❑   A. Remove the user's account from Power Users.

❑   B. Log on as administrator and install the printer yourself.

❑   C. Have the user download a new driver from the manufacturer's site on the Internet.

❑   D. Disable the computer policy that prevents users from installing print drivers for local printers.

Answer D is correct. By default, users can install only network printers. Only local administrators can install local printers and USB devices. The local policy "Devices: Prevent users from installing printer drivers, if enabled, prevents users from installing drivers for network printers. Apparently, this policy has been enabled. Answer A is incorrect. If the user were a member of the Power Users group, she would have been able to install the printer. Answer B is incorrect because installing under the administrator context would not make the printer available in the user's profile. Answer C is incorrect; a new driver will not empower a user to install a new printer.

4. You are a desktop support technician. To configure a computer running Windows XP with a USB mouse, keyboard, printer, scanner, and digital camera, you obtain a bus-powered USB hub with four ports. You connect all the devices, they are recognized and configured, and they work normally.

The user needs to back up her files and obtains a USB tape backup device. You have one remaining port on the USB hub. When you connect the device to the remaining port, it is not recognized and it does not work.

The device works when you plug it directly into the computer's USB port.

How would you configure the system to support all the devices?

❑   A.   Connect the USB tape backup device indirectly, through the printer's USB port.

❑   B.   Obtain a USB Y connector to extend the number of ports in the bus-powered hub.

❑   C.   Configure a custom hardware policy to disable the tape backup device.

❑   D.   Replace the hub with an active hub.

Answer D is correct. A hub receives its power from the computer to which it is attached or through a separate AC/DC power supply. The hub requires extra power to support the tape backup. The hub needs supplemental power provided by an external source. Answer A is incorrect because connecting a USB device through the printer does not increase the amount of available electricity. Answer B is incorrect because a USB Y connector does not increase the amount of available electricity in the USB hub. Answer C is incorrect because a custom policy that disables the tape backup device will disable the device.

5. You are a desktop support technician. You have recently upgraded a computer running Windows 98 Second Edition to Windows XP Professional. The user complains that the screen resolution is only 640×480 and 16 colors and that he is unable to change the settings in Control Panel. You log on to the computer and attempt to change the settings and are equally unsuccessful.

To enable a greater resolution and larger number of colors, what should you do?

❑   A.   Reinstall Windows XP Professional and obtain the latest service pack.

❑   B.   Restart the computer, access the Advanced Start Menu, and select VGA Mode.

❑   C.   Log on locally. Do not log onto a domain.

❑   D.   Re-install the Windows 98 video driver.

❑   E.   Install the correct video driver for the video card.

Answer E is correct; the limitation on display settings is controlled by the video driver. The driver installed on the computer might be corrupt or left over from the Windows 98 installation. Answer A is incorrect; neither a reinstallation or a service pack can provide an upgraded video driver, especially if it is unsupported hardware. Answer B is incorrect; selecting VGA mode does not enable any better video quality. Answer C is incorrect; a local logon will not enable any better video driver. Answer D is incorrect; the Windows 98 video driver more than likely is ineffective in a Windows XP environment.

6. You are a desktop support technician, and you successfully upgrade a computer running Windows 98 Second Edition to Windows XP Professional. A user complains that the display properties are stuck on 640×480 resolution and 16 colors. You obtain a Windows XP driver for the video card and complete its installation. You reboot the computer and discover that the display properties are still 640×480 and 16 colors.

   What should you do to modify the computer's display properties?

   ❑   A. Open the Display Properties in Control Panel, click Themes, and change the theme to the Windows default.

   ❑   B. Open the Display Properties in Control Panel, click Settings, and set the desired resolution and numbers of colors.

   ❑   C. Open the Display Properties in Control Panel, click Appearance, and modify the font size.

   ❑   D. Open the Display Properties in Control Panel, click Settings, click Advanced, and increase the dots per inch (DPI) setting.

   ❑   E. Reinstall the video driver.

   ❑   F. Obtain another video driver.

   Answer B is correct. Display properties are not modified immediately by Windows XP when a new driver is installed. To update the display properties, you must access the screen resolution and color quality settings in the Appearance sheet of the dialog box. Answer A is incorrect; changing themes does not necessarily update resolution and color quality. Answer C is incorrect; modifying the font size does not change resolution and color quality. Answer D is incorrect. DPI does not affect resolution nor color quality. Answers E and F are incorrect. There is no evidence that a faulty video driver needs to be reinstalled or replaced.

7. You are a desktop support technician, and a user working with a computer running Windows XP has obtained a PnP PC "combo" card that combines a modem and a NIC. She inserts the card, reboots the computer, and discovers that the devices appear in Device Manager...but they do not work.

Which of the following actions should you perform?

❑ A. Reboot the laptop again and "see what happens."

❑ B. Install the driver manually.

❑ C. Connect the mouse to a PS2/USB adapter and plug the interface into a USB port.

❑ D. Move the card to another slot on the motherboard.

Answer B is correct. You should obtain drivers from Microsoft or the manufacturer of the card and reinstall them yourself. Answer A is incorrect. There is no expectation that rebooting the computer a second time will enable the devices. After all, the devices do appear properly in Device Manager. Answer C is incorrect; diverting the mouse to a USB port will not enable the card to function properly. Windows is responsible for assigning resources to PnP devices and preventing conflicting settings. Answer D is incorrect; moving the card to another slot in the motherboard should have no impact. The devices are already recognized hardware by Windows XP.

8. You are a desktop support technician. A user has installed a new modem on his machine and complains that it is impossible to control the volume of the modem's speaker. Otherwise, the modem is working properly. You locate an updated version of the driver for the modem at the manufacturer's Web site. After you install it, the modem does not make any noise because it does not initialize! You want to restore the modem back to functionality.

What should you do?

❑ A. Restore Windows XP from the most recent backup.

❑ B. Use the Windows XP Recovery Console.

❑ C. Select Last Known Good Configuration

❑ D. Use Roll Back Driver.

Answer D is correct. The driver roll back feature is the quickest way to reset a device's settings to use the previously installed driver. Answer A is incorrect; restoring from backup is a tedious process. Answer B is incorrect; the Recovery Console is designed to remedy boot issues. It is not the first choice for a desktop support technician attempting to resolve a modem problem. Answer C is incorrect. The Last Known Good Configuration option is a troubleshooting technique used when the operating system refuses to boot.

9. You are a desktop support technician. You are installing a dozen new USB scanners on computers running Windows XP in your Windows Server 2003 domain. All goes smoothly, except on the computers running Windows XP in the Finance department, where you receive error messages which indicate that the driver for the scanner cannot be installed.

What actions should you take?

❑ A. Reinstall the driver.

❑ B. Configure the computers to display a warning if drivers are not digitally signed.

❑ C. Configure the computer to block any drivers that are not signed.

❑ D. Use the Add Hardware Wizard to install the driver.

Answer B is correct. By enabling a group policy, by configuring the local policy, or by editing System Properties of the computers running Windows XP in the Finance department, you can enable a warning message yet not block the installation of unsigned drivers with the command: "Warn: prompt me each time to choose an action." More than likely, for stability and security, the Finance department computers were configured to block the installation of all unsigned drivers. Answer A is incorrect. Installing a driver a second time will not remedy the block. Answer C is incorrect. "Blocking" all drivers is probably the current configuration. Answer D is incorrect; using the Add Hardware Wizard does not bypass the local driver signing configuration.

10. You are a desktop support technician. You have a user who works in the construction industry and travels to building sites to attend meetings. On site, she usually powers her laptop from available AC outlets. However, on occasion, power is not supplied to the building where the meeting occurs and she is forced to use battery power.

    The user complains that she has "lost" all her work when traveling on the road. You examine the dialog box in Figure 4.14. What is the most likely explanation?

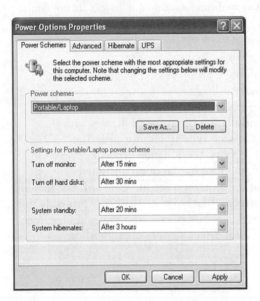

Figure 4.14   The Power Options Properties sheet.

- ❏ A. The battery life is only 4 hours.
- ❏ B. The battery life is only 2 hours.
- ❏ C. The data was never saved by the user.
- ❏ D. The battery alarm is not configured.

Answer B is correct. The battery failed before hibernation could happen. Answer A is incorrect. A battery life of 4 hours would have allowed time for hibernation to take place to preserve the files. Answer C is incorrect; a user does not have to save a file if hibernation works properly. Answer D is incorrect; a low battery alarm would not prolong battery life nor autosave files.

Need to Know More?

Wallace, Rick. *Microsoft Windows XP Professional Academic Learning Series*. Redmond, Washington: Microsoft Press, 2001.

Balter, Dan and Derek Melber. *MCSE/MCSA Exam Cram 2: Windows XP Professional*. Indianapolis, Indiana: Que Certification, 2002.

Stanek, William R. *Microsoft Windows XP Professional Administrator's Pocket Consultant*. Redmond, Washington: Microsoft Press, 2003.

Barker, Gord and Robert L. Bogue. *MCSE Training Guide (70-270): Windows XP Professional*. Indianapolis, Indiana: Que Publishing, 2002.

Microsoft Windows Team. *Microsoft Windows XP Professional Resource Kit Second Edition*. Redmond, Washington: Microsoft Press, 2003.

Search the Microsoft Product Support Services Knowledge Base on the Internet: http://support.microsoft.com. You can also search Microsoft TechNet on the Internet: http://www.microsoft.com/technet. Find technical information using keywords from this chapter such as supporting mobile users, tools for troubleshooting XP, troubleshooting XP startup, managing XP devices, and XP hardware.

Managing and Troubleshooting User and Desktop Settings

· ·

Terms you'll need to understand:

✓ Locales
✓ Language Interface Pack (LIP)
✓ StickyKeys, FilterKeys, and MouseKeys
✓ The Utility Manager
✓ The **AT** command
✓ Local, mandatory, and roaming profiles
✓ File Settings and Transfer (FAST) Wizard
✓ Fast user switching
✓ MSCONFIG

Techniques you'll need to master:

✓ Configuring desktop settings
✓ Configuring taskbar and menu settings
✓ Configuring multiple-language support
✓ Configuring Accessibility Options
✓ Configuring the fax service
✓ Configuring the Task Scheduler
✓ Configuring user profiles
✓ Configuring software installation packages
✓ Configuring program compatibility settings

As a desktop support professional, you must be able to configure and troubleshoot the desktop environment.

What follows is an overview of all the Windows XP desktop features that pays special attention to diagnostic and troubleshooting tools and techniques.

Configuring and Troubleshooting Desktop Settings

The Windows XP Professional desktop combines features of Windows 98, Windows Me, and Windows 2000. In general, local and domain user accounts that are not members of the Administrators group can configure few options on a Windows XP Professional computer. The following list is a summary of the most commonly used Control Panel applets:

➤ *Keyboard*—This option, shown in Figure 5.1, adjusts the cursor blink rate, the speed at which a character repeats when you hold down a key, and the time lapse before a character repeats.

Figure 5.1   Keyboard properties.

➤ *Display*—The Display applet, shown in Figure 5.2, has changed from Windows 2000. You can choose from five tabs to affect various aspects of the display:

Figure 5.2 Display properties.

1. *Themes* enable the user to choose from various Windows XP desktop visual display settings to customize the graphical experience. Themes consist of a background for the desktop plus a set of sounds, icons, and associated other elements that serve to personalize a Windows XP computer.

2. *Desktop* enables the user to select a background wallpaper or a background color for the Windows XP desktop. By clicking the Customize Desktop button, you can choose which icons appear on the desktop (the default is Recycle Bin only), modify the graphic for each icon, and run or schedule the Desktop Cleanup Wizard to move unused desktop items to a folder that you select.

3. *Screen Saver* selects a screen saver but is also a shortcut to the Power Options applet. The Power button on the Screen Saver tab enables you to adjust power schemes and configure Standby and Hibernate modes.

4. *Appearance* adjusts the window and button styles along with the color and font schemes that appear in all dialog boxes and windows. The *Effects* button gives the user the ability to turn on or off various effects such as menu and tooltip transitions, menu shadowing, and showing window contents while dragging. The *Advanced* button enables you to highly customize the color and fonts for the Windows XP environment.

5. *Settings* enable the user to set the screen resolution and the color quality for the video display adapter. If you encounter problems with the video display, you can click the *Troubleshoot* button to

invoke the Video Display Troubleshooter. If Windows XP doesn't detect a Plug and Play monitor, it assigns default color depths and resolutions. By clicking the *Advanced* button, you can adjust several properties for the video display and the display adapter, such as whether to apply new settings without restarting, adjusting the display mode, changing the refresh rate, altering hardware acceleration, and working with color management.

➤ *Sounds and Audio Devices*—This applet, shown in Figure 5.3, controls sounds for startup, logoff, and other Windows events. It also controls what WAV files are used for critical error alerts and general alerts. You can modify the default devices for voice playback and voice recording as well as work with the properties of various sound and audio hardware that might be installed on a particular PC.

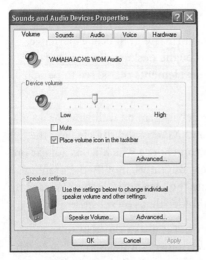

Figure 5.3   Sounds and Audio Devices properties.

➤ *Scanners and Cameras*—This applet enables you to manage scanned and photographic images. You use it to install digital cameras, scanners, or other image devices when the Plug and Play feature of Windows XP is unable to detect a device. To install an image device, you must be an administrator.

➤ *Speech*—The Speech applet invokes the Speech Properties dialog box in which you can control the text-to-speech voice selection, preview the voice selection, and specify the voice speed. You can also click the Audio Output button to specify the preferred audio output device and volume level.

➤ *Wireless Link*—The Wireless Link applet enables you to control infrared, image transfer, and wireless hardware settings for your computer's infrared port, if available.

Changing Settings for the Taskbar and Toolbars

The Taskbar and Start Menu applet, shown in Figure 5.4, gives you control over the appearance and behavior of both the taskbar and the Windows XP Start menu. Launching the Taskbar and Start Menu icon from the Control Panel invokes the Taskbar and Start Menu Properties dialog box. You can also access the Taskbar and Start Menu Properties dialog box by right-clicking a blank area on the taskbar and selecting Properties or by right-clicking a blank area on the Start menu itself and selecting Properties.

Figure 5.4 The Taskbar and Start Menu applet.

Windows XP follows in the footsteps of Windows 2000. You can easily arrange menu items by dragging and dropping them. You can drag a menu item from one submenu to another. Also, you can open context menus by right-clicking menu items.

Unlike Windows 2000, Windows XP does not hide the menu items that you've used infrequently. However, if you revert to the Classic Start Menu, Use Personalized Menus is enabled by default and items on the Start menu that are not used often are hidden. To disable this feature, right-click a blank area on the Start menu and select the Properties option to display the Start Menu tab of the Taskbar and Start Menu Properties dialog box. Click the

Customize button for the Classic Start Menu option to display the Customize Classic Start Menu dialog box. Deselect the Use Personalized Menus option.

You find more customization options when you click the Customize button for either the Start Menu or the Classic Start Menu off the Start Menu tab of the Taskbar and Start Menu Properties dialog box, as shown in Figure 5.5. On the Advanced tab of the Customize Start Menu dialog box, available options include opening submenus when you pause the mouse pointer over a parent menu item and highlighting newly installed programs on the Start menu.

Figure 5.5   The Advanced Start Menu options.

Other Taskbar Options

The taskbar serves as a multipurpose tool that makes navigating the interface easier. One of its options, Group Similar Taskbar Buttons, keeps together similar file icons on the taskbar while you are working on them. The option, located on the Taskbar tab of the Taskbar and Start Menu Properties dialog box, also automatically groups files opened with the same application into a single button if the taskbar becomes too crowded.

When you right-click a blank area on the taskbar, you can view many customization choices, including Lock the Taskbar. If you select Lock the Taskbar, you cannot move or size it; it remains stationary.

If you select the Toolbars option, you can add one or more additional toolbars onto the taskbar. You can add the Address, Links, Desktop, and Quick Launch toolbars. You can also add your own custom toolbar.

Changing Pointing Device Settings

The Mouse applet controls mouse button configuration for left-hand or right-hand use. It also adjusts the double-click speed and the rate at which the cursor moves across the screen (see Figure 5.6).

Figure 5.6 The Mouse Properties dialog box.

Configuring Support for Multiple Languages or Multiple Locations

You configure all regional and language settings through the Regional and Language Options applet, as shown in Figure 5.7, in the Control Panel folder.

The Regional Options tab on the Regional and Language Options dialog box defines the default locale.

A *locale* represents a unique language (region). As you might notice in Figure 5.7, English (United Kingdom) and English (United States) are different locales that share a common language but use different currency, date, and time formats.

To change the default settings for a locale, click the Customize button.

The choice of locales is inherited from the language collections installed in Windows XP. For example, to choose the Chinese (PRC) locale, you must install the East Asian languages collection.

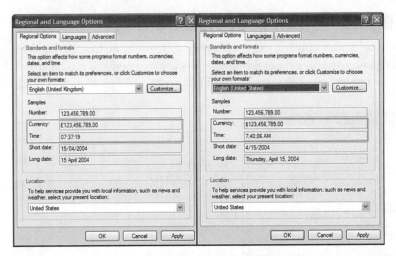

Figure 5.7 Comparing English (United Kingdom) to English (United States), an example of two different locales.

To use additional locales, install supplemental language collections using the dialog box's Language tab.

Enabling Multiple-Language Support

Microsoft has categorized the world's languages into three major language groups: Basic Collection, Complex Script Collection, and East Asian Collection.

You can add, remove, and configure support for input languages and associated keyboard layouts from the Languages tab on the Regional and Language Options dialog box, shown in Figure 5.8. From this tab, you can add supplemental language support for East Asian languages and add support for complex script and right-to-left languages.

Configuring and Troubleshooting Multiple-Language Support

After you install the necessary language groups, you can enable a specific input language by clicking the Details button to access the Text and Services and Input Languages dialog box, shown in Figure 5.9.

With the Text and Services Input Language dialog box, users can enable keyboard support for additional languages. Imagine a keyboard that can alternately type in Arabic (Saudi Arabia), Chinese (PRC), and English (United States).

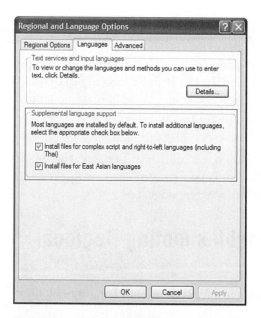

Figure 5.8   Installing supplemental support for additional languages.

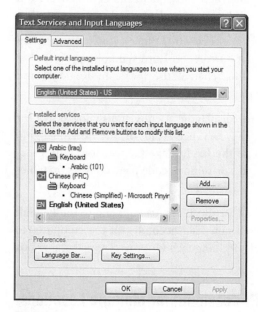

Figure 5.9   Enabling multiple input languages from the installed language groups.

After you enable an additional input language (besides the default language), an icon appears on the taskbar next to the system tray; it indicates the input language that is currently being used. A quick way to select input languages (besides assigning hotkeys) is to click the Language icon on the taskbar and then select the specific input language that you need.

The Basic language collection provides support for six language groups, which include the Russian, Greek, and Turkic. Because this language collection is installed by default, you can view documents typed in Russian, but you cannot edit the document in Russian until you add Russian as an *input* language.

By clicking the Key Settings button on the Text Services and Input Languages dialog box, you can assign keystroke combinations (hotkeys) to switch easily between different installed input languages.

Configuring and Troubleshooting Regional Settings

To troubleshoot regional settings, use the Regional and Language Options applet within the Control Panel.

The three pages of the dialog box and their subsequent submenus enable you to troubleshoot a large collection of language and regional setting options.

For example, if your selected locale is French (France), don't be surprised when you click the currency format button and Euro symbols appear rather than dollar symbols! You can either change the locale in Regional and Language Options or customize the default currency symbol.

To specify the language to use for displaying menus and dialog boxes for non-Unicode applications, use the Advanced tab of the Regional and Language Options dialog box. Use the Code Page Conversion Tables section, as shown in Figure 5.10, to add or remove code page conversion tables on Windows XP.

Click the Apply All Settings to the Current User Account and to the Default User Profile check box to allow all new user accounts on the computer to take advantage of all the Regional and Language Options regional dialog box settings that you configure.

Configuring Windows XP Professional for Multiple Locations

As a desktop support technician, you must thoroughly understand the Windows XP Professional features that you can use to benefit the mobile user.

As mentioned earlier, Windows XP provides the ability to easily switch currency and date formats and keyboard and input languages.

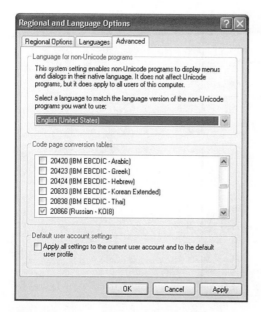

Figure 5.10   Troubleshooting non-Unicode applications.

Windows XP also supports the ability to keep in touch easily with locations elsewhere. In the Regional and Language Options program in the Control Panel, on the Regional Options page is an area entitled Location, which helps Windows Services provide you with local information such as news and weather.

For example, if you work in the United States but have family members in Vienna, you would choose Austria to view, by default, the news, sports, and weather information from there when you open a Web browser (see Figure 5.11). This feature is supported by only certain Internet providers, like Microsoft Network (MSN).

Finally, do not confuse Regional Options with localized versions of Windows XP. To provide Windows users with menu options and dialog boxes written in their own language, you must purchase a foreign-language version of Windows or the Multilingual User Interface Pack (MUI) for Windows XP or use the Windows XP Language Interface Pack (LIP), shown in Figure 5.12.

The Microsoft LIP provides a collection of foreign language skins that you can install in Windows XP Professional. For more information on these packages, go to http://www.microsoft.com/downloads/details.aspx?FamilyID= 0db2e8f9-79c4-4625-a07a-0cc1b341be7c&displaylang=en.

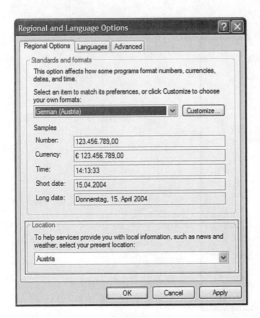

Figure 5.11   The Regional Options Location drop-down list box in Control Panel.

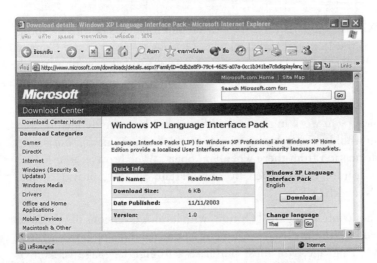

Figure 5.12   Windows XP and Internet Explorer after installing the Microsoft LIP, Thai Edition. Notice the toolbar and menus.

Configuring and Troubleshooting Accessibility Services

The Accessibility Options Control Panel applet, shown in Figure 5.13, contains five tabs: Keyboard, Sound, Display, Mouse, and General.

Figure 5.13   Configuring many accessibility options in Windows XP.

Several useful options are available on the Keyboard tab to control repeat rate and key combinations:

➤ *StickyKeys*—Enables a user to press multiple keystrokes, such as Ctrl+Alt+Del, by using one key at a time. Users also can enable StickyKeys and see the dialog box in Figure 5.14 by pressing the Shift key five times in succession. When enabled, StickyKeys displays an icon in the system tray. Double-clicking this icon opens the Accessibility Options applet.

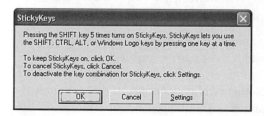

Figure 5.14   The StickyKeys message box and its system tray icon display after you press the Shift key five times in succession.

➤ *FilterKeys*—Slows down the keyboard repeat rate and makes Windows ignore repeated keystrokes. You can also enable FilterKeys and see the dialog box in Figure 5.15 by holding down the right Shift key for 8 seconds. When enabled, FilterKeys displays an icon in the shape of a stopwatch in the system tray.

Figure 5.15   The FilterKeys message box after holding down the right Shift key for 8 seconds.

➤ *ToggleKeys*—Causes Windows to play a high-pitched sound when a user presses the Num Lock, Caps Lock, or Scroll Lock key. You can also enable this feature by holding down the Num Lock key for 5 seconds.

On the Sound tab of Accessibility Options, you can enable the following two sound features to help notify users visually of warnings and other events:

➤ *SoundSentry*—Displays visual warnings when the *system* generates audible alerts. The feature is helpful for users with a hearing impairment. Users can configure when a sound is generated and how much of the screen flashes. You can Flash Active Caption Bar, Flash Active Window, or Flash Desktop.

➤ *ShowSounds*—Displays text captions as "closed captioning" on behalf of *programs* that use sounds to convey messages and information.

The Display tab of Accessibility Options enables you to aid users who are visually impaired. You can configure the following:

➤ *High Contrast*—To change the color scheme to a high-contrast scheme that allows for easier reading. As a shortcut, you can switch to high contrast by pressing the Alt + left Shift + Print Screen keys.

➤ *Cursor Options*—To adjust the blink rate for your Windows XP cursor. You can also set the cursor width to be narrower or wider.

If users are visually impaired, configure High Contrast. If the computer is a shared computer, you can configure accessibility features (including High Contrast) to turn off automatically. By default, the idle timeout interval is 5 minutes and configured in the General tab, discussed later.

The Mouse tab of Accessibility Options enables you to use the keyboard instead of a mouse to navigate:

➤ *MouseKeys*—Lets the numeric keypad replace the mouse. You can also configure the keypad to impersonate single-click, double-click, and drag-mouse actions. In addition, you also assign settings that control the pointer speed. As a shortcut, you can also enable this feature by pressing left Alt + left Shift + Num Lock.

The General tab of Accessibility Options enables a desktop support technician to specify overall settings for accessibility features:

➤ *Automatic Reset*—To turn off StickyKeys, FilterKeys, ToggleKeys, SoundSentry, High Contrast, and MouseKeys after a specified idle period passes.

➤ *Notification*—To activate alerts whenever an accessibility feature is turned on or off by having a warning message pop up or by having the system make a sound.

➤ *SerialKeys*—To provide access to alternative serial port input devices (such as puff-and-sip devices) for users who cannot use a standard keyboard

➤ *Administrative Options*—Include Apply All Settings to Logon Desktop, which allows the current user to use the accessibility options when logging on to the system. Apply All Settings to Defaults for New Users applies the accessibility options to all new user accounts.

You can configure additional security settings using the shortcuts in the Accessibility menu, shown in Figure 5.16. You can locate these tools by navigating to Start, All Programs, Accessories, Accessibility.

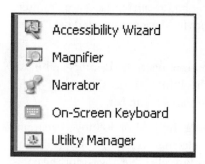

Figure 5.16 Additional accessibility options.

The menu provides three additional accessibility tools that are not available in the Accessibility Options applet in the Control Panel:

➤ *Narrator*—For people who have low vision or who are completely vision-impaired. The Narrator uses a synthesized voice to read menu options, text, dialog boxes, and alerts.

➤ *Magnifier*—Splits the screen into two regions, magnified and normal. The magnified portion of the screen magnifies the size of anything that the mouse pointer is hovering over in the normal window. You can increase or decrease the magnification level and the size of the magnification display area.

➤ *On-Screen Keyboard*—Displays a virtual keyboard on the Windows XP desktop. Users use the mouse pointer or a joystick to press the virtual keys.

The Utility Manager, located in the same menu, enables users to access and launch these three accessibility tools.

Users can start Utility Manager even before logging on to the computer by pressing the Windows key + U at the Welcome screen. Narrator, the built-in text-to-speech program, starts when Utility Manager opens so that users who have impaired vision can obtain immediate access to Utility Manager.

Using Utility Manager, you can configure Windows to automatically start accessibility programs each time you log on to your computer, when you lock your computer desktop, or when Utility Manager starts.

Configuring and Troubleshooting the Fax Service

Windows XP provides support for sending and receiving faxes via an internal or external modem or through a remote fax device connected over a network.

To install the fax service, click the Start button, open the Printers and Faxes folder, and select Set Up Faxing from the Printer Tasks section, or select File, Set Up Faxing from the Printers and Faxes menu bar.

Also, you can install fax service by opening the Add or Remove Programs applet from the Control Panel and selecting Add/Remove Windows Components. Mark the Fax Services check box, click Next, wait for the components to be installed, and then click Finish to complete the Windows Components Wizard.

After you install the fax service, you can configure the service using the Fax Console. After installing the fax service, the first time that you click Start, All Programs, Accessories, Communications, Fax, and Fax Console, the Fax Configuration Wizard launches.

By default, the fax service is configured only to allow users to send faxes, not receive them. To turn on the fax-receiving feature, mark the Enable Receive check box. A desktop support technician can also use the Fax Wizard, shown in Figure 5.17, to configure routing options—that is, whether to print a received fax on a certain print device and whether to store an additional copy of each fax within a specific folder.

Figure 5.17   The Fax Configuration Wizard enabling users to route incoming faxes to printers and shared folders.

After you complete the wizard, the Fax Console window opens. You can also access the Fax Console window by right-clicking the Fax icon in the Printers and Faxes folder and selecting Open from the pop-up menu or simply by double-clicking the Fax icon in the Printers and Faxes folder.

To fax a document, follow these steps:

1. Click File, Send a Fax from the Fax Console; click File, Print from an Application Program; or click File, Send to, and Fax Recipient.

2. If you select File, Print from within an application, select the fax printer and then click OK to submit the fax. Whichever of the options you choose, the Send Fax Wizard launches and asks you for transmission information, including the recipient's name and fax number.

You can use the Fax Console to both troubleshoot and monitor fax transmissions. With the Fax Console, you can

➤ Send a fax.

➤ Receive a fax.

➤ Change sender information.

➤ Manage personal cover pages.

➤ Check fax printer status.

➤ Run the Fax Configuration Wizard to reconfigure the fax service.

➤ Open the Fax Properties window.

➤ Launch the Fax Monitor.

The Fax Console window displays four folders named Incoming, Inbox, Outbox, and Sent Items for organizing faxes.

To troubleshoot failed faxes, verify that the user has permission to send or receive faxes and make sure that the fax device is configured to send and receive faxes.

If those settings are correct and faxes are still not being sent or received, stop and restart the fax service.

To adjust fax settings, right-click the Fax icon in the Printers and Faxes folder and select Properties.

The Fax Properties window, shown in Figure 5.18, displays seven tabs:

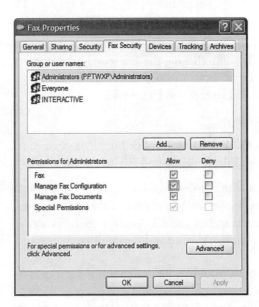

Figure 5.18 The Windows XP Professional Fax Properties window.

➤ *General*—Enables you to assign a location, comment, and configure specific fax features.

➤ *Sharing*—Not supported under Windows XP Professional.

➤ *Security*—Enables you to set printing permissions for a fax.

➤ *Fax Security*—Enables you to set fax permissions for a fax.

➤ *Devices*—Enables you to specify fax device settings and send and receive options for each device.

➤ *Tracking*—Enables you to specify a fax device to monitor and to set send and receive notification options.

➤ *Archives*—Enables you to specify whether to archive incoming and out-going faxes and where to store those archives.

You can configure fax security permissions by right-clicking the Fax icon in the Printers and Faxes folder and then selecting Properties. By default, three groups are assigned Fax Security permissions: Administrators, Everyone, and Interactive.

Members of the Everyone group, by default, can submit low- and normal-priority faxes. Interactive users, by default, can submit low-, normal-, or high-priority faxes. They can also view fax jobs, manage fax jobs, view the fax service configuration, and view incoming fax and outgoing fax archives. Administrators, by default, can additionally manage the fax service configuration and manage incoming and outgoing fax archives.

Managing and Troubleshooting the Task Scheduler

The Task Scheduler utility, designed to automatically run commands at specified times, can be useful to a desktop support technician who needs to automate repetitive procedures.

You can open the Scheduled Tasks folder, shown in Figure 5.19, from the Control Panel by double-clicking the Scheduled Tasks icon or by clicking Start, All Programs, Accessories, System Tools, Scheduled Tasks. Unlike Windows 2000 Professional, the Scheduled Tasks folder is not shared by default. You still can, however, create a task on a Windows XP computer and copy it to another Windows XP computer. This option is helpful if a similar task needs to run on many computers.

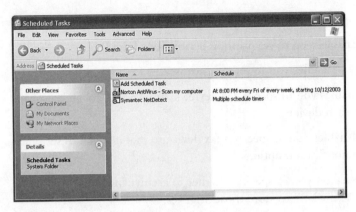

Figure 5.19 The Scheduled Tasks folder.

To create a new task, open the Scheduled Tasks folder and double-click the Add Scheduled Task icon to launch the Scheduled Task Wizard. This wizard steps you through the process of selecting a program, batch file, or a script to run automatically at a scheduled time. The Scheduled Tasks service runs under the security context of the Windows XP local system account. However, for each scheduled task, you must specify a user account and password that determines the security context under which each scheduled task will execute.

Perform the following steps to create an automated task using the Scheduled Tasks folder:

1. Double-click the Add Scheduled Task icon and then click Next at the Scheduled Task Wizard window.

2. Select the application program that you want to schedule from the list, or click Browse to locate the appropriate program and click Next.

3. Choose when the task should run and then click Next. The options are

   ➤ Daily

   ➤ Weekly

   ➤ Monthly

   ➤ One Time Only

   ➤ When My Computer Starts

   ➤ When I Log On

4. Depending on your choice in Step 3, you might have to set up what time of the day, what days of the week, or what months of the year the task should run. Choose the appropriate options and then click Next.

5. The next step requires you to enter a username and password. The username must have the right to run the selected application. Click Next.

6. The last dialog box of the wizard asks you whether to open the Advanced Properties dialog box after the task is created. The Properties dialog box enables the user to edit the schedule, delete the task if it is not scheduled to run again, stop the task, start the task during idle periods, and not start the task if the computer is running on batteries. Also, you can assign security permissions to the task to control which users can modify the task options. Click Finish.

After you close the Scheduled Task Wizard and the Advanced Properties sheet, Windows creates an icon that represents the task. After you create a task, double-click its icon to view and configure advanced properties.

 The Scheduled Task Wizard makes it easy to create tasks. However, sometimes, tasks fail to run. The most common reason is that the wrong username or password was entered for the task. If a task fails, verify that you entered the correct username and password for the security context under which the task runs.

Another area where an incorrect account can cause problems is if a task is created for old 16-bit applications. The task might fail to run because the *system* account, by default, is used on the Task Scheduler service. If a Task Scheduler service error is generated, modify the account used to run the service. To do so, go to Start, Control Panel, Administrative Tools and open the Services console. Right-click the Task Scheduler service and choose Properties. Edit the Log On properties tab highlighted in Figure 5.20.

To troubleshoot further, if a task doesn't run, you can stop and restart the Task Scheduler service. You can configure the service to restart automatically if it fails. To do so, click the Recovery tab of the Task Scheduler Properties dialog box shown in Figure 5.20 and specify actions for service failures.

 Windows XP still supports the legacy **AT** command-line utility to schedule commands and programs.

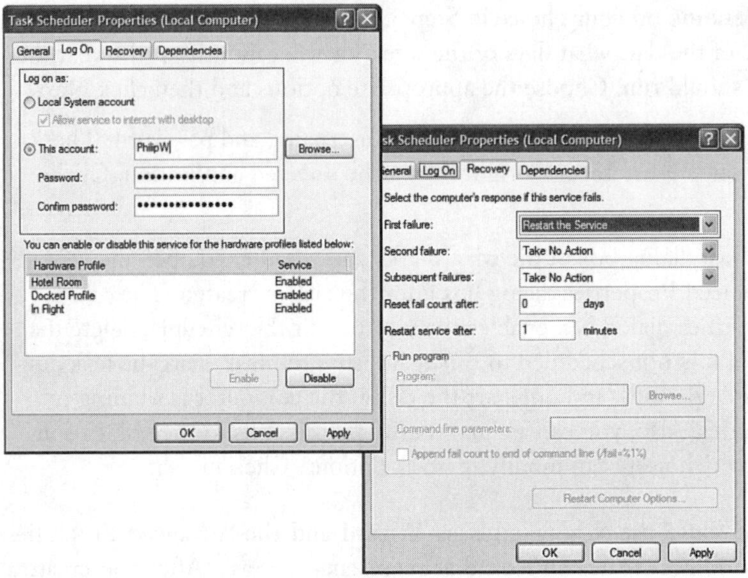

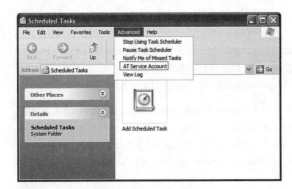

Figure 5.20 To troubleshoot task errors, customize Log On options and Recovery options for the Task Scheduler service.

Events scheduled using the AT command can run under a different security context than the Task Scheduler service. To do so, select Advanced, AT Service Account from the Scheduled Tasks folder's menu, shown in Figure 5.21. You can then specify a particular account whose security context will be used for all events that are scheduled using the AT command.

Figure 5.21 The Advanced menu of the Scheduled Tasks folder.

Configuring and Managing User Profiles

As a desktop support technician, you must understand the configuration of user profiles to troubleshoot Windows XP.

With the fundamental understanding that a profile is a collection of unique settings stored in the local Documents and Settings folder of a computer running Windows XP, a desktop support technician must be comfortable with the differences among roaming profiles, mandatory profiles, the All Users profile, and the Default User profile.

Each user of a computer running Windows XP has profile settings, originally created from the Default User profile and combined with the All Users profile. If you log on with administrative privileges, an index of all the current profiles is visible in the System Properties dialog box, as shown in Figure 5.22.

Figure 5.22 The User Profiles dialog box from the Advanced tab of the System Properties window. The user is logged in as PhilipW.

Profiles are merely a collection of folders and files stored locally or on a network server that sculpt and store each user's computer configuration.

There are three types of local profiles on a computer running Windows XP—Default User, All Users, and individual user profiles for each user who has logged on to the computer. The operating system uses the Default User profile as a template from which to establish the initial profile for all new local user accounts that do not already have a local profile. The All Users profile contains settings that are common to and shared by all users. Individual user profiles contain settings that are specific to each individual user.

Often, when you install an application on a computer running Windows XP, the program creates a Start menu shortcut and places it in the All Users profile in the `%systemdrive%\Documents and Settings` folder. Thus, the shortcut appears on everyone's Start menu. However, not all programs work in this fashion. Such programs only put a shortcut in your profile. Copy the shortcut to the All Users profile so that `all` users inherit the shortcut.

In Windows XP Professional, unlike Windows 2000 Professional, you cannot copy the profile of the current user account.

In the event that you want to copy the administrator user profile, you must log on using a different account (perhaps a temporary account) and then use the User Profiles dialog box to copy the profile for your administrator account. In Figure 5.22, a user is logged in as PhilipW; when the Administrator profile is highlighted, the Copy to button is available. After that, you can remove the temporary account.

You do not have to use the GUI Copy to feature from the User Profiles dialog to copy user profiles: you can simply use the Windows Explorer or a command-line tool such as **XCOPY** to copy user profile folders, as shown in Figure 5.23.

Figure 5.23 User Profile folder structure for the local administrator.

A user's permissions control how she can modify her Start menu because a user's Start menu is the culmination of her personal shortcuts in her profile and the short-cuts in the All Users profile. By default, members of the Power Users group on a computer running Windows XP have the Modify permission for this folder. Also, by default, users have Full Control of their own profile folders. If a user has write permissions to the All Users profile folder, she can modify those shortcuts, too.

A *mandatory* user profile enables administrators to configure standard desktop settings and apply those settings to user accounts. Users can modify their desktop settings while they are logged on to the domain, but those changes are not saved to the mandatory user profile when the users log off. To make a profile mandatory, rename the Ntuser.dat file in the profile to Ntuser.man.

According to Microsoft, if you need to maintain managed desktop configurations for groups of users or for groups of computers, you should consider using group policy settings instead of mandatory user profiles.

A *roaming* user profile is stored on a network share and is downloaded to a computer each time that a user logs on to the domain. The path to a roaming user profile is specified in the properties of the user's account. When a user logs off, the profile (along with any changes made during the session) is saved to the file server. By default, user profiles include the My Documents folder and can become very large. When a user logs on to a domain remotely over a slow connection, downloading a roaming profile could significantly impact performance.

Originally, the default behavior of roaming user profiles in Windows NT 4.0 was to include all the folders in the user profile directory. In other words, when a user logged on, all folders within the local profile folder were copied from the server to the client at logon and copied back at logoff.

In Windows XP, however, the History, Local Settings, Temp, and Temporary Internet Files folders do not roam by default. A desktop support technician can troubleshoot and configure other nonroaming folders using the group policy feature shown in Figure 5.24.

A *temporary* user profile is created any time that an error condition prevents a user's profile from being loaded. Temporary profiles are deleted at the end of each session. Hence, changes made by the user to his desktop settings or any other files in a temporary user profile are lost when the user logs off.

To prevent laptop users from downloading their roaming profiles to a laptop computer, you can enable the Only Allow Local User Profiles policy on all the laptop computers. You can configure this policy under the node Computer Configuration/Administrative Templates/System/User Profiles in the local computer policy Microsoft Management Console (MMC).

Figure 5.24 Customizing user profiles (by excluding directories) with a Windows XP local policy using **Gpedit.msc**.

You can also affect the same result by configuring other policies that define which connections should be deemed slow and that allow the use of a roaming profile only if the connection is deemed not slow.

To improve the Roaming Profile feature (which was occasionally thwarted by open Registry files after users logged off in Windows 2000), Windows XP now waits 60 seconds after a user logs off to save the user's Registry settings and then roams the profile correctly. In Windows 2000, if the profile is locked when a user logs off, Windows polls the profile for 60 seconds unsuccessfully and then quits!

Migrating User Settings with the File Settings and Transfer Wizard

The File Settings and Transfer (FAST) Wizard, shown in Figure 5.25, is a special GUI version of the User State Migration Tool that is available in the Windows 2000 Resource Kit. It enables you to migrate user files and settings from an older computer to a newer one.

Figure 5.25 FAST Wizard.

The FAST Wizard enables you to migrate Internet Explorer, Outlook Express, and Outlook settings; phone and modem options; fonts; folder options; taskbar settings; mouse and keyboard settings; network drives and printers folders; and user-specified files. The FAST Wizard supports three transfer techniques:

➤ By using direct cable connection using an RS-232 serial port or using a parallel (LPT) port

➤ By using removable media such as floppy disks or Zip disks

➤ By using other media or connections, including network drives or removable hard drives

The "source" computer that you want to transfer settings from must be running one of the following:

➤ Windows 95

➤ Windows 98/Windows 98 Second Edition (SE)

➤ Windows Millennium Edition (Me)

➤ Windows NT 4

➤ Windows 2000

➤ Windows XP

Although the FAST Wizard offers several options for copying user and application settings, the direct cable connection and the network connection options are the fastest and easiest methods.

Configuring and Troubleshooting Fast User Switching

Family members or co-workers who share one computer understand the "emergencies" that require one to use the computer while the other is still busy working on a project.

Fast user switching, a feature of Windows XP Home Edition and Windows XP Professional when it is not joined to a domain, enables you to quickly switch between users without actually logging off from the computer. Multiple users can share a computer and be logged on simultaneously, toggling back and forth without closing the programs they are running. Think of fast user switching between logons as a logon equivalent to Alt-tabbing between open applications.

When fast user switching is enabled, you can switch to another logon by clicking Start, Log Off, Switch User and then click the user account to which you want to switch.

You can configure fast user switching in the User Accounts applet in the Control Panel, shown in Figure 5.26.

Figure 5.26 Fast user switching in the User Accounts applet, which is available as long as you're not joined to a domain.

SerialKeys does not work when fast user switching is on. SerialKeys, described earlier in this chapter, is an accessibility feature that provides support so that users can use alternative input devices, such as single switch or puff-and-sip devices, in place of the computer's standard keyboard or mouse.

The fast user switching logoff option does not appear if it has not been turned on in User Accounts in Control Panel. Only administrators can turn on or off fast user switching. It cannot be turned off while multiple users are logged on to the computer. When fast user switching is disabled, programs shut down when you log off; the computer uses less overhead and generally runs faster for the next user who logs on.

Installing Applications by Using Windows Installer Packages

As a desktop support technician, you are expected to understand and troubleshoot the deployment of application packages. You must be comfortable explaining and configuring .msi files, .mst files, .zap files, and group policy objects (GPOs) within a Windows Active Directory environment.

With Windows 2000, Microsoft created a new method for installing applications called Windows Installer Service packages. This software installation service is integrated into Windows XP.

The Windows Installer Service has two essential functions:

➤ It is an operating system service that is responsible for installing, removing, and updating software by asking the Windows Installer Service package for instructions on how the application should be installed, removed, modified, or repaired.

➤ It establishes a standard method for installing, removing, or modifying applications.

After an application is installed, the Windows Installer Service checks the state of the application while it is being launched. This service provides "self-healing" capabilities to applications if they were installed as a Windows Installer Service package. The service is always checking to see whether the application needs to be repaired.

A Microsoft Installer file (MSI file) contains all the information necessary to tell the Windows Installer Service how the application should be installed. To take advantage of the features that Windows Installer Service offers, you must install an application as an MSI file. Applications such as Microsoft Office XP and Office 2003 have their own MSI files. Software developers must design their applications to use this new service. However, existing applications can still gain some of the functionality that MSI files have to offer.

A *Microsoft Transform (MST)* file can modify and customize an MSI file. Transform files contain the customizations; *MSI files themselves should never be altered.* A Microsoft Patch (MSP) file is a Windows Installer patch file used for deploying bug fixes or service releases of a software product. *Patch files* cannot remove components or features; change product codes; or remove or change the names of shortcuts, files, or Registry keys. *Application assignment scripts (AAS files)* contain instructions associated with the publication or assignment of a Windows Installer package.

You might be wondering what to do if you don't have an MSI file or if you can't repackage the file. Non-Windows Installer–based applications such as Install.exe and Setup.exe must use a ZAW down-level applications package (ZAP) file to publish a package. A *ZAP* file is just a text file with a .zap extension. The file provides information about how to install a program and the application's properties.

Publishing MSI Packages

You typically install MSI files over the network or locally on the client computer. A common method for installing MSI files in a Windows Active Directory domain environment is to *publish* or *assign* applications to users through Active Directory. Users (and computers) in Active Directory can be grouped into logical containers called organizational units (OUs). You can create a GPO setting for an OU that either publishes or assigns MSI files to users. Any users in the OU then have access to the published or assigned software programs when they log on to their Windows XP Professional computers.

Windows Installer, if an installation fails, automatically rolls back the installation. If the GPO still exists when the network connection resumes, the installation is restarted.

When you publish a software application using a GPO, you are making it available to one or more users and the *published application follows the users from workstation to workstation within an Active Directory domain.* Users install a published application from the Add/Remove Programs icon in the Windows Control Panel. *You may only publish an application to users*, not to computer objects.

 You cannot assign or publish Windows Installer packages through a local policy stored on a local computer.

When you assign a software application using a GPO, you are placing an icon for that application on the Start menu and associating its file extensions. *You may assign applications to both computers and users.* An assigned application actually gets installed the first time that a user opens the assigned program or attempts to open a file with a file extension that is registered to that application (such as sheet1.xls, which would be associated with Microsoft Excel).

A software package is typically *published* to users when it is *not mandatory* that they have a particular application installed on their computer. This is a means to make the applications available for users if they decide they want to use them. After you create a GPO to publish a software package, you can log on to your computer and find the published applications listed in the Add or Remove Programs applet in the Windows XP Control Panel.

Inside Add or Remove Programs, select the Add New Programs button to see which applications are published. Users can install a published application with user credentials because the Windows Installer Service installs the published application with elevated privileges on behalf of users.

This feature provides a central location for users to install applications. It saves users from having to search for network-shared folders that contain applications they want to install.

When an application is assigned, it is added to the Add New Programs button and a shortcut is placed on the Start, All Programs menu when users log on to their computers. The software is *not installed* until users select the shortcut for the first time.

 Software that has been published or assigned is also installed if users double-click a file with the file extension supported by the published or assigned application, such as an Excel worksheet or a Word document.

Specifying Program Compatibility Settings

Applications that worked under earlier versions of Windows might fail to operate properly under Windows XP for any one of a number of reasons: a program might expect older formats of Windows data, or it might expect user information, such as that in personal and temporary folders, to be in other locations or formats.

Under Windows XP, application programs offer a Compatibility tab on their properties sheets, shown in Figure 5.27.

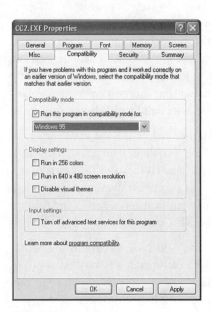

Figure 5.27   If you have trouble running a program, try editing compatibility properties.

On the Compatibility tab of an application's shortcut, you can configure several options related to compatibility. You can configure it to run in Windows 9x compatibility mode, Windows Me mode, Windows NT Workstation 4.0 with Service Pack (SP) 5 mode, or Windows 2000 mode. Under display settings, you can also specify that an application run with 256 colors and in 640×480 resolution. Making these changes, again, might enable an application to run properly that was originally written with those screen attributes in mind. This might be a solution if a legacy program, when launched, distorts your screen. You can also specify that an application run with visual themes disabled if an application's menus or other screen elements do not display properly with themes enabled.

When using the compatibility settings, the choices are applied *exclusively* to the application program when the program is launched from its customized shortcut. When the application is closed, the original settings are returned.

You can work with application compatibility settings from the GUI in one of two ways: use the Compatibility tab on the properties sheet for a program's executable file or its shortcut icon, or run the Program Compatibility Wizard, shown in Figure 5.28.

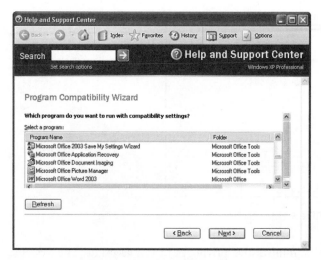

Figure 5.28 Program Compatibility Wizard.

To launch the Program Compatibility Wizard, click Start, All Programs, Accessories, Program Compatibility Wizard. The wizard leads you through all the option settings for running an older application under Windows XP. The wizard even prompts you to test the application so you can verify that it runs correctly.

When you complete the wizard, it saves the compatibility settings as part of the program's properties, which you can access by right-clicking the program's executable file, selecting properties, and clicking the Compatibility tab.

Using **MSCONFIG** for Troubleshooting and Customizing

The MSCONFIG.exe tool, shown in Figure 5.29, combines separate and important configuration files and settings into one central utility.

You can launch it from a command window or from the Start, Run box simply by typing **MSCONFIG** and clicking OK. (The file itself is located in the %systemroot%\pchealth\helpctr\binaries folder. The term %systemroot% is a Windows XP environment variable that denotes the location of the Windows folder, such as c:\windows.)

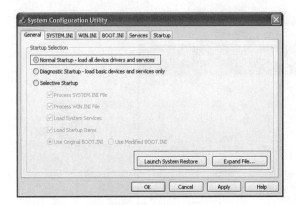

Figure 5.29 The **MSCONFIG.exe** system configuration utility.

A user does not need administrative privileges to run MSCONFIG. The System Configuration Utility has six tabs:

➤ *General*—Enables you to control system startup settings launch System Restore, and expand Windows XP setup files from compressed cabinet files.

➤ *SYSTEM.INI*—Enables you to directly edit the System.ini file instead of using Notepad or the SYSEDIT utility.

➤ *WIN.INI*—Enables you to directly edit the Win.ini file instead of using Notepad or the SYSEDIT utility.

➤ *BOOT.INI*—Enables you to modify the system's Boot.ini file, shown in Figure 5.30.

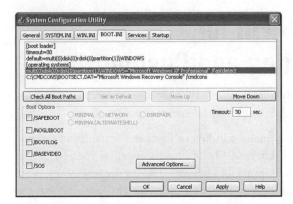

Figure 5.30 The **MSCONFIG** utility's **BOOT.INI** tab.

Although it doesn't allow you to actually edit each line-item entry, you can change many settings. You can change the default operating system, modify the timeout setting, and verify all boot paths. You can select from several predefined boot options, such as /SAFEBOOT, /NOGUIBOOT, /BOOTLOG, /BASEVIDEO (standard VGA), and /SOS (displaying system device drivers as they load into memory). You can also set advanced options such as /MAXMEM, /NUMPROC, /PCILOCK, and /DEBUG:

➤ /MAXEM—Controls the maximum amount of RAM that Windows XP Professional can use.

➤ /NUMPROC—Controls the maximum number of processors that Windows XP Professional can use.

➤ /PCILOCK—(on x86-based systems) Stops the operating system from dynamically assigning hardware input and output and interrupt request resources to PCI devices. It allows the BIOS to configure the devices.

➤ /DEBUG—Loads the Windows kernel debugger when you start Windows XP Professional.

➤ *Services*—Displays a list of all installed services and their current status (stopped or running) on the Windows XP computer. You can enable or disable each service for the next time the computer is restarted.

➤ *Startup*—Lists the programs and utilities that are configured to run at system startup. You can enable or disable each startup item to take effect at the next system restart.

Exam Prep Questions

1. You are a desktop support technician. You are asked to deploy an application to several divisions using Windows Installer and the Group Policy feature. You want to customize the appliation in different ways for different divisions. You are assured by developers that the applications can be packaged and you want to accomplish this task with the least administrative effort. How would you go about this?

   ❏ A. Use a separate **.msi** file and a separate **.mst** file for each division.

   ❏ B. Use one **.mst** file for all divisions. Use a separate **.msi** file for each division.

   ❏ C. Use one **.msi** file for all divisions. Use separate **.mst** files for each division.

   ❏ D. Use a separate **.msi** file for each division, a separate **.mst** file for each division, and one **.zap** file for all divisions.

   Answer C is correct. To customize the behavior of the .msi file, you must create a separate .mst transform file for each division. Transforms enable administrators to customize a Windows Installer package file. You can apply separate .mst files to a single .msi package. However, you must use .mst files in conjunction with .msi files at the time of deployment; you cannot apply them to existing installations. Answer A is incorrect because you don't need a separate .msi file for each division. Answer B is incorrect because you can't use one .mst file for all divisions. The .mst file is the file that customizes the generic .msi installation. Answer D is incorrect because a .zap file is used to provide installation instructions to the operating system for legacy applications. A .zap file is not necessary in this scenario.

2. You are a desktop support technician. You log on to a computer running Windows XP as the local administrator and install a specialize inventory management program. Multiple users share the computer, and afterward they complain that they cannot find a shortcut on the Start menu for the software program you installed. How do you fix the problem with the least adminitrative effort?

   ❏ A. Copy the shortcut from the Administrator profile to the All Users profile.

   ❏ B. Copy the All Users profile to the Default User profile.

   ❏ C. Copy each user's profile to All Users profile.

   ❏ D. Copy the shortcut from the Administrator profile to the the Default User profile.

Answer A is correct because the shortcut is only established in the administrator's profile. If you copy the shortcut to the All Users profile, all current and future users have the shortcut in their Start menus. Answer B is incorrect because the All Users profile does not have the shortcut created by the software installation. Answer C is incorrect because the shortcut does not exist in any user's profile. Answer D is incorrect because if you copy the shortcut to the default user profile, only new users of the computer inherit the shortcut, not current users.

3. You are a desktop support technician. One of the reporters in your news agency had been assigned to a trial in Europe. While reporting out of the Paris bureau office, the reporter's laptop was adjusted by the local desktop support technician to display the date, time, currency, and numbers in French format. With the trial concluded, the reporter returns to the States and needs her laptop to display the date, time, currency, and numbers in U.S. format. How do you make this change with the least administrative effort?

❑ A. In Regional and Language Options in Control Panel, on the Regional Options tab, select United States in Location.

❑ B. In Regional and Language Options in Control Panel, on the Settings tab, select English (United States)–US in Default Input Language.

❑ C. In Regional and Language Options in Control Panel, on the Regional Options tab, select English (United States) in Standards and Formats.

❑ D. In Regional and Language Options in Control Panel, on the Advanced tab, select English (United States) in Language for non-Unicode programs.

The correct answer is C. Settings for numbers, date, time, currency, are called locales. To switch to the U.S. English locale, you need to select Regional and Language options in the Control Panel, select Regional Options, and select English (United States) in Standards and Formats instead of France. Answer A is incorrect because location controls the location for which users want to receive weather and news, usually through a Web browser. It does not influence the way numbers, time, and so on are displayed. Answer B is incorrect because default input language specifies the language that is used to enter text, not the format of numbers, time, currency, and dates. Answer D is incorrect because there is no indication that there is a problem with a legacy application.

4. You are a desktop support technician. In accordance with the Americans with Disabilities Act, you configure a kiosk in the public library you administer with the High Contrast accessibility feature to accommodate library members who are visually challenged. All users log on to the computer in the library with the same logon name and password. You begin to receive complaints from some users who say the feature is "unnecessary" for them. How do you accommodate both sectors of the library with the least administrative effort?

❏   A.   Create separate user accounts with different color schemes.

❏   B.   Disable High Contrast when the computer is idle for 5 minutes.

❏   C.   Enable StickyKeys.

❏   D.   Enable Large Fonts.

The correct answer is B. By configuring the Accessibility options to disable high contrast when the computer is idle for 5 minutes, you can tell users to wait 5 minutes for the display to change. You can turn off accessibility features after they are idle for a specific amount of time. The feature is located on the General tab of the Accessibility Options program. This feature is useful for shared computers. Answer A is incorrect because separate accounts would be complicated to support. Answer C is incorrect because StickyKeys are designed for users with impaired dexterity. Answer D is incorrect because enabling large fonts would not provide different users with different settings.

5. You are a desktop support technician. Several users, all of whom are members of the local Power Users group, share a single computer running Windows XP. Company policy states that

➤   Users are allowed to create their own shortcuts on the Start menu.

➤   Shortcuts are available only to the user who created them.

➤   Users are not allowed to change shortcuts available to All Users.

How would ensure these stardards are met?

❏   A.   Ensure that these users do not have write permission on the **Documents and Settings\All Users** folder.

❏   B.   Disable sharing for the **Documents and Settings\Default User** folder.

❏   C.   Copy the Default User profile and use it to create each user's profile.

❏   D.   Redirect each user's **My Documents** folder to a file server.

Answer A is correct because it prevents Power Users from modifying the All Users profile folder. The All Users folder in Documents and Settings normally contains shortcuts available to all users. Removing the write ability on that folder prevents users from modifying those shortcuts. Answer B is incorrect because local profile folders are not shared by default. Answers C and D are incorrect because Power Users, by default, have modify permissions on the All Users profile folder. Answers C and D do not eliminate that permission.

6. You are a desktop support technician. After upgrading a group of computers running Windows 95 to Windows XP Professional, you are informed that a mission-critical database program no longer runs. When users start the application in Windows XP, the entire desktop becomes distorted and remains so, even when they stop the program. You need to prevent all other applications from being affected by those screen distortions. How could you do this?

❑ A. Configure the legacy database program to run in Windows 95 compatible mode.

❑ B. Modify the display settings in Compatibility.

❑ C. Change the monitor's DPI settings in Display Settings.

❑ D. Reinstall the database program.

The correct answer is B. On the Compatibility tab of a program running on computers running Windows XP (unlike in Windows 2000), you can configure display settings. Answer A is incorrect because there is nothing in the scenario that suggests the program isn't running properly; therefore, Windows 95 Compatibility mode is unnecessary. Answer C is incorrect because modifying the screen DPI just makes objects appear bigger or smaller; it doesn't affect screen resoltion or color settings. Answer D is incorrect because reinstalling the program would not remove screen distortions.

7. You are a desktop support technician. A user manages corporate insurance policies for clients throughout Europe. The user can view contracts written in Russian but cannot edit them. To enable editing of contracts written in Russian, you must configure Regional and Language Options in Control Panel.

Which of the following will enable editing of a foreign language file?

❑ A. From the Standards and Formats tab of Regional Options, select Russian.

❑ B. Enable install files for complex script and right-to-left languages (including Thai).

❑ C. On the Language Bar Settings page, enable the Russian language.

❑ D. On the Settings tab, beneath Installed Services, add Russian.

The correct answer is D. The user can view documents composed in Russian but cannot edit the document until she adds Russian as an input language. An input language specifies the language in which text is entered and the keyboard layout necessary to accommodate that language. Answer A is incorrect because if you select Russian from Standards and Formats on the Regional Options tab, the numbers, dates, time, and currency appear according to Russian language conventions. Answer B is incorrect because enabling Install Files for complex script and right-to-left languages (including Thai), you are installing the language files necessary for Arabic, Hebrew, and Vietnamese. Answer C is incorrect because the language bar settings configure options that control the location of the language bar that lists installed languages. It doesn't enable you to write in Russian.

8. You are a desktop support technician. Users report that when they launch an application on a computer running Windows XP, the screen appears distorted. What do you do to fix the problem?

   ❑ A. Change the color scheme.
   ❑ B. Configure the application to run with different display settings.
   ❑ C. Configure the application to run in a separate memory space.
   ❑ D. Obtain and install a new video driver.

The correct answer is B. This question reflects the difference between Windows 2000 and Windows XP. On the Compatibility tab of the application's shortcut, you can configure several options related to compatibility, including display settings. In the past, you might have tried to change display settings in Control Panel. That would make the changes global. In Windows XP compatibility settings are applied exclusively to the program initialized by the shortcut. When you close the application, the original settings are returned. Answer A is incorrect because changing the current color scheme should have little impact on the distorted screen appearance. Answer C is incorrect because running the program in its own memory space is applicable to 16-bit programs that run in virtual DOS machines and should have no impact. Answer D is incorrect because, according to the scenario, there is no problem with the video driver.

9. You are a desktop support technician. Your company selected a new software application and you need to deploy it with the least administrative effort. You package the program using Windows Installer, add the package to a group policy, and link the policy to an OU that encompasses the users for which the program is intended. Using network tools, you begin the rollout of the application package. Suddenly, the network connection between the file server and the workstaion fails. Once the connection to the server is restored, you must ensure that the program deployed successfully.

What should you do?

- ❏ A. Do nothing. The deployment resumes automatically when the connection is restored.
- ❏ B. Delete and re-create the installation package.
- ❏ C. Uninstall the program on each user's computer.
- ❏ D. Copy the installation package to everyone's hard drive and run the installation locally.

The correct answer is A. This is a question about the nature of Windows Installer. The benefit of the Windows installer service is that if an installation fails, it automatically rolls back the installation. Therefore, you should not need to do anything. If the group policy containing the package still exists when the netowork connection resumes, the installation restarts. Answer B is incorrect because deleting and re-creating the package does not repair an installation. There is also no indication that the problem that caused the network outage was related to a faulty installation package. Answer C is incorrect because the installation package, when it redeploys, automatically repairs a partial or incomplete installation. Answer D is incorrect because it is an unnecessary and inconvenient solution. You do not need to copy the MSI file to each user's computer.

10. You are a desktop support technician. One day, a user notices that everytime he goes to **http://www.google.com**, the menus appear in French, and the screen says Google Francais. When other users on the network navigate to **http://www.google.com**, they see a Web page written in English.

What is the most likely reason for this?

- ❏ A. The user has an incorrect default gateway address.
- ❏ B. The user has chosen, under Standards and Formats, French (France) in Regional and Language Options.
- ❏ C. The user has chosen, under Location, France in Regional and Language Options.
- ❏ D. The user has an incorrect DNS server configuration.

The correct answer is B. When you change the locale of a computer running Windows XP, not only do the default values for standards and formats change to match the chosen region, but also Google modifies its screen to match your preference. Answer A is incorrect because the default gateway, if misconfigured, would prevent Internet access, not affect the appearance of a Web page. Answer C is incorrect because modifying the location in the Regional and Language Options controls news and weather services, not the language in which a Web page is written. Answer D is incorrect; there is no evidence of a faulty Domain Name System (DNS) server. All the other users in the office are directed to a Google Web page written in English.

Need to Know More?

Wallace, Rick. *Microsoft Windows XP Professional Academic Learning Series*. Redmond, Washington: Microsoft Press, 2001.

Balter, Dan and Derek Melber. *MCSE/MCSA Exam Cram 2: Windows XP Professional*. Indianapolis, Indiana: Que Certification, 2002.

Stanek, William R. *Microsoft Windows XP Professional Administrator's Pocket Consultant*. Redmond, Washington: Microsoft Press, 2003.

Barker, Gord and Robert L. Bogue. *MCSE Training Guide (70-270): Windows XP Professional*. Indianapolis, Indiana: Que Publishing, 2002.

Microsoft Windows Team. *Microsoft Windows XP Professional Resource Kit Second Edition*. Redmond, Washington: Microsoft Press, 2003.

Search the Microsoft Product Support Services Knowledge Base on the Internet: http://support.microsoft.com. You can also search Microsoft TechNet on the Internet: http://www.microsoft.com/technet. Find technical information using keywords from this chapter, such as Accessibility Wizard, user profiles, .MSI files, multilingual solutions, Microsoft LIP, Task Scheduler, FAST, fast user switching, faxing in Windows XP, application compatibility technologies, and MSCONFIG.

6

Troubleshooting Local Security, System Startup, and User Logon Problems

. . . .

Terms you'll need to understand:

✓ Local users
✓ Local groups
✓ User profiles
✓ Log on Locally
✓ Logon Security Policy MMC
✓ Group policies
✓ Software restriction policies
✓ Security Configuration and Analysis Snap-in
✓ Security templates
✓ Last Known Good Configuration
✓ **Bootcfg**
✓ sc.exe

Techniques you'll need to master:

✓ Analyzing and modifying security settings
✓ Creating and configuring local and domain user accounts
✓ Troubleshooting software restriction policies
✓ Troubleshooting startup problems
✓ Troubleshooting logon problems
✓ Configuring user rights

As a desktop support professional, you must be able to configure and troubleshoot a variety of Windows XP security-related features, programs, and settings. This chapter focuses on security in terms of local and domain accounts, user and group rights, security configuration with group policy objects (GPOs), the Security Configuration and Analysis Microsoft Management Console (MMC) snap-in, and the logistics of logons.

Local User Accounts

If it weren't for individual user accounts, we'd all log on and have the same menu settings, privileges, and files. By enabling multiple user accounts, Windows XP provides a way for users to protect their files from others, even from another user account on the same computer. It also provides a way to differentiate the patchwork of user preferences and properties known as the user's profile.

Local user accounts that exist on a computer running Windows XP enable a user to log on by means of credentials stored in the local system, rather than by values stored centrally on an authenticating server, known as a domain controller. The Windows NT 4.0 Server, Windows 2000 Server, and Windows Server 2003 operating systems have the ability to be configured as domain controllers.

A desktop support technician must understand the distinction between a local and a domain account and how each is represented by the *user profiles* that are stored on a computer running Windows XP. The accounts are visible in the User Profiles page of the System Properties dialog box, as shown in Figure 6.1.

Figure 6.1 Multiple profiles displayed within the User Profiles dialog box.

The profiles in Figure 6.1 are the direct result of a local user named Administrator on the computer running Windows XP. There are a total of three profiles on the computer: the domain administrator, the local administrator, and a user named ExamCram.

There can be as few as one local user account on a computer running Windows XP, the local administrator account. All members of the Users local group and the Administrators local group are permitted to log on to the computer as well. In Figure 6.2, the local Administrators group consists of a local account named Administrator, a global domain group named Domain Admins, and a domain account named PhilipW. In other words, all members of the Domain Admins group, Administrator, and PhilipW have administrative privileges on this computer.

Figure 6.2 Local users group membership and local administrators group membership displayed side by side.

Microsoft provides centralized authentication services through two mechanisms: Windows NT Server domain controllers and the Active Directory service, which can only reside on computers running Windows 2000 Server and Windows Server 2003.

When a user logs on, as shown in Figure 6.3, the user can log on to a domain (if a domain exists) or onto the workstation. It all depends on whether the user account is a local account or a domain account.

Managing and Troubleshooting Local User Accounts

When users are unable to log on, check the status of their accounts. You can manage local user accounts in either the User Accounts Control Panel applet or the Local Users and Groups MMC shown in Figure 6.3. You can also manage local users remotely by configuring the Local Users and Groups snap-in to point to a different computer running Windows XP on which you have local administrative privileges, as shown in Figure 6.4.

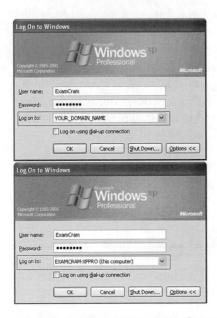

Figure 6.3 Top: logging on to a domain; Bottom: logging onto the local computer.

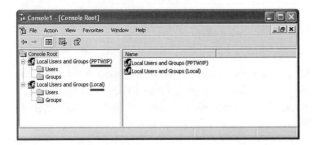

Figure 6.4 Using a custom MMC to manage local user accounts on two separate computers running Windows XP.

Creating and Modifying Local Users and Groups

Domain accounts give you access to the network and access to network resources that have been permitted to you. Local accounts are created on individual computers running Windows XP and give you access to the machine and local files you have created or those to which you've been given local permissions.

If an account is specific to a local computer, the user cannot access network-based resources *unless* the resources are configured to allow anonymous access.

Local user accounts live in a database on the local machine named the Security Accounts Manager (SAM). You create user accounts with the User Accounts applet in the Control Panel or with the Local Users and Groups MMC.

Two user accounts—administrator and guest—are created automatically when Windows XP Professional is installed. You can use the administrator account to initially log on locally and configure the computer.

There are three types of local user accounts in Windows XP Professional:

➤ *Computer administrator*—Atomatically has full and complete rights to the computer. It is created during the installation and setup of Windows XP Professional. You can't delete it, but you can rename it. You should consider renaming the administrator account to disguise it and make it more difficult for potential hackers to gain control of the system. The administrator can take ownership of files and other objects on the computer. It can also install software that will be available to all users. To create new local user accounts, first log on as the local computer administrator. To increase security, ensure that the administrator account has a complex password.

➤ *Limited*—Less powerful than the administrator account, limited accounts are used by "mere mortals" to access system resources. Limited accounts can change their own passwords. Unlike the administrator and guest accounts, they are not created by default.

➤ *Guest*—The built-in guest account allows users to log on to the computer without using a unique account. It has no password. With the guest account enabled, you can allow multiple users to log on and access local resources without having to create and manage separate accounts for each person. On the one hand, in a workgroup environment, it simplifies file and printer sharing by reducing the need to create separate user accounts. On the other hand, it sacrifices auditing information because different individuals share the same account. It is disabled by default.

The guest account is not an "authenticated user;" It is not a member of the built-in Authenticated Users group. When logged on interactively, the guest account is a member of the local security group named Guests and the local security group named Users. When logged on over the network, the local guest account is only a member of the local Guests group.

The Computer Management MMC tool provides a collection of MMC snap-ins for performing common computer-management tasks or gathering information about local or remote computers. Using Computer Management, you can quickly view information about local users and groups accounts.

To view the local user and security group information of a remote computer, right-click My Computer, and click Manage. In the Computer Management console, you can see local User and Groups, or switch to view another computer's local users and groups by right-clicking Computer Management (local) and clicking Connect to Another Computer.

 To protect files from unauthorized use, users can often password-protect those files, but password protection is not provided by Windows XP. Users can encrypt files using the Encrypted File System (EFS), a Windows XP feature of NTFS-formatted drives. When a file is encrypted, it can be viewed only by the user who encrypted it, data recovery agents, and users whom the user explicitly designates.

Managing and Troubleshooting Local Security Settings

The easiest way to manage and troubleshoot local security settings is with the Local Security Policy MMC. The Local Security Policy MMC links directly to account policies, local policies, public key policies, software restriction policies, and IPSec policies.

To launch the Local Security Policy Editor in Windows XP, choose Start, Run; type `secpol.msc`; and press Enter.

If the computer is a member of an Active Directory domain, the local policies that you see in the Local Security Policy MMC may have been created on the local machine or may be the product of a GPO. GPOs contain security settings that are inherited by domain members.

If you want to modify the local security settings of a number of computers running Windows XP, create a GPO on a domain controller and link it to the domain or an organization unit (OU) of which the computer is a member.

Editing Local Policy Settings

Local policies comprise a collection of values that control the behavior of Windows XP system. In fact, they include the local security policies.

Local policies, shown in Figure 6.5, are representations of values stored in the Registry of Windows XP. They can be edited locally or remotely. They can also be modified by a GPO that resides on a domain controller.

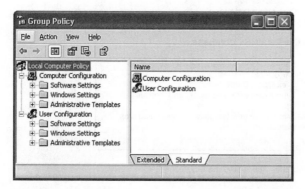

Figure 6.5   The local policy on a computer running Windows XP Professional.

To view the local policy on a Windows XP machine, you can use the MMC titled Group Policy. To launch this MMC in Windows XP, type the command **gpedit.msc** in the Run dialog box and press Enter.

Using the Security Configuration and Analysis Tool

The Security Configuration and Analysis tool, shown in Figure 6.6, is an MMC that enables desktop support technicians to compare current Windows XP configurations with predefined template settings.

You can create your own custom security configuration template or you can import a predefined Microsoft security template. The Security Configuration and Analysis tool uses a security database file generated from the template to compare the current computer settings against the database.

Several predefined security templates ship with Windows XP Professional, such as compatws.inf for compatible workstation settings, securews.inf for secure workstation settings, and hisecws.inf high-security workstation settings. You find these default security template files in the %systemroot%\security\templates folder.

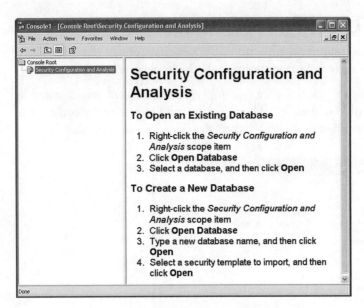

Figure 6.6 The Security Configuration and Analysis MMC snap-in.

To access the Security Configuration and Analysis tool and build an MMC that contains it, follow these steps:

1. Click Start to open the Start menu.

2. Click Run.

3. Type MMC and then click OK to open an empty console.

4. Click File and then click Add/Remove Snap In to open the Add/Remove Snap-In dialog box.

5. Click Add, scroll down the list of snap-ins, and click Security Configuration and Analysis.

6. Click Add and then click Close to close the snap-in list box.

7. Click OK to complete the adding of snap-ins.

8. Click File, Save; type `Security and Configuration and Analysis`; and then click Save to save the snap-in you've just created.

Troubleshooting Active Directory Security Policies

A desktop support technician needs to be able to analyze the effects of group policy security settings on member workstations or user accounts in a domain.

Group policies at the domain level can be linked to the domain, site, or OUs in which a computer or user account is located.

The Resultant Set of Policy (RSoP) snap-in (RSoP.msc), shown in Figure 6.7, enables a desktop support technician to poll and evaluate the cumulative effect that GPOs have on computers and users.

To start the Resultant Set of Policy snap-in, click Start, Run; type rsop.msc; and press Enter.

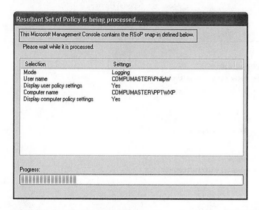

Figure 6.7 RSoP processing.

When the RSoP program completes its analysis, as shown in Figure 6.8, it displays the results.

The RSoP MMC is a recent release from Microsoft and replaces the Group Policy Result command, GPResult.exe, which also enables a desktop support technician to view and output a list, as shown in Figure 6.10, of the results of group policy settings on the local computer running Windows XP.

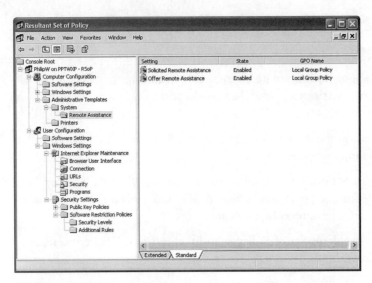

Figure 6.8 The RSoP results display.

Figure 6.9 An analysis report from the **GPResult.exe** command.

Managing and Troubleshooting Local User Rights

Local user rights represent the general privileges a user has while working at a computer. If you need to know who has the right to shut down the system or log on locally, check user rights.

Local user rights are displayed and modified within the local policy settings of the local machine, shown in Figure 6.10. They are also viewable with the Security Policy MMC tool. You can find local user rights under Security Settings/Local Policies, User Rights Assignment.

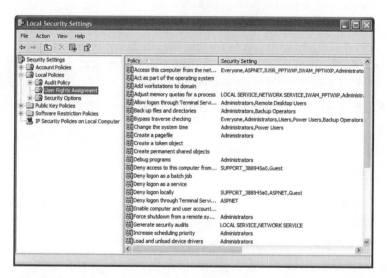

Figure 6.10   Local User Rights Assignment settings for local policy.

There are 37 separate rights built into Windows XP. Explicit Deny settings *always* take precedence over explicit or implicit Allow settings.

For example, members of the Authenticated Users group are permitted to add up to 10 computers to an Active Directory domain. To add more than 10 computers, a user must be explicitly given that permission in the Active Directory. You can do this manually or with the Active Directory Delegation Wizard. This policy would be local to a computer acting as a domain controller, where the computer accounts are stored. It is not a workstation configuration.

Managing and Troubleshooting Local User Settings

The procedures for managing and troubleshooting local user settings depend on whether the computer and user are part of a domain or a workgroup.

In a non-networked (workgroup) environment, local user accounts should be limited to an administrator account and those that are necessary for access to the computer. A user does not need to be an administrator to gain access to the machine. Logging on with unnecessary administrator rights elevates the dangers of malicious code. Consider configuring machines with a minimum of user accounts, with the least privileges necessary.

When you add a local user to a computer running Windows XP, you are allowing him or her to have access to files on the computer. If the computer is a member of a domain, you can add a domain user to the local machine or create a new user account that is not a domain account.

To add local user account to a computer running Windows XP, follow these steps:

1. In Control Panel, open User Accounts.

2. On the Users tab, click Add.

3. Type the username and the domain name to which the user belongs. (This step adds a domain account to the local computer.)

4. To create a new local account on the computer, use the Advanced tab.

5. Click the Advanced button in the Advanced user Management section of the Advanced tab, shown in Figure 6.11, to open the Local Users and Groups MMC.

6. Right-click the Users folder and click New User.

7. In the New User dialog box, provide the username, full name, description, and password and confirm the password.

8. Click Create.

When you successfully add a domain user account to the local computer, you are giving an existing user account permission to use the computer. You can only add existing domain users to the local computer by using the User Accounts applet. You should not add new a user to the Local Administrators group unless that user will be performing tasks locally that require administrative permission.

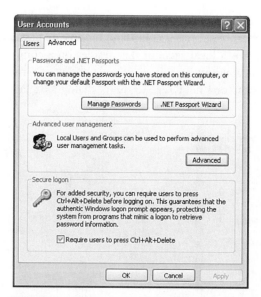

Figure 6.11 The Advanced button under Advanced User Management on the Advanced Settings tab for User Accounts.

You can also use the Users applet to modify the properties of an existing local user account domain. In the Users applet, select the User whom you want to modify and click Properties.

In the User Properties dialog box, you can control the name of the local group of which the account is a member—Standard User (Power User), Restricted User (Users), or Other (Administrators and other local groups).

In User Properties dialog box, a user can be configured to be a member of a single group.

If you use the Local Users and Groups MMC, however, you can add a single user to multiple groups. You can also make groups members of other groups. The Local Users and Groups MMC provides more flexibility than the Properties option of the User Accounts applet.

There must be at least one local administrator account (a member of the Administrators local group) on a computer running Windows XP. If you are the only user on the computer with a computer administrator account, you will not be able to change your account type in the User Accounts dialog box because there must be at least one person with a computer administrator account on the computer.

Users, on occasion, can forget their account passwords. If it is a domain account, a domain administrator can reset the account and modify its password on a domain controller. If it is a local account that resides on a computer running Windows XP, a local administrator must reset the password locally using the command button on the User Accounts dialog box, as shown in Figure 6.12.

Figure 6.12 The Reset Password button on the User Accounts dialog box.

In Windows XP, a user can make a *Forgotten Password disk* to eliminate the need for a local administrator to reset a local user's password should the user forget it. To create a Forgotten Password disk, a user can press the Ctrl+Alt+Del keys simultaneously to display the Windows Security dialog box, click Change Password, and then click Backup to access the Forgotten Password Wizard, as shown in Figure 6.13. The Forgotten Password Wizard stores password reset information on a floppy disk.

When a user creates the disk, he is asked to provide his current password. This information, encrypted, is stored on the floppy disk in a file named userkey.psw.

The user can use the disk when he attempts to log on to the local machine and does not provide the correct password. In this situation, users have the opportunity, as shown in Figure 6.14, to provide a reset disk.

Figure 6.13 The Forgotten Password Wizard.

Figure 6.14 The Logon Failed message box prompting the user to use a Forgotten Password reset disk.

If the user uses the reset disk, the process creates a new password and erases any other locally stored passwords he might have. These passwords might include security-related values, including private encryption keys needed to view encrypted files and e-mail messages. It might also include Internet-related passwords stored on the computer. These passwords will need to be re-entered by the user.

The Password Reset Wizard only works for workgroup members or standalone Windows XP computers: *computers that are domain members are not eligible*. A desktop support technician may create a Forgotten Password disk for local users by logging on locally as a member of the local Administrators group and clicking on the Prevent a Forgotten Password link located under the Related Tasks section of the task pane for the User Accounts dialog box in Control Panel, shown in Figure 6.15.

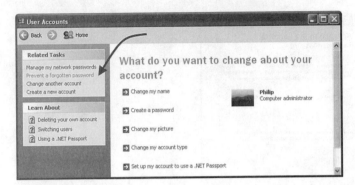

Figure 6.15 The Prevent a Forgotten Password option for local users on a workgroup or standalone computer.

Managing and Troubleshooting Local Group Settings

Two types of accounts reside locally on a computer running Windows XP. A *user account* represents an individual on the basis of her logon name and password. A *group account* is a container that links user accounts. All user accounts within a group share common privileges.

Local groups are specific to a computer and are not recognized by a domain. These groups are a primary means of managing local user rights and file and folder permissions on the computer. By default, computers running Windows XP Professional contain the following groups:

➤ *Administrators*—Full privileges. Members of this group have complete control over the computer. The first account created on a clean installation of Windows XP is a member of the Administrators group. All members of the existing Administrators group in an upgrade installation scenario maintain their Administrators group memberships in the new operating system.

A member of the Administrators group not only has unlimited powers but also imparts those powers to all programs she runs. If a hacker or virus gains access to a computer while a member of the Administrators group is logged on, the hacker or virus can use the administrator's security context to perform any task on the local computer. For this reason, administrators should rarely log onto a computer using their administrator accounts. It would be more secure to log on with an account with minimal privileges and use the **runas** command to run programs that require administrator rights.

Administrators can create and delete user accounts and add or modify permissions. Members can unload and load device drivers, manage security auditing functions, and take ownership of files and other objects. By the way, any right that administrators do not have by default, they can grant to themselves.

➤ *Backup Operators*—Can log on to the computer and run backups and restores of files to which they have no explicit permissions. Less powerful than Administrators, Backup Operators can shut down a system but not change security settings.

➤ *Guests*—Minimal access to local resources. Members cannot view system and application event logs. Members have the same access rights as members of the Local Users group when logged on locally.

➤ *Network Configuration Operators*—Less than full administrators. Members can manage network configuration settings, modify network and dial-up connections, and configure IP address assignment.

➤ *Power Users*—Less system access than Administrators but more access than users. Members of this group can share printers and share files, change the system clock, remotely shut down the system, and modify the priorities of processes. They can also run legacy applications that are not certified for Windows XP Professional and that will not run if a user is only a member of the Users group. Power Users can create user accounts and have Modify access to the %windir%\System32 folder, program files, and the HKey_Local_Machine\Software branch of the Registry, but they cannot replace operating system files or install services. They cannot run backups, load or unload device drivers, or take ownership of files or other objects.

NOTE An administrator can provide Power Users with the right to load and unload device drivers, by explicitly adding the Power Users group to the list of groups on a local machine that have the right to load and unload device drivers. You can make this addition with the Local Security Policy editor, the **Secpol.msc** snap-in tool that ships with Windows XP.

➤ *Remote Desktop Users*—Members have the right to log on remotely.

➤ *Replicator*—Its members can receive files replicated from other servers across a domain. This group, or its members, is used to empower services to replicate files.

➤ *Users*—Members can run programs and access data on the computer. They can access the computer from elsewhere on the network and remotely shut down the system. Members have Read/Write permission to only their own profiles and cannot share folders or local printers to others. (In standalone or workgroup mode, this group is referred to as Limited Users.) Default security settings are designed to prohibit members of this group from compromising the integrity of the operating system or the installed applications.

 Members of the Users group can install peripherals such as printers only if the driver is digitally signed, automatically installed, or already available on the system or though a trusted path. Applications not certified for Windows 2000 or XP Professional will not run under a User's account context.

➤ *HelpServicesGroup*—A group of users used by the Help and Support Center.

➤ *IIS_WPG*—The Internet Information Services (IIS) worker process group, available if you've installed IIS. Members of this group can manage the IIS Web server—not content, just the service.

Desktop support technicians can manage the membership of these groups by using the Local Users and Groups snap-in for the MMC or by using User Accounts in Control Panel.

If you are using Windows XP Professional in a standalone or workgroup configuration, the User Accounts applet in Control Panel allows you to manage only three of these built-in security groups—Administrators, Users (also referred to as Limited users—see Figure 6.16), and Guests. If you want to manage all the built-in groups, when Windows XP is in a standalone or workgroup configuration, you need to manage them from the Local Users and Groups snap-in.

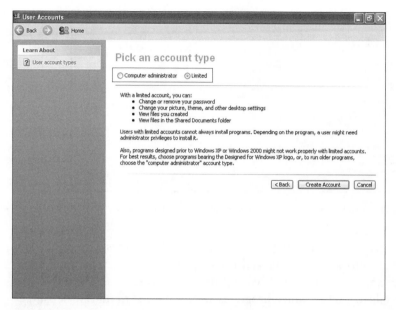

Figure 6.16 Workgroup computers support two categories of users, Computer Administrators and Limited.

Configuring Software Restriction Policies

Software restriction policies provide desktop support technicians with a policy-driven mechanism for identifying software programs running on computers in a domain and control the ability of those programs to execute. These kinds of policies can prevent hostile code from running.

The policies are provided as a precise method of limiting which programs will run in Windows XP, a filtering method more precise than one that just uses a program's name.

Software restriction policies can be created locally as shown in Figure 6.17 or delivered to computers running Windows XP using GPOs.

When a user attempts to start a program that is restricted, he is blocked by the group policy setting, and a message appears, stating "This operation has been cancelled due to restrictions in effect on this computer. Please contact your system administrator."

A software restriction policy includes a default rule that either enables or disables all programs by default. It also can include exceptions.

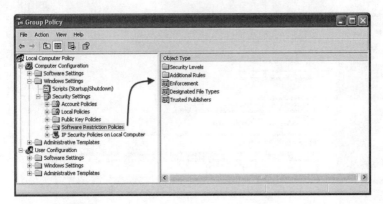

Figure 6.17 Software Restriction Policies section of the Group Policy editor.

If your goal were to create the most secure configurations, you would "disallow" all software programs and explicitly allow only certain applications that are known and trusted. If you set the default rule to "unrestricted," you must explicitly define which programs are *not* allowed to run. By default, no programs are blocked.

Rules are written by desktop support technicians to identify applications that are the explicit exceptions to the default policy. To create these rules, you must identify software that is an exception to the default rule. Rules may include text to help describe the rule.

As shown in Figure 6.18, a software restriction policy can include four types of criteria to identify software. The policy can look at a program's digital certificate, unique hash value, local source path, or network source (Internet) zone.

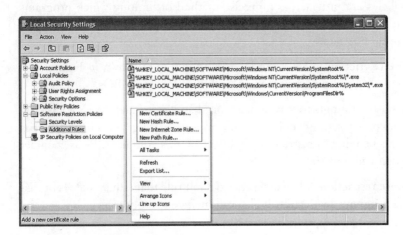

Figure 6.18 Four options for software restriction rules.

When multiple rules apply to software programs, specific rules override general rules. Here is the order of highest priority to lowest priority:

1. Hash rule

2. Certificate rule

3. Path rule

4. Internet zone rule

5. Default rule

Identifying and Troubleshooting Computer Startup Issues

To solve startup problems, a desktop support technician needs to understand the Windows XP boot sequence and determine at which stage the startup problem occurs.

Does the startup failure occur before, during, or after Windows XP Professional starts up? Is the condition due to user error, virus activity, hardware, or software failure? The more accurate the technician's diagnosis, the less likely an unneeded reinstallation of Windows XP will be prescribed.

If the error shows up before the operating system loader (Ntldr) starts, perhaps boot files are missing, have been deleted, or are unreadable. You must also suspect hard disk damage involving the master boot record (MBR), boot sector, or partition table.

If the problem occurs after the operating system launches, suspect problems involving corrupt system files, mismatched device drivers, or incompatible hardware.

A normal Windows XP startup (excluding hibernation or standby) follows the following sequence:

1. Power-on self test (POST)

2. NTLDR initial startup

3. Boot.ini read

4. NTDetect.com hardware detection

5. NTOSkrnl kernel logon

6. Logon phase

If an error occurs during the POST phase of startup, commands within or results from the computer's BIOS might be at fault.

The POST performs an initial hardware check, verifies the presence of minimum hardware, and fetches values stored in nonvolatile complementary metal-oxide semiconductor (CMOS) memory.

If there's a problem in this phase, examine the CMOS settings, or update the BIOS firmware.

Don't forget that a computer running Windows XP might fail to boot simply because the boot order in the CMOS settings specifies a floppy drive rather than the hard drive and the floppy drive is occupied by a disk that does not contain the necessary boot files.

If the boot process targets the hard drive correctly yet is unable to read instructions stored in the MBR and partition table, the boot process fails. If the MBR is read successfully, the partition table identifies the active partition where a boot sector provides necessary file system information and the location of the NTLDR file. However, if an active partition does not exist, or if the boot sector information is unreadable, users receive one or more of the following error messages:

➤ Invalid partition table

➤ Error loading operating system

➤ Missing operating system

➤ Boot: Couldn't Find NTLDR

➤ NTLDR is missing.

If the NTLDR file is successfully located, it loads files from the boot partition where the operating system files are stored. NTLDR reads the boot.ini file and launches the NTDetect.com program to detect hardware.

In a multiboot system, there is usually one boot.ini that displays the various operating system choices. The operating system you choose, or the one that is chosen by default, triggers the corresponding operating system.

When an operating system begins to load, other files become critical to the boot process. If one or more of the following operating system files become damaged or missing, Windows XP does not boot properly:

➤ %systemroot%\system32\system—The system hive of the Registry that stores the "current control set" containing the initial elements (services) with which Windows XP boots.

➤ `%systemroot%\System32\Drivers`—Keyboard, mouse, and video display driver files.

➤ `HAL.dll`—The hardware abstraction layer (HAL) dynamic-link library file that translates operating system commands into hardware instructions.

 NOTE Versions of **HAL.dll** vary. During installation of Windows XP, one of several HAL files is installed and named **HAL.dll**. To determine the version of HAL installed on a computer running Windows XP, and whether it's the appropriate version, view the properties of your computer's drivers in Device Manager, as shown in Figure 6.19.

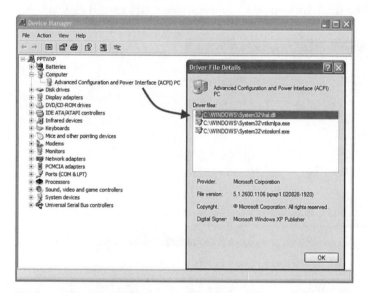

Figure 6.19 Device driver details from Device Manager.

Together, the kernel and the HAL initialize the Windows executive, a group of software components that configure driver and service information stored in the Registry control sets.

After the control set containing device and service settings is loaded, the kernel starts the Session Manager subsystem (`Smss.exe`), which performs such functions as

➤ Creating system variables.

➤ Starting the kernel mode Windows subsystem, Win32k.sys.

➤ Starting the user mode Windows subsystem, Csrss.exe.

➤ Starting the logon manager, Winlogon.exe.

From here, the logon screen usually appears. (Notable exceptions: automatic logon is configured or the computer is part of a workgroup, there is only one account on the computer, and its password is blank.)

When a successful logon occurs, the current control set used in the boot process is backed up, named LastKnownGood, and stored in the Registry for recovery purposes. When a user is unable to boot Windows and selects Last Known Good Configuration, he is interrupting the Windows startup and requesting Windows to use the Last Known Good control set, rather than the "Current Control Set." Figure 6.20 displays the Registry location where the control sets are stored and displays the index number of the control set, which would be the Last Known Good control set. (It's named ControlSet3.)

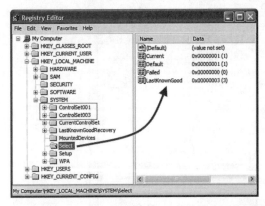

Figure 6.20 The Last Known Good configuration is **ControlSet3**. The Current Configuration is **ControlSet1**.

When Windows XP fails to start, it might reboot, apologize, and suggest remedies, as shown in Figure 6.21.

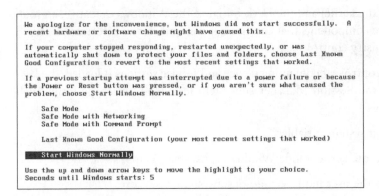

Figure 6.21 A Windows XP startup message after a failed attempt to boot the operating system.

If a startup problem occurs and suggestions don't appear, consider the following "Roadmap for Recovery" list. (You can start Windows in Safe Mode by using the Advanced Startup Options menu shown in Figure 6.22. To see the Advanced Startup Options screen, hold down the F8 function key when starting Windows.)

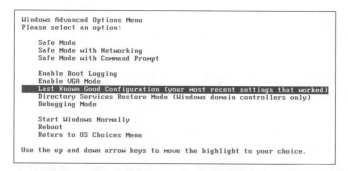

```
Windows Advanced Options Menu
Please select an option:

    Safe Mode
    Safe Mode with Networking
    Safe Mode with Command Prompt

    Enable Boot Logging
    Enable VGA Mode
    Last Known Good Configuration (your most recent settings that worked)
    Directory Services Restore Mode (Windows domain controllers only)
    Debugging Mode

    Start Windows Normally
    Reboot
    Return to OS Choices Menu

Use the up and down arrow keys to move the highlight to your choice.
```

Figure 6.22 An option in the Advanced Options Menu to start with the Last Known Good Configuration.

The following Windows XP startup solutions are listed beginning with the least invasive measures.

1. At boot up, in the Advanced Startup Options menu, use the Last Known Good Configuration.

2. Under Normal Mode or Safe Mode, use Driver Rollback to undo a device driver update.

3. In Normal Mode or Safe Mode, use System Restore.

4. Under Safe Mode, disable offending applications, device drivers, or services.

5. Under Safe Mode, remove software programs.

6. Use Recovery Console, as shown in Figure 6.23, to replace corrupted files

7. Examine `Boot.ini` settings.

8. Install a second copy of Windows XP on the system (in a different folder) and restore operating system files from a backup copy.

9. Use Automated System Recovery (ASR) in Windows XP Backup to reformat the system partition and restore operating system files from a backup.

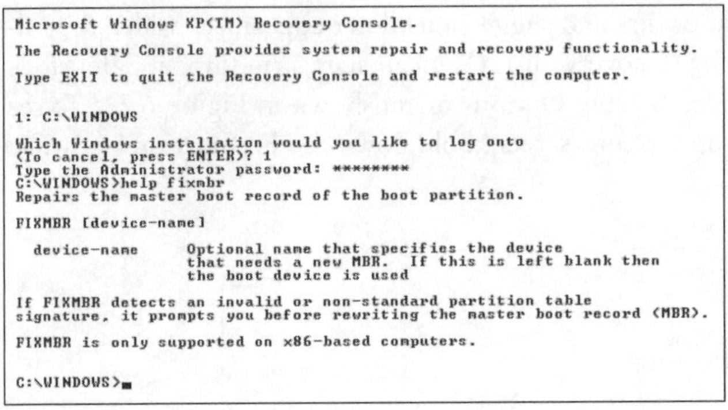

```
Microsoft Windows XP(TM) Recovery Console.

The Recovery Console provides system repair and recovery functionality.

Type EXIT to quit the Recovery Console and restart the computer.

1: C:\WINDOWS

Which Windows installation would you like to log onto
(To cancel, press ENTER)? 1
Type the Administrator password: ********
C:\WINDOWS>help fixmbr
Repairs the master boot record of the boot partition.

FIXMBR [device-name]

   device-name     Optional name that specifies the device
                   that needs a new MBR.  If this is left blank then
                   the boot device is used

If FIXMBR detects an invalid or non-standard partition table
signature, it prompts you before rewriting the master boot record (MBR).

FIXMBR is only supported on x86-based computers.

C:\WINDOWS>_
```

Figure 6.23   The Recovery Console screen.

Users can also disable misbehaving or corrupted services that are preventing the successful boot of Windows. Instead of using the Services.msc snap-in that's available only in a GUI environment, you can use sc.exe, a command-line tool that communicates with the Service Control Manager and displays information about services running on your computer. sc.exe, as shown in Figure 6.24, gathers the same type of information obtainable from the Services snap-in. For troubleshooting startup, the sc query and sc config commands are the most helpful. You can perform the following tasks by using the sc.exe command:

➤ Display service information, such as start type and whether you can pause or end a service.

➤ Modify the startup type of a service.

➤ Start, pause, or resume a service.

➤ Disable a service by using the sc config command.

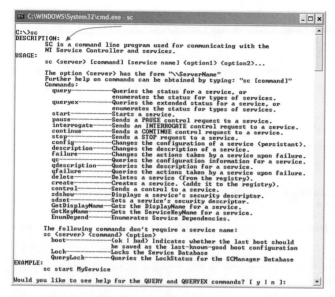

Figure 6.24 The **Sc.exe** utility for managing services.

Identifying and Troubleshooting Local User Logon Issues

Local logons are often hampered by poor typing and poor reading, so check the simplest solutions first. Is the password correct? Is the account name correct?

The interactive logon process in Windows XP Professional involves a number of components and a sequence of events that are invisible to the user. However, if it's a local account, the sources of problems are limited to settings on the local computer.

Windows XP standalone or workgroup computers may be configured with account lockout policies based on the number of failed logon attempts within a certain span of time. These settings are stored locally in the local policy of the workstation (see Figure 6.25). By default, they are configured but not enabled. The local administrator account is exempt from this policy.

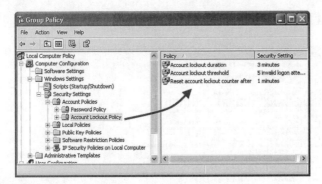

Figure 6.25 Local Account lockout policy settings.

If a user invokes a lockout by entering an incorrect password more consecutive times than the account lockout policy permits, the local administrator needs to unlock the account and modify the user's logon password by opening the Control Panel and accessing the user's account in the local User Accounts dialog box.

Identifying and Troubleshooting Domain User Logon Issues

When a local user is unable to log on locally, the problem is isolated and solvable with a limited number of variables. When a user is unable to log on to the domain, there is a larger number of causes, including network connectivity, which you must consider. Look for these common causes of logon failure:

➤ Password or username incorrectly typed.

➤ Password typed with CAPS LOCK on.

➤ No common protocol between a Windows XP Professional–based client and a domain controller.

When one of the first two items is the problem, you can expect to see a message, "Make sure your username and domain are correct." If the third item is the cause of a failure, then you should see an error message stating that the domain controller could not be contacted. If you have been able to connect to the domain controller in the past, then something must have changed in the configuration of TCP/IP. Here is a desktop support technician's network checklist for troubleshooting domain logons:

➤ Is there an incorrect static address or subnet mask?

➤ Is Dynamic Host Configuration Protocol (DHCP) enabled but there is no DHCP server available?

➤ Is the default gateway correct?

➤ Are the Windows Internet Naming Service (WINS) and Domain Name System (DNS) server addresses correct?

➤ Are the LMHosts and Hosts files configured properly?

If a user has recently renamed his computer, network logon problems can be caused by inconsistency between the local computer name and the name known to the domain. To troubleshoot this problem, rename the Windows XP Professional–based computer that belongs to a domain. To rename a Windows XP computer that is a member of a Windows domain, follow these steps:

1. Create a new computer account (or have one created for you) that uses the new computer name.

2. Disjoin the computer from the domain by temporarily joining a workgroup.

3. When prompted, restart the computer.

4. Join the domain by using the new computer name.

5. When prompted, restart the computer.

This task ought to reset any computer SIDs that might have become unsynchronized.

Timing also makes a difference in network logons. After your computer joins a Windows 2000 or later domain, and you attempt to log on to the domain, the following message may appear if the workstation's and server's time clocks are not closely synchronized:

The system cannot log you on due to the following error: There is a time difference between the client and server. Please try again or consult your system administrator.

The Kerberos authentication protocol inspects the timestamp of the authentication request sent by the logged-on client and compares it with the domain controller. If a significant difference exists between two values (the default is 5 minutes), authentication fails. To remedy the problem, someone must log on locally to an administrative account and make sure that the Windows XP computer's time clock is the same as that of the domain controller.

NOTE

You must correctly enter the time zone as well. The Kerberos protocol converts all times to Greenwich Mean Time (GMT) and then compares each computer's time settings based on GMT.

If you want to log on to a Windows domain and the name of the logon domain does not appear in the dialog box, you might need to click the Options button to open an expanded dialog box, or you can type your username and the Windows Active Directory domain name using the User Principal Name (UPN) in the User Name box in the format *MyName@MyDomain*.com at the Log On to Windows dialog box.

If you have already explored the preceding solutions, the domain account might be locked out or disabled. A locked-out account cannot be used until an administrator resets it or until the account lockout duration expires. The Account Lockout policy setting disables accounts after a set number of failed logon attempts.

The domain lockout policy, account lockout threshold, and lockout duration are all controlled at the domain level in the Active Directory. You must change them in the Default Domain Policy or in another domain-linked policy to enable lockout after a specified number of attempts.

If a user unsuccessfully attempts to log on to workstations or member servers that have been locked using either Ctrl+Alt+Del or password-protected screen savers, the attempt does not count as a failed logon attempt under this policy setting. Failed attempts to log on to the network do count.

To manually unlock an account that has been locked out, open the user's property sheet in the Active Directory Users and Computers console. On the Account tab, clear the Account Is Locked Out check box. It is a good practice to reset the user's password at the same time. However, changing the password alone does not unlock the account.

Exam Prep Questions

1. You're a desktop support technician for your company. After installing a program on his computer, a user reports he cannot reboot his computer running Windows XP. An error message appears when he attempts to reboot, saying that "The system cannot find the boot files" Which of the following actions is the easiest way to repair the boot files?

   ❑ A. Boot.cfg
   ❑ B. Recovery Console: rebuild option
   ❑ C. Editing boot.ini directly
   ❑ D. Last Known Good Configuration

   The correct answer is B. When you run the Recovery Console, you can use the `bootcfg` command to scan the hard disks in a computer running Windows XP and use the information to modify the contents of the `Boot.ini` file or rebuild a new copy. The `/rebuild` option scans all the hard disks for copies of Windows installations and enables a desktop support technician to add to the `boot.ini` file.

   Answer C is incorrect. Editing the `boot.ini` file directly is not recommended. It is easier to use a command. Answer D is incorrect. The Last Known Good Configuration option is accessible after the boot files are read and the Advanced Option menu appears. Answer A is incorrect. `Boot.cfg` is a Linux file.

2. You are a desktop support technician. For security purposes, a sales rep asks you to configure her computer running Windows XP to prevent other sales representatives from logging on to her computer.

   Which of the following actions should you perform?

   ❑ A. Configure the Interactive Logon: Require Domain Controller Authentication to Unlock Workstation.
   ❑ B. Limit the Log on Locally policy on her computer.
   ❑ C. Place her computer in an OU. Configure a Log on Locally Security Policy in a GPO and link it to the OU in which the computer resides.
   ❑ D. Place all the users to be affected by this restriction into an OU. Configure the Deny Log On Security Policy in a GPO and link it to the OU that contains the computer.

   The correct answer is B. By default, on a computer running Windows XP, the Log on Locally right is assigned to all members of the Users group, which comprises all domain users. You can remove the Users Local group from the policy and just add the sales rep's name. Answers C and D are incorrect because redesigning the Active Directory by relocating users and computers into new or different OUs is unnecessary. Answer A is incorrect. The Interactive Logon: Unlock Policy in the scenario determines whether a domain controller must validate the account before a workstation can be unlocked. It does not control who can log on locally.

3. You are a desktop support technician. A co-worker is planning to install Windows XP on 90 computers. He will also administer the computers after the upgrade.

   Which of the following actions should you perform to enable him to have the right to install and administer these computers?

   ❑ A. Since any domain user can install and administer Windows XP client computers, no action is required.

   ❑ B. Use the delegation of control to give him explicit permissions on the Computers container within the active directory.

   ❑ C. In the local group policy on each computer, grant the user Add Workstations to the Domain right.

   ❑ D. In the GPO linked to the domain, grant him Add Workstations to the Domain right.

   The correct answer is B. You can use the Delegation of Control Wizard to grant him permission to create computer objects in the OU. This action will enable him to add as many computer accounts as necessary. The right to add workstations to the domain right, by default, is granted to authenticated users in the default domain controller policy. This permission lets a user add up to 10 workstations. Answer A is incorrect because domain users can only add up to 10 computers to a domain. Answer C is incorrect because privileges for adding computers to a domain are controlled on a domain controller, not the local machine. Answer D is incorrect because domain users already have the right to add workstations to the domain.

4. You are a desktop support technician for a medical insurance company that has an Active Directory domain. Your company will be opening a new branch office where you will be deploying Windows XP, a number of applications, and data to 200 computers. You plan to use the imaging software to distribute a standard image of a prototype computer. The data that will reside on all target computers is confidential and must be encrypted.

   Which of the following actions should you perform to secure these files?

   ❑ A. Do not encrypt the data on the prototype computer. Have users individually encrypt data on their computers.

   ❑ B. Encrypt the data yourself on the prototype computer before running sysprep.exe.

   ❑ C. Encrypt the data on the prototype computer. Create local user accounts for each employee and designate those local users as trusted users of the encrypted files.

   ❑ D. Configure the prototype computer to use IPSec.

The correct answer is A. You can use the EFS to protect files stored on NTFS-formatted drives. Only the user who encrypted the file and those users the user has designated can open the file. As a desktop support technician, you should create a prototype computer with all the appropriate software, run the Sysprep utility on it, and then duplicate the resultant image to all the intended computers. Computers that are the result of sysprep.exe are members of a workgroup, not a domain. Answer B is incorrect because the users could not read files encrypted by another without explicit permission. Answer C is incorrect because it is never a good plan to create numerous local user accounts on a computer that will be part of a domain. Answer D is incorrect because IP Security (IPSec) is used to encrypt data as it traverses the network. It does not encrypt files stored locally on the hard drive.

5. You are a desktop support technician and you administer a Windows domain. Employees use a word processing program that creates temporary files in the same folder as the documents being edited. A user named Fred will be editing a number of extremely important confidential documents. You have already created a folder on Fred's computer running Windows XP and have copied the sensitive files into it. Corporate guidelines state that only Fred should be able to access the files and the temporary files in that folder.

How would you secure these files?

❏ A. Encrypt all the files yourself.
❏ B. Encrypt the folder yourself.
❏ C. Have Fred encrypt all the files.
❏ D. Have Fred encrypt just the folder.

The correct answer is D. When you attempt to encrypt a single file in a folder on an NTFS partition, Windows XP warns you of the consequences; that temporary files in the folder are not encrypted unless the folder is encrypted. To best secure files in this scenario, a user should encrypt the entire folder so that even temporary files created by an application are also encrypted. Answer A is incorrect because if you encrypt all the files, only you can read them. Answer B is incorrect because if you encrypt the folder, only you can read the folder's contents. Answer C is incorrect because it is more secure to encrypt the folder, not just the files.

6. You are a desktop support technician. Tom, an assistant of yours, will be installing Windows XP on 10 new computers. Tom has a domain user account and can install Windows XP. Following the practice of least privilege, you need to grant him only enough authority to add these computers and no other computers.

Which of the following actions should you perform to give Tom this power?

❏ A. Use the Delegation of Control Wizard in Active Directory Users and Computers to grant Tom permission on the Computers container.

❏ B. Grant Tom the Add Workstations to the Domain right in the local GPO on each of the 10 computers.

❏ C. Grant Tom the Add Workstations to the Domain right to a GPO linked to the entire domain.

❏ D. Ask Tom to begin the installations.

The correct answer is D. By default, a domain user can add up to 10 computers to the domain in which his or her account resides. Answer A is incorrect because if you were to give Tom, using the Delegation of Control Wizard, permission to add computer objects on the Computers container, it would give him unlimited abilities to add computers. Answer B is incorrect because the ability to add workstations to the domain is controlled on domain controllers, not the local computer. Answer C is incorrect because Tom already has the right to add workstations to the domain at the domain level.

7. You are a desktop support technician. Company policy states that all user account logons must be authenticated by a domain controller. You must ensure that this security policy is always enforced. All clients are computers running Windows XP.

Which of the following actions should you perform?

❏ A. Create a GPO that requires domain controller authentication before the workstation can be unlocked.

❏ B. Create a GPO that prevents any previous logons from being cached.

❏ C. Give the Full Control permission for the domain controller's OU to all users.

❏ D. Using the Security Configuration and Analysis Tool, apply the setup security.inf security template to all client computers.

The correct answer is B. Windows XP enables users to be logged on by cached credentials. That is, if a previous domain logon was successful, although the domain is currently unreachable, a domain logon is still authenticated by the cached credentials. Because of the security implications in this scenario, a desktop support technician might be compelled to eliminate cached credentials by applying the Interactive Logon: Number of Previous Logons to Cache policy and specifying 0. Answer A is incorrect because the Require Domain Controller Authentication to Unlock Workstation policy controls whether a user's logon credentials must be provided and a domain controller contacted to unlock a workstation. Answer C is incorrect because giving a user with Full Control permissions for the domain controller's OU does not impact nor affect locally cached credentials. Answer D is incorrect because the `setup security.inf` template designed to provide default workstation security settings. It does not disable authentication by cached logons.

8. You are a desktop support technician. You do nightly backups of folders stored on client workstations. Users must be allowed to work on any computer running Windows XP in your domain but must be denied the right to shut down the computers so that your backup routines run smoothly.

   How would you secure these computers to prevent unauthorized shutdowns?

   ❑ A. In the local policy settings, remove the local Users group on each computer from the Shut Down the System right.

   ❑ B. Assign necessary NTFS security properties to the System Properties applet in the Control Panel.

   ❑ C. In the local policy settings, configure the Remove and Prevent Access to the Shut Down Command policy.

   ❑ D. Delete the Power Options icon from the Control Panel

   The correct answer is A. Because all users, by default, are members of the Domain Users group, which is a member of the local Users group on every domain member computer, they have the right to shut down the system. To prevent it, you must modify that hierarchy by editing the local policy on the computers you want to control. Answer B is incorrect because NTFS security settings cannot be assigned to dialog boxes. Answer C is incorrect because the Remove and Prevent Access to the Shut Down command hides the shutdown option in the GUI. It does not prevent a user from using the command-line command `shutdown. -s`. Answer D is incorrect because power options in the Control Panel are not related to the shutdown feature.

9. You are a new desktop support technician for your company. Some users, you notice, do not have to press Ctrl+Alt+Del to log on. Your company's security policy requires that everyone use Ctrl+Alt+Del. You've set up an appropriate policy, linked it to the domain, and tested it. Unfortunately, it doesn't immediately seem to affect the problematic computer.

   You need the policy to be implemented as soon as possible.

   Which of the following actions should you perform?

   ❏ A. Run GPUpdate /force on the problematic computer.

   ❏ B. Run GPUpdate /force on a domain controller.

   ❏ C. Run secedit /refreshpolicy machine_policy on the problematic computer.

   ❏ D. Run secedit /refreshpolicy machine_policy on the domain controller.

   The correct answer is A. To "pull" machine commands established by a group policy to a workstation immediately, you can run `GPUpdate /force` on the computer running Windows XP. Answer B is incorrect because you run the command on the target machine, not the domain controller. Answers C and D are incorrect: `secedit /refreshpolicy machine_policy` and `secedit /refreshpolicy user_policy` are commands from Windows 2000. GPUpdate has replaced those commands.

10. You are a desktop support technician. All computers in the Human Resource department belong to an OU named HR. All employees in that department belong to the HR group. You suspect that a user has been trying to gain unauthorized access over the network to shared files on the HR department's computers. You want to identify that person without affecting other computers and by using the least administrative effort.

    How would you identify which user or users are responsible using the least administrative effort and without affecting other computers?

    Each correct answer represents one part of the solution. Choose two.

    ❏ A. Create and link an group policy for auditing to the HR OU.

    ❏ B. Turn on auditing for the Everyone group on the shared folders or files on the computers in HR.

    ❏ C. Configure a separate audit policy on each computer in the HR OU individually.

    ❏ D. Enable auditing for the HR group.

    The correct answers are A and B. You must configure a group policy for auditing and link it to the HR OU in Active Directory. You must also enable auditing for the Everyone group on the shared folders that you want to monitor. Answer C is incorrect because configuring each computer separately would be using excessive effort. Answer D is incorrect because you are unsure who the culprits are. Limiting your audits to just the HR group might not capture the offender.

Need to Know More?

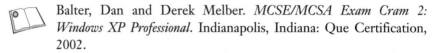 Minasi, Mark. *Mastering Windows XP Professional*. Alameda, California: Sybex, 2001.

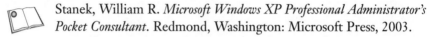 Balter, Dan and Derek Melber. *MCSE/MCSA Exam Cram 2: Windows XP Professional*. Indianapolis, Indiana: Que Certification, 2002.

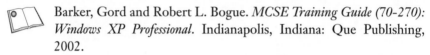 Stanek, William R. *Microsoft Windows XP Professional Administrator's Pocket Consultant*. Redmond, Washington: Microsoft Press, 2003.

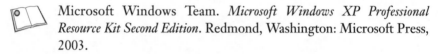 Barker, Gord and Robert L. Bogue. *MCSE Training Guide (70-270): Windows XP Professional*. Indianapolis, Indiana: Que Publishing, 2002.

Microsoft Windows Team. *Microsoft Windows XP Professional Resource Kit Second Edition*. Redmond, Washington: Microsoft Press, 2003.

Search the Microsoft Product Support Services Knowledge Base on the Internet: `http://support.microsoft.com`. You can also search Microsoft TechNet on the Internet: `http://www.microsoft.com/technet`. Find technical information using keywords from this chapter, such as XP authorization and access control, best practices guide for securing Active Directory, XP logon and authentication, and XP security event messages.

Monitoring and Analyzing Operating System Performance

Terms you'll need to understand:

✓ Event Viewer
✓ Task Manager
✓ System Monitor
✓ Performance logs and alerts
✓ Performance objects, counters, and instances
✓ **Logman.exe**
✓ **Eventtriggers.exe**
✓ **Netcap.exe**

Techniques you'll need to master:

✓ Monitoring events with the Event Viewer Microsoft Management Console (MMC)
✓ Monitoring and managing applications, processes, and current system vital signs with Task Manager
✓ Using the Performance Logs and Alerts snap-in
✓ Viewing real-time server performance data with the System Monitor ActiveX control snap-in
✓ Recording logged server performance data with Performance Logs and Alerts
✓ Identifying and troubleshooting bottlenecks

Data in a computer only travels four places: to memory, to the hard drive, to the processor, and across the network. One of these places is the *bottleneck*. A desktop support technician is a detective responsible for discovering that bottleneck and resolving it. Because of the inevitable deterioration of performance on a computer due to disk usage and file fragmentation, described later in this chapter, it is important for the desktop support technician to master the tools provided to monitor, troubleshoot, and optimize, a computer running Windows XP.

Clues and evidence are collected and displayed by the System Monitor ActiveX Control and the Task Manager. The Event Viewer, often the "smoking gun," lists recent events.

In this chapter, we explore all these tools and more.

Monitoring and Analyzing Event Logs

Many processes are constantly running on workstations. Operating system and third-party services run in the background; application programs run in the foreground. The messages that are sent back and forth between application programs and the operating system can generate different types of events.

The event log service, which is configured to run at system startup, records events and stores them in log files.

All Event Log files are stored in the `%systemroot%\system32\config` folder by default. Event log files are identified with the `.evt` filename extension. These log files are not text files; you cannot view them using a simple text editor, such as Notepad. Although you can save the `.evt` files in various text-readable formats, you can view the events stored in these log files by using the Event Viewer.

Working with the Event Viewer

You can launch the Event Viewer snap-in tool by choosing Start, Run; typing `eventvwr.msc`; and clicking OK. On Windows XP standalone computers, three different event logs appear in the viewer:

➤ *Application*—This log records events that are generated by application programs. The name of this log file stored on disk is `AppEvent.Evt`.

➤ *Security*—This log records success and failure notifications for audited events. Administrators can configure various auditing settings through local or group policies; the results of those audited events get recorded in the security log. Only users who have been granted the user right called Manage Auditing and Security Log may access the Security log; members of the Administrators group possess this right by default. The name of this log file stored on disk is SecEvent.Evt.

➤ *System*—This log records events generated by the operating system and its subsystems, such as its device drivers and services. The name of this log file stored on disk is SysEvent.Evt.

Viewing Event Logs

After you launch the Event Viewer, you can select the log you want to look at in the left pane; the events then appear in the right (details) pane, as you can see in Figure 7.1. When you double-click an event, its properties window displays the details of the event, including the date, time, computer name, event ID, and a description of the event itself. The Event Viewer displays five types of events:

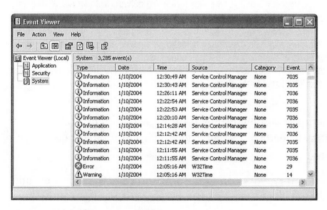

Figure 7.1 Looking at system events in the Event Viewer for a computer running Windows XP. Notice the warning and error events.

➤ *Error*—These events are recorded whenever significant problems occur, such as the loss of data or the loss of functionality. Unexpected system shutdowns and the failure of a service to start automatically at boot time are examples of events that are logged as errors.

➤ *Warning*—These events are recorded to indicate possible future problems. Low disk space for a drive volume is an example of an event that might get logged as a warning.

➤ *Information*—These events are recorded often. They indicate the successful operation of a program, a device driver, or a service. For example, Event ID 6005 indicates that "the Event Service was started"; this event usually coincides with the starting or restarting of the computer.

➤ *Failure Audit*—These events are recorded each time that any audited security event fails. For example, if a user attempts to log on to the computer with an unrecognized or incorrect username or password, a failure audit event is logged if the policy setting for Audit Account Logon Events is set to Success, Failure or if it's set only to Failure. You can configure Audit Policy settings at the local or group policy levels.

➤ *Success Audit*—These events are recorded each time that any audited security event succeeds. For example, if a user successfully logs onto the computer, a success audit event is logged if the policy setting for Audit Account Logon Events is set to Success, Failure or if it's set only to Success. You can configure Audit Policy settings at the local or group policy levels.

You can configure audit policy settings at the local, site, domain, domain controller (DC), and organizational unit (OU) policy levels in a network with an Active Directory domain controller. You can use the Local Security Settings snap-in (**secpol.msc**) or the Local Policy Settings snap-in (**gpedit.msc**) to configure audit policy settings locally. However, they might be overridden by settings enabled at the site, domain, or OU level. From one of the snap-ins just mentioned, expand the Security Settings node, expand the Local Policies subnode, and select the Audit Policy subnode. Double-click the policy setting listed in the details pane to configure it.

The new Eventtriggers.exe command-line tool, shown in Figure 7.2, displays and configures actions to be taken when events like system messages, warnings, and failures occur.

The Eventtriggers.exe utility works on both local and remote computers and monitors the application log, system log, and security log. You must be a member of the Administrators group to use Eventriggers.exe. To view a current list of event triggers, type eventtriggers (without any parameters) at a command prompt. For more details on this tool, search on the keyword "eventtriggers" in the Windows XP Professional Help and Support Center, or type eventtriggers /? at a command prompt.

Archiving Event Logs, Setting Options, and Filtering Events

Event logs fill up over time. By default, the maximum log size for each event log is 512KB. By default, when the log reaches its maximum size, it overwrites events as needed. If you want to manually clear a log, right-click the log (in the left pane of the Event Viewer) and select Clear All Events. A message box asks whether you want to save the events contained in the log before you clear them. If you click Yes, the Save As dialog prompts you to choose a location on disk, a filename for this log, and the file type to save this log as— Event Log (.evt), Text (tab delimited, *.txt), or CSV (comma-separated variable, *.csv).

Figure 7.2 The **eventtriggers.exe** command-line utility.

You can open archived logs saved in the .evt file format within the Event Viewer. You can right-click a log in the Event Viewer, select Open Log File, and then specify the location and name of the file to open. You can also right-click the Event Viewer root node and select Open Log File to open a log file without closing any of the existing logs. You can open logs saved in the .txt file format in any text editor or word-processing program. You can open logs saved in the .csv file format in applications such as Microsoft Excel or Notepad. However, the Event Viewer cannot itself open logs saved as .txt or .csv files.

You can filter the events that appear by clicking the View menu and clicking Filter. You can filter events by Event Type, Event Source, Category, Event ID, User, Computer, and time/date. To display all records in the log, click Restore Defaults and click Apply.

If you right-click a log, you can take advantage of a new feature of Windows XP called *New Log View*. When you create a new log view, you can specify how the Event Viewer presents a log instead of having to always modify the default display settings for the log. You can give this new log view a custom name, and you can manage it just like any other log, as shown in Figure 7.3.

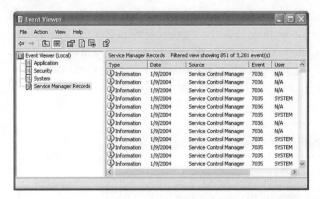

Figure 7.3 An example of a new log view (the fourth log is a custom view of the system log).

Performance Monitoring Tactics

The only way to effectively monitor performance is to compare it over an appropriate time span.

To effectively monitor a computer's performance, you must do the following:

1. Create a baseline.

2. Proactively monitor.

3. Evaluate performance.

4. Identify potential bottlenecks.

5. Take corrective action.

6. Monitor the effectiveness and stability of the change.

7. Perform Step 2 on a regular, consistent basis.

A *baseline* is a range of acceptable performance of a system component under normal working conditions. *Baselining*, or establishing a baseline, requires that you capture key counters while a system performs with normal loads and all services running. Then, you can compare future performance against the baseline to identify potential bottlenecks, troubleshoot sudden changes in performance, and justify system improvements.

A baseline should cover a relatively large timeframe so that it captures a range of data reflecting acceptable performance. You should configure the samplings interval so that the log does not become enormous. Generate baselines regularly, perhaps even once a month, to keep an eye on performance trends.

The most useful objects to understand and monitor are described and discussed later in the chapter under "Analyzing and Optimizing Windows XP Subsystems".

The Performance console enables you to monitor system performance as well as proactively configure the system to send alerts based on various performance thresholds. You can launch the console by typing `Perfmon.msc` in the Run dialog box and pressing Enter. The console also appears as an icon named Performance in the Administrative tools folder of the Control Panel.

Working with the Perfmon's System Monitor

The *System Monitor MMC ActiveX snap-in* is a node of the Performance MMC and is available for inclusion in custom MMC consoles.

The System Monitor can display performance data about the local computer, or it can display performance data on one or more remote computers in real time.

The plethora of performance metrics, or *counters*, available for monitoring can make the task a daunting one, indeed. To monitor an activity, you must select a *computer*, a category (*object*), and a specific subcategory (*counter*). Some counters are broken down into *instances*.

To learn how to add counters the System Monitor, see the section "Adding and Removing Objects, Counters, and Instances," later in this chapter.

By default, the System Monitor tool is preconfigured with three sets of performance objects, counters, and instances (object:counter:instance) each time that you launch the Performance snap-in, as shown in Figure 7.4:

➤ *Memory:Pages/sec*—This performance metric is the rate at which pages are read from or written to disk to resolve *hard page faults*. Hard page faults occur when a process requests a page from memory, but the system cannot find it and it must be retrieved from disk. This metric is a primary indicator of the kinds of faults that cause systemwide slowdowns. This value should remain consistently between 0 and 20 but not consistently higher than 20.

➤ *PhysicalDisk:Avg. Disk Queue Length:_Total*—This performance metric is the average number of both read and write requests that were queued (waiting) for the selected disk during the sample interval. This value should remain consistently between 0 and 2 but not consistently higher than 2.

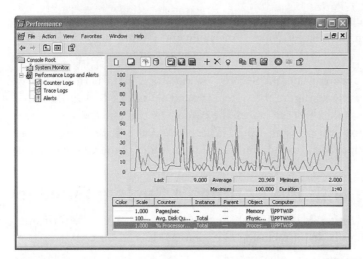

Figure 7.4 The default System Monitor in graph view with the default performance objects, counters, and instances.

➤ *Processor:% Processor Time:_Total*—This performance metric is the percentage of elapsed time that the processor spends to execute a non-idle thread. It is calculated by measuring the duration that the idle thread is active in the sample interval and subtracting that time from interval duration. (Each processor has an idle thread that consumes cycles when no other threads are ready to run.) This metric is the primary indicator of processor activity and displays the average percentage of busy time observed during the sample interval. It is calculated by monitoring the time that the service is inactive and subtracting that value from 100%. This value should remain consistently below the 85% mark.

The Windows NT **diskperf.exe -y** command is not needed to enable either LogicalDisk or PhysicalDisk counters in Windows XP. All disk objects and counters are automatically enabled on demand for Windows XP and Windows Server 2003 computers.

System Real-Time Monitoring with Task Manager

Before we discuss the customizable options available in System Monitor, keep in mind that another monitoring tool, Task Manager, shown in Figure 7.5, also enables you to view applications and processes and a number of other common performance counters in real time.

You can use either the Task Manager tool or the System Monitor tool to measure system performance in real time, but the Task Manager displays only local values; the System Monitor can display values on remote computers running Windows XP.

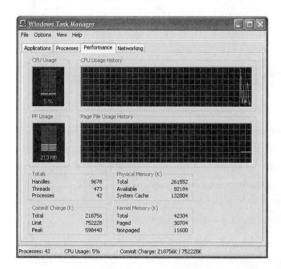

Figure 7.5   Charting and monitoring system performance in real time with Task Manager.

Access the Task Manager in any one of three ways:

➤ Right-click the taskbar and select Task Manager.

➤ Press Ctrl+Shift+Esc on the keyboard.

➤ Press Ctrl+Alt+Del on the keyboard and select Task Manager.

The Task Manager utility displays five tabs—Applications, Processes, Performance, Networking, and Users. The *Applications tab* shows the application programs that are currently running in the foreground; background services do not appear on this page. The *Processes tab* displays the processes currently running on the computer; to view all processes from all users logged on to the computer, mark the Show Processes from All Users check box.

The *Performance tab* shows current usage of the CPUs, the CPU usage history charts, current page file usage, page file usage history chart, and current memory usage statistics. The *Networking tab* is new for Windows XP; it charts the current network adapters' network traffic utilization. The *Users tab* lists the users who are currently logged on to the console or logged on via Remote Desktop connections. The Users tab appears only if the computer you are working on has Fast User Switching enabled, is a member of a workgroup, or is a standalone computer. The Users tab is unavailable on computers that are members of a network domain.

For any other vital statistics on a system, or for more detailed and in-depth inquiries, use the System Monitor and the Performance Logs and Alerts tools, which are available as part of the Performance MMC snap-in.

Customizing Real-Time Monitoring with System Monitor

As mentioned earlier, you can use the System Monitor to view the status of many system components in real time and display them in any of three different views—graph, histogram, or report. The *graph* view is the default, and it supports the most optional settings. The *histogram* view is a bar-chart configuration. The *report* view is simply a list of the performance objects, counters, and their associated instances in a report-like format.

Using the System Monitor, you can display the local computer along with several remote computers over a network connection all at the same time.

To modify the display properties of the system monitor, right-click the view (the right pane of the Performance console) and choose Properties. You can alter all properties of the System Monitor view, including the display color of counters, the scale and sample rate, and the format of the monitor's display—which can be in a graph, a histogram (bar chart), or a report (numeric display) format.

Rather than just display real-time statistics, you can also choose to record the system performance of the local or remote computers to a log file using the Performance Logs and Alerts node of the Performance snap-in. To record the values, see the section "Using Logged Monitoring with Performance Logs and Alerts," later in this chapter.

 To obtain the most accurate results when monitoring a computer's performance with System Monitor, you should monitor a computer remotely. System Monitor itself requires a certain amount of overhead to run. Therefore, when you run System Monitor on the same machine you are measuring, the performance data can be negatively affected and the results might be somewhat skewed.

Adding and Removing Objects, Counters, and Instances

System Monitor offers you a variety of ways to add objects, counters, and instances to its list of monitored items; which we simply refer to collectively as *counters*.

To add counters, you can click the plus symbol (+) on the icon bar, you can press Ctrl+I on the keyboard, or you can right-click the right (details) pane in any view and select Add Counters. To both add and remove counters, you can right-click the details pane in any view, select Properties, and click the Data tab.

Any of these methods opens the Add Counters dialog box shown in Figure 7.6.

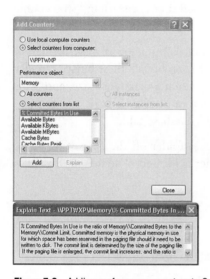

Figure 7.6 Adding performance counters to System Monitor with the Add Counters dialog box.

To remove counters from System Monitor, you can select the counter that you want to remove at the bottom of the details pane and press the Del key on the keyboard.

Using Logged Monitoring with Performance Logs and Alerts

The Performance Logs and Alerts tool in Windows XP is the other half of the Performance snap-in. Performance Logs and Alerts supports *logged monitoring* to log files whose size is only limited by the maximum supported file size for the file system on which the logs are stored. In addition, you can append performance data onto existing log files.

The Performance Logs and Alerts tool offers you three major benefits:

➤ The ability to record system performance data at specified intervals over time using *counter logs*

➤ A method to record detailed system events after specific events (triggers) occur using *trace logs*

➤ A configuration setting enabling a notification (alert) to be sent by the system when specific counters exceed certain preset thresholds

Configuring and Viewing Counter Logs

Counter logs enable you to collect performance data on systems over periods of time to create performance baselines, chart and analyze performance trends, and diagnose performance bottlenecks. You can schedule these logs to record data automatically at predetermined times or start and stop counter logs manually.

You can choose from five different types of counter log storage formats—comma-delimited text files; tab-delimited files; binary files; binary circular files that overwrite themselves when they reach a maximum size; and SQL database files, which require a connection to a Microsoft SQL Server computer and access to an accompanying SQL database table.

Logs are stored, by default, in the \Perflogs folder off the root of the same drive volume where the %systemroot% folder is located. The default format is binary (a .blg extension).

To set up a new counter log, follow these steps:

1. Launch the Performance console.

2. Expand the Performance Logs and Alerts node and select the Counter Logs subnode.

3. Right-click the Counter Logs subnode and select New Log Settings.

4. Type a name for this log in the Name box and click OK.

5. From the General tab of the properties dialog box that appears, shown in Figure 7.7, you can perform the following actions:

   ➤ Click the Add Objects button to add objects with *all* their associated counters to the log.

   ➤ Click the Add Counters button to add individual counters and instances to the log.

   ➤ Select one or more objects or counters from the Counters list and click the Remove button to delete them.

6. To change the sample interval, type a number or increment or decrement the interval using the up or down arrow on the Interval spinner box.

Figure 7.7   The General Tab of the properties box for a log named **ExamCram_000001.blg**.

7. To change the sample interval time units, click the Units drop-down list box and select from Seconds, Minutes, Hours, or Days.

8. If you want to have the counter log record data under a specific user account's security context, type the user account name in the Run as box and then click the Set Password button to specify the proper password.

9. Click the Log Files tab to specify log file options.

10. Click the Log File Type drop-down list box to select the type of log storage format that you want for this log—binary file (default), text file (comma delimited), text file (tab delimited), binary circular file, or SQL database.

11. Click the Configure button to change the location of the log file, change the log filename, or establish a maximum log file size. If the Maximum Limit (default) option is selected, the logging continues for this counter log until the log file uses all the available space on the disk where the log is located. Click OK for the Configure Log Files dialog box when finished.

12. Clear the End File Names with check box if you do not want the log file's name appended with a numeric sequence number or a date format.

13. If you leave the End File Names with check box marked, you can select from the *nnnnnn* setting or one or several date formats from the associated drop-down list box, such as *mmddhh*, which uses the current month, day, and hour, or *mmddhhmm*, which uses the current month, day, hour, and minute.

14. Optionally, you can type a description in the Comment box.

15. Mark the Overwrite Existing Log File check box if you want to overwrite an existing file that has the same name.

16. Click the Schedule tab to specify start and stop times for logging to this counter log.

17. Click OK to create the new counter log.

You can create a counter log from the current collection of counters set up in the System Monitor tool by right-clicking anywhere in the details pane of System Monitor and selecting Save As. When the Save As dialog box appears, select a location on disk to save these settings, specify the Save as Type as a Web page (***.htm**, ***.html**) file, and click Save to save the settings file. Next, go to the Performance Logs and Alerts node, right-click the Counter Logs subnode, and select New Log Settings from. Locate the settings file that you saved and click the Open button. Click OK for the message box that appears. Type a name for this new counter log in the Name box for the New Log Settings dialog box that pops up. Make any changes that you want to the new counter log's properties window that appears, and click OK when you are done.

To manually start a counter log to record performance data, right-click the counter log name in the details pane of Performance Logs and Alerts and select Start. The icon for the counter log turns to green, indicating that logging is occurring. To manually stop a counter log from logging data, right-click the counter log name and select Stop. To modify a counter log's settings, right-click the log and select Properties.

To view the results of logging, go to System Monitor and click the View Log Data icon from the icon bar or press Ctrl+L on the keyboard. Be sure that the Source tab is selected, as shown in Figure 7.8. Click the Log Files option button, if you are not using the SQL Database logging format. Next, click the Add button, locate the log file using the Select Log File dialog box, and click Open to select the file. If you are using the SQL database logging format, click the Database option button and select the SQL System DSN and Log Set from their respective drop-down list boxes.

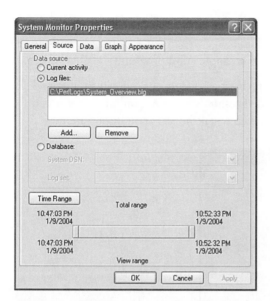

Figure 7.8 Setting the data source for a counter log to display its results in System Monitor.

To adjust the period of time view for displaying the log file's results, click the Time Range button; use the slider bar to shorten or lengthen the time window. Lengthening the time window gives you more of an overall view of a performance trend; shortening the time window lets you zoom in to analyze the details of system performance for a specific period of time.

You can also create counter logs from the command line under Windows XP using the aforementioned **logman.exe** tool. If you type **logman /?** at a command prompt, you can get help on the many "verbs," parameters, and options available with this tool. For example, the command line **logman create counter perf_log -c "\Processor(_Total)\% Processor Time** creates a new counter log named **perf log** that uses the binary file format and uses the Processor object, the % Processor Time counter, and the **_Total** instance.

Configuring Alerts

Alerts enable you to generate actions based on a counter reaching a particular threshold. For example, you might want to be notified when a disk's capacity reaches 90% so that you might work to increase the disk's capacity before it fills up completely. To do so, you specify a counter (such as %Free Space for a logical disk) and a threshold (under 10%).

Alerts send notifications whenever the predefined counter setting exceeds or falls beneath the specified alert threshold. When an alert is triggered based on its settings, it can perform several actions—create an entry in the application event log, send a network message to someone, initiate logging for a specific performance log, and run an application program.

The General tab of an alert's properties dialog box, shown in Figure 7.9, enables you to set counters and thresholds. The Action tab enables you to specify what actions should be taken when the alert conditions are met.

Figure 7.9   The General tab of an alert's properties dialog box.

To manually start an alert, right-click the alert name in the details pane of Performance Logs and Alerts and select Start. The icon for the alert turns to green, indicating that the alert is operating. To manually stop an alert from scanning the system, right-click the alert name and select Stop. To modify an alert's settings, right-click the alert and select Properties.

Monitoring Windows XP

Now that we've covered the nuts and bolts of how to monitor activity, the remaining sections focus on the meat and potatoes: what to monitor and why to monitor.

At a minimum, a desktop support technician should always monitor the four major performance areas (the "Big Four") that can have a significant impact on performance on a computer running Windows XP—processor utilization, memory utilization, disk utilization, and network utilization. These four major performance areas and the reasons for their impact on performance are covered in the remaining sections of this chapter.

Troubleshooting Performance Bottlenecks with System Monitor

By using the System Monitor and creating log files, you can determine when any of the utilization values for memory, disk, network, and processor are out of the norm.

Although the System Monitor does not remedy a bottleneck, you can use it to quantify the bottleneck. If you configure an action to be triggered by an alert, then it could be said that the System Monitor *can* remedy a bottleneck.

For example, Figure 7.10 displays a comparison that indicates an aberration in Disk Queue Length.

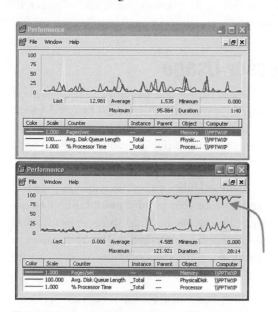

Figure 7.10 Comparing current Average Disk Queue Length performance data (top) against logged baseline performance data (bottom).

Diagnosing and Resolving Performance Bottlenecks

As a desktop support technician, you might receive comments from a user who says, "My computer *feels* slow today."

Although the Windows XP monitoring tools can enable you to identify which of the Big Four subsystems is the root cause, other "tweaks" might enable a desktop support technician to adjust the way in which the system and the applications interact.

You should diagnose system performance with the Task Manager or the System Monitor. As mentioned earlier, the System Monitor gives you a wider array of options.

Analyzing and Optimizing Windows XP Subsystems

To analyze and optimize Windows XP subsystems, you need to focus on the "usual suspects." Tables 7.1, 7.2, 7.3, and 7.4 in the following sections provide specific performance counters to analyze when checking for possible system bottlenecks. Each table lists general guidelines for performance counters that you should monitor, the threshold levels to check, and what remedial action that you can take to resolve the performance problem.

Monitoring Processor Usage

One or more CPUs are the heart of any computer system, and it's not good for a workstation to be fully utilized for prolonged periods. The CPU Usage graph in Task Manager and the % Processor Time counter in the Performance snap-in measure processor utilization. Sustained usage of 85% or more can indicate a processor bottleneck.

Large spreadsheets that employ many calculations and income tax preparation software are examples of applications that require more CPU processing power than word processing documents or slide show presentations. Keep in mind the types of software applications that each user requires to properly assess whether a dual-processor system would improve performance for certain users.

Table 7.1 contains the ways in which you can monitor processor performance.

Table 7.1 Troubleshooting Processor Usage Bottlenecks		
Performance Object: Counter	**Unacceptable Threshold Level**	**Remedy**
Processor:% User Time		
Processor:% Processor Time		
Processor:% Privileged	Sustained usage higher than 85%.	Upgrade existing CPU to a faster CPU or install additional CPUs. Time
System:Processor Queue Length		
Server Work Queues: Queue Length	Sustained usage higher than 2.	Upgrade existing CPU to a faster CPU or install additional CPUs.
Processor:Interrupts/sec	Varies by processor; however, substantially higher values than the baseline can indicate a hardware problem with another device in the computer, such as a faulty network adapter or a failing disk controller.	Locate and replace the hardware device that is generating the high number of interrupts.

As an alternative to installing another processor, you might try optimizing processor configuration.

Windows XP preemptively multitasks active processes, ensuring that all threads gain access to the processor. Processes do run at different priorities, however. Priority levels of 0 to 31 are assigned to a process, and higher-level processes are executed before lower-level processes.

As a desktop support technician, you can specify process priority using Task Manager. Right-clicking a process on the Processes tab enables you to set a process's priority. Processes are assigned a priority of Normal by default. Choosing Above Normal or High increases the priority of a process and thereby increases the frequency with which its threads are serviced. Choosing Below Normal or Low reduces the servicing of a process.

NOTE

> Do not use the Realtime priority. This priority should be reserved for real-time data gathering applications and operating system functions. Setting an application to the Realtime priority can cause system instability and can be difficult to reverse without restarting the system.

You can also control process priority when an application is launched, using the start command with the /low, /belownormal, /normal, /abovenormal, /high, and /realtime command-line switches.

On *dual-processor* Windows XP Professional computers, you can assign one or more specific processes to a specific processor. When you right-click a process in Task Manager from the Processes tab, the Set Affinity and Set Priority options are available. The Set Affinity option is not available on single CPU systems.

Monitoring Memory Usage

Memory is often the first performance bottleneck in the "real world." The counters related to processor and disk utilization (discussed later) might be well beyond their thresholds simply because inadequate memory is causing paging, which impacts those two components. You should always examine memory counters to ensure that they are not the root cause of the performance bottleneck.

Symptoms related to inadequate memory include excessive paging or a high rate of hard page faults.

To correct a memory shortage, your first reaction might be to add more RAM, which is certainly one solution. However, it is often equally valid to optimize memory usage by stopping unnecessary services, drivers, and background applications or by moving services or applications to systems with excess capacity.

Table 7.2 contains some suggested counters to monitor.

Table 7.2 Troubleshooting Memory Usage Bottlenecks		
Performance Object:Counter	**Unacceptable Threshold Level**	**Remedy**
Memory:Page Faults/sec	Consistent page fault rates higher than 5.	Identify the processes using disproportional amounts of RAM and install more memory.
Memory:Committed Bytes	Sustained value higher than 75% of total physical RAM installed.	Identify the processes using disproportional amounts of RAM and install more memory.
Memory:Available Bytes	Consistent value lower than 5% of total physical RAM installed.	Identify the processes using disproportional amounts of RAM and install more memory.
Memory:Pages/sec	Consistently higher than 20.	Identify the processes causing excessive paging and install more memory.
Memory:Pool Nonpaged Bytes	Steady increases (compared to baseline) over time without an increased workstation load can indicate a memory leak.	Identify one or more programs that might have a memory leak, stop running the programs, or get updated versions.

When installing more physical memory is not an option, consider optimizing Virtual Memory settings.

In computers running Windows XP, when physical RAM is not sufficient to support active processes, the *Virtual Memory Manager (VMM)* moves less active data or code from physical RAM to virtual memory stored in the paging file. When a process later attempts to address data or code currently in the paging file, the VMM transfers that memory space back into physical RAM. The paging file thus provides for efficient utilization of a system's physical RAM and allows a system to support more activity than its physical RAM alone would allow.

The transfer of *pages*, 4KB blocks of memory, to and from the paging file is normal on any system, but excessive paging, or thrashing, indicates a memory shortage. In addition, the paging file itself can impede performance if it is not properly optimized.

You configure the paging file using the System applet in Control Panel. Click the Advanced tab; click the Performance Options button; and then, in the Virtual Memory section, click Change.

The paging file, called `Pagefile.sys`, is created on the `%systemroot%` volume by default. Microsoft recommends that the paging file size should be 1.5 times the amount of physical RAM installed in the computer. You can configure the paging file to be placed on other volumes or to be split across multiple volumes, in which case there will be a `Pagefile.sys` file on each selected drive volume.

The total size of the paging file is considered the sum total of all the paging files that the system uses. You can also configure the paging file's *initial size* (the space created initially by the VMM and reserved for paging activity) and its *maximum size* (a setting that can permit the VMM to expand the paging file to a size greater than the initial size).

The ideal paging file configuration is to split it evenly over multiple physical disks except for the disks containing the system and boot partitions.

Optimize paging by performing the following:

➤ Remove the paging file from the system and boot partitions. The system partition is technically the partition that is used to start the system: it contains the NTLDR file and the boot sector. To make things confusing, the boot partition contains the operating system and is indicated by the variable `%systemroot%`. Luckily, most computers are configured with Windows XP on the C drive (the first partition), making the boot partition, the system partition, and `%systemroot%` all equal to C:. To remove the paging file from a partition, set its initial size and maximum size to zero (0) and click the Set button.

➤ Configure the paging file to reside on multiple physical disks, and configure the initial size and maximum size identically on all drives. The paging subsystem then spreads written pages evenly across all available Pagefile.sys files.

➤ Configure the paging file to reside on fast, less active drives. If you have drives of various speeds, put the paging file on the fastest one. If you have drives that are less active, put the paging file on those so that the paging system doesn't have to compete as often with other read or write operations.

➤ Before moving the paging file, defragment the volumes on which you will put the paging file. This practice helps prevent a fragmented paging file.

➤ Set the initial size to be sufficient for the system's paging requirements, and then set the maximum size to the same size. When the maximum size is greater than the initial size, and the system must expand the paging file, the expansion puts an additional burden on both the processor and disk subsystems. In addition, the paging file is likely to become fragmented, further hitting the performance of paging.

Monitoring Disk Usage

Disk storage can be a significant source of performance bottlenecking on a computer because disks are mechanical. Therefore, disk response times are generally much slower than the access times for nonmechanical components, such as the processor, memory, or even network I/O. You can monitor PhysicalDisk counters, LogicalDisk counters, or both. *PhysicalDisk counters* measure individual hard disk drives. *LogicalDisk counters* measure logical partitions or volumes stored on physical disks. LogicalDisk counters help you isolate the source of bottlenecks to a particular logical drive volume so that you can more easily identify where disk access requests are coming from.

 For Windows XP systems, you no longer need to enable LogicalDisk counters with the **Diskperf.exe** command so that you can monitor their performance with the System Monitor snap-in. LogicalDisk counters are automatically enabled on demand. You need **Diskperf.exe** only for the remote administration of computers running Windows NT and Windows 2000.

Table 7.3 Troubleshooting Disk Usage Bottlenecks		
Performance Object:Counter	**Unacceptable Threshold Level**	**Remedy**
PhysicalDisk:% Disk Time		
LogicalDisk:% Disk Time	Consistently higher than 50%.	First, verify that excessive paging is not the cause of this problem; if it is not the result of excessive paging, replace the disk with a faster model.
PhysicalDisk:Current Disk Queue Length		
LogicalDisk:Current Disk Queue Length	Consistently higher than 2.	Replace the disk with a faster model.
PhysicalDisk:Avg. Disk Bytes/Transfer		
LogicalDisk:Avg. Disk Bytes/Transfer	Consistently lower than the workstation's baseline.	Replace the disk with a faster model.
PhysicalDisk:Disk Bytes/sec		
LogicalDisk:Disk Bytes/sec	Consistently lower than the workstation's baseline.	Replace the disk with a faster model.

In general, when disk performance is a bottleneck, you can add capacity; replace disks with faster hardware; move applications, services, or data to underutilized disks; or implement spanned or striped volumes.

Windows XP Home Edition does not support striped or spanned dynamic disk volumes.

Monitoring Network Usage

Network throughput can have a major impact on users as they request data from network servers. Network bandwidth includes how fast bytes are sent to and from a computer and how fast data packages (packets, frames, segments, and datagrams) are transferred.

Network bottlenecks are often caused by too many requests for data on a particular network device; too much data traffic on the network segment; or a physical network problem with a hub, switch, router, or other network device.

The Network Utilization graph in Task Manager can assist you with troubleshooting a possible network bottleneck. This statistic should generally average below 30% utilization on a LAN.

For more definitive analysis, use the counters from Table 7.4 in the System Monitor.

Table 7.4 Troubleshooting Network Usage Bottlenecks		
Performance Object:Counter	Unacceptable Threshold Level	Remedy
Server:Bytes Total/sec		
Network Interface:Bytes Total/sec	Sustained usage levels higher than the baseline averages for with faster models; install	Replace the installed network adapters the workstation. another network adapter; upgrade the physical network cabling, hubs, and switches.
Server:Byte Received/sec	Sustained usage levels higher than 50% of the network adapter's bandwidth rating.	Replace the installed network adapters with faster models; upgrade the physical network cabling, hubs, and switches.
Network Interface:Bytes Sent/sec	Sustained usage levels lower than the baseline averages for the workstation.	Replace the installed network adapters with faster models; upgrade the physical network cabling, hubs, and switches.

Network usage bottlenecks can be difficult to troubleshoot because many factors can influence network bandwidth availability and because the larger networks become, the more complex they become. If you determine that network throughput is the source of your computer's bottleneck, you can take some constructive measures such as the following:

➤ Add servers to distribute network traffic.

➤ Segment the network into smaller subnets and connect each subnet to a separate network card on the workstation.

➤ Remove network bindings from unneeded network cards.

➤ Reduce network traffic by eliminating unnecessary protocols.

➤ Install the latest networking equipment such as 100Mb or 1000Mb (gigabit) switches, hubs, routers, and cabling.

Monitor these counters and watch for the threshold levels listed in Table 7.4.

 Although Windows Server 2003 and Windows 2000 Server can support Network Monitor for relatively sophisticated network traffic analysis, Windows XP Professional has fewer network performance tools. Although counters are available for the number of bytes and packets received and sent over a particular network interface, unfortunately you cannot view the contents or properties of packets from the GUI using only Windows XP Professional tools.

To conduct detailed network analysis for a Windows XP Professional system, perform the following steps:

1. Install the Network Monitor Driver.

2. From the Network Connections folder, right-click a connection, choose Properties, and then click Install.

3. Select the Protocol component and click the Add button. Select Network Monitor Driver and click OK.

4. Click Close to exit from the connection's Properties dialog box.

The Network Monitor Driver can collect packets that the Windows XP system's network interfaces send or receive. You can analyze the packet capture file (.cap) using a version of Network Monitor that ships with Systems Management Server (SMS), Windows 2000 Server, or Windows Server 2003.

You can also use a new tool that ships with Windows XP Professional, the Netcap.exe command-line utility, to analyze your system's network packets. The program installs a network driver and enables you to capture network traffic that you can later view with Microsoft's Network Monitor program. The first time you run the program, it installs the appropriate driver.

Exam Prep Questions

1. You are a desktop support technician for your company. A Windows XP user reports that his computer is responding slowly. You suspect one of several applications running on the computer. To test your theory, you log on to the computer and run the programs. You use Task Manager to view the results shown in Figure 7.11. Which of the programs listed is the probable bottleneck?

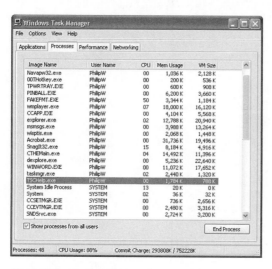

Figure 7.11   The Task Manager Processes tab.

- ❏   A. **wmplayer.exe**
- ❏   B. **FAKEFMT.exe**
- ❏   C. **Acrobat.exe**
- ❏   D. **WINWORD.exe**

The correct answer is B. The highest percentage of CPU utilization by far is associated with the FAKEFMT.exe process. If this value, 50%, is prolonged, it could indicate a program failure. Answers A, C, and D are incorrect because, although each of them occupies significant amounts of memory, they are not slowing down the processor at present.

2. You're a desktop support technician for your company. A customer named Tim reports that he has installed three new applications on the computer and that when he runs all three simultaneously, his computer and the three applications are slow to respond. He opens Task Manager and views all the values shown in Figure 7.12. Which process is most likely causing the computer to run slowly?

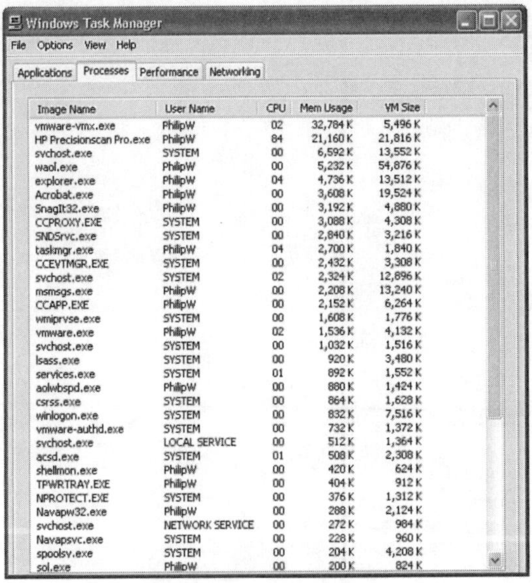

Image Name	User Name	CPU	Mem Usage	VM Size
vmware-vmx.exe	PhilipW	02	32,784 K	5,496 K
HP Precisionscan Pro.exe	PhilipW	84	21,160 K	21,816 K
svchost.exe	SYSTEM	00	6,592 K	13,552 K
waol.exe	PhilipW	00	5,232 K	54,876 K
explorer.exe	PhilipW	04	4,736 K	13,512 K
Acrobat.exe	PhilipW	00	3,608 K	19,524 K
SnagIt32.exe	PhilipW	00	3,192 K	4,880 K
CCPROXY.EXE	SYSTEM	00	3,088 K	4,308 K
SNDSrvc.exe	SYSTEM	00	2,840 K	3,216 K
taskmgr.exe	PhilipW	04	2,700 K	1,840 K
CCEVTMGR.EXE	SYSTEM	00	2,432 K	3,308 K
svchost.exe	SYSTEM	02	2,324 K	12,896 K
msmsgs.exe	PhilipW	00	2,208 K	13,240 K
CCAPP.EXE	PhilipW	00	2,152 K	6,264 K
wmiprvse.exe	SYSTEM	00	1,608 K	1,776 K
vmware.exe	PhilipW	02	1,536 K	4,132 K
svchost.exe	SYSTEM	00	1,032 K	1,516 K
lsass.exe	SYSTEM	00	920 K	3,480 K
services.exe	SYSTEM	01	892 K	1,552 K
aolwbspd.exe	PhilipW	00	880 K	1,424 K
csrss.exe	SYSTEM	00	864 K	1,628 K
winlogon.exe	SYSTEM	00	832 K	7,516 K
vmware-authd.exe	SYSTEM	00	732 K	1,372 K
svchost.exe	LOCAL SERVICE	00	512 K	1,364 K
acsd.exe	SYSTEM	01	508 K	2,308 K
shellmon.exe	PhilipW	00	420 K	624 K
TPWRTRAY.EXE	PhilipW	00	404 K	912 K
NPROTECT.EXE	SYSTEM	00	376 K	1,312 K
Navapw32.exe	PhilipW	00	288 K	2,124 K
svchost.exe	NETWORK SERVICE	00	272 K	984 K
Navapsvc.exe	SYSTEM	00	228 K	960 K
spoolsv.exe	SYSTEM	00	204 K	4,208 K
sol.exe	PhilipW	00	200 K	824 K

Figure 7.12 The Task Manager Processes tab.

❏ A. **HP Precisionscan Pro.exe**

❏ B. **Vmware-vmx.exe**

❏ C. **explorer.exe**

❏ D. **waol.exe**

The correct answer is A. At 84% CPU utilization, this program is monopolizing CPU attention and might be preventing other programs from responding in a reasonable amount of time. Although Answers B, C, and D occupy significant amounts of memory, they are probably not the bottleneck.

3. You are a desktop support technician for your company. A computer with 256MB of RAM, a 20GB hard drive, and a Pentium III 866MHz processor running Windows XP responds slowly when a user runs several applications. On the user's computer, you are examining the Performance tab information in Task Manager shown in Figure 7.13.

Which of the following upgrades would benefit the performance?

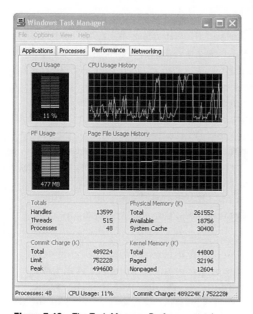

Figure 7.13   The Task Manager Performance tab.

❑   A. A second processor
❑   B. A faster processor
❑   C. A second hard drive
❑   D. Additional RAM

The correct answer is D. The high percentage of paging file usage indicates that there is an inadequate amount of RAM in this computer. Answers A and B are incorrect because CPU usage is relatively low; therefore adding a processor or upgrading the processor will not have much of an impact. Answer C is incorrect because there is no evidence of inadequate hard drive space.

4. You are a desktop support technician. After performing an installation of Windows XP, you want to create a baseline to preserve the current performance-related values for future troubleshooting. Which of the following system tools is best suited to complete this task in Windows XP Professional?

- ❑ A. Performance Logs and Alerts
- ❑ B. System Monitor
- ❑ C. Task Manager
- ❑ D. Network Monitor Driver and the **Netcap.exe** utility

Answer A is correct. The Performance Logs and Alerts snap-in captures performance activity over time and can store it in a log. By tracking activity for key components, such as memory, processor, network interfaces, and physical and logical disks, you can create a baseline against which to compare future activity. Answer B is incorrect because the System Monitor snap-in displays only current activity or past activity: it does not preserve such data. Answer C is incorrect because the Task Manager displays only current activity for applications, processes, performance, and networking: it does not save data. Answer D is incorrect because the Network Monitor Driver and the Netcap.exe utility capture and analyze network data packets: they do not save any other performance-related data.

5. You are a desktop support technician. A user complains of poor performance from a desktop publishing program running on Windows XP. By analyzing performance counters, you discover that the bottleneck is due to insufficient memory. The computer has 256MB of memory and cannot be increased. Which of the following actions represents a best-practice approach to configuring virtual memory on a Windows XP Professional computer that has three physical hard disks (assigned as drives C, D, and E), with the **%systemroot%** folder located on the C drive?

- ❑ A. Place the paging file on the C drive with an initial size of 192MB and a maximum size of 256MB.
- ❑ B. Place a paging file on the D drive with an initial size of 192MB and a maximum size of 192MB, and place a second paging file on the E drive, also with an initial size of 192MB and a maximum size of 192MB.
- ❑ C. Place a paging file on the E drive with an initial size of 128MB and a maximum size of 256MB.
- ❑ D. Place a paging file on the E drive with an initial size of 192MB and a maximum size of 192MB, and place a second paging file on the C drive, also with an initial size of 192MB and a maximum size of 192MB.

Answer B is correct. The optimal paging file configuration is to split it evenly over multiple physical disks without placing it on the system or boot volumes. The recommended paging file size is 1.5 times the installed memory. For a system with 256MB RAM installed, that would be 384MB split over two drives (192MB each). Answer A is incorrect because it is not a best practice to place the paging file on the system or boot volumes. Answer C is incorrect because it is not optimal to make the initial size lower than the maximum size; it would cause the paging file to be expanded, which takes system resources. Answer D is incorrect because it is not a best practice to place the paging file on the system or boot volumes, even if you place other paging files on different volumes.

6. You are a desktop support technician. You support a computer running Windows XP that is installed with dual processors. Which of the following Windows XP system components can you configure or monitor from the Task Manager window for a dual-processor computer? (Select all the correct answers.)

❑ A. Network utilization and current condition

❑ B. Processor usage and page file usage

❑ C. Processor affinity for specific processes

❑ D. Processor priority for specific processes

❑ E. Available system memory

❑ F. List of processes running from all users

Answers A, B, C, D, E, and F are all correct. Network utilization percentage appears on the Networking tab, processor and page file usage appears on the Performance tab, and processor affinity settings and processor priority settings for specific processes are managed on the Processes tab. Available system memory appears on the Performance tab, and you can expand the list of processes to include all users on the machine by marking the Show Processes from All Users check box at the bottom of the Processes tab.

7. You are a desktop support technician. After installing a proprietary database application on a user's computer running Windows XP, the user complains about a significant decrease in performance. To remedy the problem, you uninstall the application from the user's computer. However, after doing so, the computer's performance remains unacceptable. You want to improve the computer's performance, but you do not want to lose any of the user's data.

Which of the following should you perform?

❑ A. Delete unnecessary software branches from the Registry.

❑ B. Use the System Monitor to establish a baseline.

❑ C. Restore the computer from the most recent backup.

❑ D. Defragment the hard drive.

The correct answer is D. Defragmenting the hard drive is a practical technique after removing large numbers of files from a computer. The process of defragmenting the drive might increase the efficiency of a drive by eliminating empty space scattered on a drive. It does not eliminate files. Answer C is incorrect because restoring the computer from the last backup deletes data. Answer A is incorrect because editing the Registry is always a treacherous recommendation and might not improve performance. Answer B is incorrect because using the System Monitor to establish a performance baseline can only show current values, not improve performance.

8. You are a desktop support technician. A user alerts you that the application log on her computer is full. You want to prevent the log from growing but need to maintain the existing entries for future forensic analysis.

   Which of the following should you perform?

   ❑ A. Create a manual restore point, and then clear the application log.
   ❑ B. Back up the application log, and then archive the records.
   ❑ C. Manually clear the application log, and archive the existing records.
   ❑ D. Create a filter for the application log and apply it to the records.

   The correct answer is C. When you manually attempt to clear the application log, you are prompted to archive the existing records to an .evt file, .txt file, or .csv file. Answer A is incorrect because creating a manual restore point preserves system settings but does not archive the application log. Answer B is incorrect. You can back up the application log file and archive the existing records, but this way is not the most efficient way to achieve the objective of the scenario. Answer D is incorrect because creating a filter does not empty the application log.

9. You are a desktop support technician. A user has a computer running Windows XP with two hard disks. Two partitions, C and D, are on the same disk. Partition C holds the operating system. Partition D holds the applications. User data is stored on an E drive, which occupies the entire second disk. When the user runs more than one application, he notices that the performance of the computer is unacceptable. Page faults are occurring, and you need to improve the computer's performance.

   What should you do to improve performance?

   ❑ A. Move the paging file to drive E.
   ❑ B. Run disk cleanup on the physical disk that hosts drives C and D.
   ❑ C. Divide the physical disk, drive E, into two separate partitions.
   ❑ D. Use System Monitor to identify which application or applications are causing the performance problems.

The correct answer is A. Page faults reflect a lack of sufficient memory. In addition, with the operating system, paging file, and applications all installed on the same drive, there is an inordinate amount of disk I/O to the first disk. If you distribute the applications, system files, and paging file, performance ought to improve. Answer B is incorrect; running disk cleanup might improve performance by deleting temporary files and making more disk space available, but the improvement would not be significant. Answer C is incorrect because part of the virtual memory space would still reside on the first disk. Answer D is incorrect because the System Monitor can merely identify bottlenecks, not remedy them.

10. You are a desktop support technician. A user reports that when he runs a spreadsheet application along with a proprietary database program, performance deteriorates. Performing a test, you notice that when running the database program, CPU usage spikes to 100%. After the database program is stopped, CPU usage drops to 30%. Paging activity is high throughout the test.

To improve the computer's performance, you should

❑ A. Upgrade the computer's NIC.

❑ B. Add more RAM.

❑ C. Increase the size of the paging file.

❑ D. Add another CPU.

The correct answer is B. Adding memory is usually the first step to improving computer performance. High disk usage and CPU utilization are often values that arise because of a lack of sufficient memory and result in excessive paging. All the facts provided in the scenario—high CPU usage, high paging activity—point to a lack of sufficient memory. If, after you add more memory, CPU utilization remains high, you should consider adding another processor. Answer A is incorrect. There is no evidence that the bottleneck is network related. Answer C is incorrect because increasing a paging file does not reduce the number of page faults. Answer D is incorrect because adding another CPU does not solve the high paging activity that is resulting in slow performance.

8

Managing and Troubleshooting Network Protocols and Services

Terms you'll need to understand:

✓ Transmission Control Protocol/Internet Protocol (TCP/IP)
✓ Ping
✓ **IPCONFIG**
✓ **PATHPING**
✓ **NSLOOKUP**
✓ Internet Connection Firewall (ICF)
✓ Dynamic Host Configuration Protocol (DHCP)
✓ HOSTS
✓ LMHOSTS
✓ Windows Internet Naming Service (WINS)
✓ Domain Name System (DNS)
✓ Virtual private network (VPN)
✓ Internet Explorer Security Settings
✓ Remote Desktop
✓ Remote Assistance

Techniques you'll need to master:

✓ Troubleshooting network settings
✓ Obtaining an IP address automatically
✓ Configuring ICF
✓ Logging network security breaches
✓ Configuring host name resolution
✓ Establishing a VPN connection
✓ Enabling and troubleshooting Remote Desktop
✓ Enabling and troubleshooting Remote Assistance

Whether or not Merriam Webster is aware of it, to a desktop support technician, the opposite of *networking* is *Not Working*.

The desktop support technician needs to be able to explain and master, manage and troubleshoot the elements that enable computers running Windows XP to communicate.

Examining TCP/IP Networking Features and Tools

A large number of variables combine to affect network performance and reliability, including traffic, remote connections, network adapter configuration, and device drivers. Network problems are often related simply to protocol configuration errors.

As a desktop support technician, you have no doubt witnessed how an incorrect setting for an IP address, default gateway, or subnet mask can often be the Achilles' heel of IP addressing, routing, and security.

The components that make up a network configuration begin with the network interface and its TCP/IP settings, shown in Figure 8.1.

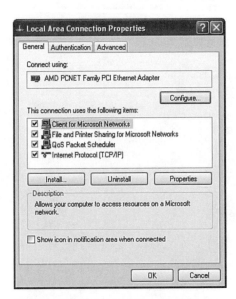

Figure 8.1   The network configuration dialog box.

Among the new features that Windows XP provides is a convenient interface with which you can troubleshoot network settings.

When you right-click a network connection either on a menu, in the system tray, or in the Network Connections Control Panel applet, a status option triggers a dialog box that reveals the condition of the network interface.

The Support tab displays the interface's current IP address values, and clicking the Details button, shown in Figure 8.2, displays other IP properties.

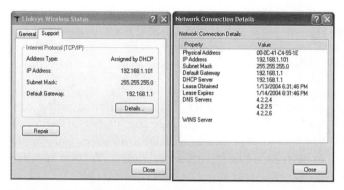

Figure 8.2 The network interface status dialog boxes.

The Repair button in the Status dialog box is a convenient way to renew an IP address obtained from a DHCP server; flush the Address Resolution Protocol (ARP), DNS, and NetBIOS name caches; and register with WINS and DNS. This button performs all those tasks at once.

Windows XP also provides wireless Institute of Electrical and Electronics Engineers (IEEE) 802.11B networking support. infrared line of sight wireless, and Network Bridge.

Network Bridge enables you to use Windows XP to connect LAN segments consisting of different media—without having to use a separate router or bridge.

Network Bridge uses the IEEE Spanning Tree Algorithm to ensure that the network is loop free.

To create a bridge between two networks, follow these steps:

1. In the Control Panel Network Connections applet, under LAN or High Speed Internet, Ctrl+click each of the network connections you want to make part of the bridge.

2. Right-click one of the connections and click Bridge Connections.

Only Ethernet adapters, IEEE 1394 adapters, or Ethernet-compatible adapters (such as wireless adapters) can be part of the network bridge.

Adapters that have ICF or Internet Connections Sharing (ICS) enabled cannot be included in the network bridge.

You may only create one single bridge on a computer running Windows XP.

You cannot create a bridge connection on computers running Windows 2000 or earlier.

Windows XP also supports a quality-of-service (QoS) packet scheduler. QoS helps Windows provide a guaranteed delivery system for network traffic such as TCP/IP packets and optimizes the utilization of shared Internet connections.

Windows XP also provides an alternate TCP/IP configuration dialog box, shown in Figure 8.3, which allows you to configure your mobile PC with two different TCP/IP settings. This is especially helpful for users with laptop computers who move between home and office. Solution: make your primary IP address dynamic, and make your alternate address static.

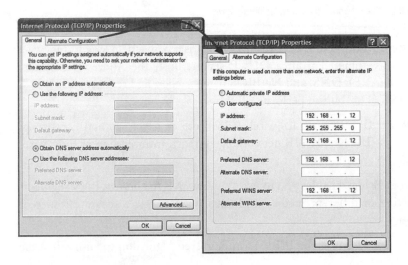

Figure 8.3 Alternate IP address configuration.

Windows XP offers a network security solution for users connected to the Internet. ICF filters inbound network traffic and by default, if enabled, filters all traffic. ICF is discussed in greater detail later in this chapter. By default, the feature is not enabled.

Understanding the TCP/IP Utilities and Their Uses

Besides carefully examining the settings of the Windows XP network configuration dialog boxes, you can use several troubleshooting tools and commands to monitor network performance.

The following is a list of those utilities:

➤*ARP (Arp.exe)*—Displays the ARP cache on the interface of the local computer. Use this tool to detect invalid entries.

➤ *GetMac (Getmac.exe)*—Displays the media access control (MAC) address for all network adapters installed on a computer.

➤ *Hostname (Hostname.exe)*—Displays the name of the computer.

➤ *IP Configuration (Ipconfig.exe)*—Displays your current IP address settings.

➤ *IP Security Monitor (Microsoft Management Console [MMC] snap-in)*— Verifies that secured communications are successfully established between devices.

➤ *Local Security Policy (secpol.msc)*—Enables you to assign or modify IP Security (IPSec) policies that can filter TCP/IP packets.

➤ *NetBT Statistics (Nbtstat.exe)*—Displays protocol statistics for current TCP/IP connections that are using NetBIOS over TCP/IP (NetBT), the status of current NetBIOS over TCP/IP connections, and the computer's registered names and scope ID. You can also use it to refresh the NetBIOS name cache.

➤*Netsh (Netsh.exe)*—Enables you to use other tools to view and modify local network interface TCP/IP configurations.

➤ *Netstat*—Displays TCP/IP protocol statistics and active connections. For example, using the command netstat -ao, you can see to whom your computer is talking and the process ID of the program that is doing the talking.

➤*Network Connectivity Tester (netdiag.exe)*—Scans your computer and runs a series of network and domain tests (from the command prompt).

➤*Network Diagnostics*—Scans and gathers (from the Help and Support Center) your computer's network-related software and hardware configurations. You can also launch it with the command netsh diag gui.

➤ *Network Monitor Capture Utility (Netcap.exe)*—Allows you to monitor (sniff) network packets and save the information to a capture (.cap) file. You can use the captured data to analyze network traffic patterns.

➤ *Nslookup.exe*—Displays information about DNS servers, performs DNS queries, and examines DNS zone files on local and remote servers.

➤ *Path Ping (Pathping.exe)*—Traces a path to a TCP/IP host, displays packet losses at each router along the way, and reveals network performance statistics. The command-line tool combines features of ping (Ping.exe) and trace route (Tracert.exe).

➤ *Ping (Ping.exe)*—Sends Internet Control Message Protocol (ICMP) echo request messages to verify that TCP/IP is configured correctly and that a TCP/IP host is available.

➤ *Port Query (portquery.exe)*—A command-line utility, available from the Microsoft Download Center, that helps you troubleshoot TCP/IP connectivity by reporting the port status of TCP and User Datagram Protocol (UDP) ports on computer that you select.

➤ *Route*—Displays the IP routing table and adds or deletes IP routes.

➤ *Tracert*—Displays the path packets travel to a TCP/IP host.

Configuring and Troubleshooting TCP/IP Settings

Truth be told, DHCP eliminates a user's need to understand many of the intricacies of TCP/IP.

But a desktop support technician needs to be comfortable with IP version 4, the 32-bit mechanism used to assigning unique addresses to devices connecting to the same network segment.

In short, no two computers on the same network segment may have the same IP address.

Subnet masks identify the size of the address range within which the individual address exists. Subnets can be big or small, depending on the number of devices they segregate from the rest of the network.

For a lengthier discussion of TCP/IP, see **http://www.microsoft.com/resources/docu-mentation/Windows/XP/all/reskit/en-us/Default.asp?url=/resources/documenta-tion/Windows/XP/all/reskit/en-us/prcc_tcp_tuoz.asp**.

After a desktop support technician has determined that there are no wiring or NIC problems (Layer 1 problems as Open Systems Interconnect [OSI] model enthusiasts would call it), he or she must examine the actual logical addresses that make up the interface's configuration.

If latency (slowness) is a problem, network protocol analyzers help you quantify the problem and locate its source. If connectivity is the problem, it's time for a ping-a-thon:

➤ Can you ping yourself (PING LOCALHOST)?

➤ Can you ping your own IP address?

➤ Can you ping a neighbor computer?

➤ Can you ping the default gateway?

➤ Can you ping a device on the other side of the default gateway?

➤ Can you ping a device using its NetBIOS name?

➤ Can you ping a device using its Fully Qualified Domain Name (FQDN)?

The ping command is one tool for connectivity troubleshooting. You can use tracert in each of the preceding scenarios to determine the pathway through which packets are traveling on their way to the destination. Tracert, shown in Figure 8.4, also reveals latency between hops, which might suggest inferior equipment or an overabundance of traffic along the packet's route.

```
C:\WINDOWS\System32\cmd.exe                                    _ □ ×

C:\>TRACERT 4.2.2.4

Tracing route to vnsc-pri-dsl.genuity.net [4.2.2.4]
over a maximum of 30 hops:

  1     1 ms     1 ms     1 ms   192.168.1.1
  2    15 ms    15 ms    15 ms   4.10.128.1
  3    17 ms    15 ms    15 ms   4.9.14.129
  4    15 ms    15 ms    15 ms   vnsc-pri-dsl.genuity.net [4.2.2.4]

Trace complete.

C:\>_
```

Figure 8.4   The **tracert** command.

If tracert fails at some point in its trace of network traffic, that information provides you with a clue to the whereabouts of the problem.

The netsh command-line utility enables you to quickly reset many TCP/IP-related values.

With the Netsh utility, a desktop support technician can reset the TCP/IP configuration to a pristine state, to the same state as when the operating system was installed. When you execute this command, Netsh rewrites pertinent Registry keys that are used by the Internet protocol (TCP/IP) stack, achieving the same effect as the removal and the reinstallation of the protocol, as shown in Figure 8.5.

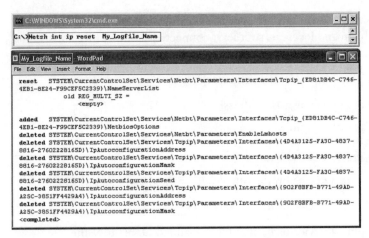

Figure 8.5 Netsh resetting network settings. The command appears above; the resultant log file appears below.

Additionally, you can access a thorough network diagnostics test by issuing the command Netsh diag gui, shown in Figure 8.6.

If latency is the problem, you can find a solution by reducing overall network traffic, reducing the number of devices that share the same network segment.

Sometimes, the only alternative to troubleshooting TCP/IP might be to revert to the tried and true NetBIOS Extended User Interface (NetBEUI).

Microsoft has discontinued support for the NetBEUI network protocol in Windows XP. However, sometimes migration to another network protocol (hmmm, such as TCP/IP), might involve significant time in planning and testing. Those who are migrating to XP by obtaining the full, retail-released version of Windows XP can find the NetBEUI protocol, lo and behold, on the Windows XP CD-ROM under the VALUEADD directory.

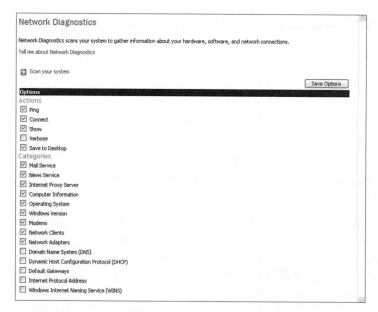

Figure 8.6 Network diagnostics test setup within Help and Support.

The files needed to install the NetBEUI protocol on Windows XP are Netnbf.inf and Nbf.sys. To install NetBEUI, follow these steps:

1. Insert the Windows XP CD-ROM into the CD-ROM drive and browse to the Valueadd\MSFT\Net\NetBEUI folder.

2. Copy Nbf.sys to the %SYSTEMROOT%\System32\Drivers directory.

3. Copy Netnbf.inf to the %SYSTEMROOT%\Inf hidden directory.

4. Click Start, click Control Panel, and then double-click Network Connections.

5. Right-click the adapter to which you want to add NetBEUI, and then click Properties.

6. On the General tab, click Install, click Protocol, and then click Add.

7. Select NetBEUI Protocol from the list and then click OK.

8. Restart Windows XP if you receive a message to complete the installation. (Some things never change!)

Choosing Between Manual and Automatic IP Address Assignments

You can assign IP addresses manually or Windows XP can acquire them automatically.

Addresses are acquired automatically for network interfaces either locally by Automatic Private IP Addressing (APIPA) or centrally by a DHCP server.

To configure a network interface to obtain an IP address automatically, click the radio button beside Obtain an IP Address Automatically in the TCP/IP configuration dialog box, shown in Figure 8.3.

There are ongoing debates about the benefits of automatic versus manual IP address acquisition. On the one hand, automatic acquisition relieves the desktop support technician of the tedious task of manually configuring workstations and effectively enables organizations to manage larger quantities of machines with fewer technicians. However, others argue with equal fervor that automatic IP address configuration introduces more, not less, complexity, due to its dependence on a computerized process.

Manually configuring IP addresses can be tedious work in all but the very smallest networks and is prone to human error. Generally, autoconfiguration is a better choice.

In short, the larger the network, the more desktop support technicians benefit from the convenience of automatic configurations. When a computer running Windows XP is configured to obtain an IP address automatically, and DHCP is unavailable to assign or renew an address, the Windows XP Professional client selects an IP address from the range of Internet Assigned Numbers Authority (IANA)–designated, private Class B addresses (169.254.0.1–169.254.255.254) with the subnet mask 255.255.0.0.

Windows then determines whether the chosen address exists elsewhere on the network by doing "duplicate-address detection." If the address is in use, then Windows selects another IP address up to 10 times. After Windows chooses an address that is not in use, it configures the interface with that address. APIPA assigns a Windows XP Professional client an IP address in the following circumstances:

➤ The client is configured to obtain a lease DHCP, but a DHCP server cannot be found, is unavailable, or is not used (for example, in a small office/home office network).

➤ The client uses DHCP to obtain a lease, but the client's attempts to renew the lease through a DHCP server have failed.

NOTE

APIPA doesn't mean the end of DHCP broadcasts. Although Windows has an APIPA address, it still continues to check for a DHCP server every five minutes. If it finds a DHCP server, it abandons the APIPA autoconfiguration information and the configuration offered by the DHCP server replaces it.

To determine whether APIPA is enabled, at the command prompt, type `ipconfig /all` and press Enter. If the text Autoconfiguration Enabled says Yes, APIPA is enabled. Addresses are assigned from the 169.254.0.1–169.254.255.254 range.

You can disable automatic private IP addressing in one of two ways:

➤ Manually configure TCP/IP. This method also disables DHCP.

➤ Disable automatic private IP addressing (but not DHCP) for a particular network interface by editing the Registry.

Configuring and Troubleshooting the ICF

With an ongoing emphasis on security, Microsoft provides many tools with which to filter traffic.

ICF, shown in Figure 8.7, provides what critics describe as a very nice basic personal firewall. Implementing ICF can pose some sudden surprises because, once enabled, it blocks all ports. If you are hosting Web or FTP services, those ports will have to be opened. To support internal applications, additional ports will need to be enabled.

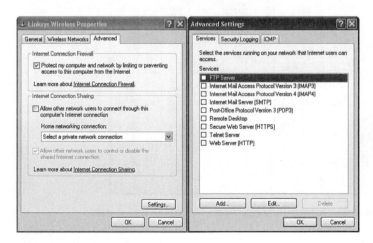

Figure 8.7   ICF configuration dialog boxes.

ICF can filter and log attempts to initiate communications from outside your computer. You can open up any port or ports. By default the firewall is not enabled in Windows XP SP1.

ICF enables a desktop support technician to configure port filtering. If, after it is enabled, users suffer connectivity problems, you can troubleshoot by either disabling ICF altogether or logging dropped packets.

In the Advanced dialog box, you can configure the following components:

- *Services*—Lists standard port assignments and enables you to create custom TCP or UDP port assignments by clicking Add.
- *Security Logging*—Controls the location, size, and contents of the log files that ICF can maintain.
- *ICMP Filtering*—Controls whether Windows XP will respond to ICMP (ping) packets. The options include both incoming and outgoing packets.

The results of aggressive filtering are always illuminating. The log file in Figure 8.8 is the result of a Port Scan attack levied from a computer that has the IP address 192.168.1.100 against a computer that has the IP address 192.168.1.101. Note: Some data has been removed for clarity.

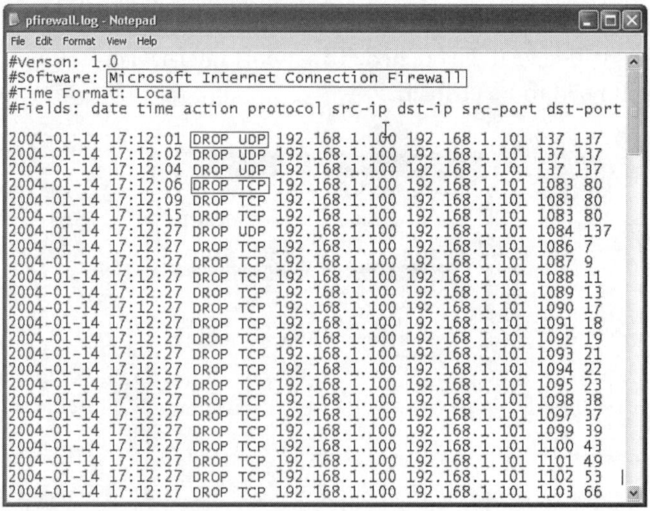


```
#Verson: 1.0
#Software: Microsoft Internet Connection Firewall
#Time Format: Local
#Fields: date time action protocol src-ip dst-ip src-port dst-port

2004-01-14 17:12:01 DROP UDP 192.168.1.100 192.168.1.101 137 137
2004-01-14 17:12:02 DROP UDP 192.168.1.100 192.168.1.101 137 137
2004-01-14 17:12:04 DROP UDP 192.168.1.100 192.168.1.101 137 137
2004-01-14 17:12:06 DROP TCP 192.168.1.100 192.168.1.101 1083 80
2004-01-14 17:12:09 DROP TCP 192.168.1.100 192.168.1.101 1083 80
2004-01-14 17:12:15 DROP TCP 192.168.1.100 192.168.1.101 1083 80
2004-01-14 17:12:27 DROP UDP 192.168.1.100 192.168.1.101 1084 137
2004-01-14 17:12:27 DROP TCP 192.168.1.100 192.168.1.101 1086 7
2004-01-14 17:12:27 DROP TCP 192.168.1.100 192.168.1.101 1087 9
2004-01-14 17:12:27 DROP TCP 192.168.1.100 192.168.1.101 1088 11
2004-01-14 17:12:27 DROP TCP 192.168.1.100 192.168.1.101 1089 13
2004-01-14 17:12:27 DROP TCP 192.168.1.100 192.168.1.101 1090 17
2004-01-14 17:12:27 DROP TCP 192.168.1.100 192.168.1.101 1091 18
2004-01-14 17:12:27 DROP TCP 192.168.1.100 192.168.1.101 1092 19
2004-01-14 17:12:27 DROP TCP 192.168.1.100 192.168.1.101 1093 21
2004-01-14 17:12:27 DROP TCP 192.168.1.100 192.168.1.101 1094 22
2004-01-14 17:12:27 DROP TCP 192.168.1.100 192.168.1.101 1095 23
2004-01-14 17:12:27 DROP TCP 192.168.1.100 192.168.1.101 1098 38
2004-01-14 17:12:27 DROP TCP 192.168.1.100 192.168.1.101 1097 37
2004-01-14 17:12:27 DROP TCP 192.168.1.100 192.168.1.101 1099 39
2004-01-14 17:12:27 DROP TCP 192.168.1.100 192.168.1.101 1100 43
2004-01-14 17:12:27 DROP TCP 192.168.1.100 192.168.1.101 1101 49
2004-01-14 17:12:27 DROP TCP 192.168.1.100 192.168.1.101 1102 53
2004-01-14 17:12:27 DROP TCP 192.168.1.100 192.168.1.101 1103 66
```

Figure 8.8 The log file of a computer running Windows XP with ICF logging enabled.

ICF is one way to filter incoming and outgoing traffic on a computer running Windows XP. You can also limit TCP/IP traffic by using TCP/IP filtering, which is available through the Advanced TCP/IP Settings dialog box's Options page, shown in Figure 8.9. Like ICF, TCP/IP filtering controls the ports and packet types for inbound traffic. You can use TCP/IP packet filtering to limit packet reception by TCP or UDP port or by IP protocol.

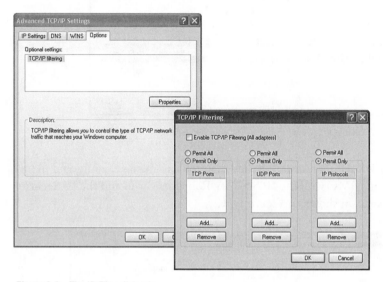

Figure 8.9 The IP Filter dialog box.

A third method of filtering is provided by IPSec, an advanced Windows XP network setting that is configured and monitored through an MMC on both Windows XP Professional and Windows XP Home Editions.

IPSec is an industry-defined set of standards that verifies, authenticates, and optionally encrypts data at the IP packet level. It can be enabled for the Windows XP Professional–based computer by using local policies or implemented by using group policy objects in Active Directory within an enterprise environment.

When you enable IPSec, built-in or custom IPSec policies determine the rules required for secured communications with other hosts. You can create or modify these rules by using the IP Security Policy Management snap-in.

You can use IPSec to filter traffic based upon encryption, authentication, and ports. Figure 8.10 shows an example of an custom IPSec filter that denies traffic to certain ports.

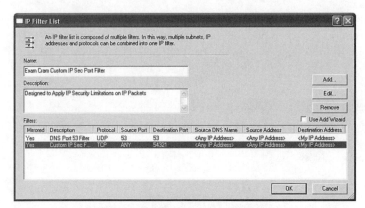

Figure 8.10 A custom IPSec filter setting within an IPSec policy.

The filter is part of an overall policy that you can manage, apply, and monitor using an MMC with the IP Security Policies snap-in and the IP Security Monitor snap-in shown in Figure 8.11.

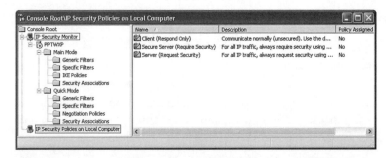

Figure 8.11 An MMC to which the IPSec Monitor and IPSec Policies snap-ins have been added.

> **NOTE**
>
> IPSec policies can be powerful. For more information, see **http://www.microsoft.com/resources/documentation/Windows/XP/all/reskit/en-us/Default.asp?url=/resources/documentation/Windows/XP/all/reskit/en-us/prcc_tcp_erqb.asp?frame=true**.

Configuring and Troubleshooting Hostname Resolution Issues

In general, users prefer names instead of numbers. In Windows XP Professional, TCP/IP supports communication over a network using a hostname, sometimes called a NetBIOS name, in place of an IP address.

Because applications might only recognize one naming convention, there are programs and files designed to translate one naming convention to another.

Windows XP Professional supports the following five ways to resolve names to IP addresses:

➤ *DNS*—Allows applications and services to convert Fully Qualified Domain Names (FQDN)to IP addresses.

➤ *WINS*—Allows applications and services to convert NetBIOS names to IP addresses. The browsing function of Microsoft Windows NT 4.0, Windows 98, and Windows 95 uses NetBIOS names.

➤ *HOSTS and LMHOSTS files*—Allow applications and services to convert FQDN and NetBIOS names into IP names using text files.

➤ *Broadcasts*—Allow applications and services to convert NetBIOS names into IP addresses by broadcasting to the local subnet.

➤ *Cache*—Allows applications and services to convert FQDN and NetBIOS names to IP addresses by looking for past associations stored in memory (DNS cache and NetBIOS cache).

For Windows XP Professional–based computers, a desktop support technician needs to understand how a client resolves names.

For an in-depth discussion of Windows XP name resolution, see **http://www.microsoft.com/resources/documentation/Windows/XP/all/reskit/ en-us/Default.asp?url=/resources/documentation/Windows/XP/all/reskit/ en-us/prjj_ipa_jhzw.asp**.

DNS is the default name-resolution method for Windows XP Professional computers and is required for their integration into an Active Directory domain.

If you can communicate with a remote machine using its IP address but not its FQDN, you need to look at the DNS tables, the local HOSTS file, and the DNS cache on the local machine. All three components contribute to DNS name resolution.

Here's the "resolution roadmap":

Windows XP first submits the name query to DNS. If DNS name resolution fails, the computer checks the length of the name.

If the name is longer than 15 bytes, and therefore a DNS-style name, resolution fails.

If the name is 15 characters or less, the computer checks whether NetBIOS is running.

If NetBIOS is not running, resolution fails; however, if NetBIOS (or NetBIOS over TCP/IP, NetBT) is running, the computer forwards the process to NetBIOS name resolution.

When Windows XP submits the name to DNS, the system checks the local DNS cache first. If the requested data is in the cache, the result is returned to the user. If the name is not its own and is not located in cache, the resolver queries the DNS servers listed in TCP/IP configuration.

When the Windows XP Professional resolver process receives either a successful or unsuccessful response to a query, it adds that information to its cache, thus creating a DNS resource record. This introduces the possibility that unsuccessful responses stored in the DNS cache might temporarily thwart troubleshooting because your system temporarily remembers failed named resolution even though you've fixed the problem.

If the name is not its own, the resolver always checks the cache first before querying any DNS server, so if a DNS resource record is in the cache, the resolver uses the record from the cache rather than query a server. This process expedites queries and decreases network traffic for DNS queries.

Keep in mind, the local cache is both the product of queries conducted by the DNS resolver and the contents of the local HOSTS file, which is preloaded into the resolver's cache and reloaded into the cache whenever it is updated.

The HOSTS file can be created and modified by a desktop support technician with a text editor. A default HOSTS file is provided in the `%systemroot%\System32\Drivers\Etc` folder under Windows XP Professional. The file can be edited to include remote host names and IP addresses for each computer with which you communicate.

However, remember that the values in the HOSTS file update the cache. Because the DNS resolver always looks in the local cache first, if the values are incorrect in the local HOSTS file, name resolution will fail.

To troubleshoot failed DNS queries, always display what is in the local DNS cache and perhaps flush the DNS cache. To display the DNS cache, enter `ipconfig /displaydns` at the command prompt. To flush the cache, enter `ipconfig /flushdns` at the command prompt. (Keep in mind that values stored in the HOSTS file automatically repopulate the DNS cache after it's been flushed.)

Configuring and Troubleshooting NetBIOS Name-Resolution Issues

Microsoft TCP/IP supports NetBIOS over TCP/IP (NetBT) to provide legacy name resolution for NetBIOS client and server programs in the LAN and wide area network (WAN) environments. This includes all Windows versions prior to Windows 2000 and all versions of Windows since Windows 2000 that are configured in a workgroup, rather than an Active Directory domain.

When DNS name resolution fails, and Windows XP attempts NetBIOS over TCP/IP (including WINS), name resolution uses one of five strategies. These strategies are defined as node types:

➤ *B-node*—Uses broadcasts to resolve names.

➤ *P-node*—Uses point-to-point communications with a NetBIOS server (such as a WINS server) to resolve names.

➤ *M-node*—Uses a mixture of broadcasts first (b-node) and then directed name queries (p-node) if broadcasts fail to resolve.

➤ *H-node*—Uses a hybrid style with a point-to-point name query first (p-node) and then broadcasts (b-node).

➤ *Microsoft-enhanced B-node*—Uses the local LMHOSTS file (this method is unique to Microsoft) before reverting to broadcasts.

 To see which node type is configured on a Windows XP Professional–based computer, type **ipconfig /all** at the command prompt. The node type appears next to the *Node type* heading.

If WINS is enabled on a Windows XP Professional–based computer, the system uses h-node by default. Without WINS, the system uses b–node by default. Using a name server to resolve names is generally preferable to broadcasting for two reasons:

➤ Broadcasts are usually blocked by routers; only local network segment NetBIOS names can be resolved.

➤ Broadcast frames are processed by all computers on a subnet and degrade network performance.

If your network doesn't have a WINS server or one is not available, configure Windows XP Professional to use LMHOSTS for NetBIOS name resolution.

If WINS is not enabled and there is no LMHOSTS file, Windows will begin broadcasting. Broadcasting will not resolve hostnames outside the local subnet. You can view NetBT name resolution statistics with the nbtstat command-line command.

To troubleshoot name resolution problems, do the following:

➤ Attempt to communicate with the remote machine by using its IP address. If you can connect with an IP address but not a name, you have a name-resolution problem.

➤ Examine the NetBT cache using the command nbtstat -c.

➤ Examine the NetBT resolver statistics using the command nbtstat -r.

Setting Up and Troubleshooting Dial-Up Connections

For the remote user, a dial-up connection is an economical and convenient method to access resources on the Internet through a telephone call to an Internet service provider (ISP). Users can also connect to office resources through a direct dial-up into a remote device.

Through the network connections applet in Control Panel, you can create, modify, and troubleshoot dial-up connections for a Windows XP user.

To configure a new dial-up connection or a new network connection, use the New Connection Wizard.

To access the Connection Wizard, follow these steps:

1. In network connections, click the Create a New Connection link in the task pane.

2. When the New Connection Wizard appears, click Next.

3. Click Connect to the Internet and then click Next.

4. Click Set Up the Connection Manually for a Dial-up Connection and then click Next.

5. Click Using a Dial-up Modem.

6. Type a name for the connection and type the phone number for the connection to dial. Click Next to continue.

7. Select whether the connection is for All Users of the Computer or just for you, and then click Next.

8. You may type in your Internet account name and password or you can leave these fields blank so that you can provide them when making the connection. Click Next to proceed and then click Finish.

When you want to connect, click the network connection settings icon you've just created. When troubleshooting connections, all the settings for the connection are nested within the connection icon in the Network Connections system folder.

The settings for a dial-up connection include configurations to be used before, during, and after connecting. The settings include the modem you use to dial, the type of password encryption you want to use upon connecting, and the network protocols you use after you connect. You can view the status of the connection, including the duration and speed of the connection from the connection itself.

To troubleshoot dial-up configuration settings, use the following dial-up dialog box properties:

➤ *General*—The minimum settings needed to connect, including phone number, alternate phone numbers, speed of dialing, flow control, speaker volume, country codes, dialing rules for different locations, area code rules, credit card dialing rules, and disabling call waiting.

➤ *Options*—Includes customizing the connection to prompt for username and phone number, to redial if unable to connect, to set the time interval between redial attempts, and to configure settings for X.25 networks.

➤ *Security*—Includes options for encryption settings and authentication protocols.

➤ *Networking*—Configures whether the connection type is Point-to-Point Protocol (PPP) or Serial Line Internet Protocol (SLIP) and whether an IP address is acquired dynamically or configured statically.

➤ *Advanced*—Enables ICF and ICS settings.

If you suspect the problem is not one of configuration but is a physical problem with the dialing device itself, you can troubleshoot by accessing the modem's properties, shown in Figure 8.12. The properties are visible through the Phone and Modem Options Control Panel Applet.

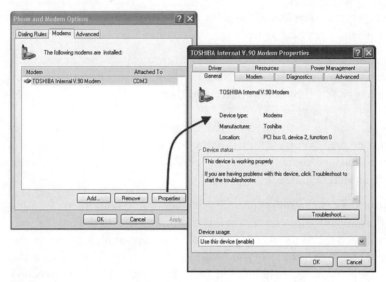

Figure 8.12   The Phone and Modem Options Applet for troubleshooting modems.

Setting Up and Troubleshooting Remote Connections over the Internet

Enabling remote users to securely connect to computers through the Internet requires the establishment of a VPN. The purpose of a VPN is to encase and conceal private data as it traverses a public network.

To create a VPN, you must create two connections for a desktop user. One connection establishes the link to the Internet. This might well be a dial-up connection. The secondary connection, shown in Figure 8.13, tunnels through the Internet, encasing the data, and ultimately connects to the remote network through a Remote Access Server, a device configured with an interface that touches the Internet with a public IP address.

To create a VPN connection, follow these steps:

1. In the Network Connections folder, click Create a New Connection from the task pane.

2. At the New Connection Wizard, click Next.

3. Click Connect to the Network at My Workplace and then click Next.

4. Click Virtual Private Network connection and click Next.

5. Type a name for the connection and click Next again.

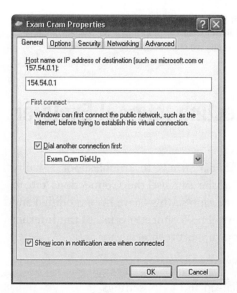

Figure 8.13 The secondary connection through the Internet to a valid IP address or FQDN of the destination computer.

6. If you would like this shortcut to automatically trigger the initial dial-up to your ISP, select it from the drop-down list box and again click Next.

7. Provide the IP address or FQDN of the remote host for which you are creating the VPN and click Next.

8. Answer the question Is the Shortcut for Your Use Alone or Shared By All Users of the Computer? and click Next.

9. Click Finish to complete the wizard.

Configuring and Troubleshooting Internet Explorer Settings

Internet Explorer, with each successive version, provides a host of options and settings enabling you to control a user's connection to the Internet. These options are all properties of the Internet Explorer application, found under Tools, Options. Each of the pages of the dialog box provides a number of entries that control Internet connectivity—connection settings, security settings, and general settings.

When troubleshooting Internet Explorer, it can be helpful to display both its current settings and the contents of the Internet cache by using the System Information Utility, **MSINFO32.exe**, and selecting the Internet Options.

Diagnosing and Correcting Internet Explorer Connection Settings

Whenever a desktop support technician needs to troubleshoot a faulty Internet Explorer connection, he or she can use the Connections tab to determine whether any network connection settings have been modified and are interrupting Internet connectivity. The Connections tab of the Internet Options dialog box enables a desktop support technician to

➤ Create a new network connection.

➤ Edit and troubleshoot existing dial-up and VPN settings.

➤ Edit and troubleshoot LAN settings.

If you are connecting to the Internet through a proxy server, ensure that the Use a Proxy Server check box is selected and that the Address and port number boxes contain the proper entries.

Diagnosing and Correcting Internet Explorer Security Settings

Security settings in Internet Explorer control how a computer running Windows XP handles content from application servers inside and outside your network. The security settings are applied separately to sites defined by four zones:

➤ *Internet*—Web sites that have not been explicitly assigned to other zones. By default, security for this collection of Web sites is set for medium enabling browsing, prompting before packets are downloaded, and blocking unsigned ActiveX controls.

➤ *Local Intranet*—Represents all the Web sites that are on your local intranet. By default, security settings for this collection of Web sites is set to medium-low. Most content runs without prompting, but ActiveX controls that are unsigned are blocked.

➤ *Trusted Sites*—Represents Web sites on which you have explicitly suspended most security settings. The default security settings on this collection of sites are minimal with minimal safeguards and allow all active content to run. It's a good place to put Web sites you absolutely trust.

➤ *Restricted Sites*—Provides the highest security by default. Being placed in this category makes a Web site safe to browse but probably less functional. It is an appropriate choice for sites that might have harmful content.

When users complain of Web sites whose functionality is reduced, a desktop support technician might want to see whether the Web site is part of a more restrictive zone or the default values on less restricted zones have been modified.

Diagnosing and Correcting Internet Explorer General Settings

The General tab of the Internet Options dialog box controls the default home page, temporary Internet files, and the History cache, as well as colors, fonts, and language and accessibility options. It is another destination for a desktop support technician when troubleshooting problems related to

➤ *Home Page*—The default page when opening the browser

➤ *Temporary Internet Files*—Controls the amount of space used to accelerate Internet access by storing cookies and cached pages

➤ *History*—A value that controls the number of days that the addresses of pages to which you've navigated remain in drop-down menus

Remotely Diagnosing and Correcting Desktop Computer Issues

When managing a help desk with no more information than an anxiety-laced email or a voice-mail message of distress, it is often difficult to translate incomplete or incoherent ramblings into meaningful solutions. Inconvenient though it might be to travel to a user's desktop to diagnose and correct problematic configurations, it was the only option until the advent of remote control software and remote desktop viewers.

With Remote Desktop and Remote Assistance, a desktop support technician can optimize his own effectiveness by remaining at his own workstation while troubleshooting remote computers. Remote Assistance and Remote Desktop are enabled separately in the System Properties of a computer running Windows XP, as shown in Figure 8.14.

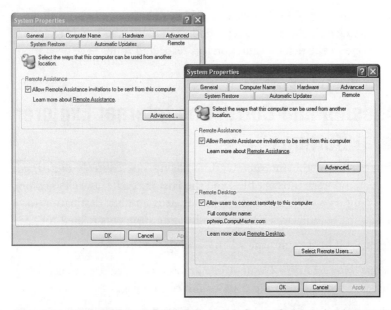

Figure 8.14 Windows XP Home Edition (left) supports Remote Assistance but does not support incoming Remote Desktop Connections. Windows XP Professional (right) supports both.

Using a Remote Desktop Connection for Troubleshooting

Remote Desktop enables an authorized remote user to connect and manage a computer through a remote console connection. This capability of Windows XP enables a computer to be managed and its programs initialized through a remote connection. Remote Desktop enables a desktop support technician to perform the following functions:

➤ Work with a computer from a remote location using a direct network, secure VPN, or Remote Access connection

➤ Manage or troubleshoot a computer remotely

➤ Access a computer remotely without letting unauthorized users view your actions

After the support person is connected, privileges are based upon the account with which she is connected. Although Remote Desktop is not specifically a troubleshooting tool, this feature does enable you to use a local keyboard, mouse, and video display to remotely diagnose and troubleshoot problems that do not require collaboration with someone logged on at the computer.

For example, while logged onto a computer running Windows XP Home, as shown in Figure 8.15, you can connect remotely to a computer running Windows XP Professional to run applications or work with files not present on your own computer.

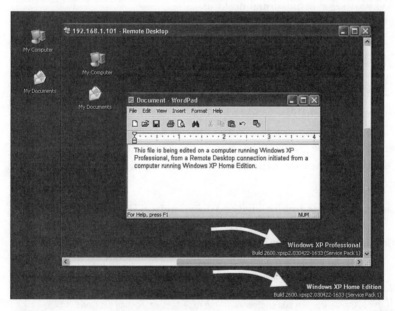

Figure 8.15 A Remote Desktop Connection window on a Windows XP Home computer connected to a remote computer running Windows XP Professional.

While you use Remote Desktop, the remote computer console remains locked and any actions that you perform are not visible on the local console monitor attached to the remote computer.

To enable incoming Remote Desktop Connections, go to the Remote tab in the System Properties dialog box. Be sure that the Allow Users to Connect Remotely to This Computer check box is marked and then click the Select Remote Users button to choose which users have remote desktop privileges.

Members of the Administrators and Domain Admins groups have Remote Desktop Connection privileges by default.

Remote Desktop uses Windows XP Professional security features to grant or deny access based on user permissions. Therefore, keep in mind the following security considerations:

➤ You cannot typically make a connection to an external, nondomain computer outside your firewall because Remote Desktop uses Terminal Services and Remote Assistance technology that requires a specific port, TCP port 3389 by default, to be open for the connection to work.

➤ Remote Desktop does not allow simultaneous remote and local access to the Windows XP professional desktop.

Using Remote Assistance for Troubleshooting

Remote Assistance enables a desktop support technician to view or share control of a user's computer running Windows XP. For remote assistance to commence, either the "novice" must invite the "expert" to view or share control of the computer or the expert must "offer assistance" to the novice, who must accept the offer.

The feature allows the user to invite a trusted person (the expert) to remotely and interactively assist them. This feature is useful in situations where collaboration with a user is required to resolve remote computer problems.

Be aware of the difference between Remote Desktop Connections and Remote Assistance. A Remote Desktop Connection establishes a new session. Remote Assistance attaches another user (the expert) to an existing session.

To use Remote Assistance, both the novice and expert need to be present at their computers and must cooperate with each other.

Remote Assistance requires that both computers are running the Microsoft Windows XP operating system or later.

The Remote Assistance session can be initiated by either the novice or the expert. A request for assistance is generally made through the local Help and Support Center (see Figure 8.16).

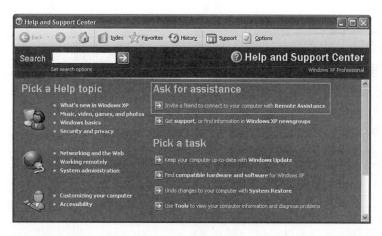

Figure 8.16 The local Help and Support Center with the Ask for Assistance option in the upper right.

A user can invite an expert by using email, Windows Messenger, or Outlook Express. If the novice is on the Internet, anyone running Windows XP or later can be invited by him to view his desktop, and with permission, the expert user can share control of the novice's computer.

An expert can offer assistance to the user first, but the option to receive an offer must first be enabled on the novice's computer by editing the local policy settings, under Computer Configuration, Administrative Templates, System, Remote Assistance, Offer Remote Assistance (Enabled).

In this scenario, the expert offers assistance through a Help and Support Center Tools in the Help and Support Center, shown in Figure 8.17. Once the offer is made and the novice accepts the offer, the expert can view and "take control" of the novice's computer.

When the novice clicks the Allow Expert Interaction button, the expert performs all actions under the novice's user security context and therefore assumes the same level of network access and local computer privileges as the novice.

To allow experts outside your organization to establish Remote Assistance connections (for example, outsourced technical support), the preferred connection method is through a VPN account because it doesn't need to open TCP Port 3389 on the firewall.

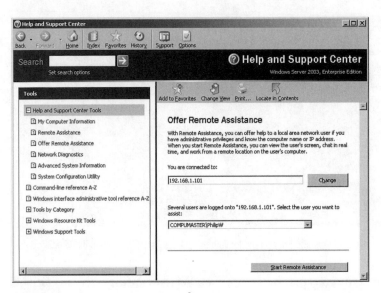

Figure 8.17 An expert's Help and Support Center displaying the Offer Remote Assistance option.

Exam Prep Questions

1. A user named Brian reports that when he types **https://www.interniche.com** in Internet Explorer's address bar and presses Enter, he receives a warning message that says, "Unable to display unsigned ActiveX controls."

   Internet Explorer is configured with default security settings. Company policy states that users are allowed to download unsigned ActiveX controls from approved Internet Web sites and **http://www.interniche.com** is an approved Web site.

   What is the best way to ensure that Brian can view the Web site?

   ❏ A. Add the Web site to the Restricted Sites list.
   ❏ B. Add the Web site to the Internet zone and modify the default security settings.
   ❏ C. Add the Web site to the Local Intranet Sites list.
   ❏ D. Add the Web site to the Trusted Sites list and modify the default security settings.

   The correct answer is D. To comply with company policy and enable users to access the Web site, add the Web site to Trusted Sites and modify the default security settings to enable downloading of unsigned ActiveX controls.

   Answer A is incorrect because Restricted Sites disable downloading of unsigned ActiveX controls by default. Answer B is incorrect because you cannot add sites to the Internet zone. Answer C is incorrect because you cannot add the Web site to the Local Intranet Sites.

2. You are a desktop support technician for your company.

All computers on the network have static addresses and use the subnet mask 255.255.255.224.

A user reports that she cannot connect to any network resources with Windows XP and cannot ping any addresses except her own.

You confirm that the computer is physically connected to the network. The network router uses the first available IP address on the subnet.

After you examine the TCP/IP settings shown in Figure 8.18, what is your conclusion?

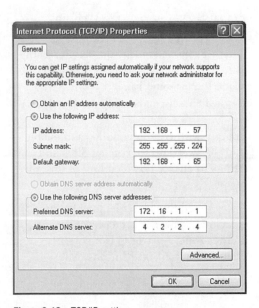

Figure 8.18 TCP/IP settings.

- ❏ A. The IP address is invalid.
- ❏ B. The subnet mask is incorrect.
- ❏ C. The default gateway address is incorrect.
- ❏ D. The DNS server address is incorrect.

The correct answer is C. Given the IP address and the subnet mask, the range of addresses for the subnet in which the computer is resident is 192.168.1.33–192.168.1.62. The default gateway must be an address within the same network as the address of the workstation. Answer A is incorrect. If the computer can ping its own IP address, then no other computer on the network has that address. Answer B is incorrect because a the subnet mask is correctly represented as 255.255.255.224. Answer D is incorrect because 192.168.1.65 is the first address in the 192.168.1.64 network.

3. You're a desktop support technician on the network.

A user working at home calls you on her cell phone to report trouble with her computer. You instruct her to send you a remote assistance invitation so that you can help her solve the problem.

While the user has you on her cell phone, she logs onto the Internet through a dial-up account, sends you a remote assistance invitation as instructed, and then disconnects from the dial-up connection.

You receive the invitation and accept it, but the connection to user's PC fails.

You need to establish a remote assistance connection with the user's computer. What do you do?

❑ A. Tell the user not to disconnect from the ISP.

❑ B. Tell the user to re-send the invitation.

❑ C. Tell the user to invite you using Remote Desktop.

❑ D. Tell the user to enable Allow Users to Remotely Connect to This Computer.

The correct answer is B. The user must reconnect to the ISP, resend an invitation, and not log off. Answer A is incorrect because the user is already disconnected from the ISP. Answer C is incorrect; Remote Desktop does not require an invitation. Answer D is incorrect because this will enable Remote Desktop and has nothing to do with Remote Assistance.

4. You're a desktop support technician for a company. A user attempts to access the company's Web site using his Windows XP laptop from a branch office in Oxnard. The company's Web site is hosted by an ISP.

Unfortunately, the user receives the error message, "Cannot Find Server or DNS Server."

You work at the main office. From your computer, how would you ensure that the user can access the Web site from the branch office network?

❑ A. Using Remote Desktop, log onto the user's machine and attempt to access the Web site.

❑ B. Using Remote Assistance, access the user's computer and attempt to access the Web site.

❑ C. Using **MSInfo32.exe**, view the settings on the remote computer.

❑ D. Ask the user to add the Web address to Trusted Sites.

The correct answer is B. Using Remote Assistance, you can view the current configuration of the user's laptop and make changes to correct the problem. Answer A is incorrect; to access the remote laptop, the desktop support technician must take control of the computer using administrative privileges, which might not reflect the user's current personal settings. Answer C is incorrect; you can use `MSInfo32.exe` to view settings on remote systems but not to control them. Answer D is incorrect because adding the Web address to Trusted Sites will not resolve DNS problems.

5. You are a desktop support technician for a company that employs 35 independent sales reps who work from home and bring their laptop computers when visiting customers.

Sales reps need to access files stored on their home-office computers from their laptops.

To protect the home-office computers from unauthorized access, though, you draw up a number of guidelines.

Which of the following actions would you recommend for the home computers to increase security.?

❑ A. Disable Allow Users to Connect Remotely to This Computer.

❑ B. Enable Allow Remote Assistance Invitations to Be Sent from This Computer.

❑ C. Enable ICF and open TCP port 3389.

❑ D. Enable Allow This Computer to Be Controlled Remotely.

The correct answer is C. ICF enables users to filter access to ports. Without ICF, all ports are available. After ICF is enabled, by default, all ports are blocked. To permit a Remote Desktop connection, you must open port 3389. Answer A is incorrect because disabling Remote Desktop connections will block, not permit, all connections. Answer B is incorrect because Remote Assistance requires someone to be at the "other" computer to permit a connection to be established. Allow Remote Assistance Invitations to Be Sent is enabled by default on computers running Windows XP. Answer D is incorrect because Allow This Computer to Be Controlled Remotely is a Remote Assistance option, not the Remote Control feature.

6. You are a desktop support technician. A Windows XP user named Mitch shares a folder on his computer. Unfortunately, nobody on the network is able to access his new share.

From your help desk, you attempt but fail to successfully ping Mitch's Windows XP computer using either the computer's name or IP address.

Mitch, however, declares that he is able to access the entire network. Which of the following actions would you recommend?

❑　A.　Install Internet Information Server on the computer.

❑　B.　Enable Allow Users to Connect Remotely to This Computer in System Properties.

❑　C.　Ask the user to disable ICF.

❑　D.　Ask the user to reboot his computer.

The correct answer is C. Whenever connectivity is a problem on computers running Windows XP, a desktop support technician must ensure that the problem is not derived from ICF, a port-filtering feature that by default blocks incoming packets. According to the scenario, the user is able to communicate using packets originating from his computer. Therefore, network connectivity has been established.

Answer A is incorrect; IIS is not necessary to share files on a computer running Windows XP. Answer B is incorrect because it is related to Remote Desktop, which is not related to file shares. Answer D is a more extreme troubleshooting measure in comparison to just disabling ICF and should usually be a last resort.

7. You are a desktop support technician. You work in the data center located at headquarters and receive an email message from a user who works in one of the company branch offices. The email message is a Remote Assistance invitation. You accept the invitation but are unable to connect to the user's computer to see her desktop.

To provide Remote Assistance support for users in the branch office, you'll need to

❑　A.　Open TCP port 25 on the firewall.

❑　B.　Open UDP port 53 on the firewall.

❑　C.　Open TCP port 3389 on the firewall.

❑　D.　Enable Allow Users to Connect Remotely to This Computer in a group policy object.

The correct answer is C. Remote Assistance connections are enabled through TCP port 3389. This port must be open for connections to be made. Answer A is incorrect; port 25 is a well-known port assigned to Simple Mail Transport Protocol (SMTP) for email, and email is working fine, as evidenced by your email invitation. Answer B is incorrect. Port 53 is a well-known port for DNS services. Answer D is incorrect because the policy is related to Remote Desktop, not Remote Assistance.

8. You are a desktop support technician. Monday, you arrive at your office, turn on your computer, and attempt unsuccessfully to access the file server. No other network users have complained about network connectivity yet. You check the wires behind your computer and they appear to be connected. You check the link lights on your network interface card and they appear to be active. You use the **ipconfig /all** command and view the results shown in Figure 8.19.

```
C:\>ipconfig /all

Windows IP Configuration

        Host Name . . . . . . . . . . . . : examcram-xppro
        Primary Dns Suffix  . . . . . . . : CompuMaster.com
        Node Type . . . . . . . . . . . . : Hybrid
        IP Routing Enabled. . . . . . . . : No
        WINS Proxy Enabled. . . . . . . . : No

Ethernet adapter Local Area Connection:

        Connection-specific DNS Suffix  . :
        Description . . . . . . . . . . . : AMD PCNET Family PCI Ethernet Adapter
        Physical Address. . . . . . . . . : 00-0C-29-D7-F4-9F
        Dhcp Enabled. . . . . . . . . . . : Yes
        Autoconfiguration Enabled . . . . : Yes
        Autoconfiguration IP Address. . . : 169.254.188.18
        Subnet Mask . . . . . . . . . . . : 255.255.0.0
        Default Gateway . . . . . . . . . :
        Primary WINS Server . . . . . . . : 192.168.1.1
```

Figure 8.19   The results of **ipconfig /all**.

What do you need to do to remedy this problem?

❑ A. Modify the subnet mask.

❑ B. Modify the default gateway.

❑ C. Modify the IP address.

❑ D. Execute the **ipconfig /renew** command.

The correct answer is D. This is a computer that is configured to obtain an IP address automatically; it has DHCP enabled. However, it has acquired an APIPA address, with no default gateway. The best way to troubleshoot connectivity is to make sure that DHCP is running properly, rather than to manually configure an IP address, default gateway, or subnet mask. To do so, use ipconfig /renew.

Answer A is incorrect because modifying the subnet mask alone will not solve the problem. Answer B is incorrect because modifying the default gateway might not solve the problem if the file server is on the same LAN segment as your PC. Answer C is incorrect because there is no indication that we have a duplicate or invalid IP address.

9. You are a desktop support technician and your computer runs Windows XP Professional. Because your company utilizes highly sensitive government data, you've been tasked to provide updated documents to your mobile workers' laptops running Windows XP using only Remote Assistance. For security reasons, email attachments are forbidden, as are sharepoints. To achieve this goal, which of the following actions should you take?

   ❑ A. Instruct the employees to use the Whiteboard feature in Windows Messenger after they have established Remote Assistance sessions.

   ❑ B. Send the documents to users as an email attachment.

   ❑ C. Place the documents on file in a shared folder on the network file server.

   ❑ D. Send the documents file during a Remote Assistance session.

   The correct answer is D. Remote Assistance enables an expert to send a file to the novice. Answer A is incorrect; the Whiteboard is a drawing program not a file transfer program. Answers B and C are incorrect; they presume users have access to the corporate network email and file servers, which is not forbidden by company policy.

10. You are a desktop support technician. Everyone in your company uses Windows XP. A user complains that he "cannot see any pictures" when browsing Web sites. Everyone else who browses to the Web site can see the pictures. To troubleshoot, you view the Internet Explorer configuration by clicking Tools and then Internet Options. What would you do next?

   ❑ A. Select Show Pictures on the Advanced tab.

   ❑ B. Click Enable on the Content tab.

   ❑ C. Add the Web sites with the pictures to the Trusted Sites Zone.

   ❑ D. Press the Clear History button on the General tab.

   The correct answer is A. Pictures on Web sites do not appear unless the Show Pictures setting is enabled on the Advanced tab of Internet Options. It is enabled by default. Answer B is incorrect because Enable is used by the Content Advisor to enable filtering of entire Web sites, not just images. Answer C is incorrect because adding the Web site to the Trusted Zone affects its security settings, not the ability to display images. Answer D is incorrect because clearing the History cache does not enable an image to appear on a Web site; it merely erases temporary files stored on the PC's hard drive.

9

Practice Exam 1

Now it's time to put to the test the knowledge that you've learned from reading this book! Write your answers to the following questions on a separate sheet of paper. You can take this sample test multiple times this way. After you answer all the questions, compare your answers to the correct answers in Chapter 10, "Answer Key for Practice Exam 1." The answer keys for both exams immediately follow each practice-exam chapter. When you can correctly answer at least 54 of the 60 practice questions (90%) in each practice exam, you are ready to start using the PrepLogic practice exams CD-ROM at the back of this *Exam Cram 2* guide. Using the practice exams for this *Exam Cram 2*, along with the PrepLogic practice exams, you can prepare yourself quite well for the actual 70-271 Microsoft certification exam. Good luck!

1. You are a desktop support technician for your company. A user is unable to install and configure a new USB printer and says that when she connects the printer to the computer with a USB cable, Windows XP asks her to insert a driver disk. Unfortunately, Windows responds that the driver is "unsigned" and the printer cannot be installed.

   The printer is on your company's supported printers list. How can you bypass the driver message?

   - ○ A. Make the user an administrator.
   - ○ B. Disable the group policy that prevents unsigned device drivers from being installed.
   - ○ C. Start Windows in Safe Mode.
   - ○ D. Copy the device into **%systemroot%** yourself.

2. You are a desktop support technician for your company. You are using Windows XP and you try to connect to a user's home computer running Windows XP using the Remote Desktop Connection client. However, you are unable to log on to the computer. Why can't you log on to the computer running Windows XP?

   - ○ A. The Windows XP computer requires Service Pack 1 (SP1).
   - ○ B. The user's home computer is running Windows XP Professional.
   - ○ C. The Allow Users to Connect Remotely to This Computer check box is unchecked on the Remote tab of the System Properties dialog box.
   - ○ D. A Terminal Services Licensing Server must be set up first.

3. You are a desktop support technician for your company. You support a user with special needs who cannot press Ctrl+Alt+Del to log on. Because of a handicap, the user needs to be able to press one key at a time.

   Which feature of Windows XP would you configure?

   - ○ A. FilterKeys
   - ○ B. StickyKeys
   - ○ C. MouseKeys
   - ○ D. ToggleKeys

4. You are a desktop support technician for your company. A user wants to add program shortcuts to his Start menu. You want to make sure that the shortcuts the user creates always show up, such as the My Computer shortcut and the My Documents shortcut. (Users have mentioned that some Start menu shortcuts "disappear.")

   How do you do this?

   - ○ A. Place a program shortcut in the Start Menu folder of the All Users profile.
   - ○ B. Place a program shortcut in the Start Menu folder for his user profile.
   - ○ C. Drag a program shortcut to the Start button.
   - ○ D. Click My Recent Documents from the Start menu.

5. You are a desktop support technician for your company. A user with a hearing impairment has just been issued a computer running Windows XP. You want to enable ShowSounds and SoundSentry included with Windows XP Professional. How would you do so?

   ○ A. Open Narrator to enable ShowSounds and SoundSentry.

   ○ B. Log on to the user's machine using her account. Open Utility Manager by pressing the Windows logo key+U, and then enable both ShowSounds and SoundSentry.

   ○ C. Open Control Panel, select Accessibility Options, click Accessibility Options and select the Sound tab.

   ○ D. Log on to the user's computer with an account with administrative privileges, open Utility Manager by pressing the Windows logo key+U, enable both ShowSounds and SoundSentry, and click OK.

6. You are a desktop support technician for your company. Using group policies, you need to provide a way for the user to be able to reset the password and view the Welcome screen rather than be logged on automatically to her computer running Windows XP. The computer is part of a workgroup, not part of a domain. How do you accomplish this task?

   ○ A. In Change the Way Users Log On or Off, select Use the Welcome Screen.

   ○ B. On a workgroup member, check the Users Must Enter a User Name and Password to Use This Computer check box, and then click OK.

   ○ C. In Group Policies, Enable "Do Not Require Ctrl+Alt+Del."

   ○ D. In Group Policies, choose Always Use Classic Logon.

7. You are a desktop support technician for your company. How can you find out which version of Windows XP is running on a user's computer? (Select all correct answers.)

   ○ A. By using the **Winver.exe** program

   ○ B. By using the **Setver.exe** program

   ○ C. In the System Properties dialog box

   ○ D. Using the **WinMSD.exe** program

   ○ E. By using the **SysKey.exe** program

8. You are a desktop support technician for your company. A user named Gregory has just installed Windows XP Professional on a new computer that is a member of a workgroup named Sales. When he goes to create a network shared folder by right-clicking a folder and selecting Sharing and Security, the Properties dialog box for the folder displays only four tabs: General, Sharing, Web Sharing, and Customize. The Sharing tab is divided into two sections: Local Sharing and Network Sharing and Security. Even when Gregory right-clicks a folder and selects Properties, he still gets the same tabbed dialog box with the same four tabs. The folder resides on an NTFS formatted volume. Gregory wants to assign NTFS security settings, although no Security tab exists for NTFS permissions. How should Gregory enable custom NTFS security?

   O A. Go to Control Panel, Administrative Tools, Local Security Policy and enable the policy for Network Access: Sharing and Security Model for Local Accounts.

   O B. Open My Computer or Windows Explorer; click Tools, Folder Options; click the View tab; and clear the check box for Use Simple File Sharing.

   O C. Open the Computer Management console, expand Services and Applications, and click the Services node. Right-click the Workstation service and select Start. Double-click the Workstation service and set the Startup Type to Automatic.

   O D. Open Control Panel and double-click Network Connections. Right-click the Local Area Connection and select Properties. Mark the check box for File and Printer Sharing for Microsoft Networks and click OK.

9. You are a desktop support technician for your company. Which of the following methods enable you to create shared network folders? (Select all correct answers.)

   ❏ A. Right-click a folder in either My Computer or Windows Explorer, select Sharing and Security, click the option button Share This Folder, and click OK.

   ❏ B. Open the Run dialog box, type **fsmgmt.msc**, press OK, right-click the Shares node, and click New File Share. Follow the onscreen instructions for the Create Shared Folder Wizard.

   ❏ C. Open the Computer Management console, expand Shared Folders, right-click the Shares node, and click New File Share. Follow the onscreen instructions for the Create Shared Folder Wizard.

   ❏ D. Open a command prompt window. Type **Net Share share_name=x:\folder_name**, where **share_name** represents the name you want to assign to the shared folder, **x:** represents the drive letter where the folder resides, and **folder_name** represents the actual name of the folder.

10. You are a desktop support technician for your company. What is the default setting for offline files under Windows XP Professional when acting as a "server" for other client computers?

   ○ A. Manual caching of documents.

   ○ B. Automatic caching of documents.

   ○ C. Caching is disabled.

   ○ D. Automatic caching of programs and documents.

11. You are a desktop support technician for your company. You want to supply permissions using **standard** security groups. Which of the following local groups are installed automatically by Windows XP Professional? (Select all correct answers.)

   ❑ A. Network Configuration Operators

   ❑ B. Replicator

   ❑ C. Authenticated Users

   ❑ D. HelpServicesGroup

   ❑ E. Remote Desktop Users

   ❑ F. Creator Group

12. You are a desktop support technician for your company. How can you determine the actual, effective NTFS permissions on a file or a folder for a user or a group with the least amount of administrative effort?

   ○ A. Log on as the specific user and test the user's permissions by attempting to read, write, modify, delete, change permissions, and take ownership of specific files and folders.

   ○ B. Log on as an administrative user, right-click a folder or file in question, choose Properties, click Security, click the Advanced button, and click the Effective Permissions tab. Select a user or group to view the effective permissions for that user or group on the specific file or folder.

   ○ C. Open the Computer Management console, click Shared Folders, and then click Effective Permissions.

   ○ D. Open the Control Panel and double-click Component Services. Right-click the NTFS Permissions node and select Effective Permissions.

   ○ E. By using the **RunAs** command, you can access a specific folder to discover the permissions associated with the account you provide in the RunAs dialog box.

13. You are a desktop support technician for your company. A user asks you to use Windows Explorer to move 7 subfolders containing 152 files from **e:\docs** to **e:\letters**. What will happen to their NTFS security permissions?

   ○ A. The folders and files moved will retain their same NTFS permissions.

   ○ B. The folders and files moved will inherit their NTFS permissions from the target (destination) folder.

   ○ C. The folders and files moved will have their NTFS permissions reset to the default settings for drive volumes, such as Allow Everyone Read and Execute and Administrators Full Control.

   ○ D. You will be prompted by a message box asking whether you want the folders and files moved to retain their permissions or to inherit their permissions from the target (destination) folder.

14. You are a desktop support technician for your company. Using the least administrative effort, you need to ensure that members of the Finance group are allowed to print documents on Printer4 only during non-business hours and that their print jobs are given a higher priority than other print jobs from any members of other groups.

   ○ A. Configure the printer properties for Printer4 on each computer for each member of all the other network groups. In the Printers and Faxes window, right-click Printer4, select Properties, click the Advanced tab, click the Available from button, and specify the business hours that the printer will be unavailable for the Finance group. Decrement the Priority counter so that each member of the other groups has a lower printing priority for Printer4 than members from the Finance groups.

   ○ B. For each user in the Finance group, open the Printers and Faxes window, right-click Printer4, select Properties, and click the Security tab. Grant the permissions Allow Print, Allow Manage Printers, and Allow Manage Documents to the Finance group.

   ○ C. Configure the printer properties for Printer4 on each computer for each member of the Finance group. In the Printers and Faxes window, right-click Printer4, select Properties, click the Advanced tab, click the Available from button, and specify the nonbusiness hours that the printer will be available. Increment the Priority counter so that each member of the Finance group has a higher printing priority for Printer4 than members from other groups.

   ○ D. For each user in the Finance group, open the Printers and Faxes window, right-click Printer4, select Properties, and click the Security tab. Click the Advanced button, click the Owner tab, and change the owner to the Finance group.

15. You are a desktop support technician for your company. Users want to manage a printer through a Web page. Which of the following statements are true about using the IPP? (Select all correct answers.)

   ❑ A. The print server computer must be running IIS 4 or later.
   ❑ B. The print server computer can be running Windows 2000 Professional or later.
   ❑ C. You can view all available printers and faxes by typing the following URL into a Web browser: **http://print_server_name/printers**.
   ❑ D. You can connect to specific printer by typing the following URL into a Web browser: **http://print_server_name/printer_share_name**.

16. You are a desktop support technician for your company. You want to access the default hidden shares on a computer running Windows XP Professional. Provided you had administrative privileges, to which of the following hidden shares would you be able to connect across a network connection? (Select three correct answers.)

   ❑ A. **SYSVOL**
   ❑ B. **ADMIN$**
   ❑ C. **CD$**
   ❑ D. **PRINTER$**
   ❑ E. **IPC$**
   ❑ F. **C$**

17. You are a desktop support technician for your company. You are explaining to a user how to use the Shared Folders snap-in. In terms of the setting of permissions for a new share, what extra feature does the snap-in provide that the Sharing tab of a folder's properties sheet lacks?

   ○ A. Setting share permissions
   ○ B. Publishing the share in Active Directory
   ○ C. Specifying offline settings
   ○ D. Specifying both share permissions and NTFS permissions
   ○ E. Specifying Web Sharing access permissions

18. You are a desktop support technician for your company. A user is trying to access a file stored in a shared folder on a remote computer running Windows XP. Both share permissions and NTFS permissions exist on the folder. How is access control to the shared folder affected by the NTFS security attached to the folder?

   ○ A. NTFS permissions always take precedence.
   ○ B. Share permissions always take precedence.
   ○ C. The most liberal permissions take precedence.
   ○ D. When both Share and NTFS permissions are combined, the permissions they have in common are the effective permissions.

19. You are a desktop support technician for your company. You are troubleshooting a subfolder that has inherited permissions from its parent folder. Which of the following characteristics apply to NTFS inherited permissions on the subfolder? (Select three correct answers.)

    ❏ A. Special permissions are inherited by default.
    ❏ B. Basic permissions are inherited by default.
    ❏ C. Explicit permissions are the same as inherited permissions.
    ❏ D. NTFS permissions are inherited by default.
    ❏ E. NTFS explicit permissions are not inherited by default.
    ❏ F. You cannot set explicit permissions on files.

20. You are a desktop support technician for your company. A user has defined the basic NTFS permission, Modify, for a folder she's shared on her computer running Windows XP. Which of the following special permissions does Modify represent? (Select three correct answers.)

    ❏ A. List Folder/Read Data
    ❏ B. Create Files/Write Data
    ❏ C. Change Permissions
    ❏ D. Delete Subfolders and Files
    ❏ E. Take Ownership
    ❏ F. Write Extended Attributes

21. You are a desktop support technician for your company. A user complains about an inability to access a file in a shared folder on your computer running Windows XP. When you view NTFS effective permissions for the user, which of the following permissions are displayed?

    ○ A. Basic permissions
    ○ B. Special permissions
    ○ C. Share permissions
    ○ D. Not inherited permissions

22. You are a desktop support technician for your company. You want to transfer ownership of a group of files. In which of the following ways can you change ownership of an NTFS file or folder? (Select three correct answers.)

    ❑ A. Any user who is a member of the Domain Users group can take ownership of any folder or file, whether or not she has permissions to the folder or file.

    ❑ B. The current owner of a file or folder can assign the Take Ownership permission to another user for the file or folder; the other user must then take ownership of the object.

    ❑ C. A member of the Administrators group can assign ownership of a file or folder to another user.

    ❑ D. Any user who is granted the Restore Files and Directories user right can assign ownership of a file or folder to another user.

    ❑ E. Any member of the Backup Operators group can take ownership of any file or folder at any time.

    ❑ F. Any member of the Authenticated Users group can assign ownership of files or folders to another user at any time.

23. You are a desktop support technician for your company. Members of the Finance Department use computers running Windows XP Professional. How can you set disk quotas on NTFS drive volumes for the Power Users group and for the Administrators group?

    ○ A. Right-click the drive letter in My Computer, select Properties, click the Quota tab, and mark the check boxes for Enable Quota Management and Deny Disk Space to Users Exceeding Quota Limit. Click Apply and click the Quota Entries button. Configure quota entries for the Power Users group and for the Administrators group.

    ○ B. Right-click the drive letter in My Computer, select Properties, click the Quota tab, and mark the check boxes for Enable Quota Management and Deny Disk Space to Users Exceeding Quota Limit. Click Apply and click the Quota Entries button. Configure quota entries for the Power Users group.

    ○ C. Right-click the drive letter in My Computer, select Properties, click the Quota tab, and mark the check boxes for Enable Quota Management and Deny Disk Space to Users Exceeding Quota Limit. Click Apply and click the Quota Entries button. Configure quota entries for each member of the Power Users group.

    ○ D. Create a new local group named Super Users and make all the members of the Power Users group and the Administrators group members of this new group. Right-click the drive letter in My Computer, select Properties, click the Quota tab, and mark the check boxes for Enable Quota Management and Deny Disk Space to Users Exceeding Quota Limit. Click Apply and click the Quota Entries button. Configure quota entries for the Super Users group.

24. You are a desktop support technician for your company. Brandy wants to move an NTFS-compressed file from NTFS drive D to an uncompressed folder on NTFS drive F. What happens to the file when she performs this operation?

    ○ A. The compressed file becomes uncompressed when it is moved to drive F.

    ○ B. The compressed file remains compressed when it is moved to drive F.

    ○ C. Windows XP prompts the user as to whether the file should remain compressed or should be uncompressed after it is moved.

    ○ D. Brandy receives an error message when she attempts to move the file to an uncompressed folder.

25. You are a desktop support technician for your company. A user, Terry, encrypts an NTFS folder named **SECRET DOCS** on the hard drive of a Windows XP Professional computer. Terry is the only user with access to all the encrypted files in the **SECRET DOCS** folder (except for the DRA). Terry shares the computer with her associate, Kim. Kim is not the DRA. Later, Kim logs on to the same computer and attempts to copy one of the files stored inside the **SECRET DOCS** folder, named **Salaries.xls**, to a floppy disk in drive A. After that, Kim tries to move the same file to an unencrypted folder on the same NTFS drive volume named **Public Docs**. What are the results of Kim's file operations?

    ○ A. Kim receives an error message for trying to copy the encrypted file to a floppy disk, but he can successfully move the encrypted file to the **PUBLIC DOCS** unencrypted NTFS folder, where the file remains encrypted.

    ○ B. Kim receives an error message for trying to copy the encrypted file to a floppy disk, and he also receives an error message for attempting to move the encrypted file to the **PUBLIC DOCS** unencrypted NTFS folder.

    ○ C. Kim receives an error message for trying to copy the encrypted file to a floppy disk, but he can successfully move the encrypted file to the **PUBLIC DOCS** unencrypted NTFS folder, where it loses its encryption attribute.

    ○ D. Kim successfully copies the encrypted file to a floppy disk, where it remains encrypted, and he can successfully move the encrypted file to the **PUBLIC DOCS** unencrypted NTFS folder.

26. You are a desktop support technician for your company. A senior vice president complains that he is unable to install software using removable media. Troubleshooting the problem, what do you suspect?

    O A. The user is not logged in with administrative privileges.
    O B. The "prevent removable media source for any install" system policy is enabled.
    O C. The computer is infected with a virus.
    O D. The user is not logged on to the domain.

27. You are a desktop support technician for your company. Joshua is unable to locate the Add Remove Programs from a CD-ROM or floppy drive option in Control Panel. What is the most likely reason?

    O A. There is no floppy drive nor CD-ROM installed in his computer.
    O B. There is never an option in Control Panel.
    O C. The policy **User Configuration\Administrative Templates\Windows Components\ControlPanel\Add/Remove Programs\Hide the Add a Program from CD-ROM or floppy disk** has been enabled.
    O D. The Registry has become corrupt.

28. You are a desktop support technician for your company. Users have computers with floppy disk drives, but they are unable to install software device drivers from floppy disk media. Looking at the floppy disk through Windows Explorer, you verify that the files are stored on the disk. What is the most likely reason for this problem?

    O A. There is a group policy that prevents installation of drivers from floppy disks.
    O B. The floppy disk is empty.
    O C. The floppy disk drive has malfunctioned.
    O D. Windows XP does not permit installation from floppy disk–based drivers.

29. You are a desktop support technician for your company. A user reports that she has "sent the document to the printer one hundred times and it still hasn't printed." As a support specialist, which of the following solutions should you consider first?

    O A. Determine that the user has permission to print files.
    O B. Determine that the correct driver is installed in the user's computer.
    O C. Determine whether the printer is plugged in, turned on, and connected to the print server.
    O D. Determine whether there is paper in the printer.

30. You are a desktop support technician for your company. One of the company's workstations has just been upgraded to Windows XP Professional from Windows 98 Second Edition. The computer is equipped with an internal SCSI adapter that cannot be installed because the new operating system cannot find a suitable driver for it. How can you tell Windows XP Professional to ignore the device until the manufacturer publishes an updated driver?

    ○ A. Uninstall the SCSI adapter in Device Manager.

    ○ B. Physically remove the SCSI adapter from the computer.

    ○ C. In Device Manager, right-click the SCSI adapter and select Disable.

    ○ D. Create a new hardware profile, restart the computer using the new hardware profile, and disable the SCSI adapter for the new hardware profile.

31. You are a desktop support technician for your company. Which of the following unsigned driver installation configurations are available under Windows XP from the graphical user interface? (Select three correct answers.)

    ❑ A. Install for administrators only

    ❑ B. Ignore

    ❑ C. Prompt

    ❑ D. Block

    ❑ E. Warn

    ❑ F. PnP drivers only

32. You are a desktop support technician for your company. You are responsible for deploying 1,000 new Windows XP Professional desktop computers within an Active Directory domain in a Windows Server 2003 network environment. What is the easiest way to ensure that all the new desktop computers do not allow unsigned device drivers to be installed?

   ○ A. Set the Unsigned Driver Options to Block in the System Properties window for a prototype computer. Then, image that model machine using the Sysprep tool and a third-party disk cloning software utility and copy the image to each of the 1,000 new workstations.

   ○ B. Use a GPO for the Default Domain Policy, or create a GPO for an OU where all the workstations will be placed. In the GPO, go to the Computer Policy, Security Settings, Local Policies, Security Options node. Set the Devices: Unsigned Driver Installation Behavior policy to Do Not Allow Installation. Mark the No Override check box for the GPO.

   ○ C. Keep the default installation setting for Unsigned Driver Options under Windows XP Professional because it is Block—Never Install Unsigned Driver Software.

   ○ D. At a local computer policy, set the Devices: Unsigned Driver Installation Behavior policy to Do Not Allow Installation for a model computer. Then, image that model machine using the Sysprep tool and a third-party disk cloning software utility and copy the image to each of the 1,000 new workstations.

33. You are a desktop support technician for your company. You are responsible for managing a computer running Windows XP that currently has several USB devices connected to several different USB hubs that are all plugged into the root USB hub on the back of the computer. Management tells you to purchase and install a USB scanner for the computer. You buy the scanner, connect it to a 12-foot USB cable, and plug the cable into one of the daisy-chained hubs. The computer does not detect the new USB scanner. What is the most likely cause of this problem?

   ○ A. The 12-foot long USB cable exceeds the supported length for USB cabling.

   ○ B. The scanner is not PnP-compliant.

   ○ C. USB scanners can only be connected to USB root hubs to function properly.

   ○ D. The USB hub, to which the scanner is connected, happens to be the sixth hub in a daisy-chained row of hubs.

34. You are a desktop support technician for your company. A user calls you complaining she is unable to locate the network settings on her computer running Windows XP. She wants to unbind obsolete protocols from her network adapter. How would you change the settings?

   ○ A. From the Network Connections window, click the Advanced menu and then select Advanced Settings.

   ○ B. From the Network Connections window, click the Advanced menu and then select Optional Networking Components.

   ○ C. In Device Manager, right-click Network Adapters and then click Properties.

   ○ D. In Device Manager, right-click a network adapter name, select Properties, and click the Advanced tab.

35. You are a desktop support technician for your company. How can you set up a new hardware profile to disable a NIC on a computer running Windows XP? (Select two correct answers.)

   ❏ A. Copy an existing profile from the Hardware Profiles dialog box and name it NIC Disabled by clicking the Hardware Profiles button on the System Properties window.

   ❏ B. Create a new hardware profile by copying the **LocalService** folder in the **%systemdrive%\Documents and Settings** folder, and name it NIC Disabled.

   ❏ C. In Device Manager, right-click the device and select Properties. Click the Log On tab, select the Hardware Profile NIC Disabled, and click Disable.

   ❏ D. Restart the system under the new profile named NIC Disabled. Open Device Manager, right-click the NIC that you want to disable, and select Disable.

   ❏ E. Create a new user account named NIC Disabled and log on using that user account each time that you want the computer to start up with the NIC disabled.

36. You are a desktop support technician for your company. Which of the following types of removable media can Windows XP write to without requiring any third-party software? (Select three correct answers.)

   ❏ A. Zip disks

   ❏ B. CD-R discs

   ❏ C. CD-RW discs

   ❏ D. DVD+R discs

   ❏ E. DVD-RW discs

   ❏ F. DVD-R discs

   ❏ G. DVD+RW discs

37. You are a desktop support technician for your company. If you add a second processor to a computer running Windows XP after the operating system is already installed, what procedure must you follow for Windows XP to take advantage of that second processor?

   ○ A. Reinstall the operating system.

   ○ B. Windows XP does not support more than one processor.

   ○ C. Upgrade the HAL driver from Uniprocessor to Multiprocessor in Device Manager.

   ○ D. Upgrade the HAL driver from Uniprocessor to DualProcessor in Device Manager.

38. You are a desktop support technician for your company. Although you recognize the usefulness of Remote Assistance as tool for users to send invitations to help desk support staff, users have been disinterested. You want to enable help desk support staff instead to initiate help desk sessions rather than require users to initially send invitations. How can you do this?

   ○ A. On the client computer, enable Remote Desktop in the System Properties.

   ○ B. In the local group policy, enable Offer Remote Assistance on the users' computers.

   ○ C. In the local group policy, enable Offer Remote Assistance on the help desk computers.

   ○ D. This cannot be done. Remote Assistance can only be started and invitations sent from the users' computers, not the help desk computers.

39. You are a desktop support technician for your company. A user reports that after upgrading from Windows NT to Windows XP, she is unable to modify her screen settings. Resolution is set for 640×480 and 16 colors. What do you recommend?

   ○ A. User driver rollback is used to revert to the Windows NT video driver.

   ○ B. Add more memory to the computer.

   ○ C. Update the driver for higher resolution and greater color depth.

   ○ D. In the Advanced tab of the Settings dialog box, disable Write Combining.

40. You are a desktop support technician for your company. Your network consists Windows XP workstations in an Active Directory domain on Windows 2000 Servers. You want to ensure that users retain their settings no matter which workstation they use to log on to the network. You also need to ensure they access their personal files from a secure network file server.

    What do you do? (Select two correct answers.)

    ❑ A. Set up each user account to use roaming profiles.

    ❑ B. Using the ClipBook Service, redirect personal folders to specific network locations.

    ❑ C. Using Accessibility Options, specify the location of roaming profile.

    ❑ D. Using group policies, redirect users' personal folders to specific network locations.

    ❑ E. Using Windows Explorer, redirect roaming profiles to network locations.

41. You are a desktop support technician for your company. You have obtained a new laptop computer on which you install a copy of Windows XP. The laptop meets all the hardware requirements of Windows XP, but when you attempt to configure Power Option Properties in Control Panel, the enable hibernation check box is unavailable. In an attempt to enable hibernation, you decide to update the BIOS of the computer. However, after doing so, when you reboot the computer, you receive a STOP error. How would you enable hibernation?

    ❑ A. Use the Windows Recovery console and replace **HAL.DLL** with an ACPI-compliant version of **HAL.dll**.

    ❑ B. Use System Restore to undo the changes made to the BIOS.

    ❑ C. Reinstall Windows XP.

    ❑ D. Restart the computer using the Last Known Good Configuration.

42. You are a desktop support technician for your company. You recently obtained a USB hard disk and attached it to an active USB hub already attached to a mouse and a Pocket PC. You install the driver for the USB device, but when you reboot the computer, the new hard driver appears neither in My Computer nor in Device Manager.

Which of the following steps would you perform first? (Select three correct answers.)

❏ A. Verify that USB support is not disabled in Device Manager.

❏ B. Verify that USB is enabled in the BIOS of the computer.

❏ C. Install the device on another PC.

❏ D. You have attached too many USB devices to the same hub. There is not enough power in the USB chain to support a mouse, Pocket PC, and disk drive at the same time. Disconnect the Pocket PC and the mouse when you want to use the hard disk.

❏ E. Disconnect the new hard disk from the hub and connect it directly to the USB port on the computer.

❏ F. Search for USB-related messages in the Application and System logs using Event Viewer.

43. You are a desktop support technician for your company. Windows XP Professional supports which of the following configurations for multiple processors?

○ A. Asymmetric multiprocessing (ASMP).

○ B. Symmetric multiprocessing (SMP).

○ C. Both ASMP and SMP.

○ D. Neither ASMP nor SMP. Windows XP supports only one processor.

44. You are a desktop support technician for your company. A user reports to you that while he was on a business trip, his laptop was stolen. Luckily, the user's data was backed up on a network server; however, the data on the stolen laptop might be at risk.

    When you install a new copy of Windows XP on the user's replacement laptop, which of the following steps should you take to protect the data? (Select two correct answers.)

    ❑   A. Install the Recovery Console and configure it for automatic administrative logon.

    ❑   B. Configure the laptop so that the Welcome screen is enabled.

    ❑   C. Use EFS and the user's logon credentials to encrypt the user's My Documents folder and any other folders that contain user data. Enable S/MIME in email client software and teach the user how to use both features.

    ❑   D. Configure the hard disk of the new laptop with one single partition formatted using the FAT32 file system.

    ❑   E. Add the computer to the corporate domain, issue user certificates for S/MIME and EFS from the Active Directory–integrated Certificate Services certificate authority. Install the certificates onto a Smart Card compatible with Windows XP Professional and Windows Server Certificate Services. Install a Smart Card reader into the new laptop computer and verify that suitable device drivers are installed.

45. You are a desktop support technician for your company. A user complains that her computer running Windows XP is unable to access a network resource. Which of the following problems might be resolved by clearing the computer's ARP cache using the command **netsh interface IP delete arpcache?**

    ○   A. User cannot connect to a server that has recently had the DNS entry changed.

    ○   B. User cannot connect to a server on the local subnet that has had its network card replaced.

    ○   C. User cannot connect to a server on the local subnet that has had its IP address changed.

    ○   D. User cannot connect to a server that has moved to a different network segment.

46. You are a desktop support technician for your company. You have been asked to explain how to configure ICS on a computer running Windows XP. Of the following scenarios, which one is best suited for ICS?

    ○ A. A small-office network that has 20 workstations and a domain controller using a single DSL connection to the Internet. All the computers are configured with static IP addresses.

    ○ B. A LAN that has 100 computers with ISP assigned IP addresses and a routed T3 connection to the Internet.

    ○ C. A home office network with four computers with static public addresses that connects to the Internet using a cable modem.

    ○ D. A home office network with four computers that connects to the Internet using a single dial-up connection.

47. You are a desktop support technician for your company. You are attempting to make a remote desktop connection using the Remote Desktop Web Connection interface. Which of the following ports and protocols are required to establish a connection? (Select two correct answers.)

    ❑ A. HTTP (TCP/IP port 80)

    ❑ B. POP3 (TCP/IP port 110)

    ❑ C. LDAP (TCP/IP port 389)

    ❑ D. RDP (TCP/IP port 3389)

    ❑ E. SMTP (TCP/IP port 25)

48. You are a desktop support technician for your company. You are training a new staff member and want to explain the advantages of standby mode over hibernation mode. How do you compare the two features? (Select two correct answers.)

    ❑ A. Standby mode does not consume hard disk space.

    ❑ B. Standby mode has no risk of data loss.

    ❑ C. Standby mode uses less power.

    ❑ D. Standby mode wakes up faster.

    ❑ E. Standby mode complies with the Federal airline regulations that all electronic devices must be turned off during take-off and landing.

49. You are a desktop support technician for your company. Before installing a new application in a computer running Windows XP, which precautions should you take? (Select two correct answers.)

    ❑ A. Boot into Safe Mode.

    ❑ B. Back up all files using NTBackup.

    ❑ C. Boot to the last known good configuration.

    ❑ D. Create a new restore point using System Restore.

    ❑ E. Boot into the Recovery Console.

50. You are a desktop support technician for your company. You have been using Windows XP with system restore for months. You now want to encrypt executable files and make sure they can never be restored to their original unencrypted state. How do you accomplish this task?

    ○ A. Encrypt the System Restore folder.

    ○ B. Turn System Restore off and on again.

    ○ C. Encrypt the folders that contain the application files.

    ○ D. Do nothing. System Restore always stores executables in an unencrypted format.

51. You are a desktop support technician for your company. From your Windows XP laptop, you work on files stored in a shared network folder and make the files available offline while out of the office. While traveling, you edit the locally cached copy of a PowerPoint 2003 presentation. However, while you are away, another user has also modified the same shared file on the server. What happens when you reconnect to the network?

    ○ A. Changes you've made to the file are automatically merged into the shared network version.

    ○ B. The original file is automatically replaced by your copy.

    ○ C. Windows XP asks you to select which version to keep and prompts you to rename the other copy of the file.

    ○ D. Windows automatically keeps whichever version of the file is newer. Changes to the older version are ignored.

52. You are a desktop support technician for your company. A user complains that during the year, his computer has "become slower." He explains that, for example, Microsoft Word takes "much" longer to open files he has created recently. Which of the following actions might improve the performance of the user's computer?

    ○ A. Enable NTFS compression.

    ○ B. Decrease the size of the paging file.

    ○ C. Run Disk Defragmenter on the computer's hard disks.

    ○ D. Set the Performance Logs and Alerts service to start automatically.

53. You are a desktop support technician for your company. You are taking over help-desk responsibilities on a Windows Server 2003 domain with computers running Windows XP. By default, which user groups have permission to make remote desktop connections to computers running Windows XP Professional? (Select two correct answers.)

    ❑ A. Administrators

    ❑ B. Remote Desktop Users

    ❑ C. Power Users

    ❑ D. Guests

    ❑ E. Users

54. You are a desktop support technician for your company. A teacher encrypts a file on her computer running Windows XP and then copies the file to an unencrypted shared folder on a Windows 2000 File Server. She later complains to you that others have read the file. Why are others able to access the file?

○ A. The file is stored on a volume that has been formatted as NTFS.

○ B. The file is stored on a volume that has been formatted as FAT32.

○ C. Network shares cannot be encrypted.

○ D. Encrypted files when copied to an unencrypted folder lose their encryption.

55. You are a desktop support technician for your company. Three employees are sharing a new computer running Windows XP that has been installed with Microsoft Office 2003. You add three more corporate applications used by your organization and want to make sure the three employees who share the computer have their data and user preferences stored separately. What should you do?

○ A. Run Sysprep.

○ B. Create local user accounts for each employee.

○ C. Create separate hardware profiles for each employee.

○ D. Manually create a new profile for each employee.

56. You are a desktop support technician for your company. You are upgrading a computer running Windows Me to the Windows XP operating system. The computer is equipped with hardware that meets the Microsoft HCL and has 128MB of RAM, a 500MHz Pentium III–compatible processor, and 12GB of disk space with 7GB free. You begin the upgrade process. The text phase of the installation goes smoothly, but as the computer begins the GUI phase, the setup program crashes. You reboot the computer several times with the same result. What is the most likely reason for the crash before the GUI phase?

○ A. You entered an invalid product key.

○ B. The Windows XP Professional installation CD-ROM is damaged.

○ C. The BIOS is incompatible with Windows XP Professional.

○ D. One or more of the memory chips installed in the computer is faulty.

57. You are a desktop support technician for your company. You are migrating settings from a group of laptop computers running Windows Me to new laptops running Windows XP. Using installation scripts, you automate much of the process, including the initial installation, joining a domain, and installing remaining applications. You are encountering trouble with the USMT. How can you troubleshoot the process that copies user data and settings to a shared folder on the network?

   ○ A. Check the local system and application logs for error messages.
   ○ B. Check the system and application logs on the domain controller where the shared network folder is stored.
   ○ C. Run the ScanState tool with verbose error logging enabled by appending the optional commands **/l scanstate.log /v 7 /u /f** to the command you use to run the tool.
   ○ D. Run the LoadState tool with verbose error logging enabled by appending the optional commands **/l scanstate.log /v 7** to the command you use to run the tool.

58. You are a desktop support technician for your company. You install the fax service on a computer running Windows XP. Because there is no printer connected locally to your fax server, you want incoming faxes printed on a network printer. How would you accomplish this task?

   ○ A. Configure the fax service to automatically print received faxes to a shared network printer that allows anonymous access to create and manage print jobs.
   ○ B. Configure the fax service to automatically print received faxes to a shared network printer that allows the local system account on your computer to create and manage print jobs.
   ○ C. Change the logon account for the fax service to an account that has permissions to log on to your computer, run the fax service, and send print jobs to the network printer. Configure the fax service to automatically print received faxes to the network printer.
   ○ D. It is impossible to configure it to automatically forward incoming fax documents to a network printer because the fax service is a local system service, not a network service. Instead, use the fax console to configure the fax service to automatically print received faxes to a local file.

59. You are a desktop support technician for your company. You want to create a shared folder on your computer running Windows XP to allow one of your co-workers to view files on your computer. You create an domain user account for this purpose and give Change permissions to the folder. Then, you share the folder, delete all the default share permissions, and assign the user Read permissions. What are the user's effective permissions when connecting to the share across the network?

   ○ A. Change
   ○ B. Read
   ○ C. No Access
   ○ D. Full Access

60. You are a desktop support technician for your company. Which of the following characteristics describe NTFS inherited permissions? (Select three correct answers.)

    ❑ A. Special permissions are inherited by default.

    ❑ B. Basic permissions are inherited by default.

    ❑ C. Explicit permissions are the same as inherited permissions.

    ❑ D. NTFS permissions are inherited by default.

    ❑ E. NTFS explicit permissions are not inherited by default.

    ❑ F. You cannot set explicit permissions on files, only on folders.

Answer Key for Practice Exam 1

1. B

2. C

3. B

4. C

5. C

6. D

7. A, C, D

8. B

9. A, B, C, D

10. A

11. A, B, D, E

12. B

13. A

14. C

15. B, D

16. B, E, F

17. D

18. D

19. A, B, D

20. A, B, F

21. B

22. B, C, D

23. C

24. A

25. A

26. B

27. C

28. A

29. C

30. C

31. B, D, E

32. B

33. D

34. A

35. A, D

36. A, B, C

37. C

38. C

39. C

40. A, D

41. C

42. C, E, F

43. B

44. C, E

45. B

46. D

47. A, D

48. A, D

49. B, D

50. B

51. C

52. C

53. A, B

54. B

55. B

56. C

57. C

58. C

59. B

60. A, B, D

1. The correct answer is B. By disabling the policy prohibiting unsigned device drivers, you can enable nonadministrators to install unsigned device drivers. Perhaps this computer was accidentally configured to "never install unsigned driver software." You control the ability to block unsigned drivers in System Properties, Hardware, Driver Signing. Answer A is incorrect; you should not elevate privileges by making a user an administrator. This violates the theory of "least privilege." Answer C is incorrect because installing a device in Safe Mode does not bypass signature requirements. Answer D is incorrect because the `%systemroot%` is not the location for device drivers. You find driver files in `%systemroot%\system32\drivers` or `%systemroot%\inf`.

2. Answer C is correct. You must mark the Allow Users to Connect Remotely to This Computer check box on the Remote tab of the System Properties window to enable Remote Desktop support. Answer A is incorrect because the Remote Desktop Connection client does not require Windows XP Service Pack 1 (SP1). Answer B is incorrect because Windows XP Home Edition does not support Remote Desktop connections. Answer D is incorrect because you do not need a licensing server for Remote Desktop connections.

3. The correct answer is B. StickyKeys lets you activate simultaneous keystrokes while pressing one key at a time. Answer A is incorrect because FilterKeys adjusts the responsiveness of the keyboard. Answer C is incorrect because MouseKeys enables the keyboard to perform mouse functions. Answer D is incorrect because ToggleKeys causes the computer to emit sounds when you press locking keys such as Caps Lock, Scroll Lock, and Num Lock.

4. The correct answer is C. When you drag a shortcut to the Start button, it automatically pins the shortcut to the pinned area of the Start menu so it always appears on the user's menu. Answer A is incorrect; the shortcut appears on all users' All Programs menus. Answer B is incorrect; a shortcut placed in the user's Start Menu folder appears in the All Programs menu. Answer D is incorrect because the My Recent Documents list contains only documents, not applications or shortcuts to applications.

5. The correct answer is C. You enable both SoundSentry, which shows visual warnings for system sounds, and ShowSounds, which instructs programs to display captions for program speech and sounds, in the Accessibility Options in Control Panel. Utility Manager enables users to check an accessibility program's status and start or stop an accessibility program. Answers B and D are both wrong because you use the Utility Manager program to enable the Narrator, Magnifier, and onscreen Keyboard features. Answer A is incorrect because the Narrator is a text-to-speech utility for vision-impaired users that reads what is displayed on your screen: the contents of the active window, menu options, or the text you have typed. Users with administrator-level access can have the program start when Utility Manager starts. Users can also start accessibility programs before logging on to the computer by pressing the Windows logo key+U at the Welcome screen.

6. Answer D is correct; this setting forces the user to log on to the computer using the classic logon screen. By default, a workgroup is set to use the simple logon screen. This setting only works when the computer is not a domain member. Answers A and B are incorrect because they do not incorporate the use of group policies. Answer C is incorrect because if this policy is enabled on a computer, a user is not required to press Ctrl+Alt+Del to log on.

7. Answers A, C, and D are correct. Both the Winver utility and WinMSD, which initializes the system information utility, display the version number and service-pack level of the operating system. MSinfo32.exe also displays the current Windows version number and service pack. The version number is also visible in the System Properties dialog box on the General tab. Answer B is incorrect because Setver.exe is an old DOS command used to define a DOS version number. Answer E is incorrect because Syskey is the tool that secures the Windows XP account database.

8. Answer B is correct. Simple File Sharing is enabled by default for standalone and workgroup-member computers. Simple File Sharing is disabled by default for domain-member computers. The Folder Options menu is the only way to enable or disable Simple File Sharing. Answer A is incorrect because the policy for Network Access: Sharing and Security Model for Local Accounts is not related to Simple File Sharing. Answer C is incorrect because the Workstation service is enabled by default. Answer D is incorrect because file and printer sharing for Microsoft Networks is enabled by default.

9. Answers A, B, C, and D are all correct. All these methods are valid ways to create shared network folders.

10. Answer A is correct. Manually caching documents is the default setting for Windows XP Professional. Answer B is incorrect because automatically caching documents is not the default setting; however, it is an option. Answer C is incorrect because caching offline files is enabled by default. Answer D is incorrect because automatically caching programs and documents is not the default setting; however, it is an option.

11. Answers A, B, D, and E are all correct. Answer C is incorrect because Authenticated Users is considered a built-in security principal, not a local group. Answer F is incorrect because Creator Group is also considered a built-in security principal, not a local group. Security principals are any account holder that is assigned an SID by Windows. It can be a user, group, computer, or service.

12. Answer B is correct. The Effective Permissions tab is a new feature in Windows XP Professional. Answer A is incorrect because it requires more administrative effort than using the Effective Permissions tab. Answer C is incorrect because no Effective Permissions tab exists for the Shared Folders snap-in. Answer D is incorrect because no Effective Permissions feature exists in the Component Services snap-in. Answer E is incorrect. The RunAs option is available for executable files, not for folders.

13. Answer A is correct. Folders and files that are moved within the same NT File System (NTFS) drive volume always retain their permissions from the source folder. Answer B is incorrect because folders and files moved to a different NTFS drive volume inherit their permissions from the target (destination) folder. Answer C is incorrect because folders and files that are moved never have their NTFS permissions reset to drive volume defaults. Answer D is incorrect because Windows Explorer does not prompt the user about retaining or inheriting NTFS permissions when moving or copying files.

14. Answer C is correct. If you set up each computer for each user who belongs to the Finance group, you can specify during which time period the printer is available and you can specify a higher priority than the default, which is 1. Answer A is incorrect because you do not need to configure computers for the users in groups other than the Finance group, and you cannot specify a priority setting lower than 1 (the default). Answer B is incorrect because printer permissions do not modify printer availability or printer priority settings. Answer D is incorrect because the printer ownership setting does not modify printer availability or printer priority settings.

15. Answers B and D are correct. Internet Printing Protocol (IPP) is supported on Windows 2000 (all editions) and later Microsoft operating systems. You can connect directly to printer by typing the URL `http://print_server_name/printer_share_name` into a Web browser. Answer A is incorrect because a print server computer must be running Internet Information Services (IIS) 5 or later to support IPP. Answer C is incorrect because IPP displays only print devices, not fax devices. However, the URL is correct.

16. Answers B, E, and F are correct. Default hidden shares include ADMIN$, IPC$, and the root of each available drive letter, such as C$. You can view them with the FSMGMT.msc Microsoft Management Console. Answer A is incorrect because SYSVOL is a default administrative share on a Windows Server. Answer C is incorrect because there is no default share named CD$. Answer D is incorrect because there is no default share named PRINTER$, but there is a default hidden share named PRINT$.

17. Answer D is correct. By clicking the Customize button from the permissions window, you can specify both share permissions and NTFS permissions when you create a new share using the Share a Folder Wizard from the Shared Folders snap-in. The Sharing tab of a folder's properties sheet provides only share permissions, not NTFS security. Answer A is incorrect because both methods allow you to set share permissions. Answer B is incorrect because publishing a share in Active Directory is not a permissions setting. Answer C is incorrect because both methods allow you to specify offline settings. Answer E is incorrect because you can only set Web Sharing access permissions from the Web Sharing tab of a folder's properties sheet.

18. Answer D is correct; when both Share and NTFS permissions are applied to an object, the permissions they have in common determine the effective permissions. Answer A is incorrect because NTFS permissions do not take precedence over share permissions. The two types of permissions work in concert with one another. Answer B is incorrect because share permissions do not take precedence over NTFS permissions either. The values they have in common determine the effective permissions on an object. Answer C is incorrect. Permissions on objects configured with Share permissions and NTFS permissions are calculated by examining the permissions they have in common. The easiest way to manage security is by sharing folders with Full Access so that NTFS security settings are the single place that effectively establish permissions.

19. Answers A, B, and D are correct. Special permissions get inherited by child objects, basic permissions get inherited by child objects, and NTFS permissions (in general) all get inherited by default. Answer C is incorrect because explicit permissions are set by users; inherited permissions are set by parent containers. Answer E is incorrect because even explicit permissions set on parent containers (folders) are inherited by child objects (subfolders and files) by default. Answer F is incorrect because you can set explicit permissions on any object or container.

20. Answers A, B, and F are correct. When set on a folder, the Modify basic NTFS permission consists of the List Folder/Read Data, Create Files/Write Data, and Write Extended Attributes special permissions, among several others. Answer C is incorrect because the Change Permissions special permissions setting is not part of the Modify permission. Answer D is incorrect because the Delete Subfolders and Files special permission is not part of the Modify permission; however, the Delete special permission is included. Answer E is incorrect because the Take Ownership special permission is not part of the Modify permission.

21. Answer B is correct; NTFS special permissions appear in the Effective Permissions dialog box. Answer A is incorrect because basic permissions do not appear in the Effective Permissions dialog box. Answer C is incorrect because share permissions do not appear in the Effective Permissions dialog box. Answer D is incorrect because both inherited and explicit NTFS permissions appear in the Effective Permissions dialog box.

22. Answers B, C, and D are correct. A user who is the current owner of an object can assign the Take Ownership permission to another user, a member of the Administrators group can assign ownership, and any user who is assigned the Restore Files and Directories right can transfer ownership to another user. Answer A is incorrect because members of the Domain Users group cannot assign the Take Ownership permission to another user for an object. Answer E is incorrect because members of the Backup Operators group cannot take ownership of files or folders at any time. Answer F is incorrect because members of the Authenticated Users group cannot assign ownership of files to other users at any time.

23. Answer C is correct. Windows XP Professional supports disk quotas on NTFS drive volumes only for individual users, not for groups. Therefore, you have to create a quota entry for each member of the Power Users group: you cannot assign a quota limit to a group. All members of the Administrators group inherit a no-limit disk quota by default, so you cannot set quotas on members of this group. Answer A is incorrect for the reasons just cited. Answer B is incorrect because you cannot set quotas on groups. Answer D is incorrect for the same reason.

24. Answer A is correct. When you move a compressed file from one NTFS volume to a different NTFS volume, the file inherits the compression attribute from the target location. Answer B is incorrect because an NTFS compressed folder or file only retains its compression attribute when it is moved to another folder on the same NTFS volume. Answer C is incorrect because Windows XP never prompts the user as to whether a folder or file should remain compressed or uncompressed. Answer D is incorrect because Windows XP does not generate error messages for moving compressed files to an uncompressed folder.

25. Answer A is correct. Only the user who originally encrypted the file (or any users given shared access to the encrypted file) may copy the file to a non-NTFS drive volume or to any type of removable media. In addition, only the user who originally encrypted the file (or any users given shared access to the encrypted file) may copy the file or move it to a folder located on a different NTFS volume. A user without shared access to an encrypted file is only permitted to move the file to another folder located on the same NTFS volume, where the file remains encrypted. Answer B is incorrect because, although Kim receives an error message when he attempts to copy the file to a floppy disk, he does not receive an error message when he attempts to move the encrypted file to an unencrypted NTFS folder located on the same NTFS volume. Answer C is incorrect because, although Kim receives an error message when he attempts to copy the file to a floppy disk, he is allowed to move the encrypted file to an unencrypted NTFS folder located on the same NTFS volume, but the file does not lose its encryption attribute. Answer D is incorrect because Kim receives an error message when he attempts to copy the encrypted file to a floppy disk.

26. Answer B is correct. If the "prevent removable media source for any install" setting (located in User Configuration\Administrative Templates\Windows Components\Windows Installer) is enabled, users cannot add programs from removable media, regardless of any other group policy settings. This policy overrides other policies related to software installation from removable media. Answer A is incorrect; administrative privileges are not required to enable someone to install software. Answer C is incorrect; there is no evidence of a virus. Answer D is incorrect. Users need not log on to the domain to be able to install software.

27. Answer C is correct. This policy controls the appearance of the feature. Answer A is incorrect; there need not be a floppy disk or a CD-ROM drive for the option to be available. Answer B is incorrect. This option is standard. Answer D is incorrect. There is no evidence that the Registry is corrupt.

28. Answer A is correct. User Configuration\Administrative Templates\ System\"configure driver search locations" options are Don't Search Floppy Disk Drives, Don't Search CD-ROM Drives, and Don't Search Windows Update. If Don't Search Floppy Disk Drives is enabled, you cannot search for new drivers on floppy disks with the Device Manager Update Driver feature. Answer B is incorrect. The disk appears to have files based on the scenario. Answer C is incorrect. The drive appears to be able to read the disk. Answer D is incorrect; Windows XP by default permits installation from removable media.

29. Answer C is correct. As a desktop support technician, you should always be aware of the physical requirements for printing and examine those first before considering more complex solutions that stem from software settings. You evaluate Answers A, B, and D after you check the physical connections.

30. Answer C is correct because it offers the easiest and fastest way to stop Windows XP from repeatedly attempting to install a driver for the small computer system interface (SCSI) device. Answer A is incorrect because it results in having the operating system redetect the device each time it restarts and then it will continue to try to install the device. Answer B is incorrect because you have to take the computer out of production to power it down and physically remove the SCSI adapter. Answer D is incorrect because it is easier to simply disable the device instead of creating a new hardware profile.

31. Answers B, D, and E are correct. Answers A, C, and F are incorrect because Windows XP offers only three options for unsigned driver installation behavior from the System Properties Window—Ignore, Warn, or Block.

32. Answer B is correct because using a group policy object (GPO) setting for the domain or for the organizational unit (OU) in which the workstations are placed is the fastest and easiest way to implement an unsigned driver signing policy. A GPO setting is also the most flexible because you can change it at any time and the change is propagated to all the workstations simultaneously. Answer A is incorrect because setting a local configuration and imaging it out is only a static solution, and the local configuration can be overridden by a GPO setting. Answer C is incorrect because the default setting for Unsigned Driver Options is not Block; it is Warn—Prompt Me Each Time to Choose an Action. Answer D is incorrect because disk-cloning solutions create static configurations rather than configurations that you can easily change later on a mass scale, such as GPO settings.

33. Answer D is correct. Windows XP only supports daisy-chained Universal Serial Bus (USB) hubs up to five levels deep in one continuous chain. Answer A is incorrect because USB cables that are 12 feet in length are supported. Answer B is incorrect because, by definition, all USB-compatible devices are Plug-and-Play (PnP)–compliant. Answer C is incorrect because USB scanners do not need to be connected to USB root hubs to function properly; however, they usually require their own separate power adapters.

34. Answer A is correct. You can change network protocol binding order, and you can bind and unbind protocols to network adapters from the Advance Settings dialog off the Advanced menu in the Network Connections window. Answer B is incorrect because the protocol binding options do not appear under Optional Networking Components. Answers C and D are incorrect because you cannot change protocol bindings from Device Manager.

35. Answers A and D are correct. You create hardware profiles by either renaming an existing profile or copying an existing profile from the Hardware Profiles dialog box. You must first create a hardware profile and then start the computer under that profile to enable or disable devices for that profile. Answer B is incorrect because you cannot create hardware profiles from the `%systemdrive%\Documents and Settings` folder. Answer C is incorrect because devices do not have a Log On tab in their properties window. Services have a Log On tab in their properties windows. Answer E is incorrect because you cannot implement a hardware profile by creating any type of user account or by logging onto the computer under a particular user account.

36. Answers A, B, and C are correct. Windows XP supports reading and writing to Zip disks, CD-R, and CD-RW media. Answers D, E, F, and G are incorrect because Windows XP does not support writing to DVD media without third-party software. Windows XP, however, can read from DVD media.

37. Answer C is correct. You use Device Manager to right-click the computer type (hardware abstraction layer [HAL]) and select Update Driver from the right-click menu to launch the Hardware Update Wizard. Answer A is incorrect because you do not need to reinstall the operating system to add support for a second processor. Answer B is incorrect because Windows XP supports two processors. Answer D is incorrect because Windows XP allows you to switch from a Uniprocessor HAL to a Multiprocessor HAL, but you cannot switch from a Uniprocessor HAL to a DualProcessor HAL. DualProcessor HAL is not a term used by Microsoft.

38. Answer C is correct. Offer Remote Assistance must be enabled on the users' computer. The help desk and the users must be using a version of Windows that is XP or newer, and the two users must be part of the same domain or within trusted domains. Answer A is incorrect because Remote Desktop is a separate remote feature that has nothing to do with Remote Assistance. Answers B and D are incorrect because it is possible for "experts" to offer assistance to "novices." You configure the option on the novice's computer, not the expert's.

39. Answer C is correct. The most likely reason for the poor video performance is an antiquated or inappropriate video driver. Answer A is incorrect because a Windows NT video driver is unlikely to improve video performance. Answer B is incorrect because adding more memory does not provide a wider array of video-resolution options. Answer D is incorrect because Write Combining is used to increase video speed. It does not affect color depth and resolution. Write Combining (WC) technology aggregates (combines) separate writes that a processor might make to a certain region of memory.

40. Answers A and D are correct. You should configure roaming profiles and redirect personal folders such as My Documents to network shares. Answer B is incorrect because the ClipBook service supports the ClipBook Viewer, which allows pages to be seen by remote ClipBooks. Answer C is incorrect because Accessibility Options in the Control Panel provide functionality, such as MouseKeys, StickyKeys, and ToggleKeys for users with special needs. Answer E is incorrect because Windows Explorer accesses local files and does not have the ability to redirect files.

41. The correct answer is C. If the computer BIOS does not support Advanced Configuration and Power Interface (ACPI) and support for power management, a non-ACPI version of HAL.dll is installed. After updating the BIOS to be ACPI-compliant, the only way to update HAL.dll is to reinstall Windows XP as an update to the current installation. Answer A is incorrect because it does not effectively install the proper HAL.dll. The ACPI version of HAL enumerates hardware differently and updates the Registry differently than a standard APM HAL. A Registry based on the original version of HAL is not the same as one on a system installed with the ACPI version of HAL. You can't just replace the HAL.dll file. Answers B and D are incorrect because you cannot boot Windows XP.

42. The correct answers are C, E, and F. As a desktop support technician, to troubleshoot hardware, you must first isolate the source of the problem. If you can install the hard disk in another PC, then the problem is not the hard disk. If you can install it directly to a USB port in the PC, then the problem is the hub. If there are error messages in the event logs, then you might discover the source of the problem. Answers A and B are incorrect; USB support is provided in the Device Manager and BIOS because the mouse and the pocket PC are already successfully connected. Answer D is incorrect because an active hub has its own power supply.

43. The correct answer is B. Windows XP Professional supports symmetrical multiprocessing (SMP). In the Windows XP family, only XP Professional supports SMP; XP Home does not. In asymmetrical multiprocessing, each CPU is dedicated to a specific function. In symmetrical multiprocessing, which is generally agreed to be superior to asymmetrical multiprocessing (but harder to implement), any CPU can handle any task if it is available to do so.

44. The correct answers are C and E. To secure a laptop computer with the features of Windows XP Professional, you can use the Encrypted File System (EFS) to encrypt all user documents and require users to be authenticated by a Smart Card. Answer A is incorrect; the Recovery Console with automatic administrative logon would make the laptop less secure because of the presence of a second operating system. Answer B is incorrect because disabling the Welcome screen only applies to workgroup members and therefore reduces security because the computer is not part of a domain. Answer D is incorrect because a FAT32-formatted drive does not support encryption.

45. The correct answer is B. A computer retains a table of IP addresses and Media Access Control (MAC) addresses representing the hardware address of other network devices. If the network interface of a network device changes, the local Address Resolution Protocol (ARP) cache is wrong temporarily. Flushing the cache purges the table and rebuilds it correctly. Answer A is incorrect; the command IPCONFIG /flushDNS deletes the local DNS cache. Answer C is incorrect; if a user cannot connect to a device whose IP address is new, a desktop support technician can resolve the problem by refreshing the NetBIOS cache with NBTSTAT - R. Answer D is incorrect. If you cannot connect to a device located on another subnet, examine the default gateway address on the local computer.

46. The correct answer is D. Internet Connection Sharing (ICS) is designed to give home office or small office computers access to the Internet through just one connection. It is not designed for networks of computers with static IP addresses, domains, or networks with gateways. Answer A is incorrect because static addresses and a domain are configured there. Answer B is incorrect because IP addresses are all static and assigned by the Internet service provider (ISP). Answer C is incorrect because all the computers have static IP addresses already assigned by an ISP.

47. The correct answers are A and D. HTTP and Remote Desktop Protocol (RDP) are required to establish a Remote Desktop Connection using Remote Desktop Web Connection. Remote Desktop Web Connection is a application hosted on a Web server that provides Remote Desktop connectivity from a browser interface. Answers B and E are incorrect. Post Office Protocol 3 (POP3) and Simple Mail Transfer Protocol (SMTP) are used for email. Answer C is incorrect because Lightweight Directory Access Protocol (LDAP) is used access to information in the Active Directory of Windows 2000 Server or Windows Server 2003.

48. The correct answers are A and D. Standby mode preserves your settings in memory and runs using reduced power. Hibernation preserves settings in a temporary file on the hard drive and turns the computer off. Answer B is incorrect because unsaved information in memory is not saved to disk and could be lost in a complete power failure. Answer C is incorrect because hibernation mode completely shuts down the computer; standby uses reduced amounts of power. Answer E is incorrect because in standby mode, the computer is not completely shut down.

49. The correct answers are B and D. Before installing applications, it is a good idea to back up your files and create a restore point using System Restore to back up system files and configurations. Answer A is incorrect. Installing a program in Safe Mode does not protect existing files, which might be overwritten by new versions. Answer C is incorrect because the last known good configuration is a repair option when you cannot get to the Windows desktop when booting Windows XP. Answer E is incorrect because the Recovery Console is a separate operating system, and installing software while it is running does not protect primary operating system. Recovery Console is used when you can't boot into the primary operating system or you need to remove or replace kernel mode drivers that are preventing you from starting Windows XP normally.

50. The correct answer is B. You must turn off System Restore to remove all old restore points, which might contain unencrypted files, and then restart the system restore feature. To permanently encrypt program files, turn off System Restore before you encrypt your files or folders, and then turn System Restore on again after the files or folders have been encrypted. When you turn off System Restore, all pre-existing restore points are deleted. Answer A is incorrect because it encrypts the storage location but does not affect the format of recovered files. Answer C is incorrect because encrypting the folders that contain the files does not remove the earlier system restore points that might contain unencrypted versions of the files. Answer D is incorrect because System Restore stores files in whichever format they have in your system.

51. The correct answer is C. When a user reconnects to the network, any changes that he made to files while offline are updated to the server. If two people made changes to the same file, you have the option to save your version of the file, keep the other version, or save both. Answer A is incorrect because changes are not automatically merged to an updated file. Answer B is incorrect because Windows XP does not automatically overwrite the file if the original has changed. Answer D is incorrect because Windows pauses before overwriting an updated original and prompts the user for a decision.

52. The correct answer is C. Running Disk Defragmenter on the drive that holds the users' files might increase the speed with which they are retrieved because the file will be stored in contiguous sectors of the drive once it is defragmented. Answer A is incorrect because NTFS compression might slow the speed with which files are retrieved because they have to be uncompressed. Answer B is incorrect because decreasing the size of the paging file results in less memory being available for programs to use. Answer D is incorrect because the Performance Logs and Alerts service, by default,starts automatically. The service collects data and can write data to a file or trigger an alert. Using Performance Logs and Alerts, however, does not speed up the computer.

53. The correct answers are A and B. Members of the Administrators and Remote Desktop Users Groups are given, by default, remote desktop privileges to computers running Windows XP Professional. Answers C, D, and E are incorrect. For best practices, add your account to the Remote Desktop Users group for your computer. After you do so, you do not have to log on as an administrator to access your computer remotely.

54. The correct answer is B. FAT32-formatted drives support sharing but do not support encryption and do not support file-level security. Answer A is incorrect because NTFS does support encryption and file-level security and enables the teacher to lock others out of the file. Answer C is incorrect. Network shares can support encryption. Answer D is incorrect because, although encrypted files do lose their encryption when copied to unencrypted folders, it is not the only reason that users can access the file. File-level security is unavailable on FAT32-formatted drives.

55. The correct answer is B. By creating local user accounts, you enable each employee to log on separately and their files are kept separate within separate user profiles. Answer A is incorrect. Sysprep is designed for deployments of Windows XP. It is a tool that prepares a prototype system to be cloned onto new computers. Answer C is incorrect because you use hardware profiles to enable or disable various hardware components. It does not create separate user settings. Answer D is incorrect. It is not necessary to manually create profiles. They are created by Windows XP the first time a user logs on.

56. The correct answer is C. When upgrading to Windows XP, it is wise to determine whether the computer manufacturer has published any BIOS upgrades. BIOS settings can prevent successful installations. Answer A is incorrect because you haven't had the opportunity to provide the product key yet. Answer B is incorrect because the initial phase of installation copies the necessary files to the computer's hard drive. The crash is occurring *after* the text phase. Answer D is incorrect because a faulty memory chip either disables all activity or provides reduced functionality.

57. The correct answer is C. The ScanState User State Migration Tool (USMT) copies data from the source computer and would be the program to troubleshoot when the read process was failing. Answer D is incorrect. LoadState.exe deposits (writes) this user-state data on a computer that is running a "clean" (not upgraded) installation of Windows XP Professional. Both of these programs are located on the Windows XP CD-ROM in the Valueadd\Msft\Usmt folder. Answers A and B are incorrect because ScanState and LoadState logs are not stored in the Event Viewer.

58. Answer C is correct. If the fax service is configured to initialize with a local account that has network printing privileges, you can configure the fax service to print to a network printer. Answers A and B are incorrect; under the guidelines of least privilege, you should never allow anonymous access to a network resources or give a local system account network privileges. Answer D is incorrect because you can configure the fax service to print to a network printer if the fax service is running with an account that has sufficient privileges.

59. The correct answer is B, Read. When combining Share permissions (Read) and NTFS permissions (Change), the permissions the settings have in common determine the effective permissions. Because you shared the folder with Read permissions, the user can get nothing other than Read permissions when accessing the folder and its files across the network. Answers A, C, and D are incorrect because Read is the only permission the folder has in common with the NTFS permissions.

60. Answers A, B, and D are correct. Special permissions, basic permissions, and NTFS permissions, by default, are inherited by child objects. Answer C is incorrect because explicit permissions are set by users; inherited permissions are set by parent containers. They are not the same. Answer E is incorrect because explicit permissions set on parent containers (folders) *are* inherited by child objects (subfolders and files) by default. Answer F is incorrect because you *can* set explicit permissions on any object or container.

Practice Exam 2

Now it's time to put to the test the knowledge that you've learned from reading this book! Write down your answers to the following questions on a separate sheet of paper. You will be able to take this sample test multiple times this way. After you answer all the questions, compare your answers with the correct answers in Chapter 12, "Answers to Practice Exam 2." The answer keys for both exams immediately follow each Practice Exam chapter.

. . . .

1. You're a desktop support technician for your company. All client computers run Windows XP. A corporate security policy change has mandated the removal of all automatic logons. Corporate headquarters wants to configure workstations to require at logon a valid username and password.

   You need to make sure that all domain users are required to log on to their computers before the desktop appears.

   How would you do this?

   ❑ A. In the Change the Way Users Log On or Off, select Use the Welcome Screen.

   ❑ B. On a workgroup computer, check the Users Must Enter a User Name and Password to Use This Computer check box, and then click OK.

   ❑ C. In Group Policy, disable the Do Not Require Ctrl+Alt+Del setting.

   ❑ D. In Group Policy, disable Always Use Classic Logon.

2. You're a desktop support technician for your company. On your network, users use Internet Explorer running on Windows XP in a Windows Server 2003 domain.

   A help desk colleague of yours moves from computer to computer, logging on from different machines throughout the day. He complains that Internet favorites created on one computer do not follow him when he logs in from others. How can you configure Internet favorites to remain consistent from login to login for a particular user?

   ❑ A. Copy the user's local profile to a network share and configure his account for roaming profiles.

   ❑ B. Use the Files and Settings Transfer Wizard to copy the Favorites folder to a network share.

   ❑ C. Configure a group policy to establish roaming profiles.

   ❑ D. On the Web pages in question, select Make Available Offline.

3. You're a desktop support technician. Users are allowed to edit their own TCP/IP settings, but one user complains to you that she is unable to edit the settings in her TCP/IP configuration.

   To troubleshoot this problem, what should you do?

   ❑ A. Log on to the machine with administrative privileges and attempt to modify TCP/IP settings.

   ❑ B. Check the security properties of the connection in Network Connections and ensure that the user account has Modify permissions.

   ❑ C. Attempt to ping the machine from a remote workstation.

   ❑ D. Log on with administrative privileges; choose Control Panel, User Accounts; and discover whether the user is a member of the Users group or has Limited User account.

4. You are a desktop support technician for your company, which requires special security settings for remote connections.

Dial-in users are required to use a Smart Card when they connect to the network, with their computers running Windows XP Professional, and to use the strongest encryption possible.

For security reasons, client computers are also required to disconnect if the remote access server doesn't support this configuration (Smart Card and strongest encryption).

To perform this setup, you've configured the EAP option Enable Smart Card Support.

How would you complete the configuration to provide the strongest encryption possible?

❑   A. Under Security Options, choose Typical and Require Data Encryption.

❑   B. Under Security Options, choose Advanced, Require Data Encryption, and MD-5 Challenge.

❑   C. Under Security Options, choose Advanced, Maximum Strength Encryption, and Smart Card or Other Certificate.

❑   D. Turn on Internet Connection Firewall.

5. You are a desktop support technician for your company. Users share their folders with co-workers. One user in the Travel department shares a folder named **Advisories**, wanting to allow other members of the department to read the travel advisories in the folder.

   All department members belong to a domain global security group named TRAVEL.

   The following is the list of security permissions that belong to the folder named **Advisories** on the network:

   Everyone ALLOW:READ

   The user reports that all network users are able to open and read the files in **Advisories**. The user needs to let only members of the Travel group access the **Advisories** share.

   How can you configure access permissions for the **Advisories** share and for the local **Advisories** folder so that only members of the Travel group can work in the **Advisories** shared folder over the network? (Select all correct answers.)

   ❑ A. Share Permissions—EVERYONE:ALLOW FULL CONTROL, NTFS permissions—EVERYONE:DENY:MODIFY, Travel:ALLOW:READ

   ❑ B. Share Permissions—EVERYONE:ALLOW FULL CONTROL, NTFS permissions—Travel:ALLOW:READ

   ❑ C. Share Permissions—EVERYONE:ALLOW:FULL CONTROL ALLOW, NTFS permissions—EVERYONE:DENY:FULL CONTROL:DENY, Travel:ALLOW:READ

   ❑ D. Share Permissions—EVERYONE:ALLOW FULL CONTROL, NTFS permissions—EVERYONE:ALLOW:FULL CONTROL

   ❑ E. Share Permissions—Travel:ALLOW:READ NTFS permissions—Travel:ALLOW:READ

6. You are a desktop support technician for your company. You log on to a Windows XP Professional workstation computer. You suspect that several different users are logging on to this workstation, so you want to view all the user profiles that are stored locally. You look in the **C:\Documents and Settings** folder, but no user profiles exist. The C: drive is the only volume on the computer. What might have happened to all the user profiles for this system?

   ❑ A. The system is configured to use only roaming profiles.

   ❑ B. The system is configured to use only mandatory roaming profiles.

   ❑ C. Fast User Switching is turned on, so user profiles exist only on a domain controller.

   ❑ D. The user profiles are located in **%systemroot%\Profiles**.

7. You are a desktop support technician for your company. WRKSTN3 is a Windows XP Professional computer that is connected to a workgroup named SALESDEPT. All computers in the workgroup are configured with default settings. A user named Alexis makes sure that she shares her GROUPDOCS folder with the network and leaves the default settings for caching. A user named Brendan, working on WRKSTN7, connects to Alexis' GROUPDOCS share. He right-clicks one of the files in the shared folder to make it available offline; however, that option does not exist on the pop-up menu. How can you help Brendan solve this problem?

❑ A. Make sure that his computer's DNS settings are correct.

❑ B. Turn off Fast User Switching.

❑ C. Run the Network Settings Wizard to enable offline files.

❑ D. Make the computer a member of an Active Directory domain.

8. You are a desktop support technician for your company. Alison always works on several Excel files and Word documents at the same time. She's tired of having so many buttons cluttering her taskbar. What can Alison do to improve the organization of the buttons representing all her open application programs on the taskbar?

❑ A. Enable DualView display.

❑ B. Enable the Taskbar Switching option.

❑ C. Turn on the Group Similar Taskbar Buttons option in Control Panel, Display Properties.

❑ D. Add the Quick Launch toolbar to the taskbar.

9. You are a desktop support technician for your company. You need to modify the Windows XP Professional boot settings so that the computer generates a boot log file each time that it restarts. You can't remember the exact boot option switch, and you'd prefer not to edit the **Boot.ini** file directly. How can you accomplish this task?

❑ A. Run the **sysedit** utility.

❑ B. Run the **msconfig** utility.

❑ C. Boot into Safe Mode and use the **bootcfg** utility.

❑ D. Use REGEDIT to modify the Registry data for the value **WindowsBoot** under **HKEY_LOCAL_MACHINE\SOFTWARE\Microsoft\Windows NT\CurrentVersion\Winlogon**.

10. You are a desktop support technician for your company. Users need to use two different legacy applications under Windows XP Professional. One application program requires a Windows NT 3.51 environment. The other program requires a Windows NT 4 SP6a environment. Which application program can Windows XP provide legacy compatibility support for?

- ❑ A. The Windows NT 4.0 SP3 application.
- ❑ B. The Windows NT 3.51 application.
- ❑ C. Both applications can be properly supported.
- ❑ D. Neither application can be properly supported.

11. You are a desktop support technician for your company. You've created a ZAP file for a legacy 16-bit application and you want to assign the application to the users in the Marketing OU within his company's Active Directory domain. How can you accomplish this using software group policy?

- ❑ A. Create a computer configuration policy to assign the application using the ZAP file.
- ❑ B. Create a user configuration policy to assign the application using the ZAP file.
- ❑ C. Create an MSI Windows Installer Package file for the legacy application using third-party repackaging software.
- ❑ D. Create an administrative template to add to the user configuration settings for the group policy of the OU.

12. You are a desktop support technician for your company. You have a computer running Windows XP Professional and several Microsoft Office 2003 applications and proprietary incident-tracking software to maintain a log of help desk support calls. You notice that when running these applications, your computer performs slowly. To improve the performance of the computer, you want to get information about these applications quickly.

Which of the following actions should you perform?

- ❑ A. Use Task Manager to get CPU usage information.
- ❑ B. Increase the priority of these programs in Task Manager.
- ❑ C. Use Dr. Watson to discover which program is creating the bottleneck.
- ❑ D. Run the programs simultaneously on another computer running Windows XP and create a performance log.

13. You are a desktop support technician for your company. You need to use the File and Settings Transfer Wizard for a user who is upgrading from an old computer running Windows 98 to a new computer running Windows XP. Which of the following computer configuration transfer techniques are supported by the FAST Wizard? (Select all correct answers.)

   ❑ A. Serial port connections (one RS-232 cable connected between two computers)

   ❑ B. Parallel port connections (one LPT cable connected between two computers)

   ❑ C. USB connections (one USB cable connected between two computers)

   ❑ D. Zip or Jaz drive cartridges

   ❑ E. IEEE 1394 (FireWire) connections (one FireWire cable connected between two computers)

   ❑ F. Infrared connections

   ❑ G. Wireless 802.11 connections

14. You are a desktop support technician for your company. You want to collect statistics on the behavior of a new computer running Windows XP. Which of the following system tools is best suited to help you create a historical baseline of overall system performance for a Windows XP Professional computer?

   ❑ A. Performance Logs and Alerts

   ❑ B. System Monitor

   ❑ C. Task Manager

   ❑ D. Network Monitor Driver and the **Netcap.exe** utility

15. You are a desktop support technician for your company. You are attempting to improve the performance of a computer running Windows XP. Which of the following actions represents a best-practice approach to configuring virtual memory on a Windows XP Professional computer that has three physical hard disks (assigned as drives C, D, and E); the **%systemroot%** folder located on the C drive; and 256MB of memory installed?

   ❑ A. Place the paging file on the C drive with an initial size of 192MB and a maximum size of 256MB.

   ❑ B. Place a paging file on the D drive with an initial size of 192MB and a maximum size of 192MB, and place a second paging file on the E drive, also with an initial size of 192MB and a maximum size of 192MB.

   ❑ C. Place a paging file on the E drive with an initial size of 128MB and a maximum size of 256MB.

   ❑ D. Place a paging file on the E drive with an initial size of 192MB and a maximum size of 192MB, and place a second paging file on the C drive, also with an initial size of 192MB and a maximum size of 192MB.

16. You are a desktop support technician for your company. You are responsible for supporting several users in the Engineering department who use a custom application program that is resource intensive. These users run several programs at once on their dual CPU systems, including the custom application. Which of the following settings can you affect in Task Manager to control the amount of resources that Windows XP Professional allocates to the custom application? (Select all correct answers.)

   ❏ A. CPU priority

   ❏ B. CPU affinity

   ❏ C. End the application program

   ❏ D. Expand the size of the paging file

   ❏ E. Increase the CPU clock speed

   ❏ F. View a disk usage chart

17. You are a desktop support technician. Your company has just bought 12 dual processor computers running Windows XP. Users complain of slow performance when running a company proprietary database program. You monitor the equipment and notice a pattern in which the first CPU on each computer, CPU1, is consistently running at 100% and CPU2 is only running at about 15%. How can you improve performance?

   ❏ A. Run the database program on CPU2.

   ❏ B. Run the database program on CPU1.

   ❏ C. Configure the application to quit using CPU affinity.

   ❏ D. Reduce the application's base priority.

18. You are a desktop support technician for your company. On a computer running Windows XP and Office 2003, you are running a proprietary program. When doing so, you notice that performance is slow. To improve the computer's performance, you want to collect information about the programs over a period of time that you can review later. Which action should you take?

   ❏ A. Use Dr. Watson to determine which program is the performance hog.

   ❏ B. Increase the priority of the programs.

   ❏ C. Use Task Manager to get information about CPU usage.

   ❏ D. Use the Performance MMC snap-in and set up appropriate objects, counters, and instances to monitor the system's use of resources.

19. You are a desktop support technician for your company. On a computer running Windows XP, you install a desktop publishing program and performance becomes much slower for the other programs on the computer. You need to run the program but also access other applications on the computer. What should you do?

   ❑ A. Reduce the priority of the desktop publishing program.
   ❑ B. Increase the priority of all programs.
   ❑ C. Reduce the priority of all programs.
   ❑ D. Increase the priority of the remaining programs.

20. You are a desktop support technician for your company. You have a 16-bit application for which there is no upgrade. You support dual processor computers running Windows XP. When the 16-bit program is running, performance is slow. After monitoring the equipment, you notice that one processor on each computer is consistently at 100% utilization. How would you improve performance?

   ❑ A. Run each 16-bit program in its own virtual MS-DOS machine.
   ❑ B. Teach users to terminate the 16-bit program and then restart the program.
   ❑ C. Increase the priority of the 16-bit program to Realtime.
   ❑ D. Assign CPU affinity to the 16-bit program.

21. You are a desktop support technician for your company. Since installing Windows XP on a computer, its performance has grown slower. Now it takes much longer to open a file. There is 3GB of disk storage remaining. The Physical Disk:% Disk Time and the Physical Disk:Current Disk Queue Length performance objects and counters display high values. Physical Disk:Reads/sec has been increasing over time, even when you access the same files from day to day. How would you improve the performance of this computer?

   ❑ A. Run Defrag.
   ❑ B. Disable disk quotas.
   ❑ C. Reformat the hard disk to FAT32.
   ❑ D. Adjust the size of the paging file.

22. You are a desktop support technician, and you support both 16- and 32-bit applications. The 32-bit programs run at an acceptable speed; the 16-bit programs are slow. CPU usage is at 75%. How can you improve the 16-bit apps without reducing the performance of the 32-bit programs?

   ❑ A. Upgrade the computer's CPU.
   ❑ B. Run the 16-bit programs in a separate memory space.
   ❑ C. Reduce the priority of the 32-bit apps.
   ❑ D. Configure the 16-bit applications to use their own CPU affinities.

23. You are a desktop support technician for your company. You need to troubleshoot a computer running Windows XP. Which of the following tools can you use to view real-time system performance data? (Select all correct answers.)
    - ❑ A. Performance Logs and Alerts
    - ❑ B. Task Manager
    - ❑ C. Event Viewer
    - ❑ D. System Monitor
    - ❑ E. **Services.msc**

24. You are a desktop support technician for your company. On a computer running Windows XP, you want to analyze events using the Event Viewer. Which of the following event items is *not* one of the five default Event Viewer event types you would find listed among the events?
    - ❑ A. Information
    - ❑ B. Error
    - ❑ C. Caution
    - ❑ D. Failure Audit
    - ❑ E. Success Audit

25. You are a desktop support technician for your company. You decide to use the System Monitor to analyze performance statistics for a computer running Windows XP. Which of the following items serve as performance metrics for specifying different computer attributes to monitor? (Select all correct answers.)
    - ❑ A. Objects
    - ❑ B. Counters
    - ❑ C. Cycles
    - ❑ D. Initiators
    - ❑ E. _Totals
    - ❑ F. Instances

26. You are a desktop support technician for a company that sells fireworks and pyrotechnical equipment. Using the Performance Logs and Alerts tool, you add performance counters such as Memory:Pages/sec, PhysicalDisk:Avg. Disk Queue Length:_Total, and Processor:% Processor Time:_Total to a new counter log. You schedule this new counter log to start on Monday morning at 8:00 a.m. and stop on Wednesday evening at 10:00 p.m. The company you work for has a seasonal business; computer usage is extremely high during this time of year due to increased marketing, sales, and accounting activities. Collecting this type of performance data is referred to as _____?
    - ❑ A. Establishing a baseline
    - ❑ B. Viewing real-time data
    - ❑ C. Logged performance monitoring
    - ❑ D. Collecting histogram data

27. You are a desktop support technician for your company. Your company has indicated a desire to update computers running Windows XP with files from Microsoft stored on intranet servers. On which of the following intranet computer systems can you install the server component of SUS? (Select all correct answers.)

    ❑ A. Windows NT Workstation 4.0 with SP5

    ❑ B. Windows XP Professional with SP1

    ❑ C. Windows 2000 Server

    ❑ D. Windows 2000 Professional

    ❑ E. Windows 98 SE

    ❑ F. Windows Me

28. You are a desktop support technician for your company. To standardize the process of updating computers running Windows operating systems on your network, management has decided to integrate SUS. Onto which of the following computer systems can you deploy Windows updates using SUS? (Select all correct answers.)

    ❑ A. Windows NT Workstation 4.0 with SP5

    ❑ B. Windows XP Professional with SP1

    ❑ C. Windows 2000 Server

    ❑ D. Windows 2000 Professional

    ❑ E. Windows 98 SE

    ❑ F. Windows Me

29. You are a desktop support technician for your company. Users are complaining about print jobs that print more slowly than expected. You've checked the hardware connections, the condition of the printer appears normal, and now you plan to relocate the print spooler folder that contains print jobs on their way to the printing device to another drive. Where in Windows XP can you modify the location of the print spooler folder?

    ❑ A. In the Registry by modifying the **Spooler** value data in **HKEY_LOCAL_MACHINE\SOFTWARE\Microsoft\Windows NT\CurrentVersion\Windows**.

    ❑ B. By clicking Start, All Programs, Administrative Tools, Computer Management and selecting Device Manager and then Printers.

    ❑ C. By opening the Printers and Faxes window; clicking File, Server Properties; clicking the Advanced tab; and typing in the new spool folder location.

    ❑ D. By going to the Control Panel, right-clicking the Printers and Faxes icon, and selecting Print Server Properties. Click the Advanced tab and type in the new spool folder location.

30. You are a desktop support technician for your company. A user complains of printing problems. You intend to examine logged events in the Event Viewer to look for clues to the cause of the problem. Which of the following print spooler events and notifications are logged or enabled by default in the Printer Server Properties dialog box of Windows XP Professional? (Select all correct answers.)

   ❑   A. Log spooler error events
   ❑   B. Log spooler warning events
   ❑   C. Notify when remote documents are printed
   ❑   D. Show informational notifications for local printers
   ❑   E. Beep on errors of remote documents
   ❑   F. Log spooler information events

31. You are a desktop support technician for your company. A remote user logged into your network from home uses Windows XP Professional. He accesses your network through a connection to his ISP and creates a VPN over the Internet into the corporate LAN. You receive an email message from the user, who complains of error messages when attempting to run an application. You reply and request that he send you a Remote Assistance invitation. The user connects to the Internet, sends the invitation, and then disconnects so that he can call for further instructions. You accept the invitation but the attempted connection fails.

   What actions should you take?

   ❑   A. Attempt to ping the user's computer to determine connectivity.
   ❑   B. Request that the user resubmit the invitation as an email attachment.
   ❑   C. Request that the user dial directly into the corporate network and resubmit the invitation.
   ❑   D. Request that the user resubmit the invitation and to remain online.

32. You are a desktop support technician. Software written for Windows 95, Windows 98, or Windows Me often will not run properly under Windows XP. Likewise, some hardware devices use drivers that are not compatible with Windows XP. If you are currently running a previous version of Windows, you can run which of the following tools before installing Windows XP to verify system hardware and software compatibility?

   ❑   A. Windows Diagnostics
   ❑   B. System Configuration Utility
   ❑   C. **CheckUpgradeOnly**
   ❑   D. Windows XP Upgrade Advisor

33. You are a desktop support technician for your company. You are performing a desktop migration for your company, which is in the process
of deploying 150 new Windows XP Professional workstations to
replace the Windows 98 SE computers currently in use. As part of this
deployment, the company wants you to migrate the following settings
from the Windows 98 SE computers to the new Windows XP
Professional systems:

> ➤ Internet Explorer settings
> ➤ Outlook Express configuration settings
> ➤ Dial-up connections
> ➤ Current display settings
> ➤ Taskbar settings

Which is the easiest tool for achieving this goal?

- ❑ A. Files and Settings Transfer Wizard
- ❑ B. NTBackup
- ❑ C. Disk Copy
- ❑ D. Third-party migration tool

34. You are a desktop support technician for your company. In Windows
XP Professional, you can use the FAST Wizard to move data files and
personal settings from your old computer to your new one. To launch
the FAST Wizard, you perform the following steps:

1. You click Start, (All) Programs, Accessories, System Tools.

2. You double-click Files and Settings Transfer Wizard.

   Windows XP Professional launches the Files and Settings Transfer
   Wizard.

3. At the Welcome to the Files and Settings Transfer Wizard page, you
   click Next.

At the What Computer Is This? dialog box, which two options are you
presented with?

- ❑ A. Copy Source / Copy Target
- ❑ B. New Computer / Old Computer
- ❑ C. Original Source / Destination Target
- ❑ D. Copy Source / Destination Target

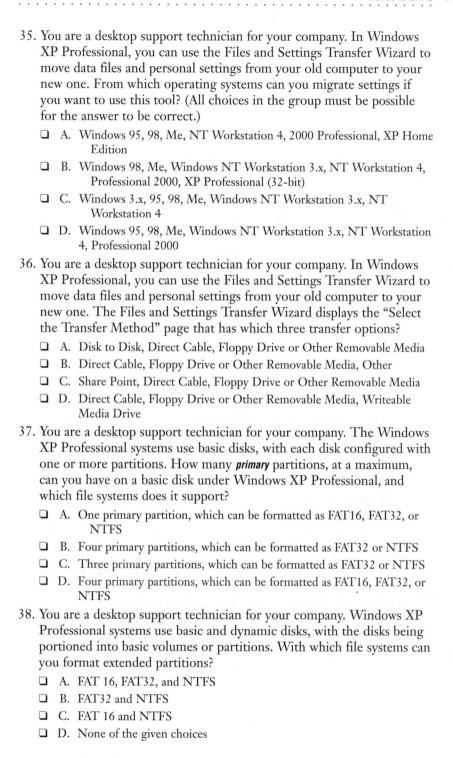

35. You are a desktop support technician for your company. In Windows XP Professional, you can use the Files and Settings Transfer Wizard to move data files and personal settings from your old computer to your new one. From which operating systems can you migrate settings if you want to use this tool? (All choices in the group must be possible for the answer to be correct.)

- ❑ A. Windows 95, 98, Me, NT Workstation 4, 2000 Professional, XP Home Edition
- ❑ B. Windows 98, Me, Windows NT Workstation 3.x, NT Workstation 4, Professional 2000, XP Professional (32-bit)
- ❑ C. Windows 3.x, 95, 98, Me, Windows NT Workstation 3.x, NT Workstation 4
- ❑ D. Windows 95, 98, Me, Windows NT Workstation 3.x, NT Workstation 4, Professional 2000

36. You are a desktop support technician for your company. In Windows XP Professional, you can use the Files and Settings Transfer Wizard to move data files and personal settings from your old computer to your new one. The Files and Settings Transfer Wizard displays the "Select the Transfer Method" page that has which three transfer options?

- ❑ A. Disk to Disk, Direct Cable, Floppy Drive or Other Removable Media
- ❑ B. Direct Cable, Floppy Drive or Other Removable Media, Other
- ❑ C. Share Point, Direct Cable, Floppy Drive or Other Removable Media
- ❑ D. Direct Cable, Floppy Drive or Other Removable Media, Writeable Media Drive

37. You are a desktop support technician for your company. The Windows XP Professional systems use basic disks, with each disk configured with one or more partitions. How many *primary* partitions, at a maximum, can you have on a basic disk under Windows XP Professional, and which file systems does it support?

- ❑ A. One primary partition, which can be formatted as FAT16, FAT32, or NTFS
- ❑ B. Four primary partitions, which can be formatted as FAT32 or NTFS
- ❑ C. Three primary partitions, which can be formatted as FAT32 or NTFS
- ❑ D. Four primary partitions, which can be formatted as FAT16, FAT32, or NTFS

38. You are a desktop support technician for your company. Windows XP Professional systems use basic and dynamic disks, with the disks being portioned into basic volumes or partitions. With which file systems can you format extended partitions?

- ❑ A. FAT 16, FAT32, and NTFS
- ❑ B. FAT32 and NTFS
- ❑ C. FAT 16 and NTFS
- ❑ D. None of the given choices

39. You are a desktop support technician. Under Windows XP Professional, dynamic disks are not supported in certain situations. Which choice is one of the situations where you cannot use dynamic disks?

   ❑ A. Laptops

   ❑ B. Internal IDE drives formatted with NTFS

   ❑ C. Internal SCSI drives formatted with NTFS

   ❑ D. Internal IDE drives formatted with FAT32

40. You are a desktop support technician. You have a 4GB drive formatted with FAT32 in your computer running Windows XP Professional, and you are attempting to convert the basic disk to a dynamic disk when you receive an error message saying that your disk does not have enough free space for the upgrade. You verify that there is 900MB of free space on the hard drive, but when you attempt the conversion again, you still receive the same answer. What is the most likely reason for the error?

   ❑ A. The minimum hard drive partition needed to convert to a dynamic disk is greater than 4GB.

   ❑ B. You need 1GB of free space or more to convert to a dynamic disk.

   ❑ C. You do not have enough unpartitioned free space available at the end of the hard drive to perform the conversion.

   ❑ D. You need to convert the partition to NTFS first before you can convert the disk to dynamic.

41. You are a desktop support technician. Dynamic disk storage is organized into volumes instead of partitions on computers running Windows XP Professional. Which type of volume combines areas of free space from two or more physical disks into a single volume where data is written across all the disks at once?

   ❑ A. Striped volume

   ❑ B. Simple volume

   ❑ C. Spanned volume

   ❑ D. Mirrored volume

42. You are a desktop support technician. A workgroup under Windows XP Professional is a small group of computers on a network that enables users to work together and does not support centralized administration. Of the following selections, which is not a characteristic of a workgroup?

   ❑ A. Resources are located on each computer in the workgroup.

   ❑ B. Resources are located on a server in the workgroup.

   ❑ C. Administration and authentication of users is performed locally on each computer in the workgroup.

   ❑ D. Each computer shares one local Security Accounts Manager (SAM) database.

43. You are a desktop support technician. You are installing Windows XP Professional from a CD-ROM to an unformatted

    40GB hard drive without an unattended setup file. Setup prompts you to select the partition on which to install Windows XP Professional. You create a new partition by using the unpartitioned free space on the hard disk. You select the maximum partition size of 4GB and FAT as the file system. You need to format the partition with FAT16 because you will install a DOS-based program that needs to be installed on such a partition to run properly. After the operating system is finished installing, you attempt to install the DOS-based program, but the program will not install and it shows an unknown error. The manufacturer of the program assures you that it will run at a command prompt within Windows XP Professional and it has been successfully installed elsewhere. What is the most likely reason this DOS program cannot install and run on this workstation?

    ❑ A. The problem is most likely a software configuration error. You need to reboot the workstation to resolve the issue.

    ❑ B. The program is based on MS-DOS and therefore cannot properly address the 4GB FAT partition.

    ❑ C. None of the available choices. MS-DOS–based programs cannot run on Windows XP Professional.

    ❑ D. None of the available choices. FAT16 partitions are limited to 2GB.

44. You are a desktop support technician for your company. The compression state of files and folders when you copy or move them within and between NTFS and FAT volumes on a Windows XP Professional system when using NTFS Compression (not the Compressed Folders feature of Windows XP Professional) depends on a number of different factors. When you copy an uncompressed file to a compressed folder in Windows XP, what happens to the new file?

    ❑ A. The file is compressed; it inherits the compression state of the target folder.

    ❑ B. The file remains uncompressed; it inherits the compression state of the target folder.

    ❑ C. The file is compressed; it keeps the compression state of the source folder.

    ❑ D. The file remains uncompressed; it keeps the compression state of the source folder.

45. You are a desktop support technician for your company. Corporate policy requires strict security guidelines. You manage a number of computers running Windows XP, which are configured as members of a workgroup, not a domain. How would you configure a password policy on a standalone computer running Windows XP Professional?

    ❏ A. Go to the User applet in the Control Panel.
    ❏ B. Use the Group Policy Object snap-in to edit local settings.
    ❏ C. Use REGEDIT to edit local settings.
    ❏ D. Use REGEDT32 to edit local settings.

46. You are a desktop support technician for your company. You are expected to design a disaster recovery plan that includes a plan for scheduling data backups. There are a number of options in the Windows Backup program. Which type of backup is normally performed once a week and upon completion resets (clears) the archive on the backed-up files?

    ❏ A. Differential
    ❏ B. Incremental
    ❏ C. Full
    ❏ D. Copy

47. You are a desktop support technician for your company. Six computers running Windows XP are in an organizational unit and have just been upgraded from Windows NT 4.0 workstation. The computers are used by employees to run 16-bit legacy applications. All six computers are configured to have the default security settings. A user tells you that she cannot install the 16-bit application on her computer running Windows XP Professional. The user is a member of the local users group. You need the 16-bit application to install and run on the user's computer. You do not want to elevate the user's privileges. Which security configuration template should you use to relax the permission settings on the computer?

    ❏ A. **basicwk**
    ❏ B. **securews**
    ❏ C. **setup security**
    ❏ D. compatws

48. You are a desktop support technician for your company. You want to map drive F on a computer running Windows XP Professional to the hidden administrative share on drive C for a file and print server named FPServer1. What command should you use?

    ❏ A. net use F:\\FPServer1\C$
    ❏ B. net view C$ \\FPServer1\F:
    ❏ C. **net view F:\\FPServer1\C$**
    ❏ D. net use C$ \\FPServer1\F:

49. You are a desktop support technician for your company. You install a copy of Windows XP Professional. When the installation finishes, you see only the Recycle Bin icon on the desktop. You do not see the My Computer, My Network Places, or My Documents icons on the desktop. You want all these icons to appear on the desktop. How would you modify the computer settings?

   ❑ A. Right-click the desktop and select Show Desktop Icons.
   ❑ B. Configure folders to use the simple folder view.
   ❑ C. Switch to the Classic Start Menu style.
   ❑ D. Enable Use Windows Classic Folders in Folder Options.

50. You are a desktop support technician for your company. A user spends half his workweek working in the office and half his workweek working at home. He uses a laptop running Windows XP Professional. While working at home over the weekend, the user logs onto his computer using a domain user account and begins creating a dial-up connection. He attempts to enable ICF on the connection but is unable to do so. In the past, the user has successfully created numerous dial-up connections and enabled ICF. Today, the user has returned to the office and notifies you of his ICF problem. How would you fix the problem?

   ❑ A. Disable the policy that prohibits ICF on your DNS domain network.
   ❑ B. Enable Allow Other Network Users to Control or Disable the Shared Internet Connection.
   ❑ C. Instruct the user to use his local account when dialing into the corporate network.
   ❑ D. Enable Web Server HTTP on Advanced Settings in the dial-up connection's Properties sheet.

51. You are a desktop support technician for your company. All users run a proprietary line-of-business accounting program that generates weekly financial reports from data that is provided by each user in a confidential file named Sales.dat. Each user's file contains unique data and is located in the C:\Accounting\Sales folder. These files must be protected from unauthorized access. You have the ability to relocate the Sales.dat file. Each user should be able to run the line-of-business software with his or her own Sales.dat file. How would you secure the files?

❑ A. On a file server, create a folder named **C:\confidential**. Copy each user's **Sales.dat** file to the folder and encrypt the folder. Map a drive letter from each user's computer to the folder.

❑ B. On a file server, create an encrypted folder named **C:\confidential**. Create a subfolder for each user and copy his or her **Sales.dat** file to the respective subfolder. On each user's computer, map a drive to the user's subfolder.

❑ C. On each user's computer, create a local folder named **C:\confidential**. Move the **Sales.dat** file to the folder and encrypt the folder.

❑ D. On each user's computer, create a folder named C:\confidential. Move the Sales.dat file to the folder and instruct the user to encrypt the folder.

52. You are a desktop support technician for your company. Your computer runs Windows XP, and sales staff members who also use laptops with Windows XP often contact you when they are on the road and repeatedly ask the same questions. You want to reduce the amount of time and effort answering technical support questions. You plan to use the Remote Assistance feature to accomplish this task. Which of the following is a solution to your problem?

❑ A. Create a simple text file that answers the most frequently asked questions and place it in a shared folder on a file server.

❑ B. Create a simple text file that answers the most frequently asked questions and send the file to users during a Remote Assistance session.

❑ C. Create a simple text file that answers the most frequently asked questions and send it to users as an email attachment.

❑ D. Create a text file that answers the most frequently asked questions, place the file on a floppy disk, and give it to users.

53. You are a desktop support technician for your company. You are responsible for developing a disaster recovery plan that includes guidelines for daily data backups. Which type of backup is normally performed once a day and upon completion does not reset (clear) the archive bit on the backed up files?

❑ A. Incremental

❑ B. Differential

❑ C. Full

❑ D. Copy

54. You are a desktop support technician for your company. You have 10 computers on which on want to install Windows XP Professional. Currently, the 10 computers are running Windows 98 SE. Each PC has the same configuration:

➤ Pentium II CPU running at 133Mhz

➤ 64MB RAM

➤ One 40GB hard disk formatted as FAT32

➤ 550MB available disk space

➤ CD-ROM drive

➤ VGA display adapter and VGA monitor

➤ Wireless keyboard and mouse combination

Based on this configuration, select the best answer that explains why you can or cannot install Windows XP Professional on each of the 10 computers.

❑ A. Yes, you can install Windows XP Professional because the configuration meets or exceeds Microsoft's minimum hardware requirements.

❑ B. No, you cannot install Windows XP Professional because Microsoft's minimum hardware requirements necessitate at least 128MB RAM.

❑ C. No, you cannot install Windows XP Professional because Microsoft's minimum hardware requirements necessitate at least a Pentium III processor.

❑ D. No, you cannot install Windows XP Professional because Microsoft's minimum hardware requirements necessitate more than 550MB of available disk space.

❑ E. No, you cannot install Windows XP Professional because the operating system cannot mount a FAT32 disk partition larger than 32GB.

55. You are a desktop support technician for your company. Your company's network infrastructure has the following components and standards:

  ➤ It's an Active Directory environment with both Windows 2000 Server and Windows Server 2003 computers.

  ➤ It uses Windows 2000 DNS servers.

  ➤ All workstations and servers use static IP addresses.

  ➤ One RIS server has been installed but is not currently used in production.

  ➤ Two terminal servers are used in Application Server mode.

  ➤ The company uses Microsoft Open Value Licensing.

  ➤ All new workstations have PXE-compliant network adapters installed.

  ➤ Workstations are standardized on Windows XP Professional SP1.

Based on the criteria listed, which of the following methods to deploy Windows XP Professional with customized applications and user settings onto 50 new computers would be the most efficient and fastest option?

❑ A. Dispatch in-house computer technicians to perform attended installations at each new computer.

❑ B. Dispatch in-house computer technicians to perform unattended installations at each new computer using a preconfigured answer file stored on a floppy disk and the Windows XP Professional CD-ROM.

❑ C. Dispatch in-house computer technicians to perform unattended installations at each new computer using a preconfigured answer file stored on a network server along with the Windows XP Professional setup files also stored on the same server.

❑ D. Dispatch in-house computer technicians to perform unattended installations at each new computer using third-party imaging software from a master system image created on a model computer prepared using the **sysprep.exe** tool.

❑ E. Instruct users how to boot their new workstations from the network and then how to start an RIS installation of a Windows XP Professional system image.

56. You are a desktop support technician for your company. You have just set up Windows XP Professional on five new computers that your company recently purchased from IBM Corporation. Just before you began the installations, the company's dedicated Internet T1 circuit went down due to a severe storm in the area. One week later, the Internet connection still does not work. How many days do you have to activate the five OEM copies of Windows XP Professional that you installed?

   ❏ A. 14 days

   ❏ B. 30 days

   ❏ C. 45 days

   ❏ D. 60 days

   ❏ E. No time limit: you only need to activate retail copies of Windows XP Professional.

57. You are a desktop support technician for your company. The server administrators for your company have installed Microsoft SQL Server 2000 using a single-processor license. The company needs 100 users to be licensed to access SQL Server data, although much of the time, only about 75 users will actually be accessing SQL Server data simultaneously. How many CALs does the company need to buy to fully comply with Microsoft licensing?

   ❏ A. 50 CALs

   ❏ B. 75 CALs

   ❏ C. 100 CALs

   ❏ D. 0 CALs

58. You are a desktop support technician for your company. You have upgraded several different computers running various Microsoft operating systems to Windows XP Professional. Unfortunately, some users have discovered that certain legacy programs will not run under Windows XP, so they have requested that you re-install their previous operating systems. For which of the following previous operating systems can you easily uninstall Windows XP and have the computer automatically revert to its previous operating system?

   ❏ A. Windows NT 4.0 Workstation

   ❏ B. Windows Me

   ❏ C. Windows 95

   ❏ D. Windows 98

   ❏ E. Windows 2000 Professional

59. You are a desktop support technician for your company. Which of the following methods is the easiest and least expensive way to centralize the authorization and deployment of Microsoft's periodic software patches (hotfixes) for Windows XP in a corporate IT environment?

   ❑ A. Install Microsoft SMS.

   ❑ B. Install Microsoft SUS.

   ❑ C. Configure a Software Deployment setting for a group policy in Active Directory.

   ❑ D. Deploy each hotfix separately as part of a new or existing logon script.

60. You are a desktop support technician for your company. You been assigned the task of installing three different operating systems on the same computer and making sure that all three can peacefully co-exist and access all drives on the computer. The operating systems are Windows 98, Windows NT 4.0 Workstation, and Windows XP Professional. Which of the following set of steps must you take to ensure operating system compatibility on this computer?

   ❑ A. First install Windows XP, next install Windows NT 4.0 Workstation, and then install Windows 98. Install each OS onto a separate folder. Format all drives as FAT32 for backward compatibility.

   ❑ B. First install Windows NT 4.0 Workstation, next install Windows 98, and then install Windows XP. Install each OS onto a separate folder. Format all drives as FAT32 for backward compatibility.

   ❑ C. First install Windows NT 4.0 Workstation, next install Windows 98, and then install Windows XP. Install each OS onto a separate drive letter. Format all drives as FAT for backward compatibility.

   ❑ D. First install Windows NT 4.0 Workstation, next install Windows 98, and then install Windows XP. Install each OS onto a separate drive letter. Format all drives as NTFS for backward compatibility.

   ❑ E. First install Windows XP, next install Windows NT 4.0 Workstation,and then install Windows 98. Install each OS onto a separate drive letter. Format all drives as FAT for backward compatibility.

Answers to
Practice Exam 2

1. C	**31.** D
2. A	**32.** D
3. D	**33.** A
4. C	**34.** B
5. B, E	**35.** A
6. D	**36.** B
7. B	**37.** D
8. C	**38.** D
9. B	**39.** A
10. D	**40.** C
11. C	**41.** A
12. A	**42.** D
13. A, B, D, F, G	**43.** B
14. A	**44.** A
15. B	**45.** B
16. A, B, C	**46.** C
17. A	**47.** D
18. D	**48.** A
19. A	**49.** C
20. D	**50.** A
21. A	**51.** D
22. B	**52.** B
23. B, D	**53.** B
24. C	**54.** D
25. A, B, F	**55.** D
26. C	**56.** B
27. B, C	**57.** D
28. B, C, D	**58.** B, D
29. C	**59.** B
30. A, B, D	**60.** C

1. Answer C is correct because if this policy is disabled, a user is required to press Ctrl+Alt+Del to log on. Answer B is incorrect because the Users Must Enter a User Name and Password for This Computer check box in the Users and Passwords tool in Control Panel only applies to local policy and is therefore overridden by group policy. Answer A is incorrect because using the Welcome screen disables the classic logon, but it has no effect for a computer that is a member of a Windows domain. Answer D is incorrect because this is a local policy setting and it is overridden by group policy.

2. Answer A is correct. To make Internet favorites available from other computers, a desktop support technician needs to configure the user's account to enable roaming profiles. Answer B is incorrect because using Files and Settings Transfer Wizard copies files and settings to a backup file, which can be restored to a destination computer. It does not, however, keep updating other machines with favorites that have been modified on a source computer. Answer C is incorrect; group policies do not control the establishment and configuration of roaming profiles. Answer D is incorrect because making Web pages available offline only makes them available on the computer on which the Web pages were originally accessed.

3. Answer D is correct. Limited users cannot edit TCP/IP settings. Answer A is incorrect. Logging onto a machine with administrator privileges and attempting to modify TCP/IP settings does not establish the capabilities of a user. Answer B is incorrect. Network Connections does not have security properties as a file or a folder do. Answer C is incorrect because neither a successful nor unsuccessful ping proves whether a user can modify TCP/IP settings. Nonadministrators generally do not have permission to access TCP/IP settings.

4. The correct answer is C. Maximum strength encryption requires secured communication and Triple Data Encryption Standard (3DES) Encapsulating Security Protocol (ESP) encryption. Answer A is incorrect because typical security settings provide a lower encryption level than the Maximum Strength encryption option. Answer B is incorrect; a Message Digest 5 (MD5) challenge is used to establish nonrepudiation, not encryption. It creates a hash value. Answer D is incorrect. Internet Connection Firewall (ICF) does not provide for data encryption; it merely opens and closes ports.

5. Answers B and E are correct. Share restrictions take priority over NT File System (NTFS) security settings. It is strongly suggested that desktop support technicians share folders to the widest audience with the most liberal permissions and limit access with the more specific NTFS security settings. In the scenario, you should share the folder to everyone with full or read permissions and then limit access to the files using NTFS read permissions. Answers B and E are the only ones that comply with that model. Explicit Deny settings always override explicit or implicit allow settings, so Answers A and C are incorrect. Answer D is incorrect because granting Full Control permission to the Everyone group for both share and NTFS permissions completely opens up the Advisories folder so that anyone can access the data stored in it.

6. Answer D is correct. The computer must have been upgraded from Windows NT Workstation 4. Upgraded systems continue to store user profiles in the same folder as the Windows NT 4 default location: %systemroot%\Profiles. All profiles get stored on the local computer, including roaming and mandatory roaming profiles, so Answers A and B are incorrect. Fast user switching, Answer C, has nothing to do with user profile locations and is only available on computers running Windows XP that are not on a domain.

7. Answer B is correct. The Offline Files feature, also known as client-side caching, is disabled whenever Fast User Switching is turned on. Answer A is incorrect because Domain Name System (DNS) settings ensure proper TCP/IP name resolution. Answer C is incorrect because the Network Settings Wizard does not configure offline file support. A Windows XP Professional computer does not need to be a member of a domain for offline files to function; therefore, Answer D is also incorrect.

8. Answer C is correct. If you enable the Group Similar Taskbar Buttons feature, all running application buttons are grouped together on the taskbar. Answer A is incorrect because DualView is related to the Multiple Monitor option that supports two displays from one video output port. Answer B is incorrect because no Taskbar Switching option exists. The Quick Launch toolbar adds icons to the taskbar for starting application programs, not for grouping program buttons that are already running. Therefore, Answer D is incorrect.

9. Answer B is correct. The msconfig utility allows you to set a variety of system startup options, including adding command-line switches to the Boot.ini file. The sysedit tool does not allow you to modify any part of the Boot.ini file, so Answer A is incorrect. The bootcfg.exe command operates in the Recovery Console of Windows XP, not Safe Mode, so Answer C is incorrect. Values for the Boot.ini file are not stored in the Windows XP Registry, so Answer D is also incorrect.

10. Answer D is correct because Windows XP does not provide program compatibility support for applications requiring a Windows NT 4.0 SP3 environment, nor for applications requiring a Windows NT 3.51 environment. Windows XP does offer program compatibility support for Windows NT 4.0 SP5, however. Answer A is incorrect because even though Windows NT 4 Service Pack 5 (SP5) applications are supported, Windows NT 4 SP3–specific programs are not explicitly supported. Answer B is incorrect because Windows NT 3.51 applications are not supported by Windows XP program compatibility. Answer C is incorrect because both Answers A and B are also incorrect. Windows XP offers program compatibility support for Windows 95, 98, Me, and 2000.

11. Answer C is correct. You can only publish, not assign, legacy applications using ZAP files. Answer A is incorrect because applications installed using ZAP files can only be published; therefore, you cannot use ZAP files for software group policies under Computer Configuration. Answer B is incorrect because you cannot assign an application using a ZAP file; it does not matter whether you want to use a computer policy setting or a user policy setting. Answer D is incorrect because you configure software deployment group policy from the Software Settings folder of the Group Policy Editor Microsoft Management Console (MMC) snap-in, not by using additional administrative templates.

12. The correct answer is A. The quickest way to discover which program or process is "stealing" the most CPU attention is to use the Task Manager. Answer B is incorrect because increasing the priority of the programs does not reveal which one is the bottleneck. Answer C is incorrect because Dr. Watson displays error reports but only when application errors occur, not for program performance problems. Answer D is incorrect because running programs on another computer, although potentially revealing, is not a quick way to solve the problem or discover its cause.

13. Answers A, B, D, F, and G are all correct. The File and Settings Transfer (FAST) Wizard supports a direct cable connection using either serial ports or parallel ports and appropriate cables. Removable media is supported, which includes Zip and Jaz drives. Infrared connections are supported indirectly because you can copy the FAST Wizard's files via an infrared connection. Wireless networking support is also included because any network connection will work. Answer C is incorrect because a direct USB connection between two computers is not supported. Answer E is incorrect because a direct FireWire connection between two computers is not supported.

14. Answer A is correct. The Performance Logs and Alerts snap-in captures performance activity for all the objects and their associated counters that you add to a performance counter log. By tracking such activity over time for key components, such as memory, processor, network interfaces, and physical and logical disks, you can create a baseline against which to compare future activity. Answer B is incorrect because the System Monitor snap-in displays only current activity or past activity: it does not store such data. Answer C is incorrect because the Task Manager displays only current activity for applications, processes, performance, and networking: it does not store such data. Answer D is incorrect because the Network Monitor Driver and the Netcap.exe utility capture and analyze network data packets: they do not store any other performance-related data.

15. Answer B is correct. The optimal paging file configuration is to split it evenly over multiple physical disks without placing it on the system or boot volumes. The recommended paging file size is 1.5 times the installed memory. For a system with 256MB RAM installed, that would be 384MB split over two drives (192MB each). Answer A is incorrect because it is not a best practice to place the paging file on the system or boot volumes. Answer C is incorrect because it is not optimal to make the initial size lower than the maximum size; such a move will cause the paging file to expand, which takes system resources. Answer D is incorrect because it is not a best practice to place the paging file on the system or boot volumes, even if you place other paging files on different volumes.

16. Answers A, B, and C are all correct. In Task Manager, you can increase or decrease an application's processor (CPU) priority by right-clicking its associated process on the Processes tab, pointing to Set Priority, and selecting one of the listed priorities. On dual-processor computers only, you can right-click an application's associated process and point to Set Affinity to choose which processor the application will use. Finally, you can right-click an application in the Applications tab and select End Task to close the running application. Answer D is incorrect because you cannot expand the size of the system's paging file from Task Manager. Answer E is incorrect because you cannot increase or decrease any of the processors' clock speeds from Task Manager. Answer F is incorrect because you cannot view a disk usage chart from Task Manager; you can only view CPU Usage and Page File Usage from the Performance tab of Task Manager.

17. The correct answer is A. The operating system is running on CPU1 and so is the application. If you can run the application on another CPU, it helps distribute the workload. Answer B is incorrect; CPU1 is already running at 100% capacity. Answer C is incorrect; CPU affinity enables technicians to associate processes with specific processors. To enable affinity, open Task Manager, right-click on the process, and choose Set Affinity. Check the CPU IDs (example CPU0, CPU1) that you want the process to run on. Answer D is incorrect because reducing the application's priority decreases its performance.

18. The correct answer is D. The Performance console offers you two options for monitoring and analyzing system responsiveness—System Monitor for observing real-time performance metrics and Performance Logs and Alerts for collecting performance data over time and for establishing a baseline of performance. Answer A is incorrect because the built-in Dr. Watson utility catalogs application errors, not application performance. Answer B is incorrect because changing the priority of a program alters its behavior; it does not reveal its behavior. Answer C is incorrect because using Task Manager to get information about processor usage only offers you current, real-time data: it does not collect data in a historical manner so that you can review it in the future in several different formats.

19. The correct answer is A. It appears that the new program is stealing processor cycles from the other applications. To reduce the affect of the new program, reduce its priority in the Task Manager. Answer B is incorrect because increasing the priority of all the applications does not benefit the ones that are becoming relatively slow. Answer C is incorrect because reducing the priority of all programs also does not improve performance of some of them relative to the new program. Answer D is incorrect; if you increase the priority of the remaining programs, they continue to compete with one another for the processor's attention.

20. The correct answer is D; assign affinities to enable the programs to run on different processors. Answer A is incorrect because there is no indication that there are multiple 16-bit programs, and if there were, running each 16-bit program in its own virtual DOS machine would take up more memory than running them in a shared virtual DOS machine space. Answer B is incorrect because starting and stopping the 16-bit application does not reduce CPU utilization, although it might recoup lost memory addresses. Answer C is incorrect because increasing the priority of an application to Realtime raises its priority to a value of 31, which is considered so high that the process might compete with operating system commands and thus can result in an operating system command timing out and making your system unstable.

21. The correct answer is A, run Defrag, because the statistics indicate slow disks even though there is 3GB of storage remaining. It appears to be a problem of file fragmentation. Answer B is incorrect because enabling users to store more files might in fact lead to greater fragmentation. Answer C is incorrect; converting to FAT32 increases the size of the clusters on the drive and in turn the volume of fragmentation. Answer D is incorrect because increasing the size of the paging file causes it to become fragmented and reduces the overall amount of available disk space. In general, as a system ages, performance is enhanced by the addition of more physical memory and the reduction of fragmentation that emerges over time.

22. The correct answer is B; run the programs in a separate memory space because doing so enables the computer processor to more efficiently multitask. Answer A is incorrect because upgrading the CPU is not warranted unless the CPU time is consistently over 85%. Answer C is incorrect because reducing the priority of a 32-bit application only serves to reduce its performance relative to the other applications. Answer D is incorrect because there is no evidence that multiple processors exist in the computer.

23. Answers B and D are correct. You can monitor a computer system in real time under Windows XP using either the Task Manager tool or the System Monitor utility. Answer A is incorrect because Performance Logs and Alerts is not designed to display performance data in real time; its results are logged. Answer C is incorrect because the Event Viewer displays system event messages, not real-time performance data. Answer E is incorrect because the Services console (`Services.msc`) does not offer real-time system performance monitoring; it merely indicates the configuration and status of services.

24. The correct answer is C. Caution is not one of the default event types for the Event Viewer; Warning, however, is one of the five default event types. Answer A is incorrect because Information is a default event type. Answer B is incorrect because Error is a default event type. Answer D is incorrect because Failure Audit is a default event type. Answer E is incorrect because Success Audit is also a default event type.

25. Answers A, B, and F are correct. You use objects, counters, and instances of objects to measure system performance using System Monitor and Performance Logs and Alerts. Answer C is incorrect because cycles are not performance metrics. Answer D is incorrect because initiators are not performance metrics. Answer E is incorrect because _Totals are not performance metrics.

26. Answer C is correct. The Performance Logs and Alerts tool collects performance data over time and records that data into log files. Answer A is incorrect because although you should use the Performance Logs and Alerts tool to create performance baseline data, you should not attempt to collect performance data as a baseline during peak usage times. Answer B is incorrect because you can only view real-time data using System Monitor or the Task Manager. Answer D is incorrect because you can view both real-time data and logged performance data as a histogram using the System Monitor tool; a histogram is a view, not a type of data.

27. Answers B and C are correct. You can only set up Software Update Services (SUS) server-side components on Windows XP SP1, Windows 2000 Server, and Windows Server 2003. Answer A is incorrect because you cannot set up SUS as a server under Windows NT Workstation 4.0. Answer D is incorrect because you cannot set up SUS as a server under Windows 2000 Professional. Answers E and F are incorrect because you cannot set up SUS as a server under either Windows 98 Second Edition (SE) or Windows Me.

28. Answers B, C, and D are correct. You can deploy Windows updates using SUS onto Windows XP, Windows 2000 Server, Windows 2000 Professional, and Windows Server 2003 computers. Answer A is incorrect because you cannot deploy updates using SUS to Windows NT Workstation 4.0 computers. Answers E and F are incorrect because you cannot deploy updates using SUS to either Windows 98 SE or Windows Me computers.

29. Answer C is correct. You can change the location of the print spooler folder from the Print Server Properties window. Answer A is incorrect because that Registry key and value name do not provide a way to change the location of the printer spool folder. Answer B is incorrect; Printers is not a node within Device Manager. Answer D is incorrect because you cannot change the location of the print spooler folder by right-clicking the Printers and Faxes icon in the Control Panel.

30. Answers A, B, and D are correct. In computers running Windows XP, error events and warning events are recorded in the Event Viewer System log by default. The Show Informational Notifications for Local Printers check box is marked (enabled) by default. You can see this configuration on the File, Printer Server Properties, Advanced dialog box. Answer C is incorrect because the Notify When Remote Documents Are Printed check box is not marked (enabled) by default. Answer E is incorrect because the Beep on Errors of Remote Documents check box is not marked (enabled) by default. Answer F is incorrect because, by default, the Log Spooler Information Events check box is not marked (enabled) by default.

31. The correct answer is D. The reason that the desktop support technician is unable to reconnect is that the user is no longer online. He must stay online to retain the IP address and connectivity needed for Remote Assistance. Answer A is incorrect because a successful ping only determines connectivity and does not correct the problem. Answer B is incorrect because the problem is not with the form of the submission; the problem is the lack of a connection. Answer C is incorrect because it does not eliminate the core source of the problem.

32. The correct answer is D. Software written for Windows 95, Windows 98, or Windows Me often does not run properly under Windows XP. In addition, some hardware devices use drivers that are not compatible with Windows XP. If you are currently running a previous version of Windows, you can run the Windows XP Upgrade Advisor before installing Windows XP to verify system hardware and software compatibility. It also identifies potential issues. Answer A is incorrect because Windows Diagnostics is a Windows NT program, WINMSD.exe, that does not determine Windows compatibility. WINMSD is also a command that launches the System Information Utility in Windows XP. Answer B, the System Configuration Utility, is incorrect because it enables you to edit system files such as Boot.ini, Win.ini, and System.ini but does not determine compatibility. Answer C, CheckUpgradeOnly, is incorrect because it is an argument used with the WINNT32.exe program to test compatibility. It cannot run on its own.

33. The correct answer is A. In Windows XP Professional, you can use the FAST Wizard to move data files and personal settings from your old computer to your new one. All the settings from the original system, including personal settings, display settings, Microsoft Internet Explorer and Microsoft Outlook Express options, dial-up connections, and your folder and taskbar options, can be migrated to your new computer. The wizard also helps you move specific files and folders to your new computer as well. Answer B is incorrect because NTBackup is a Windows NT program, not Windows 98 SE. Answer C is incorrect because Disk Copy is designed to copy entire floppy disks, not specific files on hard drives. Answer D is incorrect because third-party migration tools would be an unnecessary expense because the FAST Wizard ships with Windows XP.

34. The correct answer is B. The Files and Settings Transfer Wizard displays the What Computer Is This? dialog box, which has the following two options:

    ➤ *New Computer*—Select this option if you want to transfer your files and settings to this computer.

    ➤ *Old Computer*—Select this option if you want to transfer the files and settings on this computer to your new computer.

    Answers A, C, and D do not represent any options available in the FAST Wizard.

35. The correct answer is A. In Windows XP Professional, you can use the FAST Wizard to move data files and personal settings from your old computer to your new one. Supported source operating systems (Old Computer) are

    ➤ Windows 95
    ➤ Windows 98
    ➤ Windows 98 SE
    ➤ Windows NT 4.0 Workstation
    ➤ Windows 2000 Professional
    ➤ Windows XP Home Edition
    ➤ Windows XP Professional

    Windows 3.1 is not a valid source operating system, and therefore, answers B, C, and D are incorrect.

36. The correct answer is B. In Windows XP Professional, you can use the FAST Wizard to move data files and personal settings from your old computer to your new one. The FAST Wizard displays the "Select the Transfer Method" page, which has the following three options for performing a transfer:

    ➤ *Direct Cable*—A cable that connects your computer's serial ports.

    ➤ *Floppy Drive or Other Removable Media*—Both computers must have the same type of drive.

    ➤ *Other*—You can save files and settings to any disk drive or folder on your computer.

    Answer A is incorrect because Disk to Disk is not a valid option. Answer C is incorrect because Share Point is not a valid option. Answer D is incorrect because Writeable Media Drive is not a valid option.

37. The correct answer is D. Basic disks under Windows XP Professional can have up to four primary partitions and can use the FAT16, FAT32, or NTFS file systems. Answer A is incorrect because you can have more than one primary partition. Answer B is incorrect because FAT16 is a valid format. Answer C is incorrect because you are allowed to create up to a maximum of four primary partitions on a basic disk.

38. The correct answer is D. Basic disks under Windows XP can have up to four primary partitions or up to three primary partitions and one extended partitions with logical drives and can use FAT16, FAT32, and NTFS. Extended partitions themselves cannot be formatted. A logical drive, which can use up the entire space of the extended partition, can be formatted with any of those file systems. Answers A, B, and C are incorrect because no drives have been created on the extended partition and extended partitions cannot be formatted without logical drives.

39. The correct answer is A. Windows XP Professional does not support dynamic disks on laptops, on removable disks such as Jaz drives, or on disks using the Universal Serial Bus (USB) or Institute of Electrical and Electronics Engineers (IEEE) 1394 (FireWire) interfaces. Basic or dynamic disks can use any combination of FAT16, FAT32, or NTFS. Answers B, C, and D are incorrect; all can be configured by Windows XP as dynamic disks.

40. The correct answer is C. There must be enough unpartitioned free space available at the end of the hard drive to perform the conversion. Answer A is incorrect because disks with less than 4GB can be converted to dynamic disks. Answer B is incorrect because you do not need 1GB of free space to convert a disk to dynamic. Answer D is incorrect because partitions do not need to be NTFS to convert a disk to dynamic.

41. The correct answer is A. Striped volumes combine areas of free space from two or more physical disks into a single volume where data is written across all the disks at once, which also improves disk performance. If any one of the disks in a striped volume fails, the data on the entire striped volume is lost. Answer B is incorrect because a simple volume represents only one physical disk. Answer C is incorrect because a spanned volume represents a disk to which a partition has been expanded. The data is stored on the first disk until it is full, and then the data overflows onto the second disk. Answer D is incorrect because a mirror volume represents two drives with duplicate copies of data on them. Windows XP does not support mirrored volumes.

42. The correct answer is D. Workgroups under Windows XP Professional are small groups of computers on a network that enable users to work together and do not support centralized administration. Resources in a workgroup are located on each computer in the workgroup. A server (installed with a server operating system) could be part of a workgroup and be nothing more than a glorified workstation, except for the fact that it would not suffer the connection limitations of a desktop operating system and would be available to host additional services. Administration and authentication of users is performed locally on each computer in the workgroup. Each computer has its own local Security Accounts Manager (SAM) database. Users needing access to resources on different computers in the workgroup need to have user accounts on each computer to gain access to resources. Administering a workgroup becomes more difficult as it becomes larger because of all the different local SAM databases that need to be maintained and updated. Answer A is incorrect because, by definition, resources can be stored on each computer in the workgroup. Answer B is incorrect because, by definition, resources can be located on a server in the workgroup. That computer would be known as a workgroup server or, in some circles, a standalone server, one that is not a member of a domain. Answer C is incorrect because, by definition, each member of the workgroup maintains its own user account database. In other words, administration and authentication are decentralized in a workgroup.

43. The correct answer is B. Although Windows NT–based operating systems can access 4GB FAT16 partitions, most other operating systems cannot without issues. This includes DOS, Windows 9.x, and Windows Me, whose size limit for FAT16 volumes is 2GB. To maintain compatibility with Windows Me, Windows 98, Windows 95, or MS-DOS, a volume cannot be larger than 2GB. Answer A is incorrect because rebooting the computer does not resolve the problem of the partition size. The reason answer C, "None of the available choices: DOS programs cannot run on Windows XP Professional," is not a correct answer is that the manufacturer of the program assures you that the program will run under a command prompt within Windows XP Professional and it has been successfully installed elsewhere in your environment. Answer D is incorrect because FAT 16 partitions are not limited to 2GB in Windows NT–based operating systems such as Windows XP.

44. The correct answer is A. The compression state of files and folders when you copy or move them within and between NTFS and FAT volumes on a Windows XP Professional system when using NTFS compression (not the Compressed Folders feature of Windows XP Professional) depends on a number of factors. When you copy an uncompressed file to an uncompressed folder, the file inherits the compression state of the target folder. (The file is automatically compressed.) Answer B is incorrect because copying a file creates a new file, and therefore, the new file inherits the properties of the folder to which it is copied. Answer C is incorrect; a copied file inherits the properties of the folder to which it is copied, not the folder from which it is copied. Answer D is incorrect for the same reason.

45. The correct answer is B. You can configure password policy on a stand-alone computer running Windows XP Professional by using the Group Policy snap-in. Answers A, C, and D are incorrect because password policies are not defined in the Users applet and should not be created by editing the Registry. It is much less complicated to use the Group Policy MMC Snap-in to edit a computer's local policy settings.

46. The correct answer is C. Full backups (sometimes referred to as normal backups) are often performed once a week and supplemented by other backup types on the other days of the week. During a full restore, you need to restore the last full backup set plus the other backup tapes that had been performed since the last normal backup. The software that you use to perform a full backup resets the archive bit on files. Answers A and B are incorrect because differential and incremental backups are typically run daily. Answer D is incorrect because copy backups are done intermittently and are not scheduled.

47. The correct answer is D. If users need to install legacy applications, you can relax security by making users members of the local Power Users group or by installing the Compatibility security template (com-patws.inf). The template compatws.inf appears in the %windir%\security\templates directory. It can be applied to a system using the Security Configuration and Analysis snap-in. Answer A is incorrect because basicwk.inf does not ship with Windows XP Professional. Answer B is incorrect because securews.inf provides enhanced, not relaxed, local account policies and limits the use of LanMan authentication, enables server-side Server Message Block (SMB) signing, and provides further restrictions on anonymous users. Answer C is incorrect because setup security.inf provides "out-of-the-box" default security settings. It is used to reset permissions back to default values, not reduce security.

48. The correct answer is A. You should use the `net use F: \\FPServer1\C$` command to map the drive. By default, the root of each volume on a hard disk is shared. You create the share name by appending a dollar symbol ($) to the drive letter (c$). This technique makes the administrative share hidden so that it is not visible to network users browsing the network. Because you cannot locate the administrative share by using Explorer or My Network Places, you must use the `net use` command-line command to map a drive to the administrative share. Answers B, C, and D are incorrect because they contain the wrong syntax. The correct syntax is

    ```
    net use devicename \\ComputerName\sharename
    ```

    You use the `net view` command to display a list of domains, a list of computers, or the resource being shared by the specified computer. You cannot use this command to map drives.

49. The correct answer is C. When Windows XP Professional is installed, the default desktop displays only the Recycle Bin. To display the other desktop icons, you can right-click the taskbar, select Properties, and enable Classic Start Menu. You can also open Control Panel, start the Display program, select the Desktop tab, and click Customize Desktop to enable the appropriate icons on the General tab of the Desktop Items page. (If you enabled the desktop icons by performing those actions, then switching between the new Classic Start Menu styles has no effect on the visibility of those shortcuts.) Answer D is incorrect because enabling Use Windows Classic Folders prevents the contents of all folders from behaving as Web pages. Answer B, Display Simple Folder View, enables folders in the left pane of Windows Explorer, when selected, to display and expand in the right pane simultaneously. Answer A is incorrect because Windows XP does not have a Show Desktop Icons Menu option, although Windows 2000 does when you use Active Desktop.

50. The correct answer is A. ICF is enabled on the Properties sheet for a connection. A user's ability to enable ICF can be controlled by the local policy Prohibit Use of Internet Connection Firewall on Your DNS Domain Network. If this policy is enabled, then the ICF option located on the Advanced tab of the connection's Properties sheet becomes unavailable. This policy is available in Windows XP and is not available in Windows 2000. Answer B is incorrect because Allow the Other Network Users to Control or Disable the Shared Internet Connection allows users on home or small office networks to control Internet Connection Sharing (ICS) on the host computer. Answer C is incorrect because logging on with a local account prevents the user from accessing any resource on the corporate LAN. Answer D is incorrect because it only is available if ICF is enabled.

51. The correct answer is D. You can use the Encrypting File System (EFS) to protect files on NTFS-formatted drives. By default, when a user encrypts a folder, any existing files in that folder are encrypted and only the user can open them. Answer A is incorrect because if you copy the files into the same folder on the server, all the files overwrite one another. Answer B is incorrect because only the person who encrypts the folder (you) would be able to use the files. Answer C is incorrect because, again, the only person who could use the files would be you, the person who encrypted the folder.

52. The correct answer is B. Remote Assistance allows the transfer of files from the "expert" to the "novice." Using this technique enables a support desk technician to update the file and send it to users with the most relevant information. Answer A is incorrect because the scenario does not indicate that users can connect to the corporate LAN when traveling. (Remote Assistance does not require a domain logon.) Answer C is incorrect because the scenario does not suggest users have access to corporate email when traveling. Answer D is incorrect because the users would need the floppy disk before they began their travels, and the scenario suggests that users might have problems when already on the road.

53. The correct answer is B. A differential backup backs up files created or changed since the last full backup. (You do not normally mix incremental and differential backups, but if you do, a differential backup backs up files created or changed since the last incremental backup as well.) Differential backups do not mark files as backed up. (The archive attribute is not cleared.) If you are performing a data restore with a differential backup, it requires that you have the last normal as well as the last differential backup. It usually takes longer to create a differential backup than an incremental backup. However, the restore process is quicker because it involves only one full backup and the most recent differential (not a series of incrementals). Answers A and C are incorrect because both full and incremental backups reset the archive bit. Answer D is incorrect because a copy backup is not usually done on a regular schedule.

54. The correct answer is D. Windows XP requires a minimum of 650MB of available free disk space for installation: 550MB of free space is not enough. Answer A is incorrect because you cannot install Windows XP based on the configuration information given; a minimum of 650MB free disk space is required. Answer B is incorrect because even though you cannot install Windows XP because of its disk space requirements, it does not require 128MB RAM to install the OS. Only 64MB RAM is required. Answer C is incorrect because Windows XP Professional requires a Pentium-compatible processor to install it: a Pentium III CPU is not required. Answer E is incorrect because Windows XP Professional can mount FAT32 disk partitions larger than 32GB; it cannot *create* FAT32 disk partitions or volumes larger than 32GB.

55. The correct answer is D. Because all computers must use static IP addresses and no Dynamic Host Configuration Protocol (DHCP) server was listed as part of the network infrastructure, the most efficient method to deploy Windows XP Professional onto 50 new computers would be to use a third-party disk imaging utility, such as Ghost, and the Microsoft sysprep tool. Answer A is incorrect because attended installations are neither the fastest nor the most efficient way to deploy several computers. Answer B is incorrect because unattended installs of Windows XP using the CD-ROM media and an answer file on floppy disk is not as efficient as network installs, and you cannot deploy customized settings or applications with this method. Answer C is incorrect because although this procedure might be fairly efficient, you cannot deploy customized settings or applications with this method. Answer E is incorrect because you cannot use Remote Installation Services (RIS) in this network environment because no DHCP server is present.

56. The correct answer is B. Microsoft gives you 30 days from the installation date to activate both Original Equipment Manufacturer (OEM) and retail licensed copies of Windows XP Professional. Answers A, C, and D are all incorrect because you have up to 30 days to activate both OEM and retail licensed copies of Windows XP Professional. Answer E is incorrect because both retail and OEM copies of Windows XP require product activation; Open, Select, Enterprise, Academic, Charity, and Government license agreements do not require Microsoft product activation.

57. The correct answer is D. With Microsoft per-processor licensing, Client Access Licenses (CALs) are not required for those server products that offer a per-processor licensing option. Answers A, B, and C are incorrect for the same reason.

58. The correct answers are B and D. You can return to the previous operating system when you upgrade to Windows XP from Windows 98, Windows 98 SE, and Windows Me only. Answer A is incorrect because you cannot revert to the previous OS when you upgrade to Windows XP from Windows NT 4.0 Workstation. Answer C is incorrect because you cannot upgrade to Windows XP from Windows 95. Answer E is incorrect because you cannot revert to the previous operating system when you upgrade to Windows XP from Windows 2000 Professional.

59. The correct answer is B. Microsoft's SUS is a free download that you can install on a computer on your network to centralize and control the approval and deployment of operating system updates. In the near future, Windows Update Services (WUS) will replace SUS, offering administrators even greater features and flexibility. Answer A is incorrect because although Microsoft Systems Management Server (SMS) is a robust tool, it is a part of the Microsoft Server System and you must pay for it separately; it is not a free product. Answer C is incorrect because hotfixes are not released as .msi files; they are published as compressed executable files. To use a software deployment group policy, you have to create an .msi package file or create a .zap file to attempt to deploy it through group policy, which is not a simple task. Answer D is incorrect because deploying hotfixes through logon scripts requires more work than using SUS, and it does not offer you as much flexibility or control.

60. The correct answer is C. Microsoft recommends that you install the oldest operating system first and the newest operating system last in a dual-boot or multiboot configuration. Each operating system should be installed onto separate drive letters. The FAT (FAT16) file system is the most compatible in this scenario because Windows 98 does not natively support NTFS and Windows NT 4.0 Workstation does not natively support FAT32. Of course, Windows XP supports FAT, FAT32, and NTFS. Answer A is incorrect because you need to install the oldest operating system first, not the newest operating system first. Also, Windows NT 4.0 Workstation does not support FAT32. Answer B is incorrect because you should install each operating system onto a separate drive letter and Windows NT 4.0 Workstation does not support FAT32. Answer D is incorrect because Windows 98 does not natively support NTFS and Windows NT 4.0 Workstation does not natively support FAT32. Answer E is incorrect because you need to install the oldest operating system first, not the newest operating system first.

What's on the CD?

CD Contents and Installation Instructions

The CD features an innovative practice test engine powered by MeasureUp™, giving you yet another effective tool to assess your readiness for the exam.

Multiple Test Modes

MeasureUp practice tests are available in Study, Certification, Custom, Missed Question, and Non-Duplicate question modes.

Study Mode

Tests administered in Study Mode enable you to request the correct answer(s) and explanation to each question during the test. These tests are not timed. You can modify the testing environment *during* the test by selecting the Options button.

Certification Mode

Tests administered in Certification Mode closely simulate the actual testing environment you will encounter when taking a certification exam. These tests do not enable you to request the answer(s) and/or explanation to each question until after the exam.

Custom Mode

Custom Mode enables you to specify your preferred testing environment. Use this mode to specify the objectives you want to include in your test, the timer length, and other test properties. You can also modify the testing environment *during* the test by selecting the Options button.

Missed Question Mode

Missed Question Mode enables you to take a test containing only the questions you have missed previously.

Non-Duplicate Mode

Non-Duplicate Mode enables you to take a test containing only questions not displayed previously.

Random Questions and Order of Answers

This feature helps you learn the material without memorizing questions and answers. Each time you take a practice test, the questions and answers appear in a different randomized order.

Detailed Explanations of Correct and Incorrect Answers

You'll receive automatic feedback on all correct and incorrect answers. The detailed answer explanations are a superb learning tool in their own right.

Attention to Exam Objectives

MeasureUp practice tests are designed to appropriately balance the questions over each technical area covered by a specific exam.

Installing the CD

The minimum system requirements for the CD-ROM are

- ➤ Windows 95, 98, Me, NT 4.0, 2000, or XP

- ➤ 7MB disk space for the testing engine

- ➤ An average of 1MB disk space for each test

To install the CD-ROM, follow these instructions:

> **NOTE** If you need technical support, please contact MeasureUp at 678-356-5050 or email support@measureup.com. Additionally, you'll find Frequently Asked Questions (FAQs) at www.measureup.com.

1. Close all applications before beginning this installation.

2. Insert the CD into your CD-ROM drive. If the setup starts automatically, go to step 5. If the setup does not start automatically, continue with step 3.

3. From the Start menu, select Run.

4. In the Browse dialog box, double-click Setup.exe. In the Run dialog box, click OK to begin the installation.

5. On the Welcome screen, click Next.

6. To agree to the Software License Agreement, click Yes.

7. On the Choose Destination Location screen, click Next to install the software to C:\Program Files\Certification Preparation.

8. On the Setup Type screen, select Typical Setup. Click Next to continue.

9. After the installation is complete, verify that Yes, I Want to Restart My Computer Now is selected. If you select No, I Will Restart My Computer Later, you will not be able to use the program until you restart your computer.

10. Click Finish.

11. After restarting your computer, choose Start, Programs, MeasureUp Practice Tests.

12. Select the practice test and click Start Test.

Creating a Shortcut to the MeasureUp Practice Tests

To create a shortcut to the MeasureUp practice tests, follow these steps:

1. Right-click on your Desktop.

2. From the shortcut menu, select New, Shortcut.

3. Browse to `C:\Program Files\MeasureUp Practice Tests` and select the MeasureUpCertification.exe or Localware.exe file.

4. Click OK.

5. Click Next.

6. Rename the shortcut MeasureUp.

7. Click Finish.

After you have completed step 7, use the MeasureUp shortcut on your Desktop to access the MeasureUp practice test.

Technical Support

If you encounter problems with the MeasureUp test engine on the CD-ROM, please contact MeasureUp at 678-356-5050 or email `support@measureup.com`. Technical support hours are from 8:00 a.m. to 5:00 p.m. EST Monday through Friday. Additionally, you'll find Frequently Asked Questions (FAQs) at `www.measureup.com`.

If you'd like to purchase additional MeasureUp products, call 678-356-5050 or 800-649-1MUP (1687), or visit `www.measureup.com`.

Need to Know More?

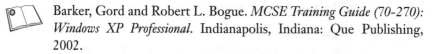

Chapter 1

Barker, Gord and Robert L. Bogue. *MCSE Training Guide (70-270): Windows XP Professional*. Indianapolis, Indiana: Que Publishing, 2002.

Bott, Ed and Carl Siechert. *Microsoft Windows XP Inside Out*. Redmond, Washington: Microsoft Press, 2001.

Microsoft Windows Team. *Microsoft Windows XP Professional Resource Kit Second Edition*. Redmond, Washington: Microsoft Press, 2003.

Minasi, Mark. *Mastering Windows XP Professional*. Alameda, California: Sybex Publishing, 2002.

Stanek, William R. *Microsoft Windows XP Professional Administrator's Pocket Consultant*. Redmond, Washington: Microsoft Press, 2003.

Search the Microsoft Product Support Services Knowledge Base on the Internet: http://support.microsoft.com. You can also search Microsoft TechNet on the Internet: http://www.microsoft.com/technet. Find technical information using keywords from this chapter, such as Windows XP installation, Setup, Setup Manager, deployment tools, unattended installation, Remote Installation Services (RIS), sysprep, licensing, upgrade installation, File Settings and Transfer (FAST) Wizard, User State Migration Tool (USMT), and Service Packs.

Chapter 2

Balter, Dan and Derek Melber. *MCSE/MCSA Exam Cram 2: Windows XP Professional.* Indianapolis, Indiana: Que Certification, 2002.

Barker, Gord and Robert L. Bogue. *MCSE Training Guide (70-270): Windows XP Professional.* Indianapolis, Indiana: Que Publishing, 2002.

Microsoft Windows Team. *Microsoft Windows XP Professional Resource Kit Second Edition.* Redmond, Washington: Microsoft Press, 2003.

Stanek, William R. *Microsoft Windows XP Professional Administrator's Pocket Consultant.* Redmond, Washington: Microsoft Press, 2003.

Wallace, Rick. *Microsoft Windows XP Professional Academic Learning Series.* Redmond, Washington: Microsoft Press, 2001.

Search the Microsoft Product Support Services Knowledge Base on the Internet: `http://support.microsoft.com`. You can also search Microsoft TechNet on the Internet: `http://www.microsoft.com/technet`. Find technical information using keywords from this chapter, such as share permissions, NTFS permissions, offline files, shadow copies, Remote Desktop Connections, and Terminal Services.

Chapter 3

Balter, Dan. *MCSE Exam Cram 2 Windows XP Professional.* Indianapolis, Indiana: Que Certification, 2002.

Bott, Ed and Carl Siechert. *Microsoft Windows XP Inside Out, Deluxe Edition.* Redmond, Washington: Microsoft Learning, 2002.

Simmons, Curt and James Causey. *Microsoft Windows XP Networking Inside Out.* Redmond, Washington: Microsoft Learning, 2002.

Stanek, William R. *Microsoft Windows XP Professional Administrator's Pocket Consultant.* Redmond, Washington: Microsoft Press, 2003.

Wallace, Rick. *Microsoft Windows XP Professional Academic Learning Series.* Redmond, Washington: Microsoft Press, 2001.

Search the Microsoft Product Support Services Knowledge Base on the Internet: `http://support.microsoft.com`. You can also search

Microsoft TechNet on the Internet: http://www.microsoft.com/ technet. Find technical information using keywords from this chapter, such as FAT, FAT32, NTFS, basic disk, dynamic disk, drive partition, drive volume, simple volume, spanned volume, and striped volume.

Chapter 5

 Balter, Dan and Derek Melber. *MCSE/MCSA Exam Cram 2: Windows XP Professional.* Indianapolis, Indiana: Que Certification, 2002.

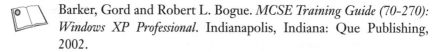 Barker, Gord and Robert L. Bogue. *MCSE Training Guide (70-270): Windows XP Professional.* Indianapolis, Indiana: Que Publishing, 2002.

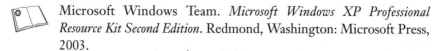 Microsoft Windows Team. *Microsoft Windows XP Professional Resource Kit Second Edition.* Redmond, Washington: Microsoft Press, 2003.

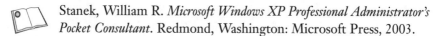 Stanek, William R. *Microsoft Windows XP Professional Administrator's Pocket Consultant.* Redmond, Washington: Microsoft Press, 2003.

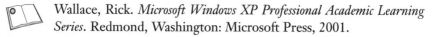 Wallace, Rick. *Microsoft Windows XP Professional Academic Learning Series.* Redmond, Washington: Microsoft Press, 2001.

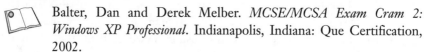 Search the Microsoft Product Support Services Knowledge Base on the Internet: http://support.microsoft.com. You can also search Microsoft TechNet on the Internet: http://www.microsoft.com/technet. Find technical information using keywords from this chapter, such as Accessibility Wizard, User Profiles, .MSI files, Multilingual Solutions, Microsoft LIP, Task Scheduler, FAST, Fast User Switching, faxing in Windows XP, Application Compatibility Technologies, and msconfig.

Chapter 6

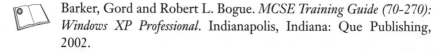 Balter, Dan and Derek Melber. *MCSE/MCSA Exam Cram 2: Windows XP Professional.* Indianapolis, Indiana: Que Certification, 2002.

Barker, Gord and Robert L. Bogue. *MCSE Training Guide (70-270): Windows XP Professional.* Indianapolis, Indiana: Que Publishing, 2002.

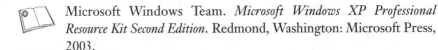 Microsoft Windows Team. *Microsoft Windows XP Professional Resource Kit Second Edition*. Redmond, Washington: Microsoft Press, 2003.

Minasi, Mark. *Mastering Windows XP Professional*. Alameda, California: Sybex, 2001.

Stanek, William R. *Microsoft Windows XP Professional Administrator's Pocket Consultant*. Redmond, Washington: Microsoft Press, 2003.

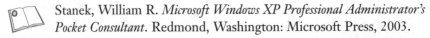 Search the Microsoft Product Support Services Knowledge Base on the Internet: `http://support.microsoft.com`. You can also search Microsoft TechNet on the Internet: `http://www.microsoft.com/technet`. Find technical information using keywords from this chapter, such as XP authorization and access control, best practices guide for securing Active Directory, XP logon and authentication, and XP security event messages.

Chapter 7

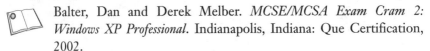 Balter, Dan and Derek Melber. *MCSE/MCSA Exam Cram 2: Windows XP Professional*. Indianapolis, Indiana: Que Certification, 2002.

Bott, Ed and Carl Siechert. *Microsoft Windows XP Inside Out*. Redmond, Washington: Microsoft Press, 2001.

Microsoft Windows Team. *Microsoft Windows XP Professional Resource Kit Second Edition*. Redmond, Washington: Microsoft Press, 2003.

Minasi, Mark. *Mastering Windows XP Professional*. Alameda, California: Sybex Publishing, 2002.

Moskowitz, Jeremy. *Group Policy, Profiles, and IntelliMirror for Windows 2003, Windows 2000, and Windows XP*. Alameda, California: Sybex Publishing, 2004.

Search the Microsoft Product Support Services Knowledge Base on the Internet: `http://support.microsoft.com`. You can also search Microsoft TechNet on the Internet: `http://www.microsoft.com/technet`. Find technical information using keywords from this chapter, such as event log, System Monitor, performance logs and alerts, baselines, performance objects and counters, and Task Manager.

Chapter 8

 Barker, Gord and Robert L. Bogue. *MCSE Training Guide (70-270): Windows XP Professional*. Indianapolis, Indiana: Que Publishing, 2002.

 Bott, Ed and Carl Siechert. *Microsoft Windows XP Inside Out*. Redmond, Washington: Microsoft Press, 2001.

 Microsoft Windows Team. *Microsoft Windows XP Professional Resource Kit Second Edition*. Redmond, Washington: Microsoft Press, 2003.

 Minasi, Mark. *Mastering Windows XP Professional*. Alameda, California: Sybex Publishing, 2002.

 Moskowitz, Jeremy. *Group Policy, Profiles, and IntelliMirror for Windows 2003, Windows 2000, and Windows XP*. Alameda, California: Sybex Publishing, 2004.

 Search the Microsoft Product Support Services Knowledge Base on the Internet: http://support.microsoft.com. You can also search Microsoft TechNet on the Internet: http://www.microsoft.com/technet. Find technical information using keywords from this chapter, such as Internet Connection Firewall, Remote Assistance, Remote Desktop Connections, configuring TCP/IP, configuring IP addressing and name resolution, and network diagnostic tools feature overview.

Glossary

. . . .

Accelerated Graphics Port (AGP)

An interface specification developed by Intel that was released in August 1997. AGP is based on peripheral connection interface (PCI) but is designed especially for the throughput demands of 3D graphics. Rather than use the PCI bus for graphics data, AGP introduced a dedicated point-to-point channel so that the graphics controller can directly access main memory. The AGP channel is 32 bits wide and runs at 66MHz, which translates into a total bandwidth of 266Mbps, as opposed to the PCI bandwidth of 133Mbps. AGP also supports two optional faster modes, with throughputs of 533Mbps and 1.07Gbps. In addition, AGP allows 3D textures to be stored in main memory rather than in video memory. AGP has a couple of important system requirements: The chipset must support AGP, and the motherboard must be equipped with an AGP bus slot or must have an integrated AGP graphics system.

access control entry (ACE)

An entry in an access control list (ACL). An ACE contains a set of access rights and a security identifier (SID) that identifies a user or group for whom the rights are allowed, denied, or audited.

access control list (ACL)

A set of data, or access control entries (ACEs), that describes which files, folders, and other resources a user or group has permission to access. Access to these objects is controlled by the operating system using the information in the ACL.

account lockout

A Windows Server security feature that locks a user account if a certain number of failed logon attempts occur within a specified amount of time, based on security-policy lockout settings. Locked accounts cannot log on.

Active Directory

The directory service that is included with Windows 2000 Server and Windows Server 2003. Active Directory is based on the X.500 standards and those of its predecessor, Lightweight Directory Access Protocol (LDAP). It stores information about objects on a network and makes this information available to applications, users, and network administrators. Active Directory is also used for authentication to network resources, using a single logon process. It provides network administrators a hierarchical view of the network and a single point of administration for all network objects.

Active Directory Users and Computers (ADUC) snap-in (console)

An administrative tool designed to perform daily Active Directory administration tasks, including creating, deleting, modifying, moving, and setting permissions on objects stored in the Active Directory database. These objects include organizational units (OUs), users, contacts, groups, computers, printers, and shared file objects.

Add Hardware Wizard

An applet in Control Panel that guides the user through connecting new hardware or removing existing hardware. The Add Hardware Wizard is triggered automatically when Windows recognizes newly attached hardware and guides the user through finding and installing any necessary drivers.

Advanced Configuration and Power Interface (ACPI)

A power-management specification developed by Intel, Microsoft, and Toshiba that enables Windows XP to control the amount of power given to each device attached to the computer. With ACPI, the operating system can turn off peripheral devices, such as CD-ROM players, when they are not in use. As another example, ACPI enables manufacturers to produce computers that automatically power up as soon as you touch the keyboard.

Advanced Power Management (APM)

An application programming interface (API) developed by Intel and Microsoft that allows developers to include power management in the BIOS. APM defines a layer between the hardware and the operating system that effectively shields programmers from hardware details. ACPI has replaced APM.

answer file

Text file that allows for unattended installations of Windows by providing answers for the questions posed by the Windows XP Setup program during the installation.

attended installation

The installation of an operating system that requires user intervention to answer questions prompted by the Setup program.

attribute

A single property that describes an object, such as the make, model, or color that describes a car. In the context of directories, an attribute is the main component of an entry in a directory, such as an email address.

auditing

The process that tracks the activities of users by recording selected types of events in the security log of a server or workstation.

Automated System Recovery (ASR)

A feature in Windows XP Professional that allows you to create a recovery backup set using the Windows Backup Utility that consists of a media backup of the system and boot drive volumes and the system state along with a backup ASR floppy disk. As a disaster-recovery option, ASR lets you restore the entire system drive volume, boot drive volume, and the computer's system state. ASR formats the system drive, re-installs Windows XP on that drive, and then restores all the configuration settings and files that existed on the system drive at the time that the ASR backup was created.

Automatic Update

A service that checks with the Windows Update Web site for critical updates and automates the process of downloading and installing the critical updates.

Automatic Private IP Addressing (APIPA)

A client-side feature of Windows Dynamic Host Configuration Protocol (DHCP) clients. If the client's attempt to negotiate with a DHCP server fails, the client computer automatically selects an IP address from the 169.254.0.0 Class B range.

Backup Utility

A Windows XP utility that helps you plan for and recover from data loss by allowing you to create backup copies of data as well as restore files, folders, and system-state data (which includes the Registry) manually or on a schedule. The Windows XP Backup Utility allows you to back up data to a variety of media types besides tape. You can also run backups from the command line using ntbackup.exe and specifying the appropriate command-line options.

baselining

The process of measuring system performance so that you can ascertain a standard or expected level of performance.

basic disk

A term that indicates a physical disk, which can have primary and extended partitions. A basic disk can contain up to three primary partitions and one extended partition, or it can have up to four primary partitions. A basic disk can also have a single extended partition with logical drives. You cannot extend a partition stored on a basic disk unless it is formatted as NTFS, and you must use the diskpart.exe command-line tool to extend a basic partition.

BIOS (Basic Input/Output System)

Built-in software that determines what a computer can do without accessing programs from a disk. On PCs, the BIOS contains all the code required to control the keyboard, display screen, disk drives, serial communications, and a number of miscellaneous functions. A BIOS that can handle Plug-and-Play devices is known as a Plug-and-Play BIOS. A Plug-and-Play BIOS is always implemented with Flash Memory rather than read-only memory (ROM). Windows XP benefits if a computer has the latest ACPI-compliant BIOS.

bootcfg

A command-line utility in Windows XP and Windows Server 2003 used to configure startup options in the boot.ini file.

boot partition or volume

The partition on a basic disk (or the volume on a dynamic disk) that contains the Windows XP operating system and its support files.

built-in security principals

Special security attributes that identify and apply to any user account which uses a Windows XP computer in a particular manner at a particular point in time. For example, when a user logs on to a Remote Desktop session, the security principal Terminal Server User is applied to that user account for the duration of her Remote Desktop session.

CD-R

A recordable CD-ROM technology using a disc that can be written to multiple times but cannot be erased.

CD/RW

A rewritable CD-ROM technology. You can also use CD/RW drives to write CD-R discs, and they can read CD-ROMs. Initially known as CD-E (for CD-Erasable), a CD/RW disk can be rewritten hundreds of times.

client-side caching (CSC)

See *offline files*.

compression

The process of making individual files and folders occupy less physical disk space. You can compress data using NT File System (NTFS) compression or through third-party utilities.

See also *NTFS data compression*.

computer account

An account that a domain administrator creates and that uniquely identifies the computer on the domain. The Active Directory computer account matches the name of the computer that joins the domain.

container

An object in a directory that contains other objects.

convert.exe

A Windows XP Professional command-line utility that turns a FAT or FAT32 drive volume into an NTFS drive volume without having to reformat or delete any data that is stored on the drive. The command-line syntax is convert.exe X: /FS:NTFS, where X: represents the drive letter that you want to convert to NTFS. There is no equivalent command to convert from NTFS to FAT or FAT32.

copy backup

A backup type that backs up all selected files, but each backed-up file's archive bit is not changed.

counter

A metric that provides information about particular aspects of system performance.

daily backup

A backup of files that have changed today which does not mark them as being backed up.

data compression

The process of making individual files and folders occupy less physical disk space. You can compress data using NTFS compression or through third-party utilities.

See also *NTFS data compression*.

data recovery agent (DRA)

A Windows XP Professional administrator or a Windows Server domain administrator who has been issued a public-key certificate for the express purpose of recovering user-encrypted data files that have been encrypted with Encrypting File System (EFS). *Data recovery* refers to the process of decrypting a file without having the private key of the user who encrypted the file. A DRA might be necessary if a user loses his or her private key for decrypting files or if a user leaves an organization without decrypting important files that other users need.

default gateway

An address that serves an important role in Transmission Control Protocol/Internet Protocol (TCP/IP) networking by providing a default route for TCP/IP hosts to use when communicating with other hosts on remote networks. A router (either a dedicated router or a computer that connects two or more network segments) generally acts as the default gateway for TCP/IP hosts. The router maintains its own routing table of other networks within an internetwork. The routing table maps the routes required to reach the remote hosts that reside on those other networks.

Device Manager

The primary tool that is used in Windows XP to configure and manage hardware devices and their settings.

DHCP server

See *Dynamic Host Configuration Protocol server*.

dial-up access

A type of access in which a remote client uses a public telephone line or Integrated Services Digital Network (ISDN) line to create a connection to a Windows Server remote access server.

differential backup

A backup that copies files created or changed since the last normal or incremental backup. A differential backup does *not* mark files as having been backed up. (In other words, the archive attribute is not cleared.) If you are performing a combination of normal and differential backups, when you restore files and folders, you need the last normal backup as well as the last differential backup.

digital signature

Public-key cryptography that authenticates the integrity and originator of a communication.

discretionary access control list (DACL)

A list of ACEs that lets administrators set permissions for users and groups at the object and attribute levels. This list represents part of an object's security descriptor that allows or denies permissions to specific users and groups.

disk defragmentation

The process of making contiguous any files that have been split, or fragmented, and stored in multiple locations on a disk. Defragmentation can improve computer performance by reducing the amount of time it takes to retrieve data from a disk.

disk group

In Windows XP Professional, a collection of multiple dynamic disks that are managed together. All dynamic disks in a computer are members of the same disk group. Each disk in a disk group stores replicas of the same configuration data, and this configuration data is stored in a 1MB region at the end of each dynamic disk.

Disk Management

A Windows XP Microsoft Management Console (MMC) snap-in that you use to perform all disk maintenance tasks, such as formatting, creating partitions, deleting partitions, and converting a basic disk to a dynamic disk.

diskpart.exe

A command-line utility that you use for managing disk storage, including creating and deleting partitions and volumes and formatting partitions and volumes.

disk quota

A control that you use in Windows XP to limit the amount of hard-disk space available for all users or an individual user. You can apply a quota on a per-user, per-volume basis only.

distribution group

A group used under Windows Server Active Directory that can contain users and other groups which cannot be assigned an access control list (ACL); no security permissions may be assigned to a distribution group. It is used as a distribution list for email purposes.

DNS

See *Domain Name System*.

domain

The fundamental administrative unit of Active Directory within a Windows Server network environment. A domain stores information about objects in the domain's partition of Active Directory. You can give user and group accounts in a domain privileges and permissions to resources on any system that belongs to the domain.

domain controller (DC)

A computer running Windows 2000 Server or Windows Server 2003 that hosts Active Directory and manages user access to a network, including logons, authentication, and access to the directory and shared resources.

Domain Name System (DNS)

DNS is used primarily for resolving fully qualified domain names (FQDNs) to IP addresses. DNS is the standard naming convention for hosts on the Internet, which have both domain names (such as `blast-throughlearning.com`) and numeric IP addresses (such as 192.168.2.8).

DRA

See *data recovery agent*.

driver rollback

A feature in Windows XP that allows a user to revert to a previous device driver when a newly installed device driver does not work properly.

driver signing

A method for marking or identifying driver files that meet certain specifications or standards. Windows XP uses a driver-signing process to make sure drivers are certified to work correctly with the Windows Driver Model (WDM) in Windows XP.

dual-boot configuration

The default operating system startup configuration for Windows NT, Windows 2000, Windows XP, and Windows Server 2003 when one Microsoft operating system is already installed on the same computer and one additional operating system is installed.

DVD (digital versatile disc or digital video disc)

An improved type of compact disc that holds a minimum of 4.7GB, enough for a full-length movie. The DVD specification supports discs with capacities from 4.7GB to 17GB and access rates of 600Kbps to 1.3Mbps. One of the best features of DVD drives is that they are backward compatible with CD-ROMs. This means that DVD players can play old CD-ROMs, CD-I disks, video CDs, and new DVDs. Newer DVD players can also read CD-R and CD-RW disks. DVD uses Moving Picture Experts Group (MPEG)-2 to compress video data.

DVD-R

One of many competing standards for writing high-capacity, write-once optical disks used to create data and video DVDs. This standard uses organic dye technology and is compatible with most DVD players and drives.It also uses a write-once optical disk to create data and video DVD discs. The DVD-R standard is a competing technology for writing data onto the disc. The DVD-R standard is not compatible with the DVD+R standard.

DVD+R

One of many competing standards for writing high-capacity, write-once optical disks used to create data and video DVDs. This standard uses dye technology and is compatible with most DVD players and drives.

A write-once optical disk used to create data and video DVD discs. DVD+R is a competing technology for writing data onto the disc. The DVD+R standard is not compatible with the DVD+R standard.

DVD-RAM

One of many competing standards for writing high-capacity, write-once optical disks used to create data and video DVDs. This standard uses phase-change and magneto-optical technology to store data but is generally not compatible with most DVD players and drives.

DVD-RW

A rewritable DVD technology. Information can be written to and erased multiple times. DVD-RW primarily is used for movies and is compatible with most of the DVD players on the market.

DVD+RW

A rewritable DVD technology. You can use DVD+RW for both data and movies, and it is compatible with most of the DVD players on the market.

dynamic disk

A physical disk in a Windows XP computer that does not use partitions or logical drives. It has dynamic volumes that you create by using the Disk Management console. A dynamic disk can contain any of five types of volumes. In addition, you can extend a volume on a dynamic disk. A dynamic disk can contain an unlimited number of volumes, so you are not restricted to four volumes per disk as you are with a basic disk.

Dynamic Host Configuration Protocol (DHCP) server

A device, workstation, or server that dynamically assigns IP addresses to clients. The DHCP server can also provide direction toward routers, Windows Internet Name Service (WINS) servers, and DNS servers. Both Windows XP Home and Professional can act as a DHCP allocator (similar to a server) when Internet Connection Sharing is enabled.

Dynamic Update

Works with Windows Update to download critical fixes and drivers needed during the setup process. Dynamic Update provides important updates to files required to minimize difficulties during setup.

dynamic volume

The only type of volume you can create on dynamic disks. There are five types of dynamic volumes: simple, spanned, mirrored, striped, and Redundant Array of Independent Disks (RAID)-5. Only computers running Windows Server 2003, Windows XP Professional, and any version of Windows 2000 can directly access dynamic volumes. Windows XP Professional and Windows 2000 Professional computers *cannot* host but *can* access mirrored and RAID-5 dynamic volumes over the network that are stored on remote Windows Server 2003 and Windows 2000 Server computers.

Encrypting File System (EFS)

A subsystem of NTFS that uses public keys and private keys to provide encryption for files and folders on computers using Windows XP, Windows 2000, and Windows Server 2003.

eventtriggers.exe

A command-line utility that allows the administration of how log events are monitored and responded to.

Event Viewer

An MMC snap-in that displays the Windows XP event logs for system, application, security, directory services, DNS server, and File Replication Service log files.

fast user switching

A feature of Windows XP and later operating systems that makes it possible for users to switch quickly between user accounts without actually logging off the computer.

FAT (file allocation table) or FAT16

A 16-bit table that many operating systems use to locate files on disk. The FAT keeps track of all the pieces of a file. The FAT file system for older versions of Windows 95 is called virtual file allocation table (VFAT); the one for Windows 95 (OEM Service Release [OSR] 2), Windows 98, and Windows Millenium Edition (Me) is called FAT32. Windows XP can use the FAT file system; however, it is often not used because the NTFS file system is preferred. FAT retains larger cluster sizes and is unable to scale to larger volume sizes. The FAT file system has no local security.

FAT32

A 32-bit version of FAT that is available in Windows 95 OSR 2 and Windows 98. FAT32 increases the number of bits used to address clusters and reduces the size of each cluster. The result is that FAT32 can support larger disks (up to 2TB) and better storage efficiency (less slack space) than the earlier version of FAT. The FAT32 file system has no local security. Windows XP can use and format partitions as FAT, FAT32, or NTFS.

Fax Console

The main utility for managing faxes in Windows XP. You can use this utility to configure fax devices and manage incoming and outgoing faxes.

fax service management console

An MMC snap-in that allows you to administer the settings for sending and receiving faxes using the fax service.

File Settings and Transfer (FAST) Wizard

A GUI tool on the Windows XP CD-ROM that allows you to copy user data and settings from a computer running Windows 9x, Windows NT 4.0, Windows 2000, or Windows XP to a different computer running Windows XP Home Edition or Windows XP Professional.

FireWire or IEEE (Institute of Electrical and Electronics Engineers) 1394a and 1394b

Very fast external bus standards that support data transfer rates of up to 400Mbps for 1394a and up to 800Mbps for 1394b. Products that support the IEEE 1394a standard have different names, depending on the company. Apple originally developed the technology and uses the trademarked name FireWire. Other companies use other names, such as i.link and Lynx, to describe their 1394a products. You can use a single 1394a port to connect up to 63 external devices. IEEE 1394b is a newer standard, which is also known as FireWire 800. Like Universal Serial Bus (USB) 1.1 and 2.0 standards, 1394a and 1394b support both Plug and Play and hot plugging, and they provide power to peripheral devices. The main difference between 1394a and USB 1.1 is that 1394a supports faster data transfer rates. USB 2.0, 1394a, and 1394b standards are great for devices that require high throughputs, such as video cameras and fast, high-capacity external storage devices.

global groups

Groups that are granted rights and permissions and can become members of local groups in their own domains and trusting domains. A global group can contain user accounts from its own domain only. Global groups provide a way to create sets of users from inside the domain that are available for use both in and out of the domain.

globally unique identifier (GUID)

A 128-byte value generated from the unique identifier on a device, the current data and time, and a sequence number. A GUID identifies a specific device or component.

group policy

A mechanism for managing change and configuration of systems, security, applications, and user environments in an Active Directory domain.

Group Policy Editor (GPE)

An MMC snap-in (gpedit.msc) that you can use under Windows XP, Windows 2000, and Windows Server 2003 that allows users to modify local policy settings on Windows computers. You cannot use the gpedit.msc tool under Windows XP Home Edition. Under Active Directory, the GPE also lets administrators create and customize group policy object (GPO) settings for entire sites, domains, and organizational units (OUs).

group policy object (GPO)

An object that is created by the GPE snap-in to hold user- and computer-specific configuration settings.

GUID

See *globally unique identifier.*

Hardware Abstraction Layer (HAL)

An underlying component of Windows NT, Windows 2000, Windows XP, and Windows Server 2003 operating systems that functions something like an application programming interface (API). In strict technical architecture, HALs reside at the device level, a layer below the standard API level. The HAL allows programmers to write applications and game titles with all the device-independent advantages of writing to an API but without the large processing overhead that APIs normally demand. Upgrading a computer's hardware from a single processor to two or more processors necessitates installing a different HAL that is compatible with more than one processor.

hardware profile

A profile that stores configuration settings for a collection of devices and services. Windows XP can store different hardware profiles so that users' needs can be met even though their computers might frequently require different device and service settings, depending on circumstances. The best example is a laptop or portable computer used in an office while in a docking station and then undocked so that the user can travel with it. The two environments require different power-management settings, possibly different network settings, and various other configuration changes.

hardware requirements for Windows XP

The minimum level of hardware (processor, storage, memory, and so on) required by Windows XP to operate.

hibernation

A power option in Windows XP Professional and Windows 2000 Professional portable computers that helps conserve battery power. Hibernation is a complete power-down while maintaining the state of open programs and connected hardware by storing the current system state to a file on the hard disk. When you bring the computer out of hibernation, the desktop is restored exactly as you left it, in less time than it takes for a complete system restart. However, it does take longer to bring the computer out of hibernation than out of standby. It's a good idea to put a computer in hibernation when you will be away from the computer for an extended time or overnight.

hidden shares

Shares that do not show up in the network browse list. Users can create their own hidden shares by appending a dollar sign ($)to any shared folder name. Windows XP creates certain hidden shares by default: these are known as hidden administrative shares because they are only accessible to members of the Administrators group.

HOSTS file

A local text file in the same format as the 4.3 Berkeley Software Distribution (BSD) Unix /etc/hosts file. This file maps hostnames to IP addresses. In Windows XP, this file is stored in the \%SystemRoot%\ System32\Drivers\Etc folder.

incremental backup

A backup that backs up only files created or changed since the last normal or incremental backup. It marks files as having been backed up. (In other words, the archive attribute is cleared.) If you use a combination of normal and incremental backups, you need to have the last normal backup set as well as all incremental backup sets to restore data.

Internet Connection Firewall (ICF)

A built-in service that monitors all aspects of the traffic that crosses the network interface, which includes inspecting the source and destination addresses, for further control.

Internet Connection Sharing (ICS)

A feature that is intended for use in a small office or home office in which the network configuration and the Internet connection are managed by the computer running Windows XP, where the shared connection resides. ICS can use a dial-up connection, such as a modem or an ISDN connection to the Internet, or it can use a dedicated connection such as a cable modem or Digital Subscriber Line (DSL) connection. It is assumed that the ICS computer is the only Internet connection—the only gateway to the Internet—and that it sets up all internal network addresses.

Internet Explorer security settings

A collection of settings in Internet Explorer used to control how the browser will respond to potentially risky activity, such as installing ActiveX components or running JScript or Java applets.

Internet Information Services (IIS)

A group of services that host Internet and intranet-related features on Windows XP computers such as File Transfer Protocol (FTP) and the World Wide Web (WWW) service under Internet Information Services. Each of these services must be installed individually; none of these features are installed by default under Windows XP, although they are installed by default under Windows 2000 Server and under Windows Server 2003, Web Edition.

Internet Printing Protocol (IPP)

A standard that allows network clients the option of entering a uniform resource locator (URL) to connect to network printers and manage their network print jobs, using an HTTP connection in a Web browser. The print server can be a Windows Server computer or a Windows XP Professional computer running IIS. You can view all shared IPP printers at `http://server-name/printers` (for example, `http://Server2/printers`).

interrupt request (IRQ)

A hardware line over which a device or devices can send interrupt signals to the microprocessor. When you add a new device to a PC, you sometimes need to set its IRQ number. IRQ conflicts used to be a common problem when you were adding expansion boards, but the Plug and Play and ACPI specifications have helped remove this headache in many cases.

I/O (input/output) port

Any socket in the back, front, or side of a computer such as a serial, parallel, or USB port that you use to connect to another piece of hardware.

IP (Internet Protocol)

One of the protocols of the TCP/IP suite. IP is responsible for determining whether a packet is for the local network or a remote network. If the packet is for a remote network, IP finds a route for it.

IP address

A 32-bit binary address that identifies a host's network and host ID. The network portion can contain either a network ID or a network ID and a subnet ID.

ipconfig

A command that allows you to view and re-negotiate IP address information for a Windows XP computer.

IPSec (Internet Protocol Security)

A TCP/IP security mechanism that provides machine-level authentication, as well as data encryption, for virtual private network (VPN) connections that use Layer 2 Tunneling Protocol (L2TP). IPSec negotiates between a computer and its remote tunnel server before an L2TP connection is established, which secures both passwords and data. IPSec is also used for data security between servers and workstations within the same LAN subnet or sets of subnets.

Last Known Good Configuration

A setting that starts Windows XP by using the Registry information that Windows saved at the last successful logon. You should use this setting only in cases when you have incorrectly configured a device or driver. Last Known Good Configuration does not solve problems caused by corrupted or missing drivers or files. Also, when you use this setting, you lose any changes made since the last successful logon.

Layer 2 Tunneling Protocol (L2TP)

An industry-standard Internet tunneling protocol that provides the same functionality as Point-to-Point Tunneling Protocol (PPTP). Unlike PPTP, L2TP does not require IP connectivity between the client workstation and the server. L2TP requires only that the tunnel medium provide packet-oriented point-to-point connectivity. You can use L2TP over media such as Asynchronous Transfer Mode (ATM), Frame Relay, and X.25.

LMHOSTS

A file used to map NetBIOS computer names to IP addresses and vice versa. On small networks, this feature is often used in lieu of a WINS server. An LMHOSTS file is different from a HOSTS file: a HOSTS file maps computer hostnames to IP addresses and vice versa. On very small networks, an LMHOSTS file may sometimes be used in lieu of a DNS server.

local group

A group account that is stored in the Security Accounts Manager (SAM) of a single system. You can give a local group access to resources only on that system.

local printers and print jobs

Digital output devices that are directly connected to a computer (by parallel or USB connection). Print jobs that are printed to local printers are sent directly to the a printer, rather than across a network.

local security policy

A feature of Windows XP Professional that provides the ability to control details of a computer or user quickly and easily through settings that are stored on the computer, rather than in Active Directory.

local user

A user account that is stored in the SAM of a single system. A local user can belong only to local groups on the same system and can be given access to resources only on that system.

logical drive

A simple volume or partition indicated by a drive letter that resides on a Windows XP basic disk.

logman.exe

A command-line utility used to manage log file data collection on remote computers, to configure and deploy log settings to multiple computers, and to extract data from existing log files.

Log on Locally

A logon right that determines which users can log on interactively. This right pertains to users who physically attempt to log on to the computer as well as to users who remotely attempt to log on using a Remote Desktop Connection (RDC). RDC users are considered interactively (locally) logged on users.

logon script

A file that you can assign to one or more user accounts. Typically a batch file, a logon script runs automatically every time the user logs on. You can use it to configure a user's working environment at every logon, and it allows an administrator to influence a user's environment without managing all aspects of it.

logon security settings

Settings that make a network recognize you so you can begin a session. Logon security settings refer to techniques for ensuring that data stored in a computer cannot be read or compromised. Most security measures involve data encryption and passwords. Data encryption is the translation of data into a form that is unintelligible without a deciphering mechanism. A password is a secret word or phrase that gives a user access to a particular program or system.

metabase

See *Internet Information Services (IIS)*.

Microsoft Management Console (MMC)

A standardized interface shell program for managing Windows XP and Windows Server computers. The MMC provides a framework for hosting administrative tools, called consoles or snap-ins, that are published by Microsoft as well as by third parties.

Microsoft Product Activation (MPA)

MPA requires that users activate their copies of retail and OEM versions of Microsoft software, such as Windows XP, Microsoft Office XP and Office 2003, and Windows Server 2003. Microsoft gives you *30 days* after the first time you use the product in which to activate *Windows XP* and *Office 2003*; Microsoft allows you *60 days* after installation in which to activate *Windows Server 2003*. If users do not activate the software within the appropriate time frame, Windows XP stops functioning; Office 2003 goes into *reduced functionality* mode (read-only mode); Windows Server 2003 can only be accessed using the Administrator account under Safe Mode.

mounted drive, mount point, or mounted volume

A pointer from one partition to another. Mounted drives are useful for increasing a drive's size without disturbing it. For example, you could create a mount point to drive E: as C:\CompanyData. Doing so makes it seem that you have increased the size available on the C: partition, specifically allowing you to store more data in C:\CompanyData than you would otherwise be able to.

MouseKeys

A feature of Windows XP, designed to provide greater accessibility to users who have difficulty using a mouse, which allows a user to position the mouse pointer using the numeric keypad. MouseKeys can also be used to provide increased accuracy in positioning the mouse pointer.

MSCONFIG utility

Also known as the System Configuration Utility. MSCONFIG allows the user to **temporarily** change the way Windows XP starts by managing services and startup entries in the Registry and various .ini files.

multiboot configuration

The default operating system startup configuration for Windows NT, Windows 2000, Windows XP, and Windows Server 2003 when two or more Microsoft operating system are already installed on the same computer and one or more additional operating systems is installed.

Multiple Processor Support (MPS) compliant

Compatible with Windows XP Professional's Symmetric Multiprocessing (SMP) capability. Windows XP Professional provides support for single or dual CPUs; Windows XP Home only supports one CPU. If you originally installed Windows XP Professional on a computer with a single CPU, you must update the HAL on the computer so that it can recognize and use multiple CPUs. Windows XP Professional supports a maximum of two processors.

name resolution

The process of mapping a computer name—either a FQDN or a NetBIOS name—to an IP address.

Narrator

An accessibility utility that translates text in an active window or menu to spoken word to aid the blind and those with impaired vision.

netcap.exe

Also known as the Network Monitor Capture Utility. Netcap.exe is used to monitor network information and traffic in a log file and is useful in troubleshooting network reliability and performance.

network directory

A file or database where users or applications can get reference information about objects on the network.

network interface card (NIC), network adapter, or adapter card

A piece of computer hardware that physically connects a computer to a network cable. It is also a device that transmits and receives electronic signals that represent data being sent from and received by the computer it is connected to. A NIC is often integrated into a computer's motherboard. Some NICs connect directly to Category 5, 5e, or 6 Ethernet cabling (or a higher grade): these are "wired" NICs. Many NICs are now "wireless" and support the 802.11a, 802.11b (Wi-Fi), or 802.11g standards; some NICs support two of these standards, and others support all three standards.

network printers and print jobs

Digital output devices that are connected to a network (by wired or wireless connection) rather than directly to a computer. Print jobs that are printed to network printers are sent across a network, rather than printed to a printer connected directly to the computer.

normal backup

A backup that copies all files and marks those files as having been backed up (in other words, clears the archive attribute). A normal backup is the most complete form of backup.

NSLOOKUP

A command-line diagnostic utility used to retrieve information from a DNS name server.

NTBackup or **NTBackup.exe**

See *Backup Utility*.

NTFS (NT File System)

An advanced file system that is designed for use specifically under the Windows NT, Windows 2000, Windows Server 2003, and Windows XP operating systems. It supports file-system recovery, extremely large storage media, and long filenames.

NTFS data compression

The process of making individual files and folders occupy less disk space with the NTFS version 5.0 file system in Windows XP. Compressed files can be read and written to over the network by any Windows- or DOS-based program *without* having to be decompressed first. Files decompress when opened and recompress when closed. The NTFS 5 file system handles this entire process. Compression is simply a file attribute that you can apply to any file or folder stored on an NTFS 5 drive volume.

NTFS data encryption

See *Encrypting File System*.

NTFS disk quota

See *disk quota*.

NTFS permission

A rule associated with a folder, file, or printer that regulates which users can gain access to the object and in what manner. The object's owner allows or denies permissions. The permissions that both NTFS permissions and Share permissions have in common take precedence if conflicting permis-

sions exist between share permissions and NTFS permissions on an object.

object

In the context of performance monitoring and optimization, a system component that has numerous counters associated with it. For example, objects include processor, memory, system, logical disk, and paging file.

offline files

A feature in Windows XP and Windows 2000 that allows users to continue to work with network files and programs even when they are not connected to the network. When a network connection is restored or when users dock their mobile computers, any changes that were made while users were working offline are updated to the network. When more than one user on the network has made changes to the same file, users are given the option of saving their specific versions of the file to the network, keeping the other version, or saving both. Also known as client-side caching (CSC).

organizational unit (OU)

A type of container object that is used within Active Directory and within the LDAP/X.500 information model to group other objects and classes together for easier administration.

pagefile

See *paging file*.

paging file

A system file that is an extension of RAM which is stored on the disk drive as a kind of virtual memory.

partition

A section on a basic disk that is created from free space so that data can be stored on it. On a basic disk, you can create up to four primary partitions or up to three primary partitions and one extended partition.

Password Authentication Protocol (PAP)

A protocol that allows clear-text authentication.

PATHPING

A command-line diagnostic utility that integrates the features of trace route and ping to identify routers that might cause network problems or congestion.

PC card

See *PCMCIA*.

PCI (peripheral component interconnect)

A local bus standard developed by Intel. Most modern PCs include a PCI bus in addition to a more general Industry Standard Architecture (ISA) expansion bus. Many analysts believe that PCI will eventually replace ISA entirely. PCI is a 64-bit bus, although it is usually implemented as a 32-bit bus. It can run at clock speeds of 33MHz or 66MHz. Although Intel developed it, PCI is not tied to any particular family of microprocessors.

PCMCIA (Personal Computer Memory Card International Association)

An organization of some 500 companies that developed a standard for small, credit-card–sized devices called PC cards. Originally designed for adding memory to portable computers, the PCMCIA standard has been expanded several times and is suitable for many types of devices. There are in fact three types of PCMCIA cards, along with three types of PC slots the cards fit into: Type I, II, and III.

Performance counters

Performance metrics that direct System Monitor about which areas of a system to track and display.

Performance logs and alerts

A component of the Performance snap-in that gives administrators the ability to record system performance data at specific intervals over time, record detailed system events after specific events have occurred,

and be notified by the system when specific counters exceed certain preset thresholds.

Performance MMC snap-in

A utility for monitoring, tracking, and displaying a computer's performance statistics, both in real time and over an extended period for establishing a system baseline. This console includes the System Monitor node and the Performance Logs and Alerts node.

Performance object instances

Terms that provide a method of identifying multiple performance objects of the same type. For example, if a computer has more than one processor installed, its processor performance object displays multiple distinct instances of this object to monitor each individual processor separately.

Performance objects

Logical collections of performance metrics associated with a computer resource (CPU, disk, memory) or service that can be monitored. Processor, Memory, PhysicalDisk, and Paging File are all examples of performance objects.

ping (packet Internet groper) utility

A utility that determines whether a specific IP address for a network device is reachable from an individual computer. Ping works by sending a data packet to the specified address and waiting for a reply. You can use ping to troubleshoot network connections in the TCP/IP network protocol.

Plug and Play

A standard developed by Microsoft, Intel, and other industry leaders to simplify the process of adding hardware to PCs by having the operating system automatically detect devices. The intent of the standard is to conceal unpleasant details, such as IRQs and Direct Memory Access (DMA) channels, from people who want to add new hardware devices to their systems. A Plug-and-Play monitor, for example, can communicate with both Windows XP and the graphics adapter to automatically set itself at the maximum refresh rate supported for a chosen resolution. Plug and Play compliance also ensures that devices are not driven beyond their capabilities.

Point-to-Point Protocol (PPP)

A method of connecting a computer to a network or to the Internet. PPP is more stable than the older Serial Line Internet Protocol (SLIP) and provides error-checking features. Windows XP Professional and Windows 2000 Professional are both PPP clients when dialing in to any network.

Point-to-Point Tunneling Protocol (PPTP)

A communication protocol that tunnels through another connection, encapsulating PPP packets. The encapsulated packets are IP datagrams that can be transmitted over IP-based networks, such as the Internet.

policy

A configuration or setting that is specified for one or more systems or users. Policies are refreshed at startup, at logon, and after a refresh interval, so if a setting is manually changed, the policy refreshes the setting automatically. Policies provide for centralized management of change and configuration.

preboot execution environment (PXE)

An industry standard for computer BIOSes and network adapter cards that supports remote (network) booting of computers. Used in conjunction with Remote Installation Services (RIS) installations.

prestaging computer accounts

A method for creating computer accounts within Active Directory in advance of installing the computers and then joining them to the domain using RIS.

primary domain controller (PDC)

In a Windows NT Server 4 or earlier domain, the computer running Windows NT Server that has read and write access to the SAM database. Both primary and backup domain controllers (BDCs) authenticate domain logons and maintain the directory database for a domain. A Windows NT domain may only have one PDC, but it may have any number of BDCs.

primary monitor

The monitor designated as the one that displays the logon dialog box when you start a computer. Most programs display their windows on the primary monitor when you first open them. A Windows XP computer can support multiple monitors or displays.

printer permissions

Restrictions placed on a printer that govern what permissions a user or group has to print to, manage, or configure a printer.

privilege or user right

The capability to perform a system behavior, such as changing the system time, backing up or restoring files, or formatting the hard drive.

RAID (Redundant Array of Independent Disks)-5 volume or striped set with parity volume

A fault-tolerant collection of equal-sized partitions on at least three physical disks, in which the data is striped and includes parity data. The parity data helps recover a member of the striped set if the member fails. Neither Windows XP Professional nor Windows 2000 Professional can host a RAID-5 volume, but Windows Server 2003 and Windows 2000 Server computers can.

Recovery Console

A command-line interface that provides a limited set of administrative commands that is useful for repairing a computer. For example, you can use the Recovery Console to start and stop services, read and write data on a local drive (including drives formatted to use NTFS), repair a master boot record (MBR), and format drives. You can start the Recovery Console from the Windows Server 2003 CD-ROM, or you can install the Recovery Console on the computer using the winnt32.exe command with the /cmdcons switch.

Remote Assistance (RA)

A built-in service that enables another user, typically a help-desk or IT employee, to remotely help the end user with an issue that she is experiencing on her Windows XP computer.

Remote Desktop Connection

Client software that enables you to access a Terminal Services session that is running on a remote computer while you are sitting at another computer in a different location. This process is extremely useful for employees who want to work from home but need to access their computers at work.

Remote Installation Services (RIS)

A server that provides Windows Server 2003, Windows XP Professional, and Windows 2000 Professional operating-system images that can be downloaded and installed by network clients using network adapters that comply with the preboot execution environment (PXE) boot ROM specifications. RIS requires Active Directory, DHCP, and DNS to serve clients.

removable storage

Allows applications to access and share the same media resources. This service is used for managing removable media. Different types of media include floppy disks, Zip disks, CD-ROMs, CD-Rs, CD-RWs, DVD media, and tape backup devices. Some include removable hard drives as removable storage.

Resultant Set of Policy

A summary of the group policies that are imposed on a particular user or computer. You can use tools such as Group Policy Result, Group Policy Update, and the RSoP snap-in to determine which policies are being applied.

runas

A Windows XP GUI and command-line tool that allows a user or an administrator to run a program or to open a file under a different user's security credentials using the appropriate user account name and password.

Safe Mode startup options

The options you get at startup when you press the F8 function key to initiate Safe Mode. When started in Safe Mode, Windows XP uses only basic files and drivers (mouse, monitor, keyboard, mass storage, base video, and default system services but no network connections) so Windows can run and you can diagnose problems with the system. You can choose the Safe Mode with Networking option, which loads all the preceding files and drivers plus the essential services and drivers to start networking. Or you can choose the Safe Mode with Command Prompt option, which is exactly the same as Safe Mode except that you get a command prompt instead of the Windows GUI. You can also choose Last Known Good Configuration, which starts the computer by using the Registry information that Windows XP saved at the last shutdown. If a symptom does not reappear when you start in Safe Mode, you can eliminate the default settings and minimum device drivers as possible causes. If a newly added device or a changed driver is causing problems, you can use Safe Mode to remove the device or reverse the change. In some circumstances, such as when Windows system files required to start the system are corrupted or damaged, the system will not start in Safe Mode.

sampling interval or update interval

The frequency with which a performance counter is logged. A shorter interval provides more detailed information but generates a larger log.

scheduled tasks

A system folder that stores scheduled jobs which run at predefined times. Administrators can create scheduled jobs.

Scheduled Tasks Wizard

A series of dialog boxes that simplify the process of creating scheduled task jobs.

Security Accounts Manager (SAM)

The database of local user and local group accounts on a Windows Server 2003 member server, Windows XP Professional, or Windows 2000 Professional computer.

Security Configuration and Analysis Snap-In

A snap-in used to analyze and configure security options on a computer-by-computer basis as well as to develop security templates that are used to lock down the security of a system with centralized group settings.

security group

A group that can contain users and other groups that can be assigned an ACL with ACEs to define security permissions on objects for the members of the group.

security identifier (SID)

A unique number that represents a security principal such as a user or group. You can change the name of a user or group account without affecting the account's permissions and privileges because the SID is what is granted user rights and resource access.

Setup Manager

A utility program that ships on the Windows XP CD-ROM and that is used to create answer files for unattended installations. Setup Manager can create answer files for unattended, sysprep, or RIS installations.

Shadow Copies of Shared Folders

A new feature under Windows Server 2003 that creates "snapshots," or copies, of original shared data folders at various scheduled intervals and during data backup operations. You can retrieve previous versions of files and folders from Shadow Copies by installing the Previous Versions Client software on Windows XP workstations and by installing the Shadow Copy Client software on Windows 2000 and previous operating

systems. In addition, the NTBACKUP utility, under Windows XP, uses the Volume Shadow Copy Service (VSS) by default for backing up files from the snapshot instead of from the original files on disk.

shared folder

A folder that is shared for use by remote users over the network.

share permission

A rule that is associated with a folder to regulate which users can gain access to the object over the network and in what manner.

Simple File Sharing

A feature of Windows XP that makes a single shared folder named Shared Documents available for any user on the network to access. Simple File Sharing hides the ability to set NTFS security directly on folders and files. This feature is enabled by default when the computer is standalone or a member of a network workgroup but is disabled when the computer is a member of a Windows domain.

simple volume

In Windows XP, the disk space on a single physical disk. A simple volume can consist of a single area on a disk or multiple areas on the same disk that are linked together. You can extend a simple volume within the same disk or among multiple disks. If you extend a simple volume across multiple disks, it becomes a spanned volume.

slipstreaming

The process of integrating a Windows XP service pack (SP) into an existing Windows XP installation folder. Subsequent installations of Windows XP do not require separate SP installations because the updated SP files are included (slipstreamed) into the original Windows XP installation files that are usually stored in a shared network folder on a server.

Smart Card

A credit-card–sized device that is used to securely store public and private keys, passwords, and other types of personal information. To use a Smart Card, you need a Smart Card reader attached to the computer and a personal identification number (PIN) for the Smart Card. In Windows XP Professional, you can use Smart Cards to enable certificate-based authentication and Single Sign-On (SSO) to the enterprise.

Smart Card reader

A small external or internal device, or even a built-in slot, into which you insert a Smart Card so that it can be read.

Software Update Services (SUS)

An add-on program that you can download from Microsoft's Web site that allows an organization to centrally manage and deploy software patches and updates for Microsoft operating systems. It works in a similar fashion to the Microsoft Windows Update Web site.

spanned volume

In Windows Server 2003 and Windows 2000 Server, the disk space on more than one physical disk. You can add more space to a spanned volume by extending it at any time. In Windows NT 4 and earlier operating systems, a spanned volume is called a volume set.

spooler service

The primary Windows XP service that controls printing functionality.

standby mode

A power-saving option in Windows XP, Windows Server 2003, and Windows 2000 computers in which a computer switches to a low-power state where devices, such as the monitor and hard disks, turn off and the computer uses less power. When you want to use the computer again, it comes out of standby quickly, and the desktop is restored exactly as you left it. Standby is useful for conserving battery power in portable computers. Standby does not save the desktop state to disk; if you experience a power failure while in standby mode, you can lose unsaved information. If there is an interruption in power, information in memory is lost.

StickyKeys

An accessibility feature of Windows XP that enables a user to press multiple keystrokes, such as Ctrl+Alt+Del, by using one key at a time.

striped volume

A volume that stores data in stripes on two or more physical disks. Data in a striped volume is allocated alternately and evenly (in stripes) to the disks of the striped volume. Striped volumes are *not fault tolerant*. Striped volumes can substantially improve the speed of access to the data on disk. You can create them on Windows Server 2003, Windows XP Professional, Windows 2000 Professional, and Windows 2000 Server computers. Striped volumes with parity, also known as RAID-5 volumes, can be created only on Windows Server 2003 and Windows 2000 Server computers. In Windows NT 4 and earlier, a striped volume is called a striped set.

subnet mask

A filter that is used to determine which network segment, or subnet, an IP address belongs to. An IP address has two components: the network address and the host (computer name) address. For example, if the IP address 209.15.17.8 is part of a Class C network, the first three numbers (209.15.17) represent the Class C network address, and the last number (8) identifies a specific host (computer) on that network. By implementing subnetting, network administrators can further divide the host part of the address into two or more subnets.

suspend mode
A deep-sleep power-saving option that does use some power.

symmetric multiprocessing (SMP)
A computer architecture that provides fast performance by making multiple CPUs available to complete individual processes simultaneously (that is, multiprocessing). Unlike with asymmetric processing, with SMP you can assign any idle processor any task as well as add additional CPUs to improve performance and handle increased loads. A variety of specialized operating systems and hardware arrangements support SMP. Specific applications can benefit from SMP if their code allows multithreading. SMP uses a single operating system and shares common memory and disk I/O resources. Windows XP Professional supports SMP; Windows XP Home Edition supports only a single CPU.

sysprep
A tool that prepares a Windows Server 2003, Windows XP Professional, or a Windows 2000 Professional computer to be imaged by using third-party disk image software. It does so by removing unique identifiers such as computer name and SIDs. Sysprep modifies the target operating system's Registry so that a unique local domain SID is created when the computer boots for the first time after the disk image is applied.

System Monitor
A node in the Performance MMC snap-in for monitoring and logging computer performance statistics using performance objects, counters, and instances.

system state
In the Windows Backup utility, a collection of system-specific data that you can back up and restore. For Windows XP/2000/2003 operating systems, the system-state data includes the Registry, the Component Object Model (COM)+ Class Registration database, and the system boot files. For Windows Server 2003 and Windows 2000 Server, the system-state data also includes

the Certificate Services database (if the server is operating as a certificate server). If the server is a DC, the system-state data also includes the Active Directory database and the `sysvol` directory.

taking ownership of objects
The act of one user account taking over ownership of files or folders from another user. Administrators must grant a user the ability to take ownership of a file or folder or make a user take ownership for himself.

Task Manager
A utility program that displays the current application programs and processes that are running on the computer. It also monitors the system's recent processor usage, recent memory usage, current network utilization, and currently logged-on users.

Terminal Server
A computer that is running Terminal Services. A Windows Server 2003 computer installs Terminal Services in Remote Desktop for Administration mode by default. You must set up Terminal Services in Application Server mode separately. Users connect to terminal servers using the Remote Desktop Client (RDC), installed by default in Windows XP.

Terminal Services
A built-in service that enables you to use the Remote Desktop Connection software to connect to a session that is running on a remote computer while you are sitting at another computer in a different location. This process is extremely useful for employees who want to work from home but need to access their computers at work.

Transmission Control Protocol/Internet Protocol (TCP/IP)
A standardized specification for data transport over a network or the Internet. TCP/IP consists of a sophisticated array of data transport services, name-resolution services, and troubleshooting utilities and is a required component for implementing Active Directory.

unattended answer file

See *answer file*.

unattended installation

The automated installation of an operating system that does not require user intervention to answer questions prompted by the Windows Setup program.

uniqueness database file

A text file that provides values which override the values stored in an unattended answer file during an automated installation of Windows XP, Windows 2000, or Windows Server 2003.

universally unique identifier (UUID)

See *globally unique identifier*.

USB (Universal Serial Bus)

An external bus standard (released in 1996) that supports data transfer rates of up to 12Mbps. The newer USB 2.0 (also known as Hi-Speed USB) standard supports data transfer rates of up to 480Mbps but is fully backward-compatible with the original USB 1.1 standard. You can use a single USB port to connect up to 127 peripheral devices, such as mice, modems, and keyboards. USB also supports Plug-and-Play installation and hot plugging. It is expected to completely replace serial and parallel ports.

user account

An object created on a local Windows XP computer or an object created within Active Directory that contains information about a user, including the user logon name, password, and group memberships. When a user account is created on a local computer's SAM database, the object contains information about the user, including the user logon name, password, and group memberships.

user profile

A collection of desktop and environmental settings that define the work area of a local computer.

user right

See *privilege*.

User State Migration Tool (USMT)

A set of tools that stores user data and settings for an upgrade or reinstallation of the computer. The tools include `scanstate` and `loadstate`, which extract the information and restore the information, respect-ively.

UUID

Universally unique identifier; see *globally unique identifier*.

video adapter

The electronic component that generates the video signal that is sent through a cable to a video display. The video adapter is usually located on the computer's main system board or on an expansion board.

virtual private network (VPN)

A private network of computers that is at least partially connected using public channels or lines, such as the Internet. A good example of a VPN is a private-office LAN that allows users to log in remotely over the Internet (an open, public system). VPNs use encryption and secure protocols such as PPTP and L2TP to ensure that unauthorized parties do not intercept data transmissions.

volume

A section on a dynamic disk that is created from unallocated space so that data can be stored on it. You can only create simple volumes, striped volumes, spanned volumes, mirrored volumes, and RAID-5 volumes on dynamic disks.

Volume Shadow Copy Service (VSS)

A new service in Windows XP and Windows Server 2003 that creates "snapshots," or copies, of original data volumes at various scheduled intervals and during data backup operations. Under Windows Server 2003, you can retrieve previous versions of files and folders from Shadow Copies; under Windows XP, Shadow Copies are used only for taking snapshots of data for backup operations.

Windows Installer Service package

A file with the .msi extension that installs applications. Such files contain summary and installation instructions as well as the actual installation files. You can install Windows Installer Service packages locally or remotely through Active Directory group policies.

Windows Internet Name Service (WINS)

A service that dynamically maps NetBIOS names to IP addresses.

Windows Messenger

The new application built into the operating system that allows for chatting, notifications, voice communication, file transfer, and sharing of applications.

Windows Product Activation (WPA)

See *Microsoft Product Activation (MPA)*.

Windows Update

Offers security-related software patches and updated device-driver support that supplements the extensive library of drivers available on the installation CD. Windows Update is an online extension, providing a central location for product enhancements.

winnt32 /cmdcons

The command and switch used to install the Recovery Console on a Windows XP computer. This command uses winnt32 on the installation media or in the distribution source.

workgroup

A peer-to-peer network in which user accounts are decentralized and stored on each individual system.

ZAP file

A file with the extension .zap that you use to allow applications without an .msi file to be deployed via Active Directory group policy. A Zero Administration Windows (ZAW) down-level applications package (ZAP) file tells a Software Deployment group policy setting how to install a legacy application program.

Index

N

O

P

Q - R

Wouldn't it be great

if the world's leading technical publishers joined forces to deliver their best tech books in a common digital reference platform?

They have. Introducing **InformIT Online Books** powered by Safari.

- **Specific answers to specific questions.**
  InformIT Online Books' powerful search engine gives you relevance-ranked results in a matter of seconds.

- **Immediate results.**
  With InformIt Online Books, you can select the book you want and view the chapter or section you need immediately.

- **Cut, paste, and annotate.**
  Paste code to save time and eliminate typographical errors. Make notes on the material you find useful and choose whether or not to share them with your workgroup.

- **Customized for your enterprise.**
  Customize a library for you, your department, or your entire organization. You pay only for what you need.

Get your first 14 days **FREE!**

InformIT Online Books is offering its members a 10-book subscription risk free for 14 days. Visit **http://www.informit.com/onlinebooks** for details.